Cambridge IGCSE™ and O level

Computer Science

Second Edition

David Watson
Helen Williams

Acknowledgements

The Publishers would like to thank the following for permission to reproduce copyright material.

p.xi © pinglabel/stock.adobe.com; **p.31** © adisa/Fotolia; **p.85** t © md3d/stock.adobe.com; **p.86** l © SergeyBitos/Shutterstock.com; **p.87** © Елена Хайруллина/stock.adobe.com; **p.92** © Romanchuck/ Fotolia; **p.94** tl © jijomathai/stock.adobe.com, bl © Dmitriy Melnikov/Fotolia.com; **p.104** © Elokua/stock.adobe.com; **p.105** © Konstantin/Fotolia; **p.106** tl © philipus.stock.adobe.com, bl © Marek/stock.adobe.com; **p.108** b © Scanrail/stock.adobe.com; **p.111** tl © Alec Romijn/Alamy Stock Photo; **p.115** t © Manfred Schmidt/Fotolia.com; **p.121** c © Mauro Rodrigues/Fotolia, l © Martin Dohrn/Science Photo Library; **p.123** © wpg77/stock.adobe.com; **p.127** © Engdao/stock.adobe.com; **p.138** c © iStockphoto.com/Karl Yamashita, b © jacobx/stock.adobe.com; **p.139** r © Cigdem Simsek / Alamy Stock Photo; **p.156** tl © Allies Interactive/Shutterstock.com; **p.201** © Andrew Brown/Fotolia; **p.202** © Stanford Eye Clinic/Science Photo Library; **p.230** cl © bobo1980/stock.adobe.com, r © Ocskay Mark/stock.adobe.com, bl © naka/stock.adobe.com; **p.231** b © Purestock/Alamy Stock Photo; **p.232** t © wellphoto/stock.adobe.com, b © Image Source/Alamy Stock Photo; **p.235** © Monica Wells/Alamy Stock Photo; **p.239** © tino168/Shutterstock.com; **p.251** © c watman/stock.adobe.com; **p.257** © Maximusdn/stock.adobe.com; **p.259** tl Cambridge map, reproduced with permission from OS © Crown copyright and database rights 2021 Hodder Education under licence to OS, tr © chagpa/stock.adobe.com.

t = top, b = bottom, l = left, r = right, c = centre

Computer hardware and software brand names mentioned in this book are protected by their respective trademarks and are acknowledged.

Scratch is developed by the Lifelong Kindergarten Group at the MIT Media Lab. See http://scratch.mit.edu

Every effort has been made to trace all copyright holders, but if any have been inadvertently overlooked, the Publishers will be pleased to make the necessary arrangements at the first opportunity.

Although every effort has been made to ensure that website addresses are correct at time of going to press, Hodder Education cannot be held responsible for the content of any website mentioned in this book. It is sometimes possible to find a relocated web page by typing in the address of the home page for a website in the URL window of your browser.

Hachette UK's policy is to use papers that are natural, renewable and recyclable products and made from wood grown in well-managed forests and other controlled sources. The logging and manufacturing processes are expected to conform to the environmental regulations of the country of origin.

Orders: please contact Hachette UK Distribution, Hely Hutchinson Centre, Milton Road, Didcot, Oxfordshire, OX11 7HH. Telephone: +44 (0)1235 827827. Email education@hachette.co.uk Lines are open from 9 a.m. to 5 p.m., Monday to Friday. You can also order through our website: www.hoddereducation.com

ISBN: 9781398318281

© David Watson and Helen Williams 2021

First published in 2014

This edition published in 2021 by
Hodder Education,
An Hachette UK Company
Carmelite House
50 Victoria Embankment
London EC4Y 0DZ

www.hoddereducation.com

Impression number   10 9 8 7 6 5 4 3 2 1

Year   2025 2024 2023 2022 2021

Cover photo © phonlamaiphoto – stock.adobe.com

Typeset by Aptara Inc.

Printed in Malaysia

A catalogue record for this title is available from the British Library.

Contents

SECTION 2 ALGORITHMS, PROGRAMMING AND LOGIC 257

SA2

Introduction

Aims

This book has been written for students of Cambridge IGCSE™ Computer Science (0478/0984) and Cambridge O Level Computer Science (2210) for examination from 2023. It fully covers the syllabus content, provides guidance to support you throughout the course and helps you to prepare for examination.

This book will help students to develop a range of skills, including programming, problem solving and testing and evaluation, as well as introducing them to automated and emerging technologies.

Assessment

The information in this section is taken from the Cambridge IGCSE and O Level Computer Science syllabuses (0478/0984/2210) for examination from 2023. You should always refer to the appropriate syllabus document for the year of examination to confirm the details and for more information. The syllabus document is available on the Cambridge International website at: www.cambridgeinternational.org

There are two examination papers:

	Paper 1 Computer Systems	**Paper 2 Algorithms, Programming and Logic**
Duration	1 hour 45 minutes	1 hours 45 minutes
Marks	75 marks	75 marks
Percentage of overall marks	50%	50%
Syllabus topics examined	1–6	7–10

How to use this book

The information in this section is taken from the Cambridge IGCSE and O Level Computer Science syllabuses (0478/0984/2210) for examination from 2023. You should always refer to the appropriate syllabus document for the year of your examination to confirm the details and for more information. The syllabus document is available on the Cambridge International website at www.cambridgeinternational.org

Organisation

The content is organised into 10 chapters, corresponding to the syllabus. The content is in the same order as the syllabus. The material directly relevant to Computer Systems is in Chapters 1–6 and the material directly relevant to Algorithms, Programming and Logic is in Chapters 7–10.

Features

Learning outline

Each chapter opens with an outline of the subject material to be covered.

In this chapter, you will learn about:
★ automated systems
- the use of sensors, microprocessors and actuators in automated systems
- the advantages and disadvantages of using automated systems in given scenarios
★ robotics
- what is meant by robotics
- the characteristics of a robot
- the roles, advantages and disadvantages of robots
★ artificial intelligence
- what is meant by artificial intelligence (AI)
- the main characteristics of AI
- the basic operation and components of AI systems to simulate intelligent behaviour.

Chapter introduction

A short introduction to the chapter topics and their focus.

This chapter considers the hardware found in many computer systems. The hardware that makes up the computer itself and the various input and output devices will all be covered.

Activity

Short questions and exercises to help recap and confirm knowledge and understanding of the concepts covered.

Activity 1.2

Convert the following denary numbers into binary (using both methods):

a	41	d	100	g	144	j	255	m	4095
b	67	e	111	h	189	k	33000	n	16400
c	86	f	127	i	200	l	889	o	62307

Example

Worked examples of technical or mathematical techniques.

❓ Example 2

A camera detector has an array of 2048 by 2048 pixels and uses a colour depth of 16. Find the size of an image taken by this camera in MiB.

1 Multiply number of pixels in vertical and horizontal directions to find total number of pixels = (2048 × 2048) = 4 194 304 pixels
2 Now multiply number of pixels by colour depth = 4 194 304 × 16 = 67 108 864 bits
3 Now divide number of bits by 8 to find the number of bytes in the file = (67 108 864)/8 = 8 388 608 bytes
4 Now divide by 1024 × 1024 to convert to MiB = (8 388 608)/(1 048 576) = **8 MiB**.

Find out more

Short activities that go a little beyond the syllabus, for those students who have a deeper interest in the subject.

 Find out more

Find out how buffers are used to stream movies from the internet to a device (such as a tablet).

Advice

As well as library routines, typical IDEs also contain an editor, for entering code, and an interpreter and/or a compiler, to run the code.

Advice

These provide tips and background, and also highlight any content that is not specifically covered in the syllabus.

Links

Numerous topics in Computer Science are connected together. The Links feature states where relevant material is covered elsewhere in the book.

Link

For more details on RAM, see Section 3.3.

Extension

Written for students interested in further study, and placed at the end of each chapter, this optional feature contains details of more sophisticated topics that are explored in the International A Level syllabus.

▶ Extension

For those students considering the study of this subject at A Level, the following section gives some insight into further study on a sub-set of machine learning called deep learning.

Deep learning

Deep learning structures algorithms in layers (input layer, output layer and hidden layer(s)) to create an artificial neural network made up of 'units' or 'nodes', which is essentially based on the human brain (i.e. its interconnections between neurons). Neural network systems are able to process more like a human and their performance improves when trained with more and more data. The hidden layers are where data from the input layer is processed into something that can be sent to the output layer. Artificial neural networks are excellent at tasks that computers normally find hard. For example, they can be used in face recognition:

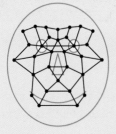

The following diagram shows an artificial neural network (with two hidden layers) – each circle, called a unit or node, is like an 'artificial neuron':

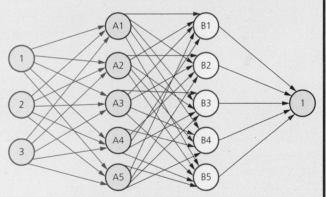

Neural networks are effective at complex visual processing such as recognising birds, for example, by their shape and colour. There are many different sizes, colours and types of bird, and machine learning algorithms struggle to successfully recognise such a wide variety of complex objects. But the hidden layers in an artificial neural network allow a deep learning algorithm to do so.

Summary

At the end of each chapter there is a list of the main points from the chapter that you should have a good understanding of.

In this chapter, you have learnt about:
- ✔ use of sensors, microprocessors and actuators in automated systems
- ✔ the advantages and disadvantages of automated systems in a number of key areas
- ✔ what is meant by robotics
- ✔ what characterises a robot
- ✔ the role of robots in a number of areas
- ✔ the advantages and disadvantages of robots in a number of areas
- ✔ the concept of artificial learning (AI)
- ✔ the main characteristics of AI
- ✔ expert systems
- ✔ machine learning.

Key terms

Key terms are in **red** throughout the book and are defined at the end of each chapter.

Key terms used throughout this chapter

bit – the basic computing element that is either 0 or 1, and is formed from the words **Bi**nary digi**t**

binary number system – a number system based on 2, in which only the digits 0 and 1 are used

hexadecimal number system – a number system based on the value 16 which uses denary digits 0 to 9 and letters A to F

error codes – error messages (in hexadecimal) generated by the computer

MAC address – *MAC address* - standing for Media Access Control, this address uniquely identifies a device on the internet; it takes the form: NN-NN-NN-DD-DD-DD, where NN-NN-NN is the manufacturer code and DD-DD-DD is the device code

IP address – *IP address* short for internet protocol address and identified as either IPv4 or IPv6; the IP address gives a unique **address** to each device connected to the **internet**, identifying its location

hypertext mark-up language (HTML) – the language used to design, display and format web pages

Exam-style questions

Chapters 1–10 conclude with exam-style questions, to help with preparation for examination.

Exam-style questions

1 A software developer is using a microphone to collect various sounds for his new game. He is also using a sound editing app.

When collecting sounds, the software developer can decide on the sampling resolution he wishes to use.

a i What is meant by **sampling resolution**? [1]

   ii Describe how sampling resolution will affect how accurate the stored digitised sound will be. [3]

The software developer will include images in his new game.

b i Explain the term **image resolution**. [1]

   ii The software developer is using 16-colour bitmap images. How many bits would be used to encode data for **one** pixel of his image? [1]

   iii One of his images is 16 384 pixels wide and 512 pixels high. He decides to save it as a 256-colour bitmap image. Calculate the size of the image file in gibibytes. [3]

   iv Describe any file compression techniques the developer may use. [3]

Pseudocode and programming languages

To succeed in your course, you will need an understanding of a particular pseudocode syntax that will be used that will be used when studying Algorithms, Programming and Logic, along with one of the following high-level programming languages: Python, VB.NET or Java. Within Chapters 7 and 8, code examples are given using the correct pseudocode syntax and all three programming languages, each in a different text colour for clarity.

▼ **Table 8.4** Examples of output statements with messages

Output the results	Language
`print("Volume of the cylinder is ", volume)`	Python uses a comma
`Console.WriteLine("Volume of the cylinder is " & volume)`	VB uses &
`System.out.println("Volume of the cylinder is " + volume);`	Java uses +

It is assumed that access to an integrated development environment (IDE) is provided by your school for the programming language in use but, if not, full instructions on how to download and run an IDE for each language are given in the *Programming, Algorithms and Logic Workbook*.

Additional support

The *Computer Systems Workbook* and *Programming, Algorithms and Logic Workbook* provide additional opportunity for practice. These write-in workbooks are designed to be used throughout the course.

Command words

Command word	What it means
Calculate	work out from given facts, figures or information
Compare	identify/comment on similarities and/or differences
Define	give precise meaning
Demonstrate	show how or give an example
Describe	state the points of a topic/give characteristics and main features
Evaluate	judge or calculate the quality, importance, amount or value of something
Explain	set out purposes or reasons/make the relationships between things evident/provide why and/or how and support with relevant evidence
Give	produce an answer from a given source or recall/memory
Identify	name/select/recognise
Outline	set out the main points
Show (that)	provide structured evidence that leads to a given result
State	express in clear terms
Suggest	apply knowledge and understanding to situations where there are a range of valid responses in order to make proposal/put forward considerations

SECTION 1

Computer systems

Chapters

Data representation

In this chapter you will learn about:
★ number systems
  - how and why computers use binary to represent data
  - the denary, binary and hexadecimal number systems
  - converting numbers between denary, binary and hexadecimal
  - how and why hexadecimal is used for data representation
  - how to add two positive 8-bit numbers
  - overflow when performing binary addition
  - logical binary shifts on positive 8-bit integers
  - two's complement notation to represent positive and negative binary numbers
★ text, sound and images
  - how and why a computer represents text
  - the use of character sets including ASCII and Unicode
  - how and why a computer represents sound
  - sound sample rate and sample resolution
  - how and why a computer represents an image
  - the effects of the resolution and colour depth on images
★ data storage and compression
  - how data storage is measured
  - calculating the file size of an image and sound file
  - the purpose of and need for data compression
  - lossy and lossless compression.

This chapter considers the three key number systems used in computer science, namely binary, denary and hexadecimal. It also discusses how these number systems are used to measure the size of computer memories and storage devices, together with how sound and images can be represented digitally.

1.1 Number systems

1.1.1 Binary represents data

As you progress through this book you will begin to realise how complex computer systems really are. By the time you reach Chapter 10 you should have a better understanding of the fundamentals behind computers themselves and the software that controls them.

You will learn that any form of data needs to be converted into a binary format so that it can be processed by the computer.

However, no matter how complex the system, the basic building block in all computers is the binary number system. This system is chosen because it only consists of 1s and 0s. Since computers contain millions and millions of tiny 'switches', which must be in the ON or OFF position, they can be represented by the binary system. A switch in the ON position is represented by 1; a switch in the OFF position is represented by 0.

Switches used in a computer make use of logic gates (see Chapter 10) and are used to store and process data.

1.1.2 Binary, denary and hexadecimal systems

The binary system

We are all familiar with the denary number system which counts in multiples of 10. This gives us the well-known headings of units, 10s, 100s, 1000s, and so on:

(10^4)	(10^3)	(10^2)	(10^1)	(10^0)
10 000	**1000**	**100**	**10**	**1**
2	5	1	7	7

Denary uses ten separate digits, 0-9, to represent all values. Denary is known as a base 10 number system.

The **binary number system** is a base 2 number system. It is based on the number 2. Thus, only the two 'values' 0 and 1 can be used in this system to represent all values. Using the same method as denary, this gives the headings 2^0, 2^1, 2^2, 2^3, and so on. The typical headings for a binary number with eight digits would be:

(2^7)	(2^6)	(2^5)	(2^4)	(2^3)	(2^2)	(2^1)	(2^0)
128	**64**	**32**	**16**	**8**	**4**	**2**	**1**
1	1	1	0	1	1	1	0

A typical binary number would be: 11101110.

Converting from binary to denary

The conversion from binary to denary is a relatively straightforward process. Each time a 1-value appears in a binary number column, the column value (heading) is added to a total. This is best shown by three examples which use 8-bit, 12-bit and 16-bit binary numbers:

❓ Example 1

Convert the binary number, 11101110, into a denary number.

128	64	32	16	8	4	2	1
1	1	1	0	1	1	1	0

The equivalent denary number is 128 + 64 + 32 + 8 + 4 + 2 = 238

❓ Example 2

Convert the following binary number, 011110001011, into a denary number.

2048	1024	512	256	128	64	32	16	8	4	2	1
0	1	1	1	1	0	0	0	1	0	1	1

The equivalent denary number is 1024 + 512 + 256 + 128 + 8 + 2 + 1 = 1931

Example 3

Convert the following binary number, 0011000111100110, into a denary number.

32768	16384	8192	4096	2048	1024	512	256	128	64	32	16	8	4	2	1
0	0	1	1	0	0	0	1	1	1	1	0	0	1	1	0

As with the two examples above, to convert this number to denary, each time a 1 appears in a column the column value is added to the total:

8192 + 4096 + 256 + 128 + 64 + 32 + 4 + 2 = 12 774

The same method can be used for a binary number of any size.

Activity 1.1

Convert the following binary numbers into denary:

a	0 0 1 1 0 0 1 1	k	0001 1110 0111
b	0 1 1 1 1 1 1 1	l	0101 0101 0100
c	1 0 0 1 1 0 0 1	m	1111 0000 1111
d	0 1 1 1 0 1 0 0	n	0111 1100 1000
e	1 1 1 1 1 1 1 1	o	0111 1111 1111
f	0 0 0 0 1 1 1 1	p	0111 1100 1111 0000
g	1 0 0 0 1 1 1 1	q	0011 1111 0000 1101
h	1 0 1 1 0 0 1 1	r	1100 0011 0011 1111
i	0 1 1 1 0 0 0 0	s	1000 1000 1000 1000
j	1 1 1 0 1 1 1 0	t	0111 1111 1111 1111

Converting from denary to binary

The conversion from denary numbers to binary numbers can be done in two different ways. The first method involves successive subtraction of powers of 2 (that is, 128, 64, 32, 16, and so on); whilst the second method involves successive division by 2 until the value "0" is reached. This is best shown by two examples:

 Example 1

Consider the conversion of the denary number, 142, into binary:

Method 1

The denary number 142 is made up of 128 + 8 + 4 + 2 (that is, 142 – 128 = 14; 14 – 8 = 6; 6 – 4 = 2; 2 – 2 = 0; in each stage, subtract the largest possible power of 2 and keep doing this until the value 0 is reached. This will give us the following 8-bit binary number:

128	64	32	16	8	4	2	1
1	0	0	0	1	1	1	0

Method 2

This method involves successive division by 2. Start with the denary number, 142, and divide it by 2. Write the result of the division including the remainder (even if it is 0) under the 142 (that is, 142 ÷ 2 = 71 remainder 0); then divide again by 2 (that is, 71 ÷ 2 = 35 remainder 1) and keep dividing until the result is zero. Finally write down all the remainders in reverse order:

2	142				read the remainders from bottom to top to get the binary number:
2	71	remainder:	0		1 0 0 0 1 1 1 0
2	35	remainder:	1		
2	17	remainder:	1		
2	8	remainder:	1		
2	4	remainder:	0		
2	2	remainder:	0		
2	1	remainder:	0		
	0	remainder:	1		

▲ **Figure 1.1**

We end up with an 8-bit binary number which is the same as that found by Method 1.

? Example 2

Consider the conversion of the denary number, 59, into binary:

Method 1

The denary number 59 is made up of 32 + 16 + 8 + 2 + 1 (that is, 59 – 32 = 27; 27 – 16 = 11; 11 – 8 = 3; 3 – 2 = 1; 1 – 1 = 0; in each stage, subtract the largest possible power of 2 and keep doing this until the value 0 is reached. This will give us the following 8-bit binary number:

128	64	32	16	8	4	2	1
0	0	1	1	1	0	1	1

Method 2

This method involves successive division by 2. Start with the denary number, 59, and divide it by 2. Write the result of the division including the remainder (even if it is 0) under the 59 (that is, 59 ÷ 2 = 29 remainder 1); then divide again by 2 (that is, 29 ÷ 2 = 14 remainder 1) and keep dividing until the result is zero. Finally write down all the remainders in reverse order:

2	59				write the remainders from bottom to top to get the binary number:
2	29	remainder:	1		1 1 1 0 1 1
2	14	remainder:	1		
2	7	remainder:	0		
2	3	remainder:	1		
2	1	remainder:	1		
	0	remainder:	1		

▲ **Figure 1.1b**

If we want to show this as an 8-bit binary number (as shown in Method 1), we now simply add two 0's from the left-hand side to give the result: 0 0 1 1 1 0 1 1. The two results from both methods clearly agree.

Both the above examples use 8-bit binary numbers. This third example shows how the method can still be used for any size of binary number; in this case a 16-bit binary number.

❓ Example 3

Consider the conversion of the denary number, 35 000, into a 16-bit binary number:

Method 1

The denary number 35 000 is made up of 32 768 + 2048 + 128 + 32 + 16 + 8 (that is, 35 000 – 32 768 = 2232; 2232 – 2048 = 184; 184 – 128 = 56; 56 – 32 = 24; 24 – 16 = 8; 8 – 8 = 0; in each stage, subtract the largest possible power of 2 and keep doing this until the value 0 is reached. This will give us the following 16-bit binary number:

32768	16384	8192	4096	2048	1024	512	256	128	64	32	16	8	4	2	1
1	0	0	0	1	0	0	0	1	0	1	1	1	0	0	0

Method 2

This method involves successive division by 2. Start with the denary number, 35000, and divide it by 2. Write the result of the division including the remainder (even if it is 0) under the 35 000 (that is, 35 000 ÷ 2 = 17 500 remainder 0); then divide again by 2 (that is, 17 500 ÷ 2 = 8750 remainder 0) and keep dividing until the result is zero. Finally write down all the remainders in reverse order:

2	35 000		
2	17 500	remainder:	0
2	8750	remainder:	0
2	4375	remainder:	0
2	2187	remainder:	1
2	1093	remainder:	1
2	546	remainder:	1
2	273	remainder:	0
2	136	remainder:	1
2	68	remainder	0
2	34	remainder	0
2	17	remainder	0
2	8	remainder	1
2	4	remainder	0
2	2	remainder	0
2	1	remainder	0
	0	remainder	1

read the remainder from bottom to top to get the binary number:

```
1 0 0 0 1 0 0 0 1 0
1 1 1 0 0 0
```

▲ Figure 1.1c

Activity 1.2

Convert the following denary numbers into binary (using both methods):

a 41	d 100	g 144	j 255	m 4095
b 67	e 111	h 189	k 33000	n 16400
c 86	f 127	i 200	l 888	o 62307

The hexadecimal system

The **hexadecimal number system** is very closely related to the binary system. Hexadecimal (sometimes referred to as simply 'hex') is a base 16 system and therefore needs to use 16 different 'digits' to represent each value.

Because it is a system based on 16 different digits, the numbers 0 to 9 and the letters A to F are used to represent each hexadecimal (hex) digit. A in hex = 10 in denary, B = 11, C = 12, D = 13, E = 14 and F = 15.

Using the same method as for denary and binary, this gives the headings 16^0, 16^1, 16^2, 16^3, and so on. The typical headings for a hexadecimal number with five digits would be:

(16^4)	(16^3)	(16^2)	(16^1)	(16^0)
65 536	4096	256	16	1
2	1	F	3	A

A typical example of hex is 2 1 F 3 A.

Since $16 = 2^4$ this means that FOUR binary digits are equivalent to each hexadecimal digit. The following table summarises the link between binary, hexadecimal and denary:

▼ **Table 1.1**

Binary value	Hexadecimal value	Denary value
0000	0	0
0001	1	1
0010	2	2
0011	3	3
0100	4	4
0101	5	5
0110	6	6
0111	7	7
1000	8	8
1001	9	9
1010	A	10
1011	B	11
1100	C	12
1101	D	13
1110	E	14
1111	F	15

Converting from binary to hexadecimal and from hexadecimal to binary

Converting from binary to hexadecimal is a fairly easy process. Starting from the right and moving left, split the binary number into groups of 4 bits. If the last group has less than 4 bits, then simply fill in with 0s from the left. Take each group of 4 bits and convert it into the equivalent hexadecimal digit using Table 1.1. Look at the following two examples to see how this works.

? Example 1

1 0 1 1 1 1 1 0 0 0 0 1

First split this up into groups of 4 bits:

1 0 1 1	1 1 1 0	0 0 0 1

Then, using Table 1.1, find the equivalent hexadecimal digits:

B	E	1

? Example 2

1 0 0 0 0 1 1 1 1 1 1 1 0 1

First split this up into groups of 4 bits:

1 0	0 0 0 1	1 1 1 1	1 1 0 1

The left group only contains 2 bits, so add in two 0s:

0 0 1 0	0 0 0 1	1 1 1 1	1 1 0 1

Now use Table 1.1 to find the equivalent hexadecimal digits:

2	1	F	D

Activity 1.3

Convert the following binary numbers into hexadecimal:

a 1 1 0 0 0 0 1 1

b 1 1 1 1 0 1 1 1

c 1 0 0 1 1 1 1 1 1 1

d 1 0 0 1 1 1 0 1 1 1 0

e 0 0 0 1 1 1 1 0 0 0 0 1

f 1 0 0 0 1 0 0 1 1 1 1 0

g 0 0 1 0 0 1 1 1 1 1 1 1 0

h 0 1 1 1 0 1 0 0 1 1 1 0 0

i 1 1 1 1 1 1 1 1 0 1 1 1 1 1 0 1

j 0 0 1 1 0 0 1 1 1 1 0 1 0 1 1 1 0

Converting from hexadecimal to binary is also very straightforward. Using the data in Table 1.1, simply take each hexadecimal digit and write down the 4-bit code which corresponds to the digit.

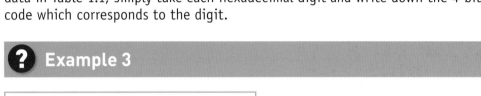

Example 3

4	5	A

Using Table 1.1, find the 4 bit code for each digit:

0 1 0 0	0 1 0 1	1 0 1 0

Put the groups together to form the binary number:

0 1 0 0 0 1 0 1 1 0 1 0

Example 4

B	F	0	8

Again just use Table 1.1:

1 0 1 1	1 1 1 1	0 0 0 0	1 0 0 0

Then put all the digits together:

1 0 1 1 1 1 1 1 0 0 0 0 1 0 0 0

Activity 1.4

Convert the following hexadecimal numbers into binary:

a	6 C		f	B A 6
b	5 9		g	9 C C
c	A A		h	4 0 A A
d	A 0 0		i	D A 4 7
e	4 0 E		j	1 A B 0

Converting from hexadecimal to denary and from denary to hexadecimal

To **convert hexadecimal numbers into denary** involves the value headings of each hexadecimal digit; that is, 4096, 256, 16 and 1.

Take each of the hexadecimal digits and multiply it by the heading values. Add all the resultant totals together to give the denary number. Remember that the hex digits A → F need to be first converted to the values 10 → 15 before carrying out the multiplication. This is best shown by two examples:

 Example 1

Convert the hexadecimal number, 4 5 A, into denary.

First of all we have to multiply each hex digit by its heading value:

256	16	1
4	5	A
(4 × 256 = 1024)	(5 × 16 = 80)	(10 × 1 = 10)	(NOTE: A = 10)

Then we have to add the three totals together (1024 + 80 + 10) to give the denary number:

1	1	1	4

 Example 2

Convert the hexadecimal number, C 8 F, into denary.

First of all we have to multiply each hex digit by its heading value:

256	16	1
C	8	F
(12 × 256 = 3072)	(8 × 16 = 128)	(15 × 1 = 15)	(NOTE: C = 12, F = 15)

Then we have to add the three totals together (3072 + 128 + 15) to give the denary number:

3	2	1	5

Activity 1.5

Convert the following hexadecimal numbers into denary:

a	6 B	f	A 0 1
b	9 C	g	B B 4
c	4 A	h	C A 8
d	F F	i	1 2 A E
e	1 F F	j	A D 8 9

To **convert from denary to hexadecimal** involves successive division by 16 until the value "0" is reached. This is best shown by two examples:

? Example 1

Convert the denary number, 2004, into hexadecimal.

This method involves successive division by 16 until the value 0 is reached. We start by dividing the number 2004 by 16. The result of the division including the remainder (even if it is 0) is written under 2004 and then further divisions by 16 are carried out (that is, 2004 ÷ 16 = 125 remainder 4; 125 ÷ 16 = 7 remainder 13; 7 ÷ 16 = 0 remainder 7). The hexadecimal number is obtained from the remainders written in reverse order:

16	2004				write the remainders from bottom to top to get the hexadecimal number:
16	125	remainder:	4	↑	
16	7	remainder:	13		7 D 4 (D=13)
	0	remainder:	7		

▲ **Figure 1.2a**

? Example 2

Convert the denary number, 8463, into hexadecimal.

We start by dividing the number 8463 by 16. The result of the division including the remainder (even if it is 0) is written under 8463 and then further divisions by 16 are carried out (that is, 8463 ÷ 16 = 528 remainder 15; 528 ÷ 16 = 33 remainder 0; 33 ÷ 16 = 2 remainder 1; 2 ÷ 16 = 0 remainder 2). The hexadecimal number is obtained from the remainders written in reverse order:

16	8463				read the remainder from bottom to top to get the hexadecimal number:
16	528	remainder:	15	↑	
16	33	remainder:	0		2 1 0 F (F=15)
16	2	remainder:	1		
	0	remainder:	2		

▲ **Figure 1.2b**

Activity 1.6

Convert the following denary numbers into hexadecimal:

a	9 8		f	1 0 0 0
b	2 2 7		g	2 6 3 4
c	4 9 0		h	3 7 4 3
d	5 1 1		i	4 0 0 7
e	8 2 6		j	5 0 0 0

1.1.3 Use of the hexadecimal system

As we have seen, a computer can only work with binary data. Whilst computer scientists can work with binary, they find hexadecimal to be more convenient to use. This is because one hex digit represents four binary digits. A complex binary number, such as 1101001010101111 can be written in hex as D2AF. The hex number is far easier for humans to remember, copy and work with. This section reviews four uses of the hexadecimal system:

>> error codes
>> MAC addresses
>> IPv6 addresses
>> HTML colour codes

The information in this section gives the reader sufficient grounding in each topic at this level. Further material can be found by searching the internet, but be careful that you don't go off at a tangent.

Error codes

Error codes are often shown as hexadecimal values. These numbers refer to the memory location of the error and are usually automatically generated by the computer. The programmer needs to know how to interpret the hexadecimal error codes. Examples of error codes from a Windows system are shown below:

Find out more

Another method used to trace errors during program development is to use memory dumps, where the memory contents are printed out either on screen or using a printer. Find examples of memory dumps and find out why these are a very useful tool for program developers.

```
 HexErrorCode  ErrorDescription
 --------------------------------
 0x0           Success
 0x1           Incorrect function.
 0x2           The system cannot find the file specified.
 0x3           The system cannot find the path specified.
 0x4           The system cannot open the file.
 0x5           Access is denied.
 0x6           The handle is invalid.
 0x7           The storage control blocks were destroyed.
 0x8           Not enough storage is available to process this command.
 0x9           The storage control block address is invalid.
 0xa           Unit test error string
 0xb           An attempt was made to load a program with an incorrect format.
 0xc           The access code is invalid.
 0xd           The data is invalid.
 0xe           Not enough storage is available to complete this operation.
 0xf           The system cannot find the drive specified.
 0x10          The directory cannot be removed.
 0x11          The system cannot move the file to a different disk drive.
 0x12          There are no more files.
 0x13          The media is write protected.
 0x14          The system cannot find the device specified.
 0x15          The device is not ready.
 0x16          The device does not recognize the command.
 0x17          Data error (cyclic redundancy check).
 0x18          The program issued a command but the command length is incorrect.
 0x19          The drive cannot locate a specific area or track on the disk.
 0x1a          The specified disk or diskette cannot be accessed.
 0x1b          The drive cannot find the sector requested.
 0x1c          The printer is out of paper.
 0x1d          The system cannot write to the specified device.
 0x1e          The system cannot read from the specified device.
 0x1f          A device attached to the system is not functioning.
 0x20          The process cannot access the file because it is being used by another process.
 0x21          The process cannot access the file because another process has locked a portion of the file.
 0x22          The wrong diskette is in the drive....
 0x24          Too many files opened for sharing.
 0x26          Reached the end of the file.
 0x27          The disk is full.
 0x32          The request is not supported.
```

▲ **Figure 1.3** Example of error codes

Media Access Control (MAC) addresses

Media Access Control (MAC) address refers to a number which uniquely identifies a device on a network. The MAC address refers to the network interface card (NIC) which is part of the device. The MAC address is rarely changed so that a particular device can always be identified no matter where it is.

A MAC address is usually made up of 48 bits which are shown as 6 groups of two hexadecimal digits (although 64-bit addresses also exist):

> NN – NN – NN – DD – DD – DD

or

> NN:NN:NN:DD:DD:DD

where the first half (NN – NN – NN) is the identity number of the manufacturer of the device and the second half (DD – DD – DD) is the serial number of the device. For example:

00 – 1C – B3 – 4F – 25 – FE is the MAC address of a device produced by the Apple Corporation (code: 001CB3) with a serial number of: 4F25FE. Very often lowercase hexadecimal letters are used in the MAC address: 00-1c-b3-4f-25-fe. Other manufacturer identification numbers include:

> 00 – 14 – 22 which identifies devices made by Dell
>
> 00 – 40 – 96 which identifies devices made by Cisco
>
> 00 – a0 – c9 which identifies devices made by Intel, and so on.

Internet Protocol (IP) addresses

Each device connected to a network is given an address known as the **Internet Protocol (IP) address**. An IPv4 address is a 32-bit number written in denary or hexadecimal form: e.g. 109.108.158.1 (or 77.76.9e.01 in hex). IPv4 has recently been improved upon by the adoption of IPv6. An IPv6 address is a 128-bit number broken down into 16-bit chunks, represented by a hexadecimal number. For example:

> a8fb:7a88:fff0:0fff:3d21:2085:66fb:f0fa

Note IPv6 uses a colon (:) rather than a decimal point (.) as used in IPv4.

HyperText Mark-up Language (HTML) colour codes

HyperText Mark-up Language (HTML) is used when writing and developing web pages. HTML isn't a programming language but is simply a mark-up language. A mark-up language is used in the processing, definition and presentation of text (for example, specifying the colour of the text).

HTML uses `<tags>` which are used to bracket a piece of text for example, <h1> and </h1> surround a top-level heading. Whatever is between the two tags has been defined as heading level 1. Here is a short example of HTML code:

Link

Refer to Chapter 3 for more detail on MAC addresses.

Find out more

Try to find the MAC addresses of some of your own devices (e.g. mobile phone and tablet) and those found in the school.

Link

Refer to Chapter 3 for more detail on IP addresses.

Find out more

Try to find the IPv4 and IPv6 addresses of some of your own devices (e.g. mobile phone and tablet) and those found in the school.

```
<h1 style="color:#FF0000;">This is a red heading</h1>


<h2 style="color:#00FF00;">This is a green heading</h2>


<h3 style="color:#0000FF;">This is a blue heading</h3>
```

▲ **Figure 1.4**

HTML is often used to represent colours of text on the computer screen. All colours can be made up of different combinations of the three primary colours (red, green and blue). The different intensity of each colour (red, green and blue) is determined by its hexadecimal value. This means different hexadecimal values represent different colours. For example:

» # FF 00 00   represents primary colour red
» # 00 FF 00   represents primary colour green
» # 00 00 FF   represents primary colour blue
» # FF 00 FF   represents fuchsia
» # FF 80 00   represents orange
» # B1 89 04   represents a tan colour,

and so on producing almost any colour the user wants. The following diagrams show the various colours that can be selected by altering the hex 'intensity' of red, green and blue primary colours. The colour *'FF9966'* has been chosen as an example:

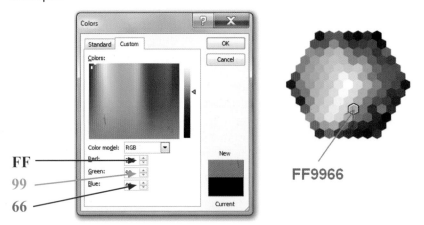

▲ **Figure 1.5** Examples of HTML hex colour codes

The # symbol always precedes hexadecimal values in HTML code. The colour codes are always six hexadecimal digits representing the red, green and blue components. There are a possible 256 values for red, 256 values for green and 256 values for blue giving a total of 256 × 256 × 256 (i.e. 16 777 216) possible colours.

Activity 1.7

1 Using software on your computer (for example, text colour option in *Word*), find out what colours would be represented by the following RGB denary value combinations:

a	Red	53	b	Red	201	c	Red	12
	Green	55		Green	122		Green	111
	Blue	139		Blue	204		Blue	81

2 Convert each of the above denary numbers into hexadecimal.

1.1.4 Addition of binary numbers

This section will look at the addition of two 8-bit positive binary numbers.

Note the following key facts when carrying out **addition** of two binary digits:

binary addition	carry	sum
0+0	0	0
0+1	0	1
1+0	0	1
1+1	1	0

This can then be extended to consider the addition of three binary digits:

binary digit	carry	sum
0+0+0	0	0
0+0+1	0	1
0+1+0	0	1
0+1+1	1	0
1+0+0	0	1
1+0+1	1	0
1+1+0	1	0
1+1+1	1	1

For comparison: if we add 7 and 9 in denary the result is: carry = 1 and sum = 6; if we add 7, 9 and 8 the result is: carry = 2 and sum = 4, and so on.

Advice

Here's a quick recap on the role of carry and sum. If we want to add the numbers 97 and 64 in decimal, we:
- add the numbers in the right hand column first
- if the sum is greater than 9 then we carry a value to the next column
- we continue moving left, adding any carry values to each column until we are finished.

For instance:

```
   9 7
 + 6 4
 _____
   1 1   CARRY VALUES

 1 6 1   SUM VALUES
```

Adding in binary follows the same rules except that we carry whenever the sum is greater than 1.

❓ Example 1

Add 00100111 + 01001010

We will set this out showing carry and sum values:

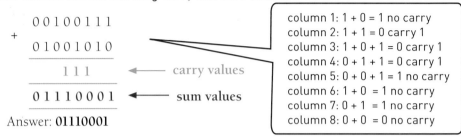

```
    00100111
  + 01001010
  _____
       1 1 1      ←  carry values
  _____
    01110001      ←  sum values
```

Answer: **01110001**

column 1: 1 + 0 = 1 no carry
column 2: 1 + 1 = 0 carry 1
column 3: 1 + 0 + 1 = 0 carry 1
column 4: 0 + 1 + 1 = 0 carry 1
column 5: 0 + 0 + 1 = 1 no carry
column 6: 1 + 0 = 1 no carry
column 7: 0 + 1 = 1 no carry
column 8: 0 + 0 = 0 no carry

❓ Example 2

a Convert 126 and 62 into binary.
b Add the two binary values in part a and check the result matches the addition of the two denary numbers

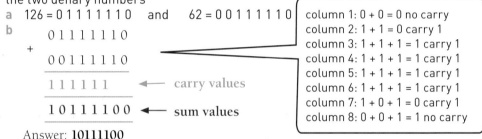

a 126 = 0 1 1 1 1 1 1 0   and   62 = 0 0 1 1 1 1 1 0

b
```
    0 1 1 1 1 1 1 0
  + 0 0 1 1 1 1 1 0
  _____
    1 1 1 1 1 1        ←  carry values
  _____
    1 0 1 1 1 1 0 0    ←  sum values
```

Answer: **10111100**

column 1: 0 + 0 = 0 no carry
column 2: 1 + 1 = 0 carry 1
column 3: 1 + 1 + 1 = 1 carry 1
column 4: 1 + 1 + 1 = 1 carry 1
column 5: 1 + 1 + 1 = 1 carry 1
column 6: 1 + 1 + 1 = 1 carry 1
column 7: 1 + 0 + 1 = 0 carry 1
column 8: 0 + 0 + 1 = 1 no carry

1 0 1 1 1 1 0 0 has the equivalent denary value of 128 + 32 + 16 + 8 + 4 = 188 which is the same as 126 + 62.

Activity 1.8

Carry out the following binary additions:

a 0 0 0 1 1 1 0 1 + 0 1 1 0 0 1 1 0   f 0 0 1 1 1 1 0 0 + 0 1 1 1 1 0 1 1

b 0 0 1 0 0 1 1 1 + 0 0 1 1 1 1 1 1   g 0 0 1 1 1 1 1 1 + 0 0 1 1 1 1 1 1

c 0 0 1 0 1 1 1 0 + 0 1 0 0 1 1 0 1   h 0 0 1 1 0 0 0 1 + 0 0 1 1 1 1 1 1

d 0 1 1 1 0 1 1 1 + 0 0 1 1 1 1 1 1   i 0 1 1 1 1 1 1 1 + 0 1 1 1 1 1 1 1

e 0 0 1 1 1 1 0 0 + 0 0 1 1 0 0 1 1   j 1 0 1 0 0 0 1 0 + 0 0 1 1 1 0 1 1

Activity 1.9

Convert the following denary numbers into binary and then carry out the binary addition of the two numbers and check your answer against the equivalent denary sum:

a 9 8 + 1 5   d 5 1 + 1 7 1   g 1 9 + 1 3 9   j 2 1 1 + 3 5

b 2 9 + 8 8   e 8 2 + 6 9   h 2 0 3 + 3 0

c 4 9 + 1 0 0   f 1 0 0 + 1 4 0   i 6 6 + 1 6 6

Overflow

Now consider the following example:

 Example 3

Add 0 1 1 0 1 1 1 0 and 1 1 0 1 1 1 1 0 (using 8 bits)

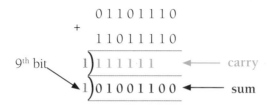

This addition has generated a 9th bit. The 8 bits of the answer are 0 1 0 0 1 1 0 0 – this gives the denary value (64 + 8 + 4) of 76 which is incorrect because the denary value of the addition is 110 + 222 = 332.

The maximum denary value of an 8-bit binary number is 255 (which is $2^8 - 1$). The generation of a 9th bit is a clear indication that the sum has exceeded this value. This is known as an **overflow error** and in this case is an indication that a number is too big to be stored in the computer using 8 bits.

The greater the number of bits which can be used to represent a number then the larger the number that can be stored. For example, a 16-bit register would allow a maximum denary value of 65 535 (i.e. $2^{16} - 1$) to be stored, a 32-bit register would allow a maximum denary value of 4 294 967 295 (i.e. $2^{32} - 1$), and so on.

Activity 1.10

1 Convert the following pairs of denary numbers to 8-bit binary numbers and then add the binary numbers. Comment on your answers in each case:

   a 89 + 175   **b** 168 + 99   **c** 88 + 215

2 Carry out the following 16-bit binary additions and comment on your answers:

   a 0111 1111 1111 0001 + 0101 1111 0011 1001

   b 1110 1110 0000 1011 + 1111 1101 1101 1001

1.1.5 Logical binary shifts

Computers can carry out a **logical shift** on a sequence of binary numbers. The logical shift means moving the binary number to the ***left*** or to the ***right***. Each shift ***left*** is equivalent to ***multiplying*** the binary number by 2 and each shift ***right*** is equivalent to ***dividing*** the binary number by 2.

As bits are shifted, any empty positions are replaced with a zero – see examples below. There is clearly a limit to the number of shifts which can be carried out if the binary number is stored in an 8-bit register. Eventually after a number of shifts the register would only contain zeros. For example, if we shift 01110000 (denary value 112) five places left (the equivalent to multiplying by 2^5, i.e. 32), in an 8-bit register we would end up with 00000000. This makes it seem as though 112 × 32 = 0! This would result in the generation of an error message.

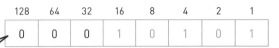

Example 1

The denary number 21 is 00010101 in binary. If we put this into an 8-bit register:

128	64	32	16	8	4	2	1
0	0	0	1	0	1	0	1

> The left-most bit is often referred to as the MOST SIGNIFICANT BIT

If we now shift the bits in this register one place to the left, we obtain:

128	64	32	16	8	4	2	1
0	0	1	0	1	0	1	0

> Note how the empty right-most bit position is now filled with a 0

> The left-most bit is now lost following a left shift

The value of the binary bits is now 21×2^1 i.e. 42. We can see this is correct if we calculate the denary value of the new binary number 101010 (i.e. 32 + 8 + 2).

Suppose we now shift the original number two places left:

128	64	32	16	8	4	2	1
0	1	0	1	0	1	0	0

The binary number 1010100 is 84 in denary – this is 21×2^2.

And now suppose we shift the original number three places left:

128	64	32	16	8	4	2	1
1	0	1	0	1	0	0	0

The binary number 10101000 is 168 in denary – this is 21×2^3.

So, let us consider what happens if we shift the original binary number 00010101 four places left:

128	64	32	16	8	4	2	1
0	1	0	1	0	0	0	0

> Losing 1 bit following a shift operation will cause an error

The left-most 1-bit has been lost. In our 8-bit register the result of 21×2^4 is 80 which is clearly incorrect. This error is because we have exceeded the maximum number of left shifts possible using this register.

Example 2

The denary number 200 is 11001000 in binary. Putting this into an 8-bit register gives:

128	64	32	16	8	4	2	1
1	1	0	0	1	0	0	0

> The right-most bit is often referred to as the LEAST SIGNIFICANT BIT

If we now shift the bits in this register one place to the right:

128	64	32	16	8	4	2	1
0	1	1	0	0	1	0	0

> Note how the left-most bit position is now filled with a 0

The value of the binary bits is now $200 \div 2^1$ i.e. 100. We can see this is correct by converting the new binary number 01100100 to denary (64 + 32 + 4).

Suppose we now shift the original number two places to the right:

128	64	32	16	8	4	2	1
0	0	1	1	0	0	1	0

The binary number 00110010 is 50 in denary – this is $200 \div 2^2$.

And suppose we now shift the original number three places to the right:

128	64	32	16	8	4	2	1
0	0	0	1	1	0	0	1

Notice the 1-bit from the right-most bit position is now lost causing an error

The binary number 00011001 is 25 in denary – this is $200 \div 2^3$.

Now let us consider what happens if we shift four places right:

128	64	32	16	8	4	2	1
0	0	0	0	1	1	0	0

The right-most 1-bit has been lost. In our 8-bit register the result of $200 \div 2^4$ is 12, which is clearly incorrect. This error is because we have therefore exceeded the maximum number of right shifts possible using this 8-bit register.

? Example 3

a Write 24 as an 8-bit register.
b Show the result of a logical shift 2 places to the left.
c Show the result of a logical shift 3 places to the right.

a

128	64	32	16	8	4	2	1
0	0	0	1	1	0	0	0

b

128	64	32	16	8	4	2	1
0	1	1	0	0	0	0	0

$\Leftarrow 24 \times 2^2 = 96$

c

128	64	32	16	8	4	2	1
0	0	0	0	0	0	1	1

$\Leftarrow 24 \div 2^3 = 3$

? Example 4

a Convert 19 and 17 into binary.
b Carry out the binary addition of the two numbers.
c Shift your result from part b two places left and comment on the result.
d Shift your result from part b three places right and comment on the result.

a

128	64	32	16	8	4	2	1	
0	0	0	1	0	0	1	1	19
0	0	0	1	0	0	0	1	17

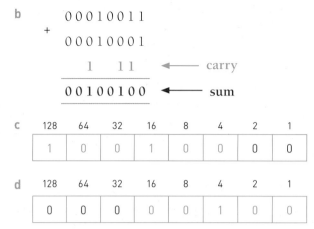

b
```
    00010011
  + 00010001
```

| | | | | | | | |
| 1 | | 11 | | | | | ← carry |

| 00100100 | ← sum |

c

128	64	32	16	8	4	2	1
1	0	0	1	0	0	0	0

d

128	64	32	16	8	4	2	1
0	0	0	0	0	1	0	0

In **c** the result is $36 \times 2^2 = 144$ (which is correct).

In **d** the result of the right shift gives a value of 4, which is incorrect since $36 \div 2^3$ is not 4; therefore, the number of possible right shifts has been exceeded. You can also see that a 1 has been lost from the original binary number, which is another sign that there have been too many right shifts.

Activity 1.11

1 a Write down the denary value of the following binary number.

0	1	1	0	1	0	0	0

   b Shift the binary number three places to the right and comment on your result.

   c Write down the denary value of the following binary number.

0	0	0	0	1	1	1	1

   d Shift the binary number four places to the left and comment on your result.

2 a Convert 29 and 51 to 8-bit binary numbers.

   b Add the two binary numbers in part **a**.

   c Shift the result in part **b** three places to the right.

   d Convert 75 to an 8-bit binary number.

   e Add the two binary numbers from parts **c** and **d**.

   f Shift your result from part **e** one place to the left.

1.1.6 Two's complement (binary numbers)

Up until now, we have assumed all binary numbers are positive integers. To allow the possibility of representing negative integers we make use of **two's complement**. In this section we will again assume 8-bit registers are being used. Only one minor change to the binary headings needs to be introduced here:

−128	64	32	16	8	4	2	1

In two's complement the left-most bit is changed to a negative value. For instance, for an 8-bit number, the value 128 is now changed to –128, but all the other headings remain the same. This means the new range of possible numbers is: –128 (10000000) to +127 (01111111).

It is important to realise when applying two's complement to a binary number that the left-most bit always determines the sign of the binary number. A 1-value in the left-most bit indicates a negative number and a 0-value in the left-most bit indicates a positive number (for example, 00110011 represents 51 and 11001111 represents –49).

Writing positive binary numbers in two's complement format

 Example 1

The following two examples show how we can write the following positive binary numbers in the two's complement format 19 and 4:

–128	64	32	16	8	4	2	1
0	0	0	1	0	0	1	1
0	0	0	0	0	1	0	0

As you will notice, for positive binary numbers, it is no different to what was done in Section 1.1.2.

Converting positive denary numbers to binary numbers in the two's complement format

If we wish to convert a positive denary number to the two's complement format, we do exactly the same as in Section 1.1.2:

 Example 2

Convert **a** 38 **b** 125 to 8-bit binary numbers using the two's complement format.

a   Since this number is positive, we must have a zero in the –128 column. It is then a simple case of putting 1-values into their correct positions to make up the value of 38:

–128	64	32	16	8	4	2	1
0	0	1	0	0	1	1	0

b   Again, since this is a positive number, we must have a zero in the –128 column. As in part **a**, we then place 1-values in the appropriate columns to make up the value of 125:

–128	64	32	16	8	4	2	1
0	1	1	1	1	1	0	1

Converting positive binary numbers in the two's complement format to positive denary numbers

? Example 3

Convert 01101110 in two's complement binary into denary:

−128	64	32	16	8	4	2	1
0	1	1	0	1	1	1	0

As in Section 1.1.2, each time a 1 appears in a column, the column value is added to the total. For example, the binary number (01101110) above has the following denary value: 64 + 32 + 8 + 4 +2 = 110.

? Example 4

Convert 00111111 in two's complement binary into denary:

−128	64	32	16	8	4	2	1
0	0	1	1	1	1	1	1

As above, each time a 1 appears in a column, the column value is added to the total. For example, the binary number (00111111) above has the following denary value: 32 + 16 + 8 + 4 +2 + 1 = 63.

Activity 1.12

1 Convert the following positive denary numbers into 8-bit binary numbers in the two's complement format:

a	39	c	88	e	111	g	77	i	49
b	66	d	102	f	125	h	20	j	56

2 Convert the following binary numbers (written in two's complement format) into positive denary numbers:

	−128	64	32	16	8	4	2	1
a	0	1	0	1	0	1	0	1
b	0	0	1	1	0	0	1	1
c	0	1	0	0	1	1	0	0
d	0	1	1	1	1	1	1	0
e	0	0	0	0	1	1	1	1
f	0	1	1	1	1	1	0	1
g	0	1	0	0	0	0	0	1
h	0	0	0	1	1	1	1	0
i	0	1	1	1	0	0	0	1
j	0	1	1	1	1	0	0	0

Writing negative binary numbers in two's complement format and converting to denary

? Example 1

The following three examples show how we can write negative binary numbers in the two's complement format:

−128	64	32	16	8	4	2	1
1	0	0	1	0	0	1	1

By following our normal rules, each time a 1 appears in a column, the column value is added to the total. So, we can see that in denary this is: −128 + 16 + 2 + 1 = −109.

−128	64	32	16	8	4	2	1
1	1	1	0	0	1	0	0

Similarly, in denary this number is −128 + 64 + 32 + 4 = −28.

−128	64	32	16	8	4	2	1
1	1	1	1	0	1	0	1

This number is equivalent to −128 + 64 + 32 + 16 + 4 + 1 = −11.

Note that a two's complement number with a 1-value in the −128 column must represent a negative binary number.

Converting negative denary numbers into binary numbers in two's complement format

Consider the number +67 in 8-bit (two's complement) binary format:

−128	64	32	16	8	4	2	1
0	1	0	0	0	0	1	1

Method 1
Now let's consider the number −67. One method of finding the binary equivalent to −67 is to simply put 1s in their correct places:

−128	64	32	16	8	4	2	1
1	0	1	1	1	1	0	1

−128 + 32 + 16 + 8 + 4 + 1 = −67

Method 2
However, looking at the two binary numbers above, there is another possible way to find the binary representation of a negative denary number:

first write the number as a positive binary value – in this case 67:	0 1 0 0 0 0 1 1
we then invert each binary value, which means swap the 1s and 0s around:	1 0 1 1 1 1 0 0
then add 1 to that number:	1
this gives us the binary for −67:	1 0 1 1 1 1 0 1

? Example 2

Convert –79 into an 8-bit binary number using two's complement format.

Method 1

As it is a negative number, we need a 1-value in the –128 column.

–79 is the same as –128 + 49

We can make up 49 from 32 + 16 + 1; giving:

–128	64	32	16	8	4	2	1
1	0	1	1	0	0	0	1

Method 2

write 79 in binary:	0 1 0 0 1 1 1 1
invert the binary digits:	1 0 1 1 0 0 0 0
add 1 to the inverted number	1
thus giving –79:	1 0 1 1 0 0 0 1

–128	64	32	16	8	4	2	1
1	0	1	1	0	0	0	1

It is a good idea to practise both methods.

When applying two's complement, it isn't always necessary for a binary number to have 8 bits:

? Example 3

The following 4-bit binary number represents denary number 6:

–8	4	2	1
0	1	1	0

Applying two's complement (1 0 0 1 + 1) would give:

–8	4	2	1
1	0	1	0

in other words: –6

? Example 4

The following 12-bit binary number represents denary number 1676:

−2048	1024	512	256	128	64	32	16	8	4	2	1
0	1	1	0	1	0	0	0	1	1	0	0

Applying two's complement (1 0 0 1 0 1 1 1 0 0 1 1 + 1) would give:

−2048	1024	512	256	128	64	32	16	8	4	2	1
1	0	0	1	0	1	1	1	0	1	0	0

In other words: −1676

Activity 1.13

Convert the following negative denary numbers into binary numbers using the two's complement format:

a	−18	c	−47	e	−88	g	−100	i	−16
b	−31	d	−63	f	−92	h	−1	j	−127

Activity 1.14

Convert the following negative binary numbers (written in two's complement format) into negative denary numbers:

a	1	1	0	0	1	1	0	1
b	1	0	1	1	1	1	1	0
c	1	1	1	0	1	1	1	1
d	1	0	0	0	0	1	1	1
e	1	0	1	0	0	0	0	0
f	1	1	1	1	1	0	0	1
g	1	0	1	0	1	1	1	1
h	1	1	1	1	1	1	1	1
i	1	0	0	0	0	0	0	1
j	1	1	1	1	0	1	1	0

1.2 Text, sound and images

1.2.1 Character sets – ASCII code and Unicode

The **ASCII code** system (American Standard Code for Information Interchange) was set up in 1963 for use in communication systems and computer systems. A newer version of the code was published in 1986. The standard ASCII code **character set** consists of 7-bit codes (0 to 127 in denary or 00 to 7F in hexadecimal) that represent the letters, numbers and characters found on a standard keyboard, together with 32 control codes (that use codes 0 to 31 (denary) or 00 to 19 (hexadecimal)).

Table 1.2 shows part of the standard ASCII code table (only the control codes have been removed).

▼ **Table 1.2** Part of the ASCII code table

Dec	Hex	Char	Dec	Hex	Char	Dec	Hex	Char
32	20	<SPACE>	64	40	@	96	60	`
33	21	!	65	41	A	97	61	a
34	22	"	66	42	B	98	62	b
35	23	#	67	43	C	99	63	c
36	24	$	68	44	D	100	64	d
37	25	%	69	45	E	101	65	e
38	26	&	70	46	F	102	66	f
39	27	'	71	47	G	103	67	g
40	28	(	72	48	H	104	68	h
41	29	)	73	49	I	105	69	i
42	2A	*	74	4A	J	106	6A	j
43	2B	+	75	4B	K	107	6B	k
44	2C	,	76	4C	L	108	6C	l
45	2D	-	77	4D	M	109	6D	m
46	2E	.	78	4E	N	110	6E	n
47	2F	/	79	4F	O	111	6F	o
48	30	0	80	50	P	112	70	p
49	31	1	81	51	Q	113	71	q
50	32	2	82	52	R	114	72	r
51	33	3	83	53	S	115	73	s
52	34	4	84	54	T	116	74	t
53	35	5	85	55	U	117	75	u
54	36	6	86	56	V	118	76	v
55	37	7	87	57	W	119	77	w
56	38	8	88	58	X	120	78	x
57	39	9	89	59	Y	121	79	y
58	3A	:	90	5A	Z	122	7A	z
59	3B	;	91	5B	[	123	7B	{
60	3C	<	92	5C	\	124	7C		
61	3D	=	93	5D	]	125	7D	}
62	3E	>	94	5E	^	126	7E	~
63	3F	?	95	5F	_	127	7F	<DELETE>

Consider the uppercase and lowercase codes in binary of characters. For example,

'a'	1	1	0	0	0	0	1	hex 61 (lower case)
'A'	1	0	0	0	0	0	1	hex 41 (upper case)
'y'	1	1	1	1	0	0	1	hex 79 (lower case)
'Y'	1	0	1	1	0	0	1	hex 59 (upper case)

The above examples show that the sixth bit changes from 1 to 0 when comparing the lowercase and uppercase of a character. This makes the conversion between the two an easy operation. It is also noticeable that the character sets (e.g. a to z, 0 to 9, etc.) are grouped together in sequence, which speeds up usability.

Extended ASCII uses 8-bit codes (0 to 255 in denary or 0 to FF in hexadecimal). This gives another 128 codes to allow for characters in non-English alphabets and for some graphical characters to be included:

DOS	WIN	Dec	Hex	DOS	WIN	Dec	Hex	DOS	WIN	Dec	Hex	DOS	WIN	Dec	Hex
Ç	€	128	80	á		160	A0	└	À	192	C0	α	à	224	E0
ü		129	81	í	¡	161	A1	┴	Á	193	C1	ß	á	225	E1
é	,	130	82	ó	¢	162	A2	┬	Â	194	C2	Γ	â	226	E2
â	ƒ	131	83	ú	£	163	A3	├	Ã	195	C3	π	ã	227	E3
ä	„	132	84	ñ	¤	164	A4	─	Ä	196	C4	Σ	ä	228	E4
à	…	133	85	Ñ	¥	165	A5	┼	Å	197	C5	σ	å	229	E5
å	†	134	86	ª	¦	166	A6	╞	Æ	198	C6	µ	æ	230	E6
ç	‡	135	87	º	§	167	A7	╟	Ç	199	C7	τ	ç	231	E7
ê	^	136	88	¿	¨	168	A8	╚	È	200	C8	Φ	è	232	E8
ë	‰	137	89	⌐	©	169	A9	╔	É	201	C9	Θ	é	233	E9
è	Š	138	8A	¬	ª	170	AA	╩	Ê	202	CA	Ω	ê	234	EA
ï	‹	139	8B	½	«	171	AB	╦	Ë	203	CB	δ	ë	235	EB
î	Œ	140	8C	¼	¬	172	AC	╠	Ì	204	CC	∞	ì	236	EC
ì		141	8D	¡	-	173	AD	═	Í	205	CD	ø	í	237	ED
Ä	Ž	142	8E	«	®	174	AE	╬	Î	206	CE	ε	î	238	EE
Å		143	8F	»	¯	175	AF	╧	Ï	207	CF	∩	ï	239	EF
É		144	90	░	°	176	B0	╨	Ð	208	D0	≡	ð	240	F0
æ	'	145	91	▒	±	177	B1	╤	Ñ	209	D1	±	ñ	241	F1
Æ	'	146	92	▓	²	178	B2	╥	Ò	210	D2	≥	ò	242	F2
ô	"	147	93	│	³	179	B3	╙	Ó	211	D3	≤	ó	243	F3
ö	"	148	94	┤	´	180	B4	╘	Ô	212	D4	⌠	ô	244	F4
ò	•	149	95	╡	µ	181	B5	╒	Õ	213	D5	⌡	õ	245	F5
û	–	150	96	╢	¶	182	B6	╓	Ö	214	D6	÷	ö	246	F6
ù	—	151	97	╖	·	183	B7	╫	×	215	D7	≈	÷	247	F7
ÿ	~	152	98	╕	,	184	B8	╪	Ø	216	D8	°	ø	248	F8
Ö	™	153	99	╣	¹	185	B9	┘	Ù	217	D9	•	ù	249	F9
Ü	š	154	9A	║	º	186	BA	┌	Ú	218	DA	·	ú	250	FA
¢	›	155	9B	╗	»	187	BB	█	Û	219	DB	√	û	251	FB
£	œ	156	9C	╝	¼	188	BC	▄	Ü	220	DC	ⁿ	ü	252	FC
¥		157	9D	╜	½	189	BD	▌	Ý	221	DD	²	ý	253	FD
Pts	ž	158	9E	╛	¾	190	BE	▐	Þ	222	DE	■	þ	254	FE
ƒ	Ÿ	159	9F	┐	¿	191	BF	▀	ß	223	DF		ÿ	255	FF

▶ **Figure 1.6** Extended ASCII code table

ASCII code has a number of disadvantages. The main disadvantage is that it does not represent characters in non-Western languages, for example Chinese characters. As can be seen in Figure 1.6 where DOS and Windows use different characters for some ASCII codes. For this reason, different methods of coding have been developed over the years. One coding system is called **Unicode**. Unicode can represent all languages of the world, thus supporting many operating systems, search engines and internet browsers used globally. There is overlap with standard ASCII code, since the first 128 (English) characters are the same, but Unicode can support several thousand different characters in total. As can be seen in Table 1.2 and Figure 1.6, ASCII uses one byte to represent a character, whereas Unicode will support up to four bytes per character.

The Unicode consortium was set up in 1991. Version 1.0 was published with five goals; these were to:

- create a universal standard that covered all languages and all writing systems
- produce a more efficient coding system than ASCII
- adopt uniform encoding where each character is encoded as 16-bit or 32-bit code
- create unambiguous encoding where each 16-bit and 32-bit value always represents the same character
- reserve part of the code for private use to enable a user to assign codes for their own characters and symbols (useful for Chinese and Japanese character sets, for example).

Find out more

DOS appears in the ASCII extended code table. Find out what is meant by DOS and why it needs to have an ASCII code value.

A sample of Unicode characters are shown in Figure 1.7. As can be seen from the figure, characters used in languages such as Russian, Romanian and Croatian can now be represented in a computer).

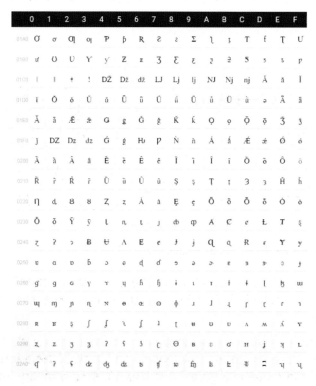

▲ **Figure 1.7** Sample of Unicode characters

1.2.2 Representation of sound

Soundwaves are vibrations in the air. The human ear senses these vibrations and interprets them as sound.

Each sound wave has a frequency, wavelength and amplitude. The amplitude specifies the loudness of the sound.

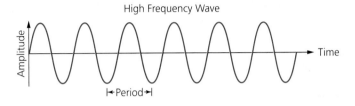

High Frequency Wave

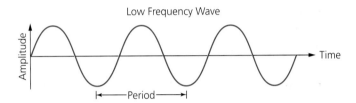

Low Frequency Wave

▲ **Figure 1.8** High and low frequency wave signals

Sound waves vary continuously. This means that sound is analogue. Computers cannot work with analogue data, so sound waves need to be sampled in order to be stored in a computer. Sampling means measuring the amplitude of the sound wave. This is done using an analogue to digital converter (ADC).

To convert the analogue data to digital, the sound waves are sampled at regular time intervals. The amplitude of the sound cannot be measured precisely, so approximate values are stored.

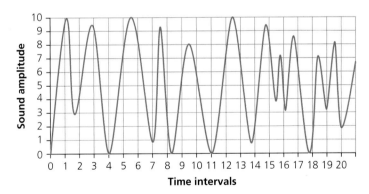

▲ **Figure 1.9** A sound wave being sampled

Figure 1.9 shows a sound wave. The x-axis shows the time intervals when the sound was sampled (1 to 21), and the y-axis shows the amplitude of the sampled sound to 10.

At time interval 1, the approximate amplitude is 10; at time interval 2, the approximate amplitude is 4, and so on for all 20 time intervals. Because the amplitude range in Figure 1.9 is 0 to 10, then 4 binary bits can be used to represent each amplitude value (for example, 9 would be represented by the binary value 1001). Increasing the number of possible values used to represent sound amplitude also increases the accuracy of the sampled sound (for example, using a range of 0 to 127 gives a much more accurate representation of the sound sample than using a range of, for example, 0 to 10). The number of bits per sample is known as the **sampling resolution** (also known as the **bit depth**). So, in our example, the sampling resolution is 4 bits.

Sampling rate is the number of sound samples taken per second. This is measured in hertz (Hz), where 1 Hz means 'one sample per second'.

So how is sampling used to record a sound clip?

» the amplitude of the sound wave is first determined at set time intervals (the sampling rate)
» this gives an approximate representation of the sound wave
» each sample of the sound wave is then encoded as a series of binary digits.

Using a higher sampling rate or larger resolution will result in a more faithful representation of the original sound source. However, the higher the sampling rate and/or sampling resolution, the greater the file size.

▼ **Table 1.3** The benefits and drawbacks of using a larger sampling resolution when recording sound

Benefits	Drawbacks
larger dynamic range	produces larger file size
better sound quality	takes longer to transmit/download music files
less sound distortion	requires greater processing power

Link
See Section 1.3 for a calculation of file sizes.

CDs have a 16-bit sampling resolution and a 44.1 kHz sample rate – that is 44 100 samples every second. This gives high-quality sound reproduction.

1.2.3 Representation of (bitmap) images

Bitmap images are made up of **pixels** (picture elements); an image is made up of a two-dimensional matrix of pixels. Pixels can take different shapes such as:

▲ **Figure 1.10**

Each pixel can be represented as a binary number, and so a bitmap image is stored in a computer as a series of binary numbers, so that:

» a black and white image only requires 1 bit per pixel – this means that each pixel can be one of two colours, corresponding to either 1 or 0
» if each pixel is represented by 2 bits, then each pixel can be one of four colours ($2^2 = 4$), corresponding to 00, 01, 10, or 11
» if each pixel is represented by 3 bits then each pixel can be one of eight colours ($2^3 = 8$), corresponding to 000, 001, 010, 011, 100, 101, 110, 111.

The number of bits used to represent each colour is called the **colour depth**. An 8 bit colour depth means that each pixel can be one of 256 colours (because

$2^8 = 256$). Modern computers have a 24 bit colour depth, which means over 16 million different colours can be represented With x pixels, 2^x colours can be represented as a generalisation. Increasing colour depth also increases the size of the file when storing an image.

Image resolution refers to the number of pixels that make up an image; for example, an image could contain 4096 × 3072 pixels (12 582 912 pixels in total).

The resolution can be varied on many cameras before taking, for example, a digital photograph. Photographs with a lower resolution have less detail than those with a higher resolution. For example, look at Figure 1.11:

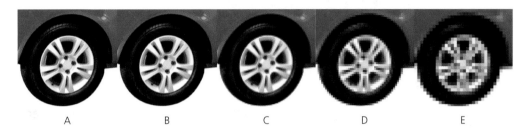

A   B   C   D   E

▲ **Figure 1.11** Five images of the same car wheel using different resolutions

Image 'A' has the highest resolution and 'E' has the lowest resolution. 'E' has become pixelated ('fuzzy'). This is because there are fewer pixels in 'E' to represent the image.

The main drawback of using high resolution images is the increase in file size. As the number of pixels used to represent the image is increased, the size of the file will also increase. This impacts on how many images can be stored on, for example, a hard drive. It also impacts on the time to download an image from the internet or the time to transfer images from device to device. A certain amount of reduction in resolution of an image is possible before the loss of quality becomes noticeable.

Activity 1.15

1 Explain each of the following terms:
   i colour depth
   ii ASCII code and Extended ASCII code
   iii Unicode
   iv sampling rate
   v bitmap image
2 A colour image is made up of red, green and blue colour combinations. 8 bits are used to represent each of the colour components.
   i How many possible variations of red are there?
   ii How many possible variations of green are there?
   iii How many possible variations of blue are there?
   iv How many different colours can be made by varying the red, green and blue values?
3 Describe the effect of increasing resolution and sampling rate on the size of a file being stored in a computer.

1.3 Data storage and file compression

1.3.1 Measurement of data storage

A **bit** is the basic unit of all computing memory storage terms and is either 1 or 0. The word comes from **b**inary dig**it**. The byte is the smallest unit of memory in a computer. 1 byte is 8 bits. A 4-bit number is called a nibble – half a byte.

1 byte of memory wouldn't allow you to store very much information so memory size is measured in the multiples shown in Table 1.4:

▼ **Table 1.4** Memory size using denary values

Name of memory size	Equivalent denary value	
1 kilobyte (1 KB)	1 000	bytes
1 megabyte (1 MB)	1 000 000	bytes
1 gigabyte (1 GB)	1 000 000 000	bytes
1 terabyte (1 TB)	1 000 000 000 000	bytes
1 petabyte (1 PB)	1 000 000 000 000 000	bytes
1 exabyte (1 EB)	1 000 000 000 000 000 000	bytes

The above system of numbering now only refers to some storage devices but is technically inaccurate. It is based on the SI (base 10) system of units where 1 kilo is equal to 1000.

A 1 TB hard disk drive would allow the storage of 1×10^{12} bytes according to this system.

However, since memory size is actually measured in terms of powers of 2, another system has been adopted by the IEC (International Electrotechnical Commission) that is based on the binary system (Table 1.5):

▼ **Table 1.5** IEC memory size system

Name of memory size	Number of bytes	Equivalent denary value	
1 kibibyte (1 KiB)	2^{10}	1 024	bytes
1 mebibyte (1 MiB)	2^{20}	1 048 576	bytes
1 gibibyte (1 GiB)	2^{30}	1 073 741 824	bytes
1 tebibyte (1 TiB)	2^{40}	1 099 511 627 776	bytes
1 pebibyte (1 PiB)	2^{50}	1 125 899 906 842 624	bytes
1 exbibyte (1 EiB)	2^{60}	1 152 921 504 606 846 976	bytes

Advice

Only the IEC system is covered in the syllabus.

This system is more accurate. Internal memories (such as RAM and ROM) should be measured using the IEC system. A 64 GiB RAM could, therefore, store 64×2^{30} bytes of data (68 719 476 736 bytes).

1.3.2 Calculation of file size

In this section we will look at the calculation of the file size required to hold a bitmap image and a sound sample.

The file size of an image is calculated as:

image resolution (in pixels) × colour depth (in bits)

The size of a mono sound file is calculated as:

sample rate (in Hz) × sample resolution (in bits) × length of sample (in seconds)

For a stereo sound file, you would then multiply the result by two.

? Example 1

A photograph is 1024 × 1080 pixels and uses a colour depth of 32 bits. How many photographs of this size would fit onto a memory stick of 64 GiB?
1. Multiply number of pixels in vertical and horizontal directions to find total number of pixels = (1024 × 1080) = 1 105 920 pixels
2. Now multiply number of pixels by colour depth then divide by 8 to give the number of bytes = 1 105 920 × 32 = 35 389 440/8 bytes = 4 423 680 bytes
3. 64 GiB = 64 × 1024 × 1024 × 1024 = 68 719 476 736 bytes
4. Finally divide the memory stick size by the files size = 68 719 476 736/4 423 680 = 15 534 photos.

? Example 2

A camera detector has an array of 2048 by 2048 pixels and uses a colour depth of 16. Find the size of an image taken by this camera in MiB.
1. Multiply number of pixels in vertical and horizontal directions to find total number of pixels = (2 048 × 2 048) = 4 194 304 pixels
2. Now multiply number of pixels by colour depth = 4 194 304 × 16 = 67 108 864 bits
3. Now divide number of bits by 8 to find the number of bytes in the file = (67 108 864)/8 = 8 388 608 bytes
4. Now divide by 1024 × 1024 to convert to MiB = (8 388 608)/(1 048 576) = 8 MiB.

? Example 3

An audio CD has a sample rate of 44 100 and a sample resolution of 16 bits. The music being sampled uses two channels to allow for stereo recording. Calculate the file size for a 60-minute recording.
1. Size of file =

sample rate (in Hz) × sample resolution (in bits) × length of sample (in seconds)

2. Size of sample = (44 100 × 16 × (60 × 60)) = 2 540 160 000 bits
3. Multiply by 2 since there are two channels being used = 5 080 320 000 bits
4. Divide by 8 to find number of bytes = (5 080 320 000)/8 = 635 040 000
5. Divide by 1024 × 1024 to convert to MiB = 635 040 000 / 1 048 576 = 605 MiB.

Activity 1.16

1 A camera detector has an array of 1920 by 1536 pixels. A colour depth of 16 bits is used. Calculate the size of a photograph taken by this camera, giving your answer in MiB.

2 Photographs have been taken by a smartphone which uses a detector with a 1024 × 1536 pixel array. The software uses a colour depth of 24 bits. How many photographs could be stored on a 16 GiB memory card?

3 Audio is being sampled at the rate of 44.1 kHz using 8 bits. Two channels are being used. Calculate:

a the size of a one second sample, in bits

b the size of a 30-second audio recording in MiB.

4 The typical song stored on a music CD is 3 minutes and 30 seconds. Assuming each song is sampled at 44.1 kHz (44 100 samples per second) and 16 bits are used per sample. Each song utilises two channels.

Calculate how many typical songs could be stored on a 740 MiB CD.

1.3.3 Data compression

The calculations in Section 1.3.2 show that sound and image files can be very large. It is therefore necessary to reduce (or **compress**) the size of a file for the following reasons:

» to save storage space on devices such as the hard disk drive/solid state drive
» to reduce the time taken to stream a music or video file
» to reduce the time taken to upload, download or transfer a file across a network
» the download/upload process uses up network bandwidth – this is the maximum rate of transfer of data across a network, measured in bits per second. This occurs whenever a file is downloaded, for example, from a server. Compressed files contain fewer bits of data than uncompressed files and therefore use less bandwidth, which results in a faster data transfer rate.
» reduced file size also reduces costs. For example, when using cloud storage, the cost is based on the size of the files stored. Also an internet service provider (ISP) may charge a user based on the amount of data downloaded.

1.3.4 Lossy and lossless file compression

File compression can either be **lossless** or **lossy**.

Lossy file compression

With this technique, the file compression algorithm eliminates unnecessary data from the file. This means the original file cannot be reconstructed once it has been compressed.

Lossy file compression results in some loss of detail when compared to the original file. The algorithms used in the lossy technique have to decide which parts of the file need to be retained and which parts can be discarded.

For example, when applying a lossy file compression algorithm to:

» an image, it may reduce the resolution and/or the bit/colour depth
» a sound file, it may reduce the sampling rate and/or the resolution.

Lossy files are smaller than lossless files which is of great benefit when considering storage and data transfer rate requirements.

Common lossy file compression algorithms are:

» MPEG-3 (MP3) and MPEG-4 (MP4)
» JPEG.

MPEG-3 (MP3) and MPEG-4 (MP4)

MP3 files are used for playing music on computers or mobile phones. This compression technology will reduce the size of a normal music file by about 90%. While MP3 music files can never match the sound quality found on a DVD or CD, the quality is satisfactory for most general purposes.

But how can the original music file be reduced by 90% while still retaining most of the music quality? Essentially the algorithm removes sounds that the human ear can't hear properly. For example:

» removal of sounds outside the human ear range
» if two sounds are played at the same time, only the louder one can be heard by the ear, so the softer sound is eliminated. This is called perceptual music shaping.

MP4 files are slightly different to MP3 files. This format allows the storage of multimedia files rather than just sound – music, videos, photos and animation can all be stored in the MP4 format. As with MP3, this is a lossy file compression format, but it still retains an acceptable quality of sound and video. Movies, for example, could be streamed over the internet using the MP4 format without losing any real discernible quality.

JPEG

When a camera takes a photograph, it produces a raw bitmap file which can be very large in size. These files are temporary in nature. **JPEG** is a lossy file compression algorithm used for bitmap images. As with MP3, once the image is subjected to the JPEG compression algorithm, a new file is formed and the original file can no longer be constructed.

The JPEG file reduction process is based on two key concepts:

» human eyes don't detect differences in colour shades quite as well as they detect differences in image brightness (the eye is less sensitive to colour variations than it is to variations in brightness)
» by separating pixel colour from brightness, images can be split into 8 × 8 pixel blocks, for example, which then allows certain 'information' to be discarded from the image without causing any real noticeable deterioration in quality.

Lossless file compression

With this technique, all the data from the original uncompressed file can be reconstructed. This is particularly important for files where any loss of data would be disastrous (e.g. when transferring a large and complex spreadsheet or when downloading a large computer application).

Lossless file compression is designed so that none of the original detail from the file is lost.

Run-length encoding (RLE) can be used for lossless compression of a number of different file formats:

» it is a form of lossless/reversible file compression
» it reduces the size of a string of adjacent, identical data (e.g. repeated colours in an image)
» a repeating string is encoded into two values:
 – the first value represents the number of identical data items (e.g. characters) in the run
 – the second value represents the code of the data item (such as ASCII code if it is a keyboard character)
» RLE is only effective where there is a long run of repeated units/bits.

Using RLE on text data

Consider the following text string: 'aaaaabbbbccddddd'. Assuming each character requires 1 byte then this string needs 16 bytes. If we assume ASCII code is being used, then the string can be coded as follows:

a	a	a	a	A	b	b	b	b	c	c	d	d	d	d	d
05 97					04 98				02 99		05 100				

This means we have five characters with ASCII code 97, four characters with ASCII code 98, two characters with ASCII code 99 and five characters with ASCII code 100. Assuming each number in the second row requires 1 byte of memory, the RLE code will need 8 bytes. This is half the original file size.

One issue occurs with a string such as 'cdcdcdcdcd' where RLE compression isn't very effective. To cope with this, we use a flag. A flag preceding data indicates that what follows are the number of repeating units (for example, 255 05 97 where 255 is the flag and the other two numbers indicate that there are five items with ASCII code 97). When a flag is not used, the next byte(s) are taken with their face value and a run of 1 (for example, 01 99 means one character with ASCII code 99 follows).

Consider this example:

String	aaaaaaaa	bbbbbbbbbb	c	d	c	d	c	d	eeeeeeee
Code	08 97	10 98	01 99	01 100	01 99	01 100	01 99	01 100	08 101

The original string contains 32 characters and would occupy 32 bytes of storage.

The coded version contains 18 values and would require 18 bytes of storage.

Introducing a flag (255 in this case) produces:

```
255  08  97 ||  255  10  98 ||  99  100  99  100  99  100 ||  255  08  101
```

This has 15 values and would, therefore, require 15 bytes of storage. This is a reduction in file size of about 53% when compared to the original string.

Using RLE with images

? Example 1: Black and white image

Figure 1.12 shows the letter 'F' in a grid where each square requires 1 byte of storage. A white square has a value 1 and a black square a value of 0:

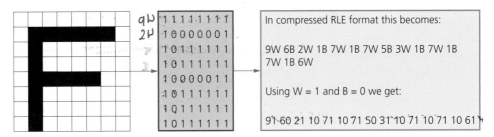

▲ **Figure 1.12** Using RLE with a black and white image

The 8 × 8 grid would need 64 bytes; the compressed RLE format has 30 values, and therefore needs only 30 bytes to store the image.

? Example 2: Coloured images

Figure 1.13 shows an object in four colours. Each colour is made up of red, green and blue (RGB) according to the code on the right.

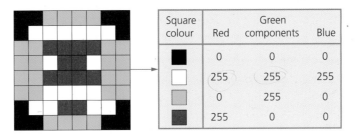

Square colour	Red	Green components	Blue
■	0	0	0
□	255	255	255
▨	0	255	0
▧	255	0	0

▲ **Figure 1.13** Using RLE with a coloured image

This produces the following data: 2 0 0 0 4 0 255 0 3 0 0 0 6 255 255 255 1 0 0 0 2 0 255 0 4 255 0 0 4 0 255 0 1 255 255 255 2 255 0 0 1 255 255 255 4 0 255 0 4 255 0 0 4 0 255 0 4 255 255 255 2 0 255 0 1 0 0 0 2 255 255 255 2 255 0 0 2 255 255 255 3 0 0 0 4 0 255 0 2 0 0 0.

The original image (8 × 8 square) would need 3 bytes per square (to include all three RGB values). Therefore, the uncompressed file for this image is 8 × 8 × 3 = 192 bytes.

The RLE code has 92 values, which means the compressed file will be 92 bytes in size. This gives a file reduction of about 52%. It should be noted that the file reductions in reality will not be as large as this due to other data which needs to be stored with the compressed file (e.g. a file header).

Extension

For those students considering the study of this subject at A Level, the following section gives some insight into further study on data representation.

The following two exercises are designed to help students thinking of furthering their study in Computer Science at A Level standard. The two topics here are not covered in the syllabus and merely show how some of the topics in this chapter can be extended to this next level. The two topics extend uses of the binary number system and using two's complement format to do binary addition.

Topic 1: Binary Coded Decimal (BCD)

The **Binary Coded Decimal (BCD)** system uses a 4-bit code to represent each denary digit, i.e.:

0 0 0 0 = 0	0 1 0 1 = 5
0 0 0 1 = 1	0 1 1 0 = 6
0 0 1 0 = 2	0 1 1 1 = 7
0 0 1 1 = 3	1 0 0 0 = 8
0 1 0 0 = 4	1 0 0 1 = 9

Therefore, the denary number, 3 1 6 5, would be 0 0 1 1 0 0 0 1 0 1 1 0 0 1 0 1 in BCD format.

Uses of BCD

The most obvious use of BCD is in the representation of digits on a calculator or clock display. For example:

Each denary digit will have a BCD equivalent value which makes it easy to convert from computer output to denary display.

Questions to try

1 Convert the following denary numbers into BCD format:

    a 2 7 1   **b** 5 0 0 6   **c** 7 9 9 0

2 Convert the following BCD numbers into denary numbers:

    a 1 0 0 1 0 0 1 1 0 1 1 1
    b 0 1 1 1 0 1 1 1 0 1 1 0 0 0 1 0

Topic 2: Subtraction using two's complement notation

To carry out subtraction in binary, we convert the number being subtracted into its negative equivalent using two's complementation and then **add** the two numbers.

? Example 1

Carry out the subtraction 95 – 68 in binary.

First convert the two numbers into binary:

    95 = 0 1 0 1 1 1 1 1
    68 = 0 1 0 0 0 1 0 0

Now find the two's complement of 68:

           1 0 1 1 1 0 1 1
    +   1
  –68 = 1 0 1 1 1 1 0 0

Then add 95 and –68:

	–128	64	32	16	8	4	2	1
	0	1	0	1	1	1	1	1
+								
	1	0	1	1	1	1	0	0
=								
1	0	0	0	1	1	0	1	1

The additional ninth bit is simply ignored leaving the binary number: 0 0 0 1 1 0 1 1 (denary equivalent of 27 which is the correct result of the subtraction).

Example 2

Carry out the subtraction 49 – 80 in binary.

First convert the two numbers into binary:

49 = 0 0 1 1 0 0 0 1
80 = 0 1 0 1 0 0 0 0

Now find the two's complement of 68:

1 0 1 0 1 1 1 1
+   1
–80 = 1 0 1 1 0 0 0 0

Now add 49 and –80:

–128	64	32	16	8	4	2	1
0	0	1	1	0	0	0	1
+				+			
1	0	1	1	0	0	0	0
=				=			
1	1	1	0	0	0	0	1

This gives us 1 1 1 0 0 0 0 1 which is –31 in denary; the correct answer.

Questions to try

1 Carry out the following binary additions and subtractions using the 8-bit column weightings:

–128   64   32   16   8   4   2   1

a 0 0 1 1 1 0 0 1 + 0 0 1 0 1 0 0 1
b 0 1 0 0 1 0 1 1 + 0 0 1 0 0 0 1 1
c 0 1 0 1 1 0 0 0 + 0 0 1 0 1 0 0 0

d 0 1 1 1 0 0 1 1 + 0 0 1 1 1 1 1 0
e 0 0 0 0 1 1 1 1 + 0 0 0 1 1 1 0 0
f 0 1 1 0 0 0 1 1 – 0 0 1 1 0 0 0 0
g 0 1 1 1 1 1 1 1 – 0 1 0 1 1 0 1 0
h 0 0 1 1 0 1 0 0 – 0 1 0 0 0 1 0 0
i 0 0 0 0 0 0 1 1 – 0 1 1 0 0 1 0 0
j 1 1 0 1 1 1 1 1 – 1 1 0 0 0 0 1 1

In this chapter, you have learnt how to:
✔ use the binary and hexadecimal number systems
✔ convert numbers between the binary, denary and hexadecimal numbers systems
✔ add together two binary numbers
✔ carry out a logical shift
✔ store negative binary numbers using two's complement
✔ interpret ASCII and Unicode character tables
✔ understand the way a computer stores image and sound files
✔ represent the size of a computer memory using KiB, GiB, and so on
✔ calculate the size of an image and sound file taking into account a number of factors
✔ understand the effect of sampling rates and resolution on the size of a sound file
✔ understand the effect of resolution and colour depth on the size of an image file
✔ understand the advantages and disadvantages of reducing the size of a file
✔ apply lossless and lossy file reduction techniques.

Key terms used throughout this chapter

bit – the basic computing element that is either 0 or 1, and is formed from the words **Bi**nary digi**t**

binary number system – a number system based on 2 and can only use the values 0 and 1

hexadecimal number system – a number system based on the value 16 which uses denary digits 0 to 9 and letters A to F

error code – an error message generated by the computer

MAC address – standing for Media Access Control, this address (given in hexadecimal) uniquely identifies a device on the internet; it takes the form: NN-NN-NN-DD-DD-DD, where NN-NN-NN is the manufacturer code and DD-DD-DD is the device code NN-NN-NN-DD-DD-DD

IP address – *Internet Protocol* identified either as IPv4 or IPv6; it gives a unique address to each device connected to a network identifying their location

HTML – *HyperText Mark-up Language* is used in the design of web pages and to write, for example, http(s) protocols; in the context of this chapter, colours used in web pages are assigned a hexadecimal code based on red, green and blue colours

overflow error – the result of carrying out a calculation that produces a value that is too large for the computer's allocated word size (8-bit, 16-bit, 32-bit, and so on)

logical shift – an operation that shifts bits to the left or right in a register; any bits shifted out of a register (left or right) are replaced with zeroes

two's complement – a method of representing negative numbers in binary; when applied to an 8-bit system, the left-most bit (most significant bit) is given the value –128

ASCII code – *a character set* for all the characters on a standard keyboard and control codes

character set – a list of characters that have been defined by computer hardware and software. The character set is necessary so that the computer can understand human characters

Unicode – *a character set* which represents all the languages of the world (the first 128 characters are the same as ASCII code)

sampling resolution – the number of bits used to represent sound amplitude in digital sound recording (also known as bit depth)

bit depth – the number of bits used to represent the smallest unit in a sound file

colour depth – the number of bits used to represent the colours of a pixel

sampling rate – the number of sound samples taken per second in digital sound recording

bitmap image – an image made up of pixels

pixel – derived from the term 'picture element', this is the smallest element used to make up an image on a display

image resolution – the number of pixels in the X–Y direction of an image, for example, 4096 × 3192 pixels

pixelated (image) – this is the result of zooming into a bitmap image; on zooming out the pixel density can be diminished to such a degree that the actual pixels themselves can be seen

pixel density – number of pixels per square inch

compression – reduction of the size of a file by removing repeated or redundant pieces of data; this can be lossy or lossless

bandwidth – the maximum rate of transfer of data across a network, measured in kilobits per second (kbps) or megabits per second (Mbps)

lossy (file compression) – a file compression method in which parts of the original file cannot be recovered during the decompression process for example, JPEG, mp3

lossless (file compression) – a file compression method that allows the original file to be fully restored during the decompression process, for example, run length encoding (RLE)

audio compression – a method used to reduce the size of a sound file using perceptual music shaping

MP3 – a lossy file compression method used for music files

MP4 – a lossy file compression method used for multimedia files

JPEG – from Joint Photographic Expert Group; a form of lossy file compression used with image files which relies on the inability of the human eye to distinguish certain colour changes and hues

run length encoding (RLE) – a lossless file compression technique used to reduce the size of text and photo files in particular

Exam-style questions

1 A software developer is using a microphone to collect various sounds for his new game. He is also using a sound editing app.

When collecting sounds, the software developer can decide on the sampling resolution he wishes to use.

a i What is meant by *sampling resolution*? [1]

ii Describe how sampling resolution will affect how accurate the stored digitised sound will be. [3]

The software developer will include images in his new game.

b i Explain the term *image resolution*. [1]

ii The software developer is using 16-colour bitmap images. How many bits would be used to encode data for **one** pixel of his image? [1]

iii One of his images is 16 384 pixels wide and 512 pixels high. He decides to save it as a 256-colour bitmap image. Calculate the size of the image file in gibibytes. [3]

iv Describe any file compression techniques the developer may use. [3]

2 The editor of a movie is finalising the music score. He will send the final version of his score to the movie producer by email attachment.

a Describe how *sampling* is used to record the music sound clips. [3]

b The music sound clips need to undergo some form of data compression before the music editor can send them via email. Which type of compression, *lossy* or *lossless*, should he use? Give a justification for your answer. [3]

c One method of data compression is known as *run length encoding (RLE)*.

i What is meant by RLE? [3]

ii The following image is being developed:

Show how RLE would be used to produce a compressed file for the above image. Write down the data you would expect to see in the RLE compressed format (you may assume that the grey squares have a code value of 0 and the white squares have a code value of 1). [4]

3 An 8-bit binary register contains the value:

0	0	1	1	0	1	1	0

    a Write down the denary value of this register. [1]

    b The contents of this register undergo a logical shift *one place* to the right.

      i Show the result of this right shift.

      ii Write down the denary value following this right shift. [2]

    c The contents of this register, at the start of the question, now undergo a logical shift *two places* to the left.

      i Show the contents of the register after this left shift operation. [1]

      ii State, with reasons, the effect of this shift on the denary value in *part a*. [2]

4 **a** Convert the following denary numbers into 8-bit binary numbers:

      i 123   **ii** 55   **iii** 180 [3]

    b Carry out the following additions using your binary values from *part a*:

      i 123 + 55   **ii** 123 + 180 [4]

    c **i** Write down the two's complement value of: 0 1 1 1 0 1 0 0 [2]

      ii Write down the binary value of −112 using two's complement notation. [1]

      iii Write down the denary value of the following binary number, which is using two's complement notation: [1]

1	0	1	1	1	0	0	1

    d **i** Convert the following denary number into an 8-bit binary number using two's complement notation: 104.

      ii Use two's complement notation to find the 8-bit binary value of −104. [2]

5 A bitmap image has the following resolution: 1140 × 1080 pixels. The image uses a colour depth of 24 bits.

    a Explain the term **pixel**. [1]

    b Explain the term **colour depth**. [1]

    c Calculate how many of these images could be stored on a 32-GiB memory stick. [3]

    d Describe how it would be possible to increase the number of these images which could be stored on this memory stick. [3]

6 **a** Nancy has captured images of her holiday with her camera. The captured images are stored as digital photo files on her camera. Explain how the captured images are converted to digital photo files. [4]

    b Nancy wants to email photos to Nadia. Many of the photos are very large files, so Nancy needs to reduce their file size as much as possible. Identify which type of file compression would be most suitable for Nancy to use. Explain your choice. [4]

Cambridge IGCSE Computer Science 0478, Paper 12 Q2, May/June 2018

7 A stopwatch uses six digits to store hours, minutes and seconds. The stopwatch stopped at:

02	:	**31**	:	**58**

Hours   Minutes   Seconds

An 8-bit register is used to store each pair of digits.

a Write the 8-bit binary numbers that are currently stored for the **Hours, Minutes** and **Seconds**.

Hours								
Minutes								
Seconds								

[3]

b The stopwatch is started again and then stopped. When the watch is stopped, the 8-bit binary registers show:

Hours:	0	0	0	0	0	1	0	1
Minutes:	0	0	0	1	1	0	1	0
Seconds:	0	0	1	1	0	1	1	1

Write the denary values that will now be shown on the stopwatch.

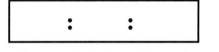

Hours   Minutes   Seconds   [3]

Cambridge IGCSE Computer Science 0478, Paper 12 Q3, May/June 2018

8 A memory stick is advertised as having a capacity of 64 GiB.
   a How many photographs of size 10 KiB could be stored on this memory stick? [2]
   b John wants to store 400 photographs in a folder on his solid state drive (SSD). Each photograph is 10 KiB in size.
      i Name **one** way of reducing the size of this file. [1]
      ii Give **two** advantages of reducing the size of his photography files. [2]
      iii Give **one** disadvantage of reducing files using the method named in **part b i**. [1]
   c The original photographs were stored as bitmap images.
      i Explain why 3 bytes of data would be needed to store each pixel in the bitmap image. [2]
      ii Calculate how many different pixel colours could be formed if one of the bytes gives the intensity of the red colour, one of the bytes gives the intensity of the green colour and one of the bytes gives the intensity of the blue colour. [3]

9 Six calculations are shown on the left and eleven denary values are shown on the right.

By drawing arrows, connect each calculation to its correct denary value.

An 8-bit register uses two's complement notation. What is the denary value of: 0 0 1 0 1 1 0 1 ?

10

16

Convert the following into GiB: 59 055 800 320 bytes

20

28

If 2^x = 1 048 576 bytes What is the value of x?

45

46

Give the denary equivalent of the following hexadecimal number: 3F

55

57

What is the denary result of the following binary addition: 0 0 0 1 0 0 1 1 +0 0 0 1 1 0 1 1

60

Find the hexadecimal value of the following denary number: 40

63

80

[6]

2 Data transmission

In this chapter you will learn about:
★ types and methods of data transmission
  – how data is broken up into data packets before transmission
  – the structure of data packets (header, payload and trailer)
  – packet switching (including the role of the router in the process)
  – methods of data transmission (serial, parallel, simplex, half-duplex and full-duplex)
  – the Universal Serial Bus (USB)
★ methods of error detection
  – why error checking methods are needed
  – error checking methods following data transmission:
    – parity checks
    – checksum
    – echo check
  – use of check digits to detect data entry errors
  – use of automatic repeat requests (ARQs) to detect errors
★ encryption
  – the need for and the purpose of encryption
  – symmetric and asymmetric encryption
  – use of public and private keys.

Data is frequently transferred from one device to another. The two devices could be in the same building or thousands of kilometres away. Irrespective of the distance travelled, the transmission of data needs to be considered with respect to:

● how the data is transmitted
● how can errors following transmission be detected and can the data be recovered
● the role of encryption to make sure data that falls into the wrong hands can't be used

It is also important to consider ways of checking for errors in data once it has been entered into a computer.

2.1 Types and methods of data transmission

2.1.1 Data packets

> Data packets are usually referred to simply as 'packets'

Data sent over long distances is usually broken up into **data packets** (sometimes called datagrams). The packets of data are usually quite small, typically 64 KiB, which are much easier to control than a long continuous stream of data. The idea of splitting up data in this way means each packet can be sent along a different route to its destination. This would clearly be of great benefit if a particular transmission route was out of action or very busy. The only obvious drawback of

45

splitting data into packets is the need to reassemble the data when it reaches its destination.

Packet structure

A typical packet is split up into:

» a packet header
» the payload
» a trailer.

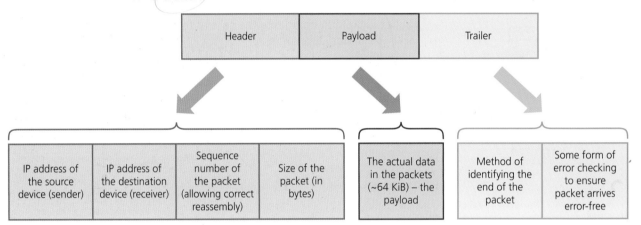

▲ **Figure 2.1** Packet structure

For **each** packet, the **packet header** consists of:

» the IP address of the sending device
» the IP address of the receiving device
» the sequence number of the packet (this is to ensure that all the packets can be reassembled into the correct order once they reach the destination)
» packet size (this is to ensure the receiving station can check if all of the packets have arrived intact).

(Note: the header often also contains another value indicating how many packets there are in total for this transmission.)

For **each** packet, the **payload** consists of the actual data being sent in the packet (this is usually about 64 KiB).

For **each** packet, the **packet trailer** consists of:

» some way of identifying the end of the packet; this is essential to allow each packet to be separated from each other as they travel from sending to receiving station
» an error checking method; **cyclic redundancy checks** (CRCs) are used to check data packets:
  – this involves the sending computer adding up all the 1-bits in the payload and storing this as a hex value in the trailer before it is sent
  – once the packet arrives, the receiving computer recalculates the number of 1-bits in the payload
  – the computer then checks this value against the one sent in the trailer
  – if the two values match, then no transmission errors have occurred; otherwise the packet needs to be re-sent.

Packet switching

Let us now consider what happens when a photograph, for example, is sent from computer 'A' to computer 'B'. The photograph will be split up into a number of packets before it is sent. There will be several possible routes for the packets, between computer 'A' (sender) and computer 'B' (receiver). Each stage in the route contains a router. A router receives a data packet and, based on the information in the header, decides where to send it next. For example:

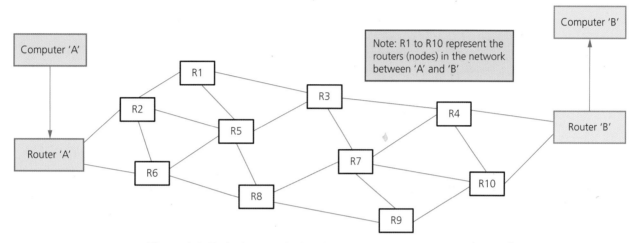

▲ **Figure 2.2** Typical network showing possible routes between 'A' and 'B'

Packet switching is a method of data transmission in which a message is broken up into a number of packets. **Each** packet can then be sent independently from start point to end point. At the destination, the packets will need to be reassembled into their correct order (using the information sent in the header). At each stage in the transmission, there are **nodes** that contain a router. Each router will determine which route the packet needs to take, in order to reach its destination (the destination IP address is used in this part of the process).

Suppose our photograph (Figure 2.3) has been split up into five packets that have been sent in the following order:

■ ■ ■ ■ ■

▲ **Figure 2.3**

» each packet will follow its own path (route)
» routers will determine the route of each packet
» routing selection depends on the number of packets waiting to be processed at each node
» the shortest possible path **available** is always selected – this may not always be the shortest path that **could** be taken, since certain parts of the route may be too busy or not suitable
» unfortunately, packets can reach the destination in a different order to that in which they were sent.

Figure 2.5 shows one possible scenario. Notice the different paths taken by each packet from computer 'A' to computer 'B'. Also notice that the packets have arrived in a different order compared to the way they were sent, namely:

■ ■ ■ ■ ■

▲ **Figure 2.4**

Computer 'B' will now have to reassemble the packets into the original sequence.

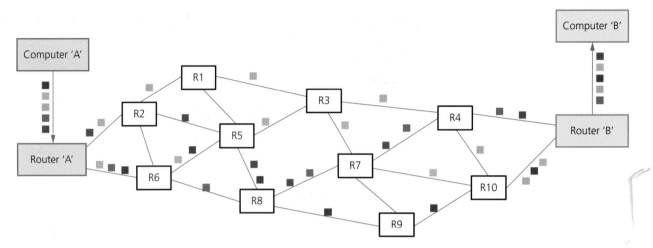

▲ **Figure 2.5** Typical network showing possible paths taken by each packet

The benefits of packet switching are:

» there is no need to tie up a single communication line
» it is possible to overcome failed, busy or faulty lines by simply re-routing packets
» it is relatively easy to expand package usage
» a high data transmission rate is possible.

The drawbacks of packet switching include:

» packets can be lost and need to be re-sent
» the method is more prone to errors with **real-time streaming** (for example, a live sporting event being transmitted over the internet)
» there is a delay at the destination whilst the packets are being re-ordered.

Sometimes it is possible for packets to get lost because they keep 'bouncing' around from router to router and never actually reach their destination. Eventually the network would just grind to a halt as the number of **lost packets** mount up, clogging up the system. To overcome this, a method called **hopping** is used. A **hop number** is added to the header of each packet, and this number is reduced by 1 *every time it leaves a router* (Figure 2.6).

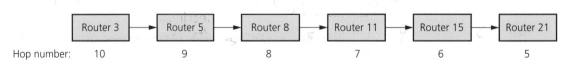

| Router 3 | Router 5 | Router 8 | Router 11 | Router 15 | Router 21 |

Hop number: 10   9   8   7   6   5

▲ **Figure 2.6** Hop numbers between routers

Each packet has a maximum hop number to start with. Once a hop number reaches zero, and the packet hasn't reached its destination, then the packet is deleted when it reaches the next router. The missing packets will then be flagged by the receiving computer and a request to re-send these packets will be made.

Find out more

Another method of sending packets is called circuit switching. Find out how this differs to packet switching, and then re-draw Figure 2.5 showing the route the packets take when using circuit switching.

Advice

Hopping is not included on the syllabus but is included here for completeness (to help understand how packets can get lost).

Activity 2.1

1 Suppose a video conference is taking place between delegates in two different countries. Packet switching is being used to send video and sound data between the delegates:

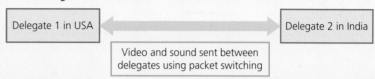

| Delegate 1 in USA | ⟷ | Delegate 2 in India |

Video and sound sent between delegates using packet switching

▲ **Figure 2.7**

Describe:

i any potential problems with sound and video quality

ii how these problems could be caused.

2 Explain how packet switching could be used to download a large web page from a website.

3 a The trailer in a packet will use one form of error checking.

Explain what is meant by a cyclic redundancy check.

b The payload contains the following data:

```
11110000 10000011 00110011 00111111 11111110 11100011
```

Use this data to show how the receiving computer can verify that the received payload was error-free.

4 a Explain how it is possible for packets to be lost during their transmission across a network.

b Describe how it is possible for a system to deal with lost packets and prevent them from slowing down the transmission process.

c Explain why you think packet switching might improve data security.

2.1.2 Data transmission

Data transmission can be either over a short distance (for example, computer to printer) or over longer distances (for example, from one computer to another in a global network). Essentially, three factors need to be considered when transmitting data:

➤ the direction of data transmission (for example, can data transmit in one direction only, or in both directions)

➤ the method of transmission (for example, how many bits can be sent at the same time)

➤ how will data be synchronised (that is, how to make sure the received data is in the correct order).

These factors are usually considered by a communication protocol.

Simplex, half-duplex and full-duplex

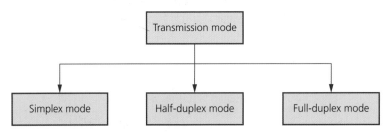

▲ **Figure 2.8** Transmission modes

Simplex data transmission

Simplex mode occurs when data can be sent in **ONE DIRECTION ONLY** (for example, from sender to receiver). An example of this would be sending data from a computer to a printer.

Half-duplex data transmission

Half-duplex mode occurs when data is sent in **BOTH DIRECTIONS** but **NOT AT THE SAME TIME** (for example, data can be sent from 'A' to 'B' and from 'B' to 'A' along the same transmission line, but they can't both be done at the same time). An example of this would be a walkie-talkie where a message can be sent in one direction only at a time; but messages can be both received and sent.

Full-duplex data transmission

Full-duplex mode occurs when data can be sent in **BOTH DIRECTIONS AT THE SAME TIME** (for example, data can be sent from 'A' to 'B' and from 'B' to 'A' along the same transmission line simultaneously). An example of this would be a broadband internet connection.

Serial and parallel data transmission

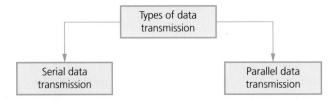

▲ **Figure 2.9** Types of data transmission

Serial data transmission occurs when data is sent **ONE BIT AT A TIME** over a **SINGLE WIRE/CHANNEL**. Bits are sent one after the other as a single stream.

▲ **Figure 2.10** Serial data transmission

(Note: Serial data transmission can be simplex, half-duplex or full-duplex.)

Serial data transmission works well over long distances. However, the data is transmitted at a slower rate than parallel data transmission. Because only one channel/wire is used, data will arrive at its destination fully synchronised (i.e. in the correct order). An example of its use is when connecting a computer to a printer via a USB connection (see Section 2.1.3).

Parallel data transmission occurs when **SEVERAL BITS OF DATA** (usually one byte) are sent down **SEVERAL CHANNELS/WIRES** all at the same time. Each channel/wire transmits one bit:

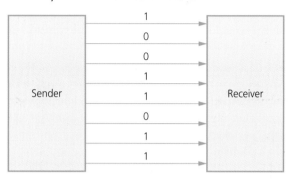

▲ **Figure 2.11** Parallel data transmission

(Note: Parallel data transmission can be simplex, half-duplex or full-duplex.)

Parallel data transmission works well over short distances. Over longer distances (for example, over 20 metres), data can become **skewed** (that is, the data can arrive unsynchronised) and bits can arrive out of order. The longer the wire, the worse this can become. It is, however, a faster method of data transmission than serial. The internal circuits in a computer use parallel data transmission since the distance travelled between components is very short and high-speed transmission is essential.

> ## Link
> For more on data transmission within the CPU refer to Chapter 3.

Activity 2.2

1 Explain what is meant by:
   i   serial, half-duplex data transmission
   ii   parallel, full-duplex data transmission
   iii serial, simplex data transmission.

2 Which types of data transmission are being described:
   i   data is sent one bit at a time in one direction only
   ii   data is being sent 8 bits at a time in one direction only
   iii data is being sent 16 bits at a time in both directions simultaneously
   iv   data is sent one bit at a time in both directions simultaneously
   v   data is sent 16 bits at a time in one direction only?

Table 2.1 shows the comparison between serial and parallel data transmission.

▼ **Table 2.1** Comparison of serial and parallel data transmission methods

Serial	Parallel
less risk of external interference than with parallel (due to fewer wires)	faster rate of data transmission than serial
more reliable transmission over longer distances	works well over shorter distances (for example, used in internal pathways on computer circuit boards)
transmitted bits won't have the risk of being skewed (that is, out of synchronisation)	since several channels/wires used to transmit data, the bits can arrive out of synchronisation (skewed)
used if the amount of data being sent is relatively small since transmission rate is slower than parallel (for example, USB uses this method of data transmission)	preferred method when speed is important
used to send data over long distances (for example, telephone lines)	if data is time-sensitive, parallel is the most appropriate transmission method
less expensive than parallel due to fewer hardware requirements	parallel ports require more hardware, making them more expensive to implement than serial ports
	easier to program input/output operations when parallel used

2.1.3 Universal serial bus (USB)

Link

....

Also refer to Section 4.1 on software drivers regarding devices plugged into USB ports.

As the name suggests, the **universal serial bus (USB)** is a form of serial data transmission. USB is now the most common type of input/output port found on computers and has led to a standardisation method for the transfer of data between devices and a computer. It is important to note that USB allows both half-duplex and full-duplex data transmission.

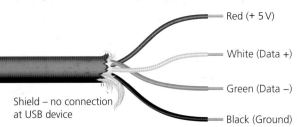

Red (+ 5 V)

White (Data +)

Green (Data −)

Black (Ground)

Shield – no connection at USB device

▲ **Figure 2.12** Typical USB cable

As Figure 2.12 shows, the USB cable consists of a four-wired shielded cable, with two wires for power (red and black). The other two wires (white and green) are for data transmission. When a device is plugged into a computer using one of the USB ports:

» the computer automatically detects that a device is present (this is due to a small change in the voltage on the data signal wires in the USB cable)
» the device is automatically recognised, and the appropriate device driver software is loaded up so that the computer and device can communicate effectively
» if a new device is detected, the computer will look for the device driver that matches the device; if this is not available, the user is prompted to download the appropriate driver software (some systems do this automatically and the user will see a notice asking for permission to connect to the device website).

We will now consider the benefits and drawbacks of using the USB system:

▼ **Table 2.2** Benefits and drawbacks of USB systems

Benefits	Drawbacks
devices plugged into the computer are automatically detected and device drivers are automatically loaded up	standard USB only supports a maximum cable length of 5 m; beyond that, USB hubs are needed to extend the cable length
connections can only fit one way preventing incorrect connections being made	
it has become an industry standard, which means considerable support is available	even though USB is backward compatible, very early USB standards (V1) may not always be supported by the latest computers
can support different data transmission rates (from 1.5 Mbps to 5 Gbps)	
no need for external power source since cable supplies +5 V power	even the latest version 3 (V3) and version 4 (V4) USB-C systems have a data transfer rate which is slow compared to, for example, Ethernet connections (Note: USB V2 has a maximum data transfer rate of 480 Mbps.)
USB protocol notifies the transmitter to re- transmit data if any errors are detected; this leads to error-free data transmission	
it is relatively easy to add more USB ports if necessary, by using USB hubs	
USB is backward compatible (that is, older versions are still supported)	

A new type of USB connector, referred to as USB-C, is now becoming more common in laptops and tablets/phones. This is a 24-pin symmetrical connector which means it will fit into a USB-C port either way round. It is much smaller and thinner than older USB connectors, offers 100 watt (20 volt) power connectivity, which means full-sized devices can now be charged and it can carry data at 10 gigabits per second (10 Gbps); this means it can now support 4K video delivery.

USB-C is backward compatible (to USB 2.0 and 3.0) provided a suitable adaptor is used, and is expected to become the new industry standard (universal) format.

Activity 2.3

Ten statements are shown on the left in the table. Each of these statements is either True or False. For each statement, tick (✔) the appropriate column to indicate which statements are true and which are false.

Statement	True	False
Packets have a header which contains the IP address of the sender and the receiver		
Packets don't require any form of error checking		
USBs use a protocol that allows for error-free data transmission between device and computer		
Serial data transmission suffers from data skewing		
The longest cable length supported by USB is 5 metres or less		
Simplex data transmission occurs when data is transmitted one bit at a time		
Full-duplex data transmission involves sending 8 bits of data at a time		
USB uses serial data transfer		
Packet switching prevents loss of any data packets		
USB connections can transfer data using half-duplex or full-duplex		

2.2 Methods of error detection

2.2.1 The need to check for errors

When data is transmitted, there is always a risk that it may be corrupted, lost or even gained.

Errors can occur during data transmission due to:

» interference (all types of cable can suffer from electrical interference, which can cause data to be corrupted or even lost)
» problems during packet switching (this can lead to data loss – or it is even possible to gain data!)
» skewing of data (this occurs during parallel data transmission and can cause data corruption if the bits arrive out of synchronisation).

Checking for errors is important since computers are unable to understand text, for example, if the words are not recognised by its built-in dictionary. Look at the following example of some corrupted text:

> Can you raed tihs?
>
> "I cnduo't bvleiee taht I culod aulaclty uesdtannrd waht I was rdnaieg. Unisg the icndeblire pweor of the hmuan mnid, aocdcrnig to rseecrah at Cmabridge Uinervtisy, it dseno't mttaer in waht oderr the lterets in a wrod are, the olny irpoamtnt tihng is taht the frsit and lsat ltteer be in the rhgit pclae. The rset can be a taotl mses and you can sitll raed it whoutit a pboerlm.
>
> Tihs is bucseae the huamn mnid deos not raed ervey ltteer by istlef, but the wrod as a wlohe.
>
> Aaznmig, huh? Yeah and I awlyas tghhuot slelinpg was ipmorantt! See if yuor fdreins can raed tihs too"
>
> (from an unknown source at Cambridge University)

▲ **Figure 2.13** Example of data corruption on a message

Whilst you probably had little problem understanding this text, a computer would be unable to make any sense of it. Data corruption is therefore a very real problem to a computer. Figure 2.13 could be the result of some data corruption following transmission which would make the text unintelligible to a computer. This is why error checking is such an important part of computer technology. The following section considers a number of ways that can be used to check for errors, so that you don't end up with text as shown in Figure 2.13 above!

There are a number of ways data can be checked for errors following transmission:

» parity checks
» checksum
» echo check.

2.2.2 Parity checks, checksum and echo checks

Parity checks

Parity checking is one method used to check whether data has been changed or corrupted following data transmission. This method is based on the number of 1-bits in a byte of data.

The parity can be either called **EVEN** (that is, an even number of 1-bits in the byte) or **ODD** (that is, an odd number of 1-bits in the byte). One of the bits in the byte (usually the most significant bit or left-most bit) is reserved for a **parity bit**. The parity bit is set according to whether the parity being used is even or odd. For example, consider the byte:

	1	1	0	1	1	0	0

parity bit

Advice

Note for the 7 bit number 1110000, the even parity bit would be 1 and the odd parity bit would be 0. The parity bit can be set as a 1 or a 0 for either choice of parity – it just depends on how many 1s are in the byte.

In this example, if the byte is using even parity, then the parity bit needs to be set to 0, since there is already an even number of 1-bits in the byte (four 1-bits). We thus get:

0	1	1	0	1	1	0	0

parity bit

In this example, if the byte is using odd parity, then the parity bit needs to be set to 1, since we need to have an odd number of 1-bits in the byte. We thus get:

1	1	1	0	1	1	0	0

parity bit

Before data is transferred, an agreement is made between sender and receiver regarding which type of parity is being used. Parity checks are therefore being used as a type of transmission protocol.

Activity 2.4

Find the parity bits for each of the following bytes:

	1	1	0	1	1	0	1	even parity being used
	0	0	0	1	1	1	1	even parity being used
	0	1	1	1	0	0	0	even parity being used
	1	1	1	0	1	0	0	odd parity being used
	1	0	1	1	0	1	1	odd parity being used
	1	1	1	1	1	1	0	even parity being used
	1	1	1	1	1	1	0	odd parity being used
	1	1	0	1	0	0	0	odd parity being used
	0	0	0	0	1	1	1	even parity being used
	1	1	1	1	1	1	1	odd parity being used

If a byte has been transmitted from 'A' to 'B', and if even parity is used, an error would be flagged if the byte now had an odd number of 1-bits at the receiver's end. For example (assuming even parity is being used):

byte being sent:

0	1	0	1	1	1	0	0

parity bit

byte being received:

0	1	0	0	1	1	0	0

parity bit

In this case, the byte received has three 1-bits, which means it now has odd parity; while the sender's byte was using even parity (four 1-bits). This means an error has occurred during the transmission of the byte. The error is detected by the recipient's computer re-calculating the parity of the byte sent. If even parity had been agreed between sender and receiver, then a change in parity in the received byte indicates that a transmission error has occurred.

Activity 2.5

1   Which of the following received bytes indicate an error has occurred following data transmission?

1	1	1	0	1	1	0	1	even parity being used
0	1	0	0	1	1	1	1	even parity being used
0	0	1	1	1	0	0	0	even parity being used
1	1	1	1	0	1	0	0	odd parity being used
1	1	0	1	1	0	1	1	odd parity being used
1	1	1	1	1	1	1	1	odd parity being used
0	0	0	0	0	0	0	0	even parity being used
1	1	1	0	0	0	0	0	odd parity being used
0	1	0	1	0	1	0	1	even parity being used
1	1	1	0	0	0	1	1	odd parity being used

2   In each case, in **question 1**, where an error occurred, can you work out which bit in the byte was changed during data transmission?

If two of the bits change value following data transmission, it may be impossible to locate the error using parity checking.

Let us imagine we are transmitting the following byte, using even parity:

0	1	0	1	1	1	0	0

Suppose more than one bit has been modified during data transmission. This means the byte could have reached the destination as any of the following:

0	1	1	1	1	1	0	1	six 1-bits

| 0 | 1 | 0 | 1 | 0 | 0 | 0 | 0 | two 1-bits |

| 0 | 1 | 0 | 1 | 0 | 1 | 1 | 0 | four 1-bits |

In all these cases, the byte has clearly been corrupted, but the bytes have retained even parity. Therefore, no error would be flagged in spite of the obvious errors in transmission. Clearly it will be necessary to have other ways to complement parity when it comes to error checking to ensure errors are never missed. One such method is called checksum – see the next section.

You should have concluded that *any* of the bits in question 2 (Activity 2.5) could have been changed where there was a transmission error. Therefore, even though an error has been flagged, it is impossible to know **exactly** which bit is in error.

One of the ways round this problem is to use **parity blocks**. In this method, a block of data is sent and the number of 1-bits are totalled horizontally and vertically (in other words, a parity check is done in both horizontal and vertical directions). As the following example shows, this method not only identifies that an error has occurred but also indicates where the error is.

? Example 1

In this example, nine bytes of data have been transmitted. Agreement has been made that **even parity** will be used. Another byte, known as the **parity byte**, has also been sent. This byte consists entirely of the parity bits produced by the vertical parity check. The parity byte also indicates the end of the block of data.

Table 2.3 shows how the data arrived at the receiving end. It is now necessary to check the parity of each byte horizontally (bytes 1 to 9) and vertically (columns 1 to 8). Each row and column where the parity has changed from even to odd should be flagged:

▼ **Table 2.3** Parity block showing nine bytes and parity byte

	Parity bit	Bit 2	Bit 3	Bit 4	Bit 5	Bit 6	Bit 7	Bit 8
Byte 1	1	1	1	1	0	1	1	0
Byte 2	1	0	0	1	0	1	0	1
Byte 3	0	1	1	1	1	1	1	0
Byte 4	1	0	0	0	0	0	1	0
Byte 5	0	1	1	0	1	0	0	1
Byte 6	1	0	0	0	1	0	0	0
Byte 7	1	0	1	0	1	1	1	1
Byte 8	0	0	0	1	1	0	1	0
Byte 9	0	0	0	1	0	0	1	0
Parity byte	1	1	0	1	0	0	0	1

A careful study of Table 2.3 shows the following:
» byte 8 (row 8) now has incorrect parity (there are three 1-bits)
» bit 5 (column 5) also now has incorrect parity (there are five 1-bits).

First of all, the table shows that an error has occurred following data transmission (there has been a change in parity in one of the bytes).

Secondly, at the intersection of row 8 and column 5, the position of the incorrect bit value (which caused the error) can be found. The 1-bit at this intersection should be a 0-bit; this means that byte 8 should have been:

0	0	0	1	0	0	1	0

which would also correct column 5 giving an even vertical parity (now has four 1-bits).

This byte could therefore be corrected automatically as shown above, or an error message could be relayed back to the sender asking them to re-transmit the block of data.

Activity 2.6

1 The following block of data was received after transmission from a remote computer; **odd parity** was being used by both sender and receiver. One of the bits has been changed during the transmission stage. Locate where this error is and suggest a corrected byte value:

	Parity bit	Bit 2	Bit 3	Bit 4	Bit 5	Bit 6	Bit 7	Bit 8
Byte 1	0	1	1	0	0	0	1	0
Byte 2	1	0	1	1	1	1	1	1
Byte 3	1	0	0	1	1	0	0	0
Byte 4	0	1	1	0	1	0	1	0
Byte 5	1	1	1	0	0	1	1	0
Byte 6	1	0	0	0	0	1	0	1
Byte 7	0	1	1	1	0	0	0	0
Byte 8	0	0	0	0	0	0	0	1
Byte 9	0	1	1	1	1	0	1	0
Parity byte	1	0	1	1	1	1	0	0

2 The following block of data was received after transmission from a remote computer. Even parity was being used by both sender and receiver. One of the bytes has been changed during the transmission stage. Locate where this error is and suggest a corrected byte value.

	Parity bit	Bit 2	Bit 3	Bit 4	Bit 5	Bit 6	Bit 7	Bit 8
Byte 1	1	1	0	0	0	0	0	0
Byte 2	0	0	1	1	1	1	0	0
Byte 3	0	1	0	0	0	1	1	1
Byte 4	1	0	1	0	1	1	1	1
Byte 5	0	0	0	1	0	0	0	1
Byte 6	0	0	1	1	1	1	1	1
Byte 7	1	0	1	1	0	1	0	0
Byte 8	0	1	0	1	0	0	0	1
Byte 9	1	1	1	0	0	1	0	0
Parity byte	0	0	1	1	1	0	0	1

Checksum

A **checksum** is a method used to check if data has been changed or corrupted following data transmission. Data is sent in blocks, and an additional value, called the checksum, is sent at the end of the block of data.

The checksum process is as follows:

» when a block of data is about to be transmitted, the checksum is calculated from the block of data
» the calculation is done using an agreed algorithm (this algorithm has been agreed by sender and receiver)
» the checksum is then transmitted with the block of data
» at the receiving end, the checksum is recalculated by the computer using the block of data (the agreed algorithm is used to find the checksum)
» the re-calculated checksum is then compared to the checksum sent with the data block
» if the two checksums are the same, then no transmission errors have occurred; otherwise a request is made to re-send the block of data.

Echo check

With **echo check**, when data is sent to another device, this data is sent back again to the sender. The sender's computer compares the two sets of data to check if any errors occurred during the transmission process.

As you will have no doubt worked out, this isn't very reliable. If the two sets of data are different, it isn't known whether the error occurred when sending the data in the first place, or if the error occurred when sending the data back for checking.

However, if no errors occurred, then it is another way to check that the data was transmitted correctly. In summary:

» a copy of the data is sent back to the sender
» the returned data is compared with the original data by the sender's computer
» if there are no differences, then the data was sent without error
» if the two sets of data are different, then an error occurred at some stage during the data transmission.

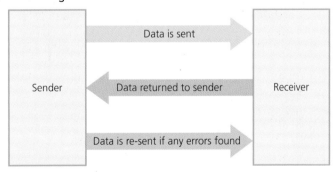

▲ **Figure 2.14** Echo check diagram

2.2.3 Check digits

A **check digit** is the final digit included in a code; it is calculated from all the other digits in the code. Check digits are used for barcodes on products, such as International Standard Book Numbers (ISBN) and Vehicle Identification Numbers

(VIN). Check digits are used to identify errors in *data entry* caused by mis-typing or mis-scanning a barcode. They can usually detect the following types of error:

» an incorrect digit entered, for example 5327 entered instead of 5307
» transposition errors where two numbers have changed order, for example 5037 instead of 5307
» omitted or extra digits, for example 537 instead of 5307 or 53107 instead of 5307
» phonetic errors, for example 13 (thirteen), instead of 30 (thirty).

▲ **Figure 2.15** Sample barcode (ISBN 13 code with check digit)

There are a number of different methods used to generate a check digit. Two common methods will be considered here:

» ISBN 13
» Modulo-11

? Example 1: ISBN 13

The check digit in ISBN 13 is the thirteenth digit in the number. We will now consider two different calculations. The first calculation is the generation of the check digit. The second calculation is a verification of the check digit (that is, a recalculation).

Calculation 1 – Generation of the check digit from the other 12 digits in a number
The following algorithm generates the check digit from the 12 other digits:
1 add all the odd numbered digits together
2 add all the even numbered digits together and multiply the result by 3
3 add the results from 1 and 2 together and divide by 10
4 take the remainder, if it is zero then use this value, otherwise subtract the remainder from 10 to find the check digit.

Using the ISBN **9 7 8 0 3 4 0 9 8 3 8 2** (note this is the same ISBN as in Figure 2.15):

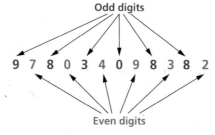

▲ **Figure 2.16** ISBN (no check digit)

1 **9 + 8 + 3 + 0 + 8 + 8 = 36**
2 $3 \times (7 + 0 + 4 + 9 + 3 + 2) = 75$
3 $(36 + 75)/10 = 111/10 = 11$ remainder 1
4 $10 - 1 = 9$ the check digit

So we end up with the following thirteen-digit number (which matches the number shown in Figure 2.15):

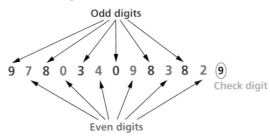

▲ **Figure 2.17** ISBN (including the check digit)

Calculation 2 – Re-calculation of the check digit from the thirteen-digit number (which now includes the check digit)

To check that an ISBN 13-digit code is correct, including its check digit, a similar process is followed:
1 add all the odd numbered digits together, **including** the check digit
2 add all the even number of digits together and multiply the result by 3
3 add the results from **1** and **2** together and divide by 10
4 the number is correct if the remainder is zero.

Using the ISBN **9 7 8 0 3 4 0 9 8 3 8 2 9** (including its check digit) from Figure 2.17:
1 **9 + 8 + 3 + 0 + 8 + 8 + 9 = 45**
2 3 × (7 + 0 + 4 + 9 + 3 + 2) = 75
3 (45 + 75)/10 = 120/10 = 12 remainder 0
4 remainder is 0, therefore number is correct.

❓ Example 2: Modulo-11

The modulo-11 method can have varying lengths of number which makes it suitable for many applications, such as product codes or VINs. The first calculation is the generation of the check digit. The second calculation is a verification of the check digit (that is, a recalculation).

Calculation 1 – Generation of the check digit from the other digits in a number

(In this example, we will assume the original number contained only 7 digits.)

The following algorithm generates the check digit from the other 7 digits:
1 each digit in the number is given a weighting of 8, 7, 6, 5, 4, 3 or 2 starting from the left (weightings start from 8 since the number will become eight-digit when the check digit is added)
2 the digit is multiplied by its weighting and then each value is added to make a total
3 the total is divided by 11
4 the remainder is then subtracted from 11 to find the check digit (note if the remainder is 10 then the check digit 'X' is used).

The example to be used has the following seven-digit number:
1 7-digit number: 4 1 5 6 7 1 0

weighting values: 8 7 6 5 4 3 2

2 sum: (8 × 4) + (7 × 1) + (6 × 5) + (5 × 6) + (4 × 7) + (3 × 1) + (2 × 0)
      = 32 + 7 + 30 + 30 + 28 + 3 + 0
total = 130
3 divide total by 11: 130/11 = 11 remainder 9
4 subtract remainder from 11: 11 – 9 = 2 (check digit)

So we end up with the following eight-digit: 4 1 5 6 7 1 0 2

Calculation 2 – Re-calculation of the check digit from the eight-digit number (which now includes the check digit)

To check that the eight-digit number is correct, including its check digit, a similar process is followed:

1 each digit in the number is given a weighting of 8, 7, 6, 5, 4, 3, 2 or 1 starting from the left
2 the digit is multiplied by its weighting and then each value is added to make a total
3 the total is divided by 11
4 the number is correct if the remainder is zero

Using the 8-digit number: 4   1   5   6   7   1   0   2
1 weighting values: 8   7   6   5   4   3   2   1
2 sum: $(8 \times 4) + (7 \times 1) + (6 \times 5) + (5 \times 6) + (4 \times 7) + (3 \times 1) + (2 \times 0) + (1 \times 2)$
        = 32 +   7 + 30 + 30 + 28 + 3 + 0 + 2
   total = 132
3 divide total by 11: 132/11 = 12 remainder 0
4 remainder is 0, therefore number is correct

Activity 2.7

1 Using the algorithm for ISBN-13 calculate the check digit for:

   978151045759

2 Find the check digits for the following numbers using **both** modulo-11 and ISBN 13 methods:
   i   2 1 3 1 1 1 0 0 0 4 2 8
   ii 9 0 9 8 1 2 1 2 3 5 4 4

2.2.4 Automatic Repeat Requests (ARQs)

We have already considered parity checks and echo checks as methods to verify that data has arrived at its destination unchanged. An **Automatic Repeat Request (ARQ)** is a third way used to check data following data transmission. This method can best be summarised as follows:

» ARQ uses positive and negative **acknowledgements** (messages sent to the receiver indicating that data has/has not been received correctly) and **timeout** (this is the time interval allowed to elapse before an acknowledgement is received)
» the receiving device receives an error detection code as part of the data transmission (this is typically a Cyclic Redundancy Check – refer to Section 2.1.1); this is used to detect whether the received data contains any transmission errors
» if no error is detected, a positive acknowledgement is sent back to the sending device
» however, if an error is detected, the receiving device now sends a negative acknowledgement to the sending device and requests re-transmission of the data
» a time-out is used by the sending device by waiting a pre-determined amount of time ....
» ... and if no acknowledgement of any type has been received by the sending device within this time limit, it automatically re-sends the data until a positive acknowledgement is received ....
» ... or until a pre-determined number of re-transmissions has taken place
» ARQ is often used by mobile phone networks to guarantee data integrity.

2.3 Symmetric and asymmetric encryption

2.3.1 The purpose of encryption

When data is transmitted over any public network (wired or wireless), there is always a risk of it being intercepted by, for example, a hacker. Under these circumstances, a hacker is often referred to as an **eavesdropper**. Using **encryption** helps to minimise this risk.

Encryption alters data into a form that is unreadable by anybody for whom the data is not intended. It cannot prevent the data being intercepted, but it stops it from making any sense to the eavesdropper. This is particularly important if the data is sensitive or confidential (for example, credit card/bank details, medical history or legal documents).

> **Link**
> ....
> For more on cyber security see Chapter 5.

Plaintext and ciphertext

The original data being sent is known as **plaintext.** Once it has gone through an **encryption algorithm**, it produces **ciphertext**:

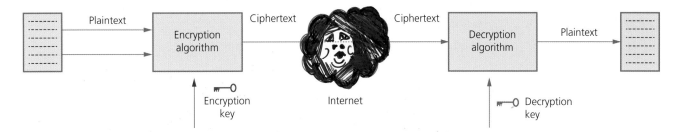

▲ **Figure 2.18** Plaintext and ciphertext

2.3.2 Symmetric and asymmetric encryption

Symmetric encryption

Symmetric encryption uses an encryption key; the same key is used to encrypt and decrypt the encoded message. First of all, consider a simple system that uses a 10-digit denary encryption key (this gives 1×10^{10} possible codes); and a decryption key. Suppose our encryption key is:

$$4\ 2\ 9\ 1\ 3\ 6\ 2\ 8\ 5\ 6$$

which means every letter in a word is shifted across the alphabet +4, +2, +9, +1, and so on, places. For example, here is the message COMPUTER SCIENCE IS EXCITING (plaintext on the top line of Figure 2.19) before and after applying the encryption key (forming the ciphertext shown on the bottom line of Figure 2.19):

C	O	M	P	U	T	E	R		S	C	I	E	N	C	E		I	S		E	X	C	I	T	I	N	G
4	2	9	1	3	6	2	8		5	6	4	2	9	1	3		6	2		8	5	6	4	2	9	1	3
G	Q	V	Q	X	Z	G	Z		X	I	M	G	W	D	H		O	U		M	C	I	M	V	R	O	J

▲ **Figure 2.19** Plaintext into ciphertext using 10-digit encryption key

To get back to the original message, it will be necessary to apply the same decryption key; that is, 4 2 9 1 3 6 2 8 5 6. But in this case, the decryption process would be the reverse of encryption and each letter would be shifted –4, –2, –9, –1, and so on. For example, 'G' ⟶ 'C', 'Q' ⟶ 'O', 'V' ⟶ 'M', 'Q' ⟶ 'P', and so on.

However, modern computers could 'crack' this encryption key in a matter of seconds. To try to combat this, we now use 256-bit binary encryption keys that give 2^{256} (approximately, 1.2×10^{77}) possible combinations. (Even this may not be enough as we head towards **quantum computers**.)

The real difficulty is keeping the encryption key a secret (for example, it needs to be sent in an email or a text message which can be intercepted). Therefore, the issue of security is always the main drawback of symmetrical encryption, since a single encryption key is required for both sender and recipient.

Asymmetric encryption

Asymmetric encryption was developed to overcome the security problems associated with symmetric encryption. It makes use of two keys called the **public key** and the **private key**:

» public key (made available to everybody)
» private key (only known to the computer user).

Both types of key are needed to encrypt and decrypt messages.

We will use an example to explain how this works; suppose Tom and Jane work for the same company and Tom wishes to send a confidential document to Jane:

1 Jane uses an algorithm to generate a **matching pair of keys** (private and public) that they must keep stored on their computers; the matching pairs of keys are mathematically linked but can't be derived from each other.
2 Jane now sends her public key to Tom.

▲ **Figure 2.20** Jane sends Tom her public key

3 Tom now uses Jane's public key (⟞—o) to encrypt the document he wishes to send to her. He then sends his encrypted document (ciphertext) back to Jane.

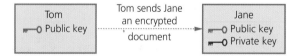

▲ **Figure 2.21** Encrypted document sent from Tom to Jane

4 Jane uses her **matching** private key (⟞—o) to unlock Tom's document and decrypt it; this works because the public key used to encrypt the document and the private key used to decrypt it are a matching pair generated on Jane's computer. (Jane can't use the public key to decrypt the message.)

 Find out more

One of the ways of mitigating the risk of symmetric keys falling into the wrong hands (known as the key distribution problem) is to use a system based on modulo-11, where both sender and receiver can calculate the encryption key without it actually being exchanged in any way. Find out how this system works.

Activity 2.8

1   At the moment Jane can only receive encrypted documents from Tom.
    Describe what would need to happen for Jane to be able to **send** encrypted documents back to Tom.

2   Explain why this method is much more secure than symmetric encryption.

Jane can also exchange her public key with any number of people working in the company, so she is able to receive encrypted messages (which have been encrypted using her public key ⊶) and she can then decrypt them using her matching private key:

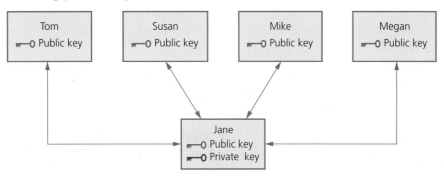

▲ **Figure 2.22** The sharing of Jane's public key

However, if a two-way communication is required between all five workers, then they all need to generate their own matching public and private keys. Once this is done, all users then need to swap public keys so that they can send encrypted documents/files/messages between each other. Each worker will then use their own private key to decrypt information being sent to them.

➡ Find out more

1   Using Figure 2.22 as your template, draw a new diagram showing the public keys and private keys that need to be swapped if Jane wishes to have a two-way exchange of encrypted documents between Tom, Susan, Mike and Megan.
2   Consider the complexity, if all five people want to have secure two-way communication between each other (and not just with Jane). This would mean each of the five workers sharing their own public keys with each of the other workers.

Activity 2.9

For each of the following ten questions, choose which of the five options corresponds to the correct response.

a   What is meant by the term **ciphertext** when used in encryption?

   A an encryption or decryption algorithm

   B an encrypted message

   C a type of session key

   D another name for plaintext

   E text following an encryption algorithm

b When carrying out asymmetric encryption, which of the following users would keep the private key?

    A the sender   **D** all recipients of the message

    B the receiver   **E** none of the above

    C both sender and receiver

c In encryption, which of the following is the term used to describe the message before it is encrypted?

    A simpletext   **D** ciphertext

    B plaintext   **E** firsttext

    C notext

d Which of the following is the biggest disadvantage of using symmetric encryption?

    A it is very complex and time consuming

    B it is rarely used anymore

    C the value of the key reads the same in both directions

    D it only works on computers with older operating systems

    E there is a security problem when transmitting the encryption key

e Which of the following is the correct name for a form of encryption in which both the sender and the recipient use the same key to encrypt and decrypt?

    A symmetric key encryption   **D** same key encryption

    B asymmetric key encryption   **E** block cipher encryption

    C public key encryption

f What of the following is the final number in a code, which is calculated from all the numbers in the code; its purpose is to find errors in data entry?

    A parity check   **D** parity bit

    B checksum   **E** check digit

    C cyclic redundancy check

g Which of the following is a form of error detection that makes use of a system of acknowledgements and timeouts?

    A automatic repeat request   **D** parity bit

    B echo check   **E** cyclic redundancy check

    C check digit

h Which of the following methods uses an extra bit added to a byte to ensure it contains an even number of 1s or odd number of 1s?

    A cyclic redundancy check   **D** check digit

    B parity check   **E** echo check

    C checksum

i Which of the following uses a calculated value which is sent after a block of data; the receiving computer also calculates the value from the block of data and compares the values?

    A parity check   **D** checksum

    B check digit   **E** automatic repeat request

    C packet switching

j Which of the following describes the check where the receiving computer sends back a copy of the data to the sending computer to allow it to compare the data?

A echo check

B automatic repeat request

C checksum

D parity check

E check digit

Extension

For those students considering the study of this subject at A Level, the following section gives some insight into further study on encryption.

Quantum cryptography exploits the laws of quantum mechanics to improve on the security of data. Quantum cryptography is based on the use of particles of light called photons (with energy calculated according to the formula: $E = hf$) and their physical quantum properties to produce a virtually unbreakable encryption system. This helps protect the security of data being transmitted over fibre optic cables. The technology is based on the laws of physics, rather than mathematics which is how the current cryptography methods already covered in this chapter work.

One of the uses of quantum cryptography is when sending encryption keys across a network – this uses a **Quantum Key Distribution (QKD)** protocol (one of the most common is called BB84).

QKD uses quantum mechanics to ensure a secure transmission of encryption keys. They use a **Qubit (Quantum bit)** which is the basic unit of quantum 'data'. Unlike normal binary (which uses discrete 0s and 1s), the state of a Qubit is **both** 0 and 1 until the photon is measured.

A photon normally vibrates or oscillates in all different directions. Polarisation restricts these vibrations to particular directions. The following diagram shows how a photon can be polarised in one of two **bases** – the rectilinear (up/down and side-to-side) basis and the diagonal basis. Do not worry too much about what a basis is – you can just think of them as two different ways of preparing and measuring the photon.

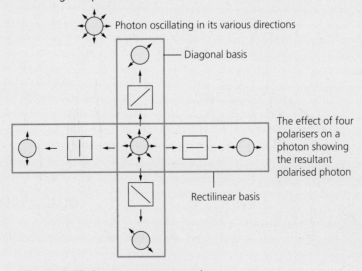

▲ **Figure 2.23** Quantum cryptography

So how do we use quantum cryptography to send an encryption key from 'A' to 'B' using the QKD protocol? To understand this we need to note that:

» Photons can be polarised in one of two bases – rectilinear or diagonal.
» In the rectilinear basis, 1 can be represented by ↕ and 0 by ↔. In the diagonal basis 1 is ⤢ and 0 is ⤡.
» A photon that is polarised in the rectilinear basis will always give the same result when measured in the rectilinear basis. So, if a photon is polarised as '1' in the rectilinear basis (↕) it will always be measured in the rectilinear basis to have the polarisation ↕.
» Similarly, a photon that is polarised in the diagonal basis will always give the same result when measured in the diagonal basis. So, if a photon is polarised as '1' in the diagonal basis (⤢) it will always be measured in the diagonal basis to have the polarisation ⤢.
» However, if a photon is polarised in the rectilinear basis but measured in the diagonal basis then information about the original polarisation is lost. The result of the measurement has a 50-50 chance of being ⤢ or ⤡ because in the diagonal basis the photon is in both 1 and 0 states **at the same time!** This measurement tells the receiver nothing about the photon's original polarisation in the rectilinear basis.
» Similarly, if a photon is polarised in the diagonal basis but measured in the rectilinear basis then information about the original polarisation is lost. The result of the measurement has a 50-50 chance of being ↕ or ↔ because in the rectilinear basis the photon is in both 1 and 0 states **at the same time**! This tells the receiver nothing about the photon's original polarisation in the diagonal basis.

1 So, the sender polarises each photon using a basis that is selected at random.
2 The receiver measures each photon using a basis that is selected at random.
3 The sender and receiver publicly exchange which basis they used for each photon.

Only when the sender and receiver use the same basis for measurement can they be sure that are both reading a 1 or 0. When they used the same basis the receiver knows they have measured a '1' or '0' correctly.

In this chapter, you have learnt about:
✔ the use of data packets when sending data over networks
✔ packet switching
✔ types of data transmission (serial, parallel, simplex, half-duplex and full-duplex)
✔ the universal serial bus (USB)
✔ how errors during transmission can occur and how to recognise them and recover from them (using parity check, checksum and echo check)
✔ the use of check digits to identify errors following data entry
✔ how automatic repeat requests are used to find errors in transmitted data
✔ why encryption of data is used
✔ symmetric and asymmetric encryption
✔ the use of public keys and private keys in asymmetric encryption.

Key terms used throughout this chapter

data packet – a small part of a message/data that is transmitted over a network; after transmission all the data packets are reassembled to form the original message/data

packet header – the part of the data packet that contains the IP addresses of the sender and receiver, and includes the packet number which allows reassembly of the data packets

packet trailer – the part of a data packet that indicates the end of the data packet and cyclic redundancy check error check

cyclic redundancy check (CRC) – an error checking method in which all the 1-bits in the data packet payload are added and the total is stored in the packet trailer; the same calculation is repeated at the receiving station

payload – the actual data being carried in a data packet

node – stages in a network that can receive and transmit data packets; routers are nodes in communication networks

packet switching – a method of transmission in which a message is broken into many data packets which can then be sent along pathways independently of each other

router – a device that enables data packets to be moved between different networks, for example to join a LAN to a WAN

real time streaming – the transmission of data over a network for live events where the data is sent as soon as it is received or generated

hopping/hop number – a number in a data packet header used to stop data packets that never reach their destination from 'clogging up' the data paths/routes

simplex – data that can be sent on one direction only

half-duplex – data that can be sent in both directions but not at the same time

full-duplex – data that can be sent in both directions at the same time (simultaneously)

serial data transmission – sending data down one channel/wire one bit at a time

parallel data transmission – sending data down several channels/wires several bits at a time (usually 1 byte)

skewed (data) – data that arrives at the destination with the bits no longer synchronised

universal serial bus (USB) – a type of serial data transmission which has become the industry standard for connecting computers to devices via a USB port

parity check – a method used to check if data has been transferred correctly; it makes use of even parity (an even number of 1-bits) or odd parity (an odd number of 1-bits)

parity bit – a bit (either 0 or 1) added to a byte of data in the most significant bit position; this ensures that the byte follows the correct even parity or odd parity protocol

parity block – a horizontal and vertical parity check on a block of data being transmitted

parity byte – an extra byte of data sent at the end of a parity block; it is composed of the parity bits generated from a vertical parity check of the data block

checksum – a verification method used to check if data transferred has been altered or corrupted; calculated from the block of data of data being sent; the checksum value is sent after each data block

automatic repeat request (ARQ) – a method of checking transmitted data for errors; it makes use of acknowledgement and timeout to automatically request re-sending of data if the time interval before positive acknowledgement is too long

acknowledgement – a message sent to the receiver indicating that data has been received correctly (used in the ARQ error detection method)

timeout – the time interval allowed to elapse before an acknowledgement is received (in the ARQ error detection method)

echo check – a method used to check if data has been transferred correctly; data is sent to a receiver and then immediately sent back to the sender; the sender then checks if the received data matches the sent data

check digit – an additional digit appended to a number to check if the entered number is error-free; check digit is a data entry check and not a data transmission check

eavesdropper – another name for a hacker who intercepts data being transmitted on a wired or wireless network

encryption – the process of making data meaningless using encryption keys; without the correct decryption key the data cannot be decoded (unscrambled)

plaintext – the original text/message before it is put through an encryption algorithm

ciphertext – encrypted data that is the result of putting a plaintext message through an encryption algorithm

encryption algorithm – a complex piece of software that takes plaintext and generates an encrypted string known as ciphertext

symmetric encryption – a type of encryption in which the same encryption key is used both to encrypt and decrypt a message

asymmetric encryption – a type of encryption that uses public keys and private keys to ensure data is secure

public key – a type of encryption key that is known to all users

private key – a type of encryption key which is known only to the single computer/user

quantum computer – a computer that can perform very fast calculations; it can perform calculations that are based on probability rather than simple 0 or 1 values; this gives a quantum computer the potential to process considerably more data than existing computers

Exam-style questions

1 A company owns a number of vending machines. Data is sent from each of these machines at the end of the day. The data contains amount of money taken, products sold and any error conditions/reports.

    a The company uses both echo checking and automatic repeat requests (ARQs).

        i Describe how echo checks work. Explain whether this is a suitable error checking method in this application. [2]

        ii Describe how automatic repeat request (ARQ) works. [3]

    b *Checksum* and *check digit* are two terms often confused by students.

      Describe **three** differences of the two techniques. [3]

2 Explain each of the following computer terms:

    i packet switching

    ii cyclic redundancy check

    iii data skewing

    iv universal serial bus

    v parity bit. [10]

3 Eight descriptions are given in the following table. The table columns are labelled checksum, parity check and ARQ.
Tick (✓) the appropriate column which correctly matches each description to the error-checking technique. For each description, it is possible to match 1, 2, 3 or none of the error-checking methods. [8]

Description	Checksum ✓	Parity check ✓	ARQ ✓
extra bit sent with each byte of data			
makes use of timeout and acknowledgement			
if an error is found, a request is made to re-send the data			
check on whether a data packet has been changed following transmission			
re-calculation made on any additional data values sent to the recipient			
data is transmitted in blocks or packets			
a method that can determine which bit in a data stream has been changed			
additional value sent at the end of a block of data to be used to check if any data transmission errors occurred			

4 a Four statements about automatic repeat requests (ARQs) are given below, but they are not in the correct order. Put the statements into their correct sequence.

        i the sending computer waits for a period of time to see if the receiving computer acknowledges receipt of the data

        ii after a set time period, a timeout occurs which automatically triggers the re-sending of the data

  iii the sending computer transmits a block of data to the receiving computer

  iv this continues until the receiving computer sends an acknowledgement that the data has been received [3]

b Five statements about checksum error checking are given below, but they are not in the correct order. Put the statements into their correct sequence.

  i if the two checksum values don't match, the receiving computer requests the data to be re-transmitted

  ii the sending computer sends a block of data together with the checksum value

  iii the receiving computer uses the block of data it receives to re-calculate the checksum using the same method as the sending computer

  iv the two checksum values are compared by the receiving computer

  v the sending computer uses the block of data to calculate the checksum using an agreed method [4]

c Five statements about parity checking are given below, but they are not in the correct order. Put the statements into their correct sequence.

  i the sending computer sends the binary data including the parity bits

  ii the sending and receiving computers agree the parity protocol (odd or even)

  iii the sending computer adds a parity bit to each byte to make the byte odd or even parity

  iv the receiving computer checks the parity of each byte received and checks it against the agreed protocol

  v if the parity of the byte is incorrect, the receiving computer requests the data to be re-sent [4]

d Six statements about check digits are given below, but they are not in the correct order. Put the statements into their correct sequence.

  i a human operator will be asked by the computer to re-enter the numerical code

  ii the computer calculates the check digit based on the numerical code entered into the computer by a human operator

  iii if the two check digits don't match, the human operator has made an error when entering the numerical code

  iv the computer compares the calculated check digit with the check digit typed in by the human operator

  v a human operator types in the numerical code into the computer

  vi the check digit is calculated and added to the numerical code [5]

5 **a** Describe what is meant by *symmetric encryption*. [2]

  b Describe what is meant by *asymmetric encryption*. [3]

  c Explain why encryption is used when transmitting data over a network. [2]

6 Six descriptions are shown on the left and ten computer terms on the right.

By drawing lines, connect each description to the correct computer term (not all of the computer terms will be used). [6]

a method of error detection; a value is calculated from a block of data and is sent with the block of data during data transmission	skewed data
	half-duplex
a method of error detection; it is based on counting the number of 1-bits; uses an additional bit which is the most significant bit in the byte	checksum
	ARQ
a data transmission method where data can be sent in both directions at the same time (simultaneously)	full-duplex
	check digit
a data transmission method where data is sent one bit at a time over a single channel/wire	universal serial bus
	encryption
a data error occurring when data arrives at the destination out of synchronisation	serial
a form of serial data transmission which allows devices to communicate with a computer; it has become the industrial standard	parity check

7 A file server is used as a central data store for a network of computers. Rory sends data from his computer to a file server that is approximately 100 metres away. It is important that the data is transmitted accurately. Rory needs to be able to read data from and write data to the file server at the same time.

a i Use ticks (✓) to identify the most suitable data transmission methods for this application. [2]

Method 1	Tick ✓	Method 2	Tick ✓
Serial		Simplex	
Parallel		Half-duplex	
		Duplex	

ii Explain why your answer to **a i** is the most suitable data transmission. [4]

b Identify and describe **two** methods of error checking that can be used to make sure that the data stored after transmission is accurate. [6]

Cambridge O Level Computer Science 2210, Paper 12 Q4, Oct/Nov 2017

8 Maisey purchases a new router and attaches it to her computer.
The connection she sets up uses duplex data transmission.

   a **Five** statements are given about duplex data transmission.
   Tick (✓) to show if the statement is **True** or **False**. [5]

Statement	True ✓	False ✓
Duplex data transmission can be either serial or parallel		
Duplex data transmission is when data is transmitted both ways, but only one way at a time		
Duplex transmission is always used to connect a device to a computer		
Duplex data transmission is when data is transmitted both ways at the same time		
Duplex data transmission automatically detects any errors in data		

   b Maisey's computer uses an integrated circuit (IC) for data transmission
   that sends multiple bits at the same time.
   State whether the IC uses **serial** or **parallel** data
   transmission. [1]

   c Maisey purchases a new printer and connects it to her computer
   using the USB port.
   Explain **two** benefits of using a USB connection. [4]

Cambridge O Level Computer Science 2210, Paper 12 Q9, Oct/Nov 2019

Hardware

> **In this chapter you will learn about:**
> ★ computer architecture
> - the Central Processing Unit (CPU)/microprocessor
> - von Neumann architecture
> - arithmetic and logic unit (ALU), control unit (CU) and registers
> - control bus, address bus, data bus
> - cores, cache and the internal clock
> - Fetch–Decode–Execute cycle
> - instruction set for a CPU
> - embedded systems
> ★ input and output devices
> - the following input devices: barcode and QR code scanners, digital cameras, keyboards, microphones, mouse, 2D/3D scanners and touch screens
> - the following output devices: actuators, light projectors, inkjet and laser printers, LED and LCD screens, speakers and 3D printers
> - sensors and their use in control and monitoring
> ★ data storage
> - primary storage (RAM and ROM)
> - secondary storage (magnetic, optical and solid state)
> - virtual memories
> - cloud storage
> ★ network hardware
> - network systems (NIC, MAC address, IP address and routers).

This chapter considers the hardware found in many computer systems. The hardware that makes up the computer itself and the various input and output devices will all be covered.

3.1 Computer architecture

3.1.1 The central processing unit (CPU)

The **central processing unit (CPU)** (also known as a microprocessor or processor) is central to all modern computer systems (including tablets and smartphones). The CPU is very often installed as an integrated circuit on a single microchip. The CPU has the responsibility for the execution or processing of all the instructions and data in a computer application. As Figure 3.1 shows, the CPU consists of:

» control unit (CU)
» arithmetic and logic unit (ALU)
» registers and buses.

3.1.2 Von Neumann architecture

Early computers were fed data while the machines were actually running; it wasn't possible to store programs or data, which meant they couldn't operate without considerable human intervention. In the mid-1940s, John von Neumann developed the concept of the 'stored program computer', which has been the basis of computer architecture ever since. The von Neumann architecture had the following main novel features (none of which were available in computers prior to the mid-1940s):

>> the concept of a central processing unit (CPU or processor)
>> the CPU was able to access the memory directly
>> computer memories could store programs as well as data
>> stored programs were made up of instructions which could be executed in sequential order.

There are many diagrams of von Neumann CPU architecture in other textbooks and on the internet. The following diagram is one example of a simple representation of von Neumann architecture:

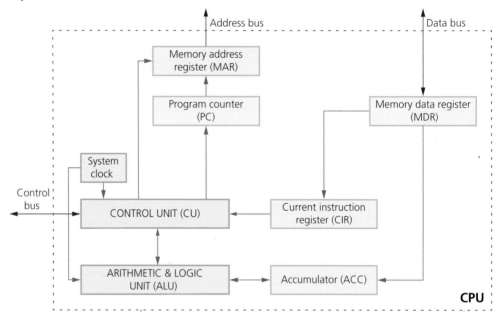

▲ **Figure 3.1** Von Neumann architecture

Components of the central processing unit (CPU)

The main components of the CPU are the Control Unit (CU), Arithmetic & Logic Unit (ALU) and system clock.

Arithmetic & Logic Unit (ALU)

The **Arithmetic & Logic Unit (ALU)** allows the required arithmetic (e.g. +, - and shifting) or logic (e.g. AND, OR) operations to be carried out while a program is being run; it is possible for a computer to have more than one ALU to carry out specific functions. Multiplication and division are carried out by a sequence of addition, subtraction and left or right logical shift operations.

Control Unit (CU)

The **control unit** reads an instruction from memory. The address of the location where the instruction can be found is stored in the Program Counter (PC). This instruction is then interpreted using the Fetch–Decode–Execute cycle (see later in this section). During that process, signals are generated along the control bus to tell the other components in the computer what to do. The control unit ensures synchronisation of data flow and program instructions throughout the computer. A

Link
....
For more arithmetic operations, please refer to Chapter 1.

Link

For more details of the system clock, see Section 3.1.3.

Link

For more details on RAM, see Section 3.3.

system clock is used to produce timing signals on the control bus to ensure this vital synchronisation takes place – without the clock the computer would simply crash!

The RAM holds all the data and programs needed to be accessed by the CPU. The RAM is often referred to as the **Immediate Access Store (IAS)**. The CPU takes data and programs held in **backing store** (e.g. a hard disk drive) and puts them into RAM temporarily. This is done because read/write operations carried out using the RAM are considerably faster than read/write operations to backing store; consequently, any key data needed by an application will be stored temporarily in RAM to considerably speed up operations.

Registers

One of the most fundamental components of the von Neumann system are the **registers**. Registers can be general or special purpose. We will only consider the special purpose registers. A full list of the registers used in this textbook are summarised in Table 3.1. The use of these registers is explained more fully in the Fetch–Decode–Execute cycle (see later in this section).

▼ **Table 3.1** Specific purpose registers

Register	Abbreviation used	Function/purpose of register
current instruction register	CIR	this register stores the current instruction being decoded and executed
accumulator	ACC	this register is used when carrying out ALU calculations; it stores data temporarily during the calculations
memory address register	MAR	this register stores the address of the memory location currently being read from or written to
memory data/ buffer register	MDR	this register stores data which has just been read from memory or data which is about to be written to memory
program counter	PC	this register stores the address where the next instruction to be read can be found

System buses and memory

Earlier on, Figure 3.1 referred to some components labelled as buses. Figure 3.2 shows how these buses are used to connect the CPU to the memory and to input/output devices.

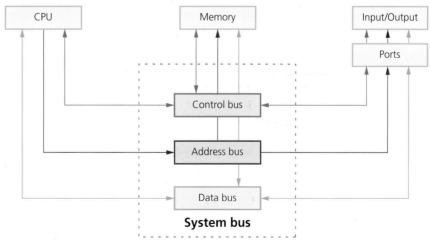

▲ **Figure 3.2** System buses and memory

Address	Contents
1111 0000	0111 0010
1111 0001	0101 1011
1111 0010	1101 1101
1111 0011	0111 1011
1111 1100	1110 1010
1111 1101	1001 0101
1111 1110	1000 0010
1111 1111	0101 0101

Memory

The computer memory is made up of a number of partitions. Each partition consists of an **address** and its contents. Table 3.2 uses 8 bits for each address and 8 bits for the content. In a real computer memory, the address and its contents are actually much larger than this.

The address will uniquely identify every **location** in the memory and the contents will be the binary value stored in each location.

Let us now consider two examples of how the MAR and MDR registers can be used when carrying out a read and write operation to and from memory:

First, consider the **READ** operation. We will use the memory section shown in Table 3.2. Suppose we want to read the contents of memory location **1111 0001**; the two registers are used as follows:

» the address of location 1111 0001 to be read from is first written into the MAR (memory address register):

MAR:	1	1	1	1	0	0	0	1

» a 'read signal' is sent to the computer memory
» the contents of memory location 1111 0001 are then put into the MDR (memory data register):

MDR:	0	1	0	1	1	0	1	1

Now let us now consider the **WRITE** operation. Again, we will use the memory section shown in Table 3.2. Suppose this time we want to show how the value 1001 0101 was written into memory location 1111 1101:

» the data to be stored is first written into the MDR (memory data register):

MDR:	1	0	0	1	0	1	0	1

» this data has to be written into location with address: 1111 1101; so this address is now written into the MAR:

MAR:	1	1	1	1	1	1	0	1

» finally, a 'write signal' is sent to the computer memory and the value 10010101 will then be written into the correct memory location.

Input and output devices

The input and output devices will be covered in more detail in Section 3.2. They are the main method of entering data into and getting data out of computer systems. Input devices convert external data into a form the computer can understand and can then process (e.g. keyboards, touch screens and microphones). Output devices show the results of computer processing in a human understandable form (e.g. printers, monitors and loudspeakers).

(System) buses

(System) buses are used in computers as parallel transmission components; each wire in the bus transmits one bit of data. There are three common buses used in the von Neumann architecture known as: address bus, data bus and control bus.

Address bus

As the name suggests, the **address bus** carries addresses throughout the computer system. Between the CPU and memory, the address bus is **unidirectional** (i.e. bits can travel in one direction only); this prevents addresses being carried back to the CPU, which would be an undesirable feature.

The width of a bus is very important. The wider the bus, the more memory locations that can be directly addressed at any given time, e.g. a bus of width 16 bits can address 2^{16} (65 536) memory locations whereas a bus width of 32 bits allows 4 294 967 296 memory locations to be **simultaneously** addressed. However, even this isn't large enough for modern computers but the technology behind even wider buses is outside the scope of this book.

Data bus

The **data bus** is **bidirectional** (allowing data to be sent in both directions along the bus). This means data can be carried from CPU to memory (and vice versa) and to and from input/output devices. It is important to point out that data can be an address, an instruction or a numerical value. As with the address bus, the width of the data bus is important; the wider the bus the larger the **word length** that can be transported. (A **word** is a group of bits which can be regarded as a single unit e.g. 16-bit, 32-bit or 64-bit word lengths are the most common.) Larger word lengths can improve the computer's overall performance.

Control bus

The **control bus** is also bidirectional. It carries signals from the control unit (CU) to all the other computer components. It is usually 8-bits wide. There is no real need for it to be any wider since it only carries control signals.

Fetch–Decode–Execute cycle

To carry out a set of instructions, the CPU first of all **fetches** some data and instructions from memory and stores them in suitable registers. Both the address bus and data bus are used in this process. Once this is done, each instruction needs to be **decoded** before finally being **executed**. This is all known as the **Fetch–Decode–Execute cycle**.

Fetch

Both data and instruction can be stored in MDR. In the **Fetch–Decode–Execute cycle**, the next instruction is **fetched** from the memory address currently stored in the MAR and the instruction is stored in the MDR. The contents of the MDR are then copied to the Current Instruction Register (CIR). The PC is then incremented (increased by 1) so that the next instruction can be then be processed.

Decode

The instruction is then decoded so that it can be interpreted in the next part of the cycle.

Execute

The CPU passes the decoded instruction as a set of control signals to the appropriate components within the computer system. This allows each instruction to be carried out in its logical sequence.

> **Link**
> ....
> See Section 4.2.2 for more details about these instructions.

Figure 3.3 shows how the Fetch–Decode–Execute cycle is carried out in the von Neumann computer model.

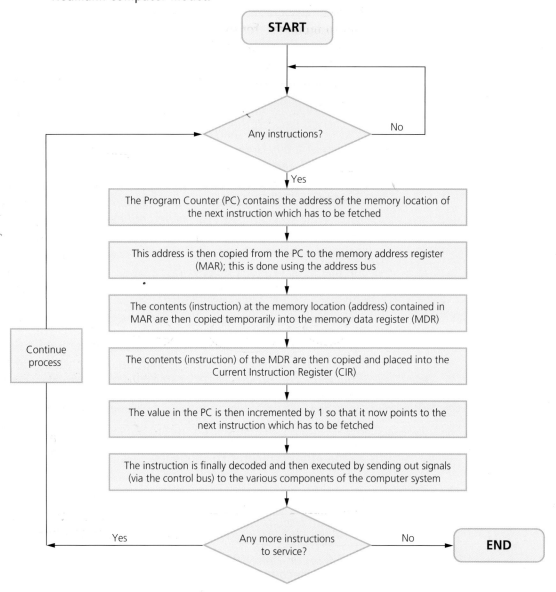

▲ **Figure 3.3** Fetch–Decode–Execute cycle flowchart

3.1.3 Cores, cache and internal clock

We will now consider the factors that determine the performance of a CPU. The first thing to consider is the role of the **system clock**. The clock defines the **clock cycle** that synchronises all computer operations. As mentioned earlier, the control bus transmits timing signals ensuring everything is fully synchronised. By increasing clock speed, the processing speed of the computer is also increased (a typical current value is 3.5 GHz – which means 3.5 billion clock cycles a second). Although the speed of the computer may have been increased, it isn't possible to say that a computer's overall *performance* is necessarily increased by using a higher clock speed. Other factors need to be considered, for example:

1 The width of the address bus and data bus (as mentioned earlier) can also affect computer performance and needs to be taken into account.

2 **Overclocking** is a factor to consider. The clock speed can be changed by accessing the **BIOS (Basic Input/Output System)** and altering the settings. However, using a clock speed higher than the computer was designed for can lead to problems, for example:

i   execution of instructions outside design limits can lead to seriously unsynchronised operations (i.e. an instruction is unable to complete in time before the next one is due to be executed) – the computer would frequently crash and become unstable

ii overclocking can lead to serious overheating of the CPU again leading to unreliable performance.

3 The use of **cache** memories can also improve CPU performance. Unlike RAM, cache memory is located within the CPU itself, which means it has much faster data access times than RAM. Cache memory stores frequently used instructions and data that need to be accessed faster, which improves CPU performance. When a CPU wishes to read memory, it will first check out the cache and then move on to main memory/RAM if the required data isn't there. The larger the cache memory size the better the CPU performance.

4 The use of a different number of **cores** can improve computer performance. One core is made up of an ALU, a control unit and the registers. Many computers are dual core (the CPU is made up of two cores) or quad core (the CPU is made up of four cores). The idea of using more cores alleviates the need to continually increase clock speeds. However, doubling the number of cores doesn't necessarily double the computer's performance since we have to take into account the need for the CPU to communicate with each core; this will reduce overall performance.

For example, with a **dual core** the CPU communicates with both cores using one channel reducing some of the potential increase in its performance:

(1 channel)

Core 1   Core 2

▲ **Figure 3.4**

while, with a **quad core** the CPU communicates with all four cores using six channels, considerably reducing potential performance:

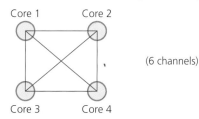

(6 channels)

Core 1   Core 2

Core 3   Core 4

▲ **Figure 3.5**

So all these factors need to be taken into account when considering computer performance. Summarising these points:

» increasing bus width (data and address buses) increases the performance and speed of a computer system

» increasing clock speed will potentially increase the speed of a computer

» a computer's performance can be changed by altering bus width, clock speed and use of multi-core CPUs

» use of cache memories can also speed up a CPU's performance.

Activity 3.1

1 a Name three buses used in the von Neumann architecture.

  b Describe the function of each named bus.

  c Describe how bus width and clock speed can affect computer performance.

2 Complete the following paragraph by using terms from this chapter:

The CPU .... data and instructions required for an application and temporarily stores them in the .... until they can be processed. The .... is used to hold the address of the next instruction to be executed. This address is copied to the .... using the .... The contents at this address are stored in the .... Each instruction is then .... and finally .... by sending out .... using the .... Any calculations carried out are done using the .... During any calculations, data is temporarily held in a special purpose register known as the ....

3.1.4 Instruction set

In a computer system, instructions are a set of operations which are decoded in sequence. Each operation will instruct the ALU and CU (which are part of the CPU). An operation is made up of an **opcode** and an **operand**.

> The opcode informs the CPU what operation needs to be done

> The operand is the data which needs to be acted on or it can refer to a register in the memory

Since the computer needs to understand the operation to be carried out, there is actually a limited number of opcodes that can be used; this is known as the **instruction set**. All software running on a computer will contain a set of instructions (which need to be converted into binary). The Fetch–Decode–Execute cycle is the sequence of steps used by the CPU to process each instruction in sequence.

One example of an instruction set is the X86, a common CPU standard used in many modern computers. Although different computer manufacturers will adopt their own internal electronic design, if the computer is based on the X86 CPU then all designs will share almost identical instruction sets. For example, Intel Pentium and AMD Athlon CPUs use almost identical X86 instruction sets even though they are based on very different electronic designs.

(Note of caution: do not confuse instruction sets with programming code; instruction sets are the low-level language instructions that instruct the CPU how to carry out an operation. Program code needs interpreters or compilers to convert the code into the instruction set understood by the computer. Some examples of instruction set operations include: ADD, JMP, LDA, and so on.)

Link

See Section 4.2.2 for examples of opcodes and operands in assembly language.

Link

For more on interpreters and compilers see Section 4.2.3.

3.1.5 Embedded systems

An embedded system is a combination of hardware and software which is designed to carry out a specific set of functions. The hardware is electronic, electrical or electro-mechanical. Embedded systems can be based on:

microcontrollers:	this has a CPU in addition to some RAM and ROM and other peripherals all embedded onto one single chip (together they carry out a specific task)
microprocessor:	integrated circuit which only has a CPU on the chip (there is no RAM, ROM or peripherals – these need to be added)
system on chips (SoC):	this may contain a microcontroller as one of its components (they almost always will include CPU, memory, input/output (I/O) ports and secondary storage on a single microchip)

An embedded system will have a specific set of tasks; Figure 3.6 summarises how embedded systems work in general:

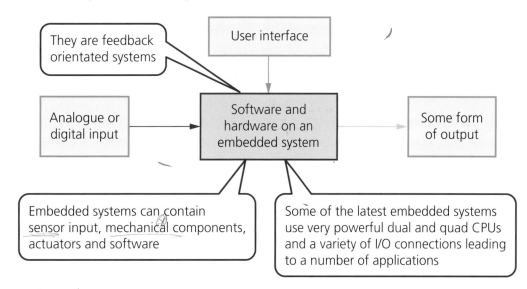

▲ **Figure 3.6** Embedded systems

When installed in a device, either an operator can input data manually (for example, select a temperature from a keypad or turn a dial on an oven control panel) or the data will come from an automatic source, such as a sensor. This sensor input will be analogue or digital in nature, for example, inputs such as oxygen levels or fuel pressure in a car's engine management system. The output will then carry out the function of the embedded system by sending signals to the components that are being controlled (for example, increase the power to the heating elements in an oven or reduce fuel levels in the engine).

Depending on the device, embedded systems are either programmable or non-programmable. Non-programmable devices need, in general, to be replaced if they require a software upgrade. Programmable devices permit upgrading by two methods:

» connecting the device to a computer and allowing the download of updates to the software (for example, this is used to update the maps on a GPS system used in a vehicle)

>> automatic updates via a Wi-Fi, satellite or cellular (mobile phone network) link (for example, many modern cars allow updates to engine management systems and other components via satellite link). ✈

There are definite benefits and drawbacks of devices being controlled using embedded systems:

▼ **Table 3.3** Benefits and drawbacks of using embedded systems

Benefits	Drawbacks
they are small in size and therefore easy to fit into devices	it can be difficult to upgrade some devices to take advantage of new technology
compared to other systems, they are relatively low cost to make	troubleshooting faults in the device becomes a specialist task
they are usually dedicated to one task allowing simple interfaces and often no requirement for an operating system	although the interface can appear to be more simple (e.g. a single knob) in reality it can be more confusing (e.g. changing the time on a cooker clock can require several steps!)
they consume very little power	any device that can be accessed over the internet is also open to hackers, viruses, etc.
they can be controlled remotely using a mobile phone, for example	due to the difficulty in upgrading and fault finding, devices are often just thrown away rather than being repaired (very wasteful)
very fast reaction to changing input (operate in real time and are feedback orientated)	can lead to an increase in the 'throw away' society if devices are discarded just because they have become out-of-date
with mass production comes reliability	

Because embedded systems can be connected to the internet, it is possible to control them remotely using a smartphone or computer. For example, setting the central heating system to switch on or off while away from home or remotely instructing a set top box to record a television programme. Since embedded systems are dedicated to a specific set of tasks, engineers can optimise their designs to reduce the physical size and cost of the devices. The range of applications are vast, ranging from a single microcontroller (for example, in an MP3 player) to a complex array of multiple units (for example, in a medical imaging system).

It is worth mentioning here that a computer is **not** an example of an embedded system. Computers are multi-functional (that is, they can carry out many different tasks which can be varied by using different software) which means they can't be classed as embedded systems.

Examples of the use of embedded systems

Motor vehicles
Modern cars have many parts that rely on embedded systems to function correctly. Figure 3.7 shows some of the many components that are controlled in this way.

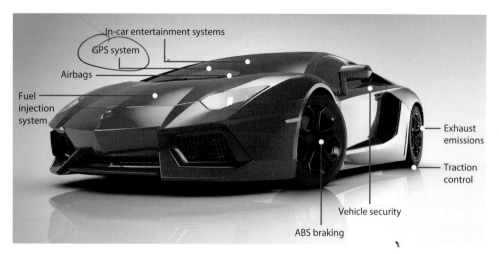

▲ **Figure 3.7** Embedded systems found in a car

Set-top box

In this example, a set-top box uses an embedded system to allow, for example, recording and playback of television programmes. This can be operated remotely by the user when not at home using an internet-enabled device or by using the interface panel when at home. The embedded system will look after many of the functions involving inputs from a number of sources such as a Solid State Device (SSD) (where television programmes can be stored or retrieved) or a satellite signal (where it will be necessary to decode the incoming signal).

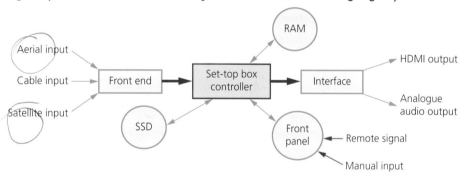

▲ **Figure 3.8** Embedded system found in a set-top box

Security systems

Embedded systems are used in many security devices:

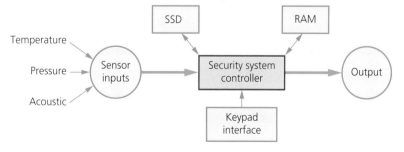

▲ **Figure 3.9** Embedded system found in a security system

The security code is set in RAM and the alarm activated or deactivated using the keypad. Data from sensors is sent to the controller which checks against values stored on the SSD (these settings are on SSD rather than RAM in case the sensitivity needs to be adjusted). An output can be a signal to flash lights, sound an alarm or send a message to the home owner via their mobile phone. Again, the home owner can interface with the system remotely if necessary.

Lighting systems

Embedded systems are used in modern sophisticated lighting systems from simple home use to major architectural lighting systems. We will concentrate here on a lighting system used in a large office. The system needs to control the lighting taking into account:

» the time of day or day of the week
» whether the room is occupied
» the brightness of the natural light.

An embedded system can automatically control the lighting using a number of inputs (such as light sensors) and key data stored in memory. Again, this fits very well into the system described in Figure 3.6.

The time of day or day of the week is important data in an office environment since energy is saved if the system switches to low lighting levels when unoccupied. This can be over-ridden by the second bullet point (above); if there is movement in the office then correct lighting levels will be automatically restored. On a very bright sunny day, the system could automatically dim the lights, only increasing the light output if natural light levels fall below a set value. There are many internal and external lighting systems that could be controlled by embedded systems (e.g. a fountain light display or a light show on a building to commemorate a special occasion). They are also used to trigger emergency lighting in, for example, aeroplanes in case of an emergency.

Some lighting systems use Bluetooth light bulbs. This allows the embedded system to control each bulb independently. Many of the bulbs available today use LEDs and many come in a number of colours to change the mood.

Vending systems

Vending machines make considerable use of embedded systems. They usually use microcontrollers to control a number of functions that we all associate with vending machines:

Link

See Section 3.2.3 for sensors used in security systems.

▲ **Figure 3.10** LED light bulb

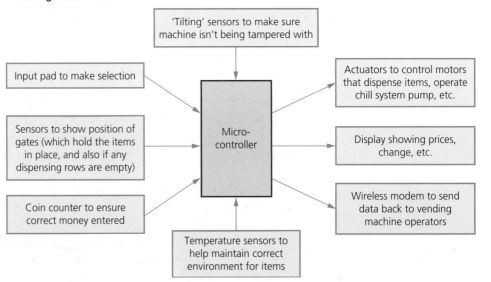

▲ **Figure 3.11** Embedded system found in a vending machine

At the heart of the vending machine is an embedded system in the form of a microcontroller. Inputs to this system come from the keypad (item selection) and from sensors (used to count the coins inserted by the customer, the temperature inside the machine and a 'tilt sensor' for security purposes). The outputs are:

» actuators to operate the motors, which drive the helixes (see figure below) to give the customers their selected item(s)
» signals to operate the cooling system if the temperature is too high
» item description and any change due shown on an LCD display panel
» data sent back to the vending machine company so that they can remotely check sales activity (which could include instructions to refill the machine) without the need to visit each machine.

▲ **Figure 3.12** Helix used in a typical vending machine

All of this is controlled by an embedded system which makes the whole operation automatic but also gives immediate sales analysis which would otherwise be very time consuming.

Washing machines

Many 'white goods' (such as refrigerators, washing machines, microwave ovens, and so on) are controlled by embedded systems. They all come with a keypad or dials that are used to select the temperature, wash cycle or cooking duration. This data forms the input to the embedded system, which then carries out the required task without any further human intervention. As with other devices, these 'white goods' can also be operated remotely using an internet-enabled smartphone or computer.

Activity 3.2

1 a Explain how it is possible to increase the performance of a CPU/ microprocessor. In your explanation, include some of the risks associated with your suggestions to improve performance.

 b What is meant by the term *instruction set*?

2 A car is fitted with the latest GPS navigation system. This device is controlled by an embedded system in the form of a microcontroller.

 a Describe the inputs needed by the embedded system and describe which outputs you would expect it to produce.

 b Since updates to the GPS device are required every six months, explain how the device is updated without the need to take the car to the garage every six months.

3.2 Input and output devices

3.2.1 Input devices

Barcode scanners (readers)

A **barcode** is a series of dark and light parallel lines of varying thickness. The numbers 0 to 9 are each represented by a unique series of lines. Various barcode methods for representing these digits exist. The example we shall use adopts different codes for digits appearing on the left and for digits appearing on the right of the barcode:

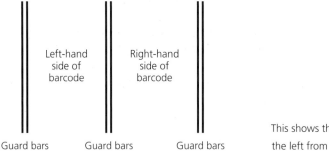

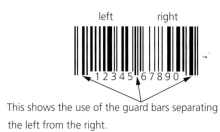

This shows the use of the guard bars separating the left from the right.

▲ **Figure 3.13** Diagram of guard bars

▲ **Figure 3.14** Sample barcode

Each digit in the barcode is represented by bars of 1 to 4 blocks thick as shown in Figure 3.15. Note there are different patterns for digits on the left-hand side and for digits on the right-hand side.

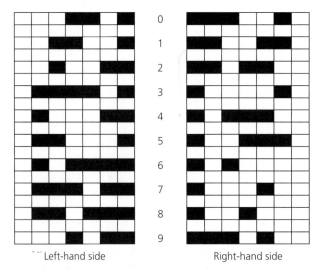

▲ **Figure 3.15** Barcode digit patterns

The section of barcode to represent the number 5 4 3 0 5 2 would therefore be:

▲ **Figure 3.16** Sample barcode section using patterns from Figure 3.15

Each digit is made up of 2 dark lines and two light lines. The width representing each digit is the same. The digits on the left have an odd number of dark elements and always begin with a light bar; the digits on the right have an even number of dark elements and always begin with a dark bar. This arrangement allows a barcode to be scanned in any direction.

So what happens when a barcode is scanned?

» the barcode is first of all read by a red laser or red LED (light emitting diode)
» light is reflected back off the barcode; the dark areas reflect little or no light, which allows the bars to be read
» the reflected light is read by sensors (photoelectric cells)
» as the laser or LED light is scanned across the barcode, a pattern is generated, which is converted into digital data – this allows the computer to understand the barcode
» for example: the digit '3' on the left generates the pattern: `L D D D D L D`
(where L = light and D = dark),
this has the binary equivalent of: `0 1 1 1 1 0 1`
(where L = 0 and D = 1).

Barcodes are most commonly found at the checkout in supermarkets. There are several other input and output devices at the checkout:

▼ **Table 3.4** Input and output devices at a checkout

Input/output device	How it is used
keypad	to key in the number of same items bought; to key in a weight, to key in the number under the barcode if it cannot be read by the barcode reader/scanner
screen/monitor	to show the cost of an item and other information
speaker	to make a beeping sound every time a barcode is read correctly; but also to make another sound if there is an error when reading the barcode
printer	to print out a receipt/itemised list
card reader/chip and PIN	to read the customer's credit/debit card (either using PIN or contactless)
touchscreen	to select items by touching an icon (such as fresh fruit which may be sold loose without packaging)

So the barcode has been read, then what happens?

» the barcode number is looked up in the stock database (the barcode is known as the key field in the stock item record); this key field uniquely identifies each stock item
» when the barcode number is found, the stock item record is looked up
» the price and other stock item details are sent back to the checkout (or point of sale terminal (POS))
» the number of stock items in the record is reduced by 1 each time the barcode is read
» this new value for number of stock is written back to the stock item record
» the number of stock items is compared to the re-order level; if it is less than or equal to this value, more stock items are ***automatically*** ordered

» once an order for more stock items is generated, a flag is added to the record to stop re-ordering every time the stock item barcode is read

» when new stock items arrive, the stock levels are updated in the database.

Advantages to the management of using barcodes

» much easier and faster to change prices on stock items
» much better, more up-to-date sales information/sales trends
» no need to price every stock item on the shelves (this reduces time and cost to the management)
» allows for automatic stock control
» possible to check customer buying habits more easily by linking barcodes to, for example, customer loyalty cards.

Advantages to the customers of using barcodes

» faster checkout queues (staff don't need to remember/look up prices of items)
» errors in charging customers is reduced
» the customer is given an itemised bill
» cost savings can be passed on to the customer
» better track of 'sell by dates' so food should be fresher.

The barcode system is used in many other areas. For example, barcodes can be utilised in libraries where they are used in books and on the borrower's library card. Every time a book is taken out, the borrower is linked to the book automatically. This allows automatic checking of when the book is due to be returned.

▲ **Figure 3.17** Sample QR code

Quick response (QR) codes

Another type of barcode is the **quick response (QR) code**. This is made up of a matrix of filled-in dark squares on a light background. For example, the QR code in Figure 3.17 is a website advertising rock music merchandise. It includes a web address in the code.

QR codes can hold considerably more information than the more conventional barcodes described earlier.

Description of QR codes

» A QR code consists of a block of small squares (light and dark) known as pixels. It can presently hold up to 4296 characters (or up to 7089 digits) and also allows internet addresses to be encoded within the QR code. This compares to the 30 digits that is the maximum for a barcode. However, as more and more data is added, the structure of the QR code becomes more complex.
» The three large squares at the corners of the code function as a form of alignment; the remaining small corner square is used to ensure the correct size and correct angle of the camera shot when the QR code is read.

Because of modern smartphones and tablets, which allow internet access on the move, QR codes can be scanned anywhere. This gives rise to a number of uses:

» advertising products (for example, the QR code in Figure 3.17)
» giving automatic access to a website or contact telephone number
» storing boarding passes electronically at airports and train stations (Figure 3.18).

▲ **Figure 3.18** Sample boarding pass

By using the built-in camera on a mobile smartphone or tablet and by downloading a QR app (application), it is possible to read QR codes on the move using the following method:

» point the phone or tablet camera at the QR code
» the app will now process the image taken by the camera, converting the squares into readable data
» the browser software on the mobile phone or tablet automatically reads the data generated by the app; it will also decode any web addresses contained within the QR code
» the user will then be sent to a website automatically (or if a telephone number was embedded in the code, the user will be sent to the phone app 📞)
» if the QR code contained a boarding pass, this will be automatically sent to the phone/tablet.

Advantages of QR codes compared to traditional barcodes

» They can hold much more information
» There will be fewer errors; the higher capacity of the QR code allows the use of built-in error-checking systems – normal barcodes contain almost no data redundancy (data which is duplicated) therefore it isn't possible to guard against badly printed or damaged barcodes
» QR codes are easier to read; they don't need expensive laser or LED (light emitting diode) scanners like barcodes – they can be read by the cameras on smartphones or tablets
» It is easy to transmit QR codes either as text messages or images
» It is also possible to encrypt QR codes which gives them greater protection than traditional barcodes.

Disadvantages of QR codes compared to traditional barcodes

» More than one QR format is available
» QR codes can be used to transmit malicious codes – known as attagging. Since there are a large number of free apps available to a user for generating QR codes, that means anyone can do this. It is relatively easy to write malicious code and embed this within the QR code. When the code is scanned, it is possible the creator of the malicious code could gain access to everything on the user's phone (for example, photographs, address book, stored passwords, and so on). The user could also be sent to a fake website or it is even possible for a virus to be downloaded.

▲ **Figure 3.19** Frame QR code

New developments
Newer QR codes (called **frame QR codes**) are now being used because of the increased ability to add advertising logos (see Figure 3.19). Frame QR codes come with a 'canvas area' where it is possible to include graphics or images inside the code itself. Unlike normal QR codes, software to do this isn't usually free.

Activity 3.3

1 Using the data in Figure 3.14, design the barcodes for:

 a 9 0 0   3 4 0   (3 digits on the left; 3 digits on the right)

 b 1 2 5 7   6 6 4 8   (4 digits on the left; 4 digits on the right)

 c 0 5 8 8 9   0 2 9 1 8   (5 digits on the left; 5 digits on the right)

2 a Describe one advantage of using QR codes rather than traditional bar codes. Explain how barcodes bring the advantage you have described.

 b A square QR code contains 40 × 40 tiny squares (pixels) where each tiny square represents a 0 or a 1. Calculate how many bytes of data can be stored on the QR code.

 c Describe the purpose of the three large squares at the corners of the QR code.

 d Describe one disadvantage of using QR codes.

▲ **Figure 3.20** Digital camera

Digital cameras

Digital cameras have essentially replaced the more traditional camera that used film to capture the images. The film required developing and then printing before the photographer could see the result of their work.

This made these cameras expensive to operate since it wasn't possible to delete unwanted photographs.

Modern digital cameras simply link to a computer system via a USB port or by using Bluetooth (which enables wireless transfer of photographic files).

These cameras are controlled by an embedded system which can automatically carry out the following tasks:

 »» adjust the shutter speed
 »» focus the image automatically
 »» operate the flash gun automatically
 »» adjust the aperture size
 »» adjust the size of the image
 »» remove 'red eye' when the flash gun has been used
 »» and so on.

What happens when a photograph is taken

 »» the image is captured when light passes through the lens onto a light-sensitive cell; this cell is made up of millions of tiny sensors which are acting as photodiodes (i.e. **charge couple devices (CCD)** which convert light into electricity)
 »» each of the sensors are often referred to as pixels (picture elements) since they are tiny components that make up the image
 »» the image is converted into tiny electric charges which are then passed through an **analogue to digital converter (ADC)** to form a digital image array
 »» the ADC converts the electric charges from each pixel into levels of brightness (now in a digital format); for example, an 8-bit ADC gives 2^8 (256) possible brightness levels per pixel (for example, brightness level 01110011)

» apart from brightness, the sensors also measure colour which produces another binary pattern; most cameras use a 24-bit RGB system (each pixel has 8 bits representing each of the 3 primary colours), which means each pixel has a red value (0 to 255 in denary), a green value (0 to 255) and a blue value (0 to 255); for example, a shade of orange could be 215 (red), 165 (green) and 40 (blue) giving a binary pattern of 1101 0111 1010 0101 0010 1000 (or D7A528 written in hex)

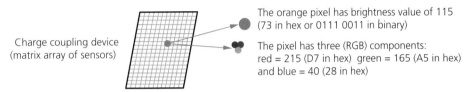

Charge coupling device (matrix array of sensors)

The orange pixel has brightness value of 115 (73 in hex or 0111 0011 in binary)

The pixel has three (RGB) components: red = 215 (D7 in hex) green = 165 (A5 in hex) and blue = 40 (28 in hex)

▲ **Figure 3.21** Typical pixel brightness and colour values

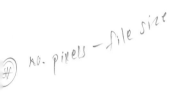

» the number of pixels determines the size of the file used to store the photograph
» the quality of the image depends on the recording device (how good the camera lens is and how good the sensor array is), the number of pixels used (the more pixels used, the better the image), the levels of light and how the image is stored (JPEG, raw file, and so on).

Mobile phones have caught up with digital cameras as regards number of pixels. But the drawback is often inferior lens quality and limited memory for the storage of photos. But this is fast changing and, at the time of writing, many smartphones now have very sophisticated optics and photography software as standard.

> **Link**
>
> For an explanation of how pixels affect file size see Chapter 1.

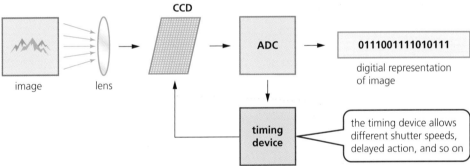

image   lens

CCD

ADC

0111001111010111

digitial representation of image

timing device

the timing device allows different shutter speeds, delayed action, and so on

▲ **Figure 3.22** Diagram of how a digital camera works

Keyboards

Keyboards are by far the most common method used for data entry. They are used as the input devices on computers, tablets, mobile phones and many other electronic items.

The keyboard is connected to the computer either by using a USB connection or by wireless connection. In the case of tablets and mobile phones, the keyboard is often **virtual** or a type of **touch screen** technology.

▲ **Figure 3.23** Keyboard

▲ **Figure 3.24** Ergonomic keyboard

As shown in Chapter 1, each character on a keyboard has an ASCII value. Each character pressed is converted into a digital signal, which the computer interprets.

They are a relatively slow method of data entry and are also prone to errors, however keyboards are probably still the easiest way to enter text into a computer. Unfortunately, frequent use of these devices can lead to injuries, such as **repetitive strain injury (RSI)** in the hands and wrists.

Ergonomic keyboards can help to overcome this problem – these have the keys arranged differently as shown in Figure 3.24. They are also designed to give more support to the wrists and hands when doing a lot of typing.

The following diagram (Figure 3.25) and description summarises how the computer recognises a letter pressed on the keyboard:

>> There is a membrane or circuit board at the base of the keys
>> In Figure 3.25, the 'H' key is pressed and this completes a circuit as shown
>> The CPU in the computer can then determine which key has been pressed
>> The CPU refers to an index file to identify which character the key press represents
>> Each character on a keyboard has a corresponding ASCII value (see Chapter 1).

compilation of values corresponding

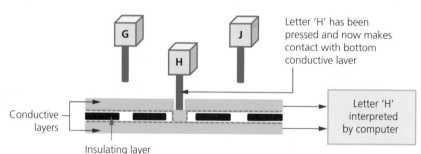

Letter 'H' has been pressed and now makes contact with bottom conductive layer

Letter 'H' interpreted by computer

Conductive layers

Insulating layer

▲ **Figure 3.25** Diagram of a keyboard

Microphones

Microphones are either built into the computer or are external devices connected through the USB port or using Bluetooth connectivity. Figure 3.26 shows how a microphone can convert sound waves into an electric current. The current produced is converted to a digital format so that a computer can process it or store it (on, for example, a CD).

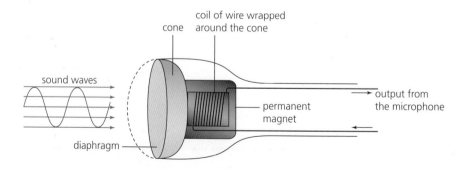

coil of wire wrapped around the cone

cone

sound waves

output from the microphone

permanent magnet

diaphragm

▲ **Figure 3.26** Diagram of how a microphone works

» When sound is created, it causes the air to vibrate.
» When a diaphragm in the microphone picks up the air vibrations, the diaphragm also begins to vibrate.
» A copper coil is wrapped around the cone which is connected to the diaphragm. As the diaphragm vibrates, the cone moves in and out causing the copper coil to move backwards and forwards.
» This forwards and backwards motion causes the coil to cut through the magnetic field around the permanent magnet, inducing an electric current.
» The electric current is then either amplified or sent to a recording device. The electric current is analogue in nature.

The electric current output from the microphone can also be sent to a computer where a sound card converts the current into a digital signal which can then be stored in the computer. The following diagram shows what happens when the word 'hut' is picked up by a microphone and is converted into digital values:

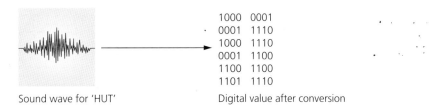

Sound wave for 'HUT'

1000	0001
0001	1110
1000	1110
0001	1100
1100	1100
1101	1110

Digital value after conversion

▲ **Figure 3.27** Analogue to digital conversion

Look at Figure 3.27. The word 'hut' (in the form of a sound wave) has been picked up by the microphone; this is then converted using an analogue to digital converter (ADC) into digital values which can then be stored in a computer or manipulated as required using appropriate software.

Optical mouse

An **optical mouse** is an example of a **pointing device**. It uses tiny cameras to take 1500 images per second. Unlike an older mechanical mouse, the optical mouse can work on virtually any surface.

A red LED is used in the base of the mouse and the red light is bounced off the surface and the reflection is picked up by a **complementary metal oxide semiconductor (CMOS)**. The CMOS generates electric pulses to represent the reflected red light and these pulses are sent to a **digital signal processor (DSP)**. The processor can now work out the coordinates of the mouse based on the changing image patterns as it is moved about on the surface. The computer can then move the on-screen cursor to the coordinates sent by the mouse.

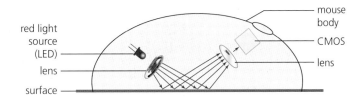

▲ **Figure 3.28** Diagram of an optical mouse

Benefits of an optical mouse over a mechanical mouse

» There are no moving parts, therefore it is more reliable.
» Dirt can't get trapped in any of the mechanical components.
» There is no need to have any special surfaces.

Most optical mice use Bluetooth connectivity rather than using a USB wired connection. While this makes the mouse more versatile, a wired mouse has the following advantages:

» no signal loss since there is a constant signal pathway (wire)
» cheaper to operate (no need to buy new batteries or charge batteries)
» fewer environmental issues (no need to dispose of old batteries).

2D and 3D scanners

Scanners are either two dimensional (2D) or three dimensional (3D).

2D scanners

These types of scanner are the most common form and are generally used to input hard copy (paper) documents. The image is converted into an electronic form that can be stored in a computer.

A number of stages occur when scanning a document:

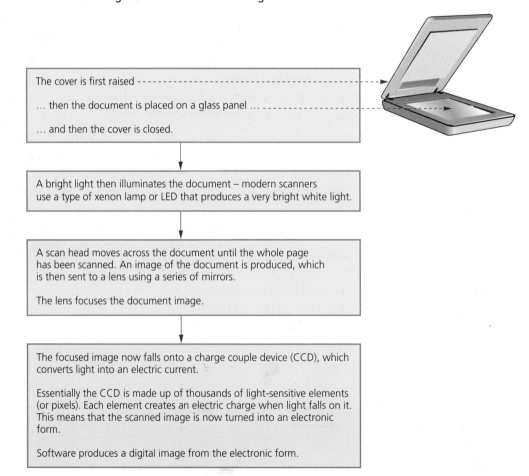

The cover is first raised -

... then the document is placed on a glass panel ... - - - - - - - - - - - - - - - -

... and then the cover is closed.

A bright light then illuminates the document – modern scanners use a type of xenon lamp or LED that produces a very bright white light.

A scan head moves across the document until the whole page has been scanned. An image of the document is produced, which is then sent to a lens using a series of mirrors.

The lens focuses the document image.

The focused image now falls onto a charge couple device (CCD), which converts light into an electric current.

Essentially the CCD is made up of thousands of light-sensitive elements (or pixels). Each element creates an electric charge when light falls on it. This means that the scanned image is now turned into an electronic form.

Software produces a digital image from the electronic form.

▲ **Figure 3.29** How a 2D scanner works

Computers equipped with **optical character recognition (OCR)** software allow the scanned text from the document to be converted into a **text file format.** This means the scanned image can now be edited and manipulated by importing it into a word processor.

If the original document was a photograph or image, then the scanned image forms an image file such as JPEG.

3D scanners

3D scanners scan solid objects and produce a three-dimensional image. Since solid objects have x, y and z coordinates, these scanners take images at several points along these three coordinates. A digital image which represents the solid object is formed.

The scanned images can be used in **computer aided design (CAD)** or, more recently, sent to a 3D printer (see Section 3.2.2) to produce a working model of the scanned image.

There are numerous technologies used in 3D scanners – lasers, magnetic resonance, white light, and so on. It is beyond the scope of this book to look at these in any great depth; however, the second application that follows describes the technology behind one form of 3D scanning.

Application of 2D scanners at an airport

2D scanners are used at airports to read passports. They make use of OCR technology to produce digital images which represent the passport pages. Because of the OCR technology, these digital images can be manipulated in a number of ways.

For example, the OCR software is able to review these images, select the text part, and then automatically put the text into the correct fields of an existing database. It is possible for the text to be stored in an ASCII format – it all depends on how the data is to be used.

At many airports the two-dimensional photograph in the passport is scanned and stored as a JPEG image. The passenger's face is also photographed using a digital camera (a 2D image is taken so it can be matched to the image taken from the passport). The two digital images are compared using face recognition/detection software. Key parts of the face are compared.

The face in Figure 3.30 shows several of the positions used by the face recognition software. Each position is checked when the software tries to compare two facial images. Data, such as:

>> distance between the eyes
>> width of the nose
>> shape of the cheek bones
>> length of the jaw line
>> shape of the eyebrows,

are all used to uniquely identify a given face.

When the image from the passport and the image taken by the camera are compared, these key positions on the face determine whether or not the two images represent the same face.

Link

For more on ASCII, please see Chapter 1.

▲ **Figure 3.30** Face recognition

Application of 3D scanning – computed tomographic (CT) scanners

Computed tomographic (CT) scanners are used to create a 3D image of a solid object. This is based on tomography technology, which basically builds up an image of the solid object through a series of very thin 'slices'. Each of these 2D 'slices' make up a representation of the 3D solid object.

Each slice is built up by use of X-rays, radio frequencies or gamma imaging; although a number of other methods exist. Each 'slice' is then stored as a digital image in the computer memory. The whole of the solid object is represented digitally in the computer memory.

Depending on how the image is formed, this type of tomographic scanner can have different names. For example:

Name	CT Scanner	MRI	SPECT
Stands for	computerised tomography	magnetic resonance images	single photon emission computer tomography
Uses	X-rays	radio frequencies	gamma rays

Here is a simple example of how tomography works:

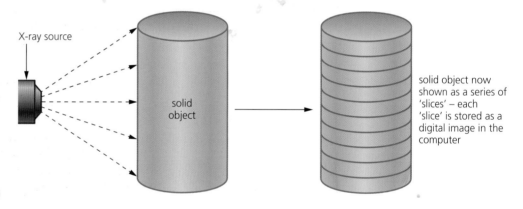

▲ **Figure 3.31** Tomography

Touch screens

Touch screens are now a very common form of input device. They allow simple touch selection from a menu to launch an application (app). Touch screens allow the user to carry out the same functions as they would with a pointing device, such as a mouse. There are three common types of touch screen technologies currently being used by mobile phone and tablet manufacturers. Similar technologies are used in other touch screen applications (for example, food selection at a fast food restaurant):

» capacitive
» infrared
» resistive (most common method at the moment).

Capacitive touch screens

Capacitive touch screens are composed of a layer of glass (protective layer), a transparent electrode (conductive) layer and a glass substrate (see Figure 3.32). Since human skin is a conductor of electricity, when bare fingers (or a special stylus) touch the screen, the electrostatic field of the conductive layer is changed. The installed microcontroller is able to calculate where this change took place and hence determine the coordinates of the point of touching.

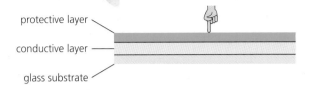

protective layer

conductive layer

glass substrate

▲ **Figure 3.32** Capacitive touch screen

There are presently two main types of capacitive touch screens:

» surface
» projective.

The two methods work in a slightly different way but they both have the same general structure as shown in Figure 3.32.

With **surface capacitive screens**, sensors are placed at the corners of a screen. Small voltages are also applied at the corners of the screen creating an electric field. A finger touching the screen surface will draw current from each corner reducing the capacitance. A microcontroller measures the decrease in capacitance and hence determines the point where the finger touched the screen. This system only works with a bare finger or stylus.

Projective capacitive screens work slightly differently to surface capacitive screens. The transparent conductive layer is now in the form of an X-Y matrix pattern. This creates a three dimensional (3D) electrostatic field. When a finger touches the screen, it disturbs the 3D electrostatic field allowing a microcontroller to determine the coordinates of the point of contact. This system works with bare fingers, stylus and thin surgical or cotton gloves. It also allows multi-touch facility (for example, pinching or sliding).

Advantages compared to the other two technologies

» Better image clarity than resistive screens, especially in strong sunlight
» Very durable screens that have high scratch resistance
» Projective capacitive screens allow multi-touch.

Disadvantages compared to the other two technologies

» Surface capacitive screens only work with bare fingers or a special stylus
» They are sensitive to electromagnetic radiation (such as magnetic fields or microwaves).

Infrared touch screens
Infrared touch screens use a glass screen with an array of sensors and infrared transmitters.

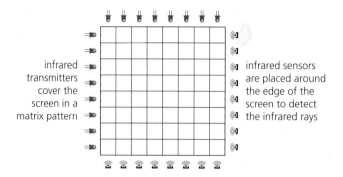

▲ **Figure 3.33** Array of infrared transmitters and sensors surrounding the screen

The sensors detect the infrared radiation. If any of the infrared beams are broken (for example, with a finger touching the screen), the infrared radiation reaching the sensors is reduced. The sensor readings are sent to a microcontroller that calculates where the screen was touched:

◀ **Figure 3.34** Infrared screen touched causing sensors (shown in red) to show a reduction in infrared radiation – thus the exact position where the screen was touched can be calculated

Advantages compared to the other two technologies

>> Allows multi-touch facilities
>> Has good screen durability
>> The operability isn't affected by a scratched or cracked screen.

Disadvantages compared to the other two technologies

>> The screen can be sensitive to water or moisture
>> It is possible for accidental activation to take place if the infrared beams are disturbed in some way
>> Sometimes sensitive to light interference.

Resistive touch screens

Resistive touch screens are made up of two layers of electrically resistive material with a voltage applied across them. The upper layer is made of flexible polyethylene (a type of polymer) with a resistive coating on one side (see Figure 3.35). The bottom layer is made of glass also with a resistive coating (usually indium tin oxide) on one side. These two layers are separated by air or an inert gas (such as argon). When the top polyethylene surface is touched, the two layers make contact. Since both layers are coated in a resistive material a circuit is now completed which results in a flow of electricity. The point of contact is detected where there was a change in voltage.

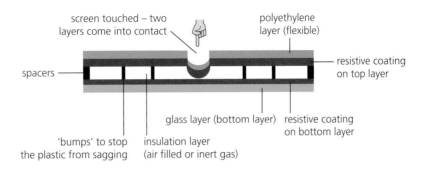

▲ **Figure 3.35** Resistive touch screen

A microcontroller converts the voltage (created when the two resistive layers touch) to digital data, which it then sends to the microprocessor.

Advantages compared to the other two technologies

» Good resistance to dust and water
» Can be used with bare fingers, stylus and gloved hand.

Disadvantages compared to the other two technologies

» Low touch sensitivity (sometimes have to press down harder)
» Doesn't support multi-touch facility
» Poor visibility in strong sunlight
» Vulnerable to scratches on the screen (made of polymer).

3.2.2 Output devices

Actuators

When a computer is used to control devices, such as a conveyer belt or a valve, it is usually necessary to use an **actuator** to, for example, start/stop the conveyer belt or open/close the valve. An actuator is a mechanical or electromechanical device such as a relay, solenoid or motor. We will consider a solenoid as the example; this converts an electrical signal into a magnetic field producing linear motion:

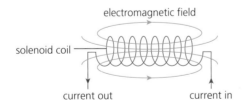

▲ **Figure 3.36** A solenoid

If a plunger (for example, a magnetised metal bar) is placed inside the coil, it will move when a current is applied to the coil (see Figure 3.36). This would allow the solenoid to operate a valve or a switch, for example. There are also examples of rotary solenoids where a cylindrical coil is used. In this case, when a current is supplied to the coil, it would cause a rotational movement of the plunger.

Light projectors

There are two common types of light projector:

» digital light projector (DLP)

» liquid crystal display (LCD) projector.

Projectors are used to project computer output onto larger screens or even onto interactive whiteboards. They are often used in presentations and in multimedia applications. The next section compares the basic operation of the two projector technologies.

Digital light projectors (DLP)

The use of millions of micro mirrors on a small **digital micromirror device** (DMD chip) is the key to how these devices work.

The number of micro mirrors and the way they are arranged on the DMD chip determines the resolution of the digital image. When the micro mirrors tilt towards the light source, they are ON. When the micro mirrors tilt away from the light source, they are OFF. This creates a light or dark pixel on the projection screen. The micro mirrors can switch on or off several thousand times a second creating various grey shades – typically 1024 grey shades can be produced (for example, if the mirror switches on more often than it switches off, it will produce a lighter shade of grey). This is known as a greyscale image.

A bright white light source (for example, from a xenon bulb) passes through a colour filter on its way to the DMD chip. The white light is split into the primary colours: red, green and blue – the DLP projector can create over 16 million different colours. The ON and OFF states of each micro mirror are linked with colours from the filter to produce the coloured image.

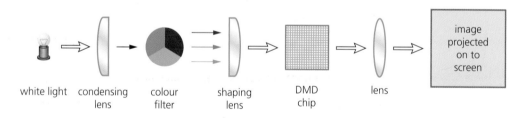

white light   condensing lens   colour filter   shaping lens   DMD chip   lens   image projected on to screen

▲ **Figure 3.37** A digital light projector (DLP)

Note: The DMD chip is a microoptoelectromechanical system (MOEMS) that contains several thousand microscopic mirrors (made out of polished aluminium metal) arranged on the chip surface. They are each about 16 µm (16×10^{-6} metres) in size and each corresponds to a pixel in the displayed screen image.

Liquid crystal display (LCD) projector

These are older technology than DLP. Essentially a high-intensity beam of light passes through an LCD display and then onto a screen. How this works in principle is described below:

» a powerful beam of white light is generated from a bulb or LED inside the projector body

» this beam of light is then sent to a group of chromatic-coated mirrors (known as dichromic mirrors); these reflect the light back at different wavelengths

» when the white light hits these mirrors, the reflected light has wavelengths corresponding to red, green and blue light components
» these three different coloured light components pass through three LCD screens (each screen is composed of thousands of tiny pixels which can either block light or let it through; this produces a **monochromatic** image)...
» ... consequently, three different versions of the same image are now produced – one is the whole image in different shades of red, one is the whole image in different shades of green and one is the whole image in different shades of blue
» these images are then re-combined using a special prism to produce a full colour image
» finally, the image passes through the projector lens onto a screen.

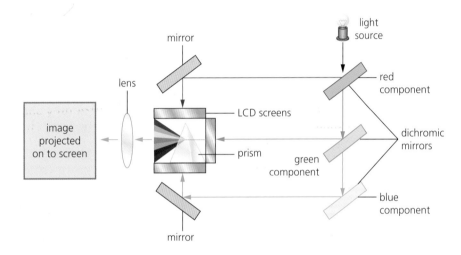

▲ **Figure 3.38** LCD projector

Advantages and disadvantages of the two types of projector

▼ **Table 3.5** Advantages and disadvantages of DLP and LCD projectors

	Advantages	Disadvantages
Digital light projector (DLP)	higher contrast ratios	image tends to suffer from 'shadows' when showing a moving image
	higher reliability/longevity	
	quieter running than LCD projector	DLP do not have grey components in the image
	uses a single DMD chip, which mean no issues lining up the images	the colour definition is frequently not as good as LCD projectors because the colour saturation is not as good (colour saturation is the intensity of a colour)
	smaller and lighter than LCD projector	
	they are better suited to dusty or smoky atmospheres than LCD projectors	
LCD projector	give a sharper image than DLP projectors	although improving, the contrast ratios are not as good as DLPs
	have better colour saturation than DLP projectors	LCD projectors have a limited life (that is, the longevity is not as good as DLPs)
	more efficient in their use of energy than DLP technology – consequently they generate less heat	since LCD panels are organic in nature, they tend to degrade with time (screens turn yellow and the colours are subsequently degraded over time)

▲ **Figure 3.39** Inkjet printer

Inkjet and laser printers

Inkjet printers

Inkjet printers are essentially made up of:

» a print head, which consists of nozzles that spray droplets of ink onto the paper to form characters
» an ink cartridge or cartridges; either one cartridge for each colour (blue, yellow and magenta) and a black cartridge or one single cartridge containing all three colours + black (Note: some systems use six colours)
» a stepper motor and belt, which moves the print head assembly across the page from side to side
» a paper feed, which automatically feeds the printer with pages as they are required.

The ink droplets are produced currently using two different technologies:

Thermal bubble – tiny resistors create localised heat which makes the ink vaporise. This causes the ink to form a tiny bubble; as the bubble expands, some of the ink is ejected from the print head onto the paper. When the bubble collapses, a small vacuum is created which allows fresh ink to be drawn into the print head. This continues until the printing cycle is completed.

Piezoelectric – a crystal is located at the back of the ink reservoir for each nozzle. The crystal is given a tiny electric charge which makes it vibrate. This vibration forces ink to be ejected onto the paper; at the same time more ink is drawn in for further printing.

When a user wishes to print a document using an inkjet printer, the following sequence of events takes place. Whatever technology is used, the basic steps in the printing process are the same.

▼ **Table 3.6** Steps in inkjet printing process

Stage in process	Description of what happens
1	the data from the document is sent to a printer driver
2	the printer driver ensures that the data is in a format that the chosen printer can understand
3	a check is made by the printer driver to ensure that the chosen printer is available to print (e.g. is it busy, is it off-line, is it out of ink, and so on)
4	the data is then sent to the printer and it is stored in a temporary memory known as a printer buffer
5	a sheet of paper is then fed into the main body of the printer; a sensor detects whether paper is available in the paper feed tray – if it is out of paper (or the paper is jammed) then an error message is sent back to the computer
6	as the sheet of paper is fed through the printer, the print head moves from side to side across the paper printing the text or image; the four ink colours are sprayed in their exact amounts to produce the desired final colour
7	at the end of each full pass of the print head, the paper is advanced very slightly to allow the next line to be printed; this continues until the whole page has been printed
8	if there is more data in the printer buffer, then the whole process from stage 5 is repeated until the buffer is finally empty
9	once the printer buffer is empty, the printer sends an interrupt to the CPU in the computer; this is a request for more data to be sent to the printer; the whole process continues until the whole of the document has been printed

Laser printers

Laser printers use dry powder ink rather than liquid ink and make use of the properties of static electricity to produce the text and images. Unlike inkjet printers, laser printers print the whole page in one go. Colour laser printers use 4 toner cartridges – blue, cyan, magenta and black. Although the actual technology is different to monochrome printers, the printing method is similar but coloured dots are used to build up the text and images.

The following table describes briefly the stages that occur when a document is printed using a laser printer:

▲ **Figure 3.40** Laser printer

▼ **Table 3.7** Steps in laser printing process

Stage in process	Description of what happens
1	the data from the document is sent to a printer driver
2	the printer driver ensures that the data is in a format that the chosen printer can understand
3	a check is made by the printer driver to ensure that the chosen printer is available to print (e.g. is it busy, is it off-line, is it out of ink, and so on)
4	the data is then sent to the printer and it is stored in a temporary memory known as a printer buffer
5	the start of the printing process involves a printing drum being given a positive charge; as this drum rotates, a laser beam is scanned across it removing the positive charge in certain areas; this leaves negatively charged areas that exactly match the text/images of the page to be printed
6	the drum is then coated with positively charged toner (powdered ink); since the toner is positively charged, it only sticks to the negatively charged parts of the drum
7	a negatively charged sheet of paper is then rolled over the drum
8	the toner on the drum now sticks to the paper to produce an exact copy of the page sent to the printer
9	to prevent the paper sticking to the drum, the electric charge on the paper is removed after one rotation of the drum
10	the paper finally goes through a fuser which is a set of heated rollers; the heat melts the ink so that it fixes permanently to the paper
11	at the very end, a discharge lamp removes all the electric charge from the drum making it ready to print the next page

Applications of inkjet and laser printers

The choice of whether to use an inkjet printer or a laser printer depends on which features make it the most appropriate output device for the given application.

Inkjet printer – inkjet printers are often used for printing one-off photos or where only a few pages of good quality, colour printing is needed; the small ink cartridges or small paper trays would not be an issue with such applications.

Laser printer – these devices produce high quality printouts and are very fast when making multiple copies of a document; any application that needs high volume printing (in colour or monochrome) would choose the laser printer (for example, producing a large number of high-quality flyers or posters for advertising). Laser printers have two advantages: they have large toner cartridges and large paper trays (often holding more than a ream of paper).

▲ **Figure 3.41** Typical 3D printer

▲ **Figure 3.42** An alloy wheel

3D printers

3D printers are used to produce solid objects that actually work. They are primarily based on inkjet and laser printer technology. The solid object is built up layer by layer using materials such as: powdered resin, powdered metal, paper or ceramic.

The alloy wheel in Figure 3.42 was made using an industrial 3D printer.

It was made from many layers (0.1 mm thick) of powdered metal using a technology known as **binder 3D printing**.

Other examples are discussed below.

The following information describes some of the features of 3D printing:

» Various types of 3D printers exist; they range from the size of a microwave oven up to the size of a small car.
» 3D printers use additive manufacturing (i.e. the object is built up layer by layer); this is in sharp contrast to the more traditional method of subtractive manufacturing (i.e. removal of material to make the object). For example, making a statue using a 3D printer would involve building it up layer by layer using powdered stone until the final object was formed. The subtractive method would involve carving the statue out of solid stone (i.e. removing the stone not required) until the final item was produced. Similarly, CNC machining removes metal to form an object; 3D printing would produce the same item by building up the object from layers of powdered metal.
» **Direct 3D printing** uses inkjet technology; a print head can move left to right as in a normal printer. However, the print head can also move up and down to build up the layers of an object.
» **Binder 3D printing** is similar to direct 3D printing. However, this method uses two passes for each of the layers; the first pass sprays dry powder and then on the second pass a binder (a type of glue) is sprayed to form a solid layer.
» Newer technologies are using lasers and UV light to harden liquid polymers; this further increases the diversity of products which can be made.

How to create a solid object using 3D printers

There are a number of steps in the process of producing an object using 3D printers. The steps are summarised below:

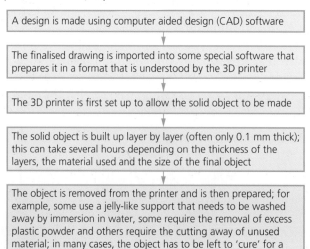

A design is made using computer aided design (CAD) software

The finalised drawing is imported into some special software that prepares it in a format that is understood by the 3D printer

The 3D printer is first set up to allow the solid object to be made

The solid object is built up layer by layer (often only 0.1 mm thick); this can take several hours depending on the thickness of the layers, the material used and the size of the final object

The object is removed from the printer and is then prepared; for example, some use a jelly-like support that needs to be washed away by immersion in water, some require the removal of excess plastic powder and others require the cutting away of unused material; in many cases, the object has to be left to 'cure' for a few hours.

◀ **Figure 3.43** How to create an object using a 3D printer

Uses of 3D printing

3D printing is regarded as being possibly the next 'industrial revolution' since it will change the manufacturing methods in many industries. The following list is just a glimpse into what we know can be made using these printers; in the years that follow, this list will probably fill an entire book:

>> the covering of prosthetic limbs can be made to exactly fit the limb
>> making items to allow precision reconstructive surgery (e.g. facial reconstruction following an accident); the parts made by this technique are more precise in their design since they can be made from exact scanning of the skull
>> in aerospace, manufacturers are looking at making wings and other parts using 3D technology; the bonus will be lightweight precision parts
>> fashion and art – 3D printing allows new creative ideas to be developed
>> making parts for items no longer in production e.g. suspension parts for a vintage car.

These are just a few of the exciting applications which make use of this new technology.

 Find out more

The reader is invited to do a search on the internet to find out new and innovative research into 3D printing applications.

LED and LCD screens

LED screens

An LED screen is made up of tiny light emitting diodes (LEDs). Each LED is either red, green or blue in colour. By varying the electric current sent to each LED, its brightness can be controlled, producing a vast range of colours.

This type of screen tends to be used for large outdoor displays due to the brilliance of the colours produced. Recent advancements in LED technology have led to the introduction of OLED (organic LED) screens (see later).

The reader needs to be very careful here. Many television screens are advertised as LED when in fact they are LCD screens which are *backlit* using LEDs.

LCD screens

LCD screens are made up of tiny liquid crystals. These tiny crystals make up an array of pixels that are affected by changes in applied electric fields. How this works is outside the scope of this book. But the important thing to realise is that for LCD screens to work, they require some form of backlighting.

Because LCD's don't produce any light, LCD screens are back-lit using light emitting diode (LED) technology and must not be confused with pure LED screens. Use of LED backlighting gives a very good contrast and brightness range. Before the use of LEDs, LCD screens used cold cathode fluorescent lamp (CCFL) as the back-lit method.

Essentially, CCFL uses two fluorescent tubes behind the LCD screen which supply the light source. When LEDs are used, a matrix of tiny blue-white LEDs is used behind the LCD screen.

LEDs have become increasingly more popular, as the method of back lighting, due to a number of advantages over older CCFL technology:

>> LEDs reach their maximum brightness almost immediately (there is no need to 'warm up' before reaching full efficiency)
>> LEDs give a whiter light that sharpens the image and makes the colours appear more vivid; CCFL had a slightly yellowish tint
>> LEDs produce a brighter light that improves the colour definition
>> monitors using LED technology are much thinner than monitors using CCFL technology
>> LEDs last indefinitely; this makes the technology more reliable and makes for a more consistent product
>> LEDs consume very little power which means they produce less heat as well as using less energy.

Organic light emitting diodes (OLED)

Newer LED technology is making use of **organic light emitting diodes (OLEDs)**. These use organic materials (made up of carbon compounds) to create semi-conductors that are very flexible. Organic films are sandwiched between two charged electrodes (one is a metallic **cathode** and the other a glass **anode**). When an electric field is applied to the electrodes, they give off light. This means that no form of backlighting is required. This allows for very thin screens. It also means that there is no longer a need to use LCD technology, since OLED is a self-contained system.

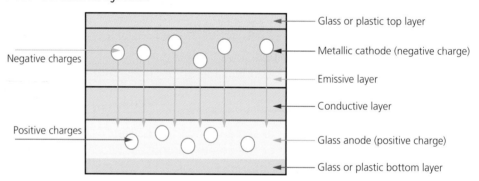

▲ **Figure 3.44** How an OLED screen works

But the important aspect of OLED technology is how thin this makes the screen. It is possible, using OLED technology, to bend screens to any shape (see Figure 3.45). When this is adopted by mobile phone manufacturers, it makes it possible to develop phones that can wrap around your wrist – much like a watch strap. Imagine screens so thin that they can be folded up and placed in your pocket until they are needed. Or how about using folding OLED displays attached to fabrics creating 'smart' clothing (this could be used on outdoor survival clothing where an integrated circuit, mobile phone, GPS receiver and OLED display could all be sewn into the clothing)?

▲ **Figure 3.45** OLED television (curved screen)

Advantages of using OLED compared to existing LEDs and LCDs:

» The plastic, organic layers of an OLED are thinner, lighter and more flexible than the crystal structures used in LEDs or LCDs.
» The light-emitting layers of an OLED are lighter; OLED layers can be made from plastic rather than the glass as used in LED and LCD screens.
» OLEDs give a brighter light than LEDs.
» OLEDs do not require backlighting like LCD screens – OLEDs generate their own light.
» Since OLEDs require no backlighting, they use much less power than LCD screens (most of the LCD power is used to do the backlighting); this is very important in battery-operated devices such as mobile phones.
» Since OLEDs are essentially plastics, they can be made into large, thin sheets (this means they could be used on large advertising boards in airports, subways, and so on).
» OLEDs have a very large field of view, about 170 degrees, which makes them ideal for use in television sets and for advertising screens.

(Loud) speakers

Loudspeakers are output devices that produce sound. When connected to a computer system, digitised sound stored on a file needs to be converted into sound as follows:

» The digital data is first passed through a digital to analogue converter (DAC) where it is changed into an electric current.
» This is then passed through an amplifier (since the current generated by the DAC will be very small); this creates a current large enough to drive a loudspeaker.
» This electric current is then fed to a loudspeaker where it is converted into sound.

The following schematic shows how this is done:

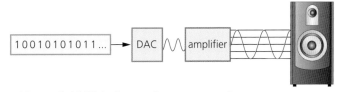

▲ **Figure 3.46** Digital to analogue conversion

As Figure 3.46 shows, if the sound is stored in a computer file, it must pass through a **digital to analogue converter (DAC)** to convert binary (digital) data into an analogue form (electric current) that can then drive the loudspeaker. Figure 3.47 shows how the loudspeaker converts the electric current into sound:

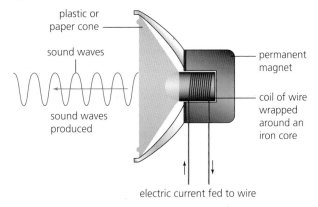

▲ **Figure 3.47** Diagram showing how a loudspeaker works

>> When an electric current flows through the coil of wire that is wrapped around an iron core, the core becomes a temporary electromagnet; a permanent magnet is also positioned very close to this electromagnet.

>> As the electric current through the coil of wire varies, the induced magnetic field in the iron core also varies. This causes the iron core to be attracted towards the permanent magnet and as the current varies this will cause the iron core to vibrate.

>> Since the iron core is attached to a cone (made of paper or thin synthetic material), this causes the cone to vibrate, producing sound waves.

Activity 3.4

1 a Explain the main differences in operation of a laser printer compared to an inkjet printer.

   b i Name one application of a laser printer and one application of an inkjet printer.

     ii For each of your named applications in **b i**, give a reason why the chosen printer is the most suitable.

2 The nine stages in printing a page using an inkjet printer are shown below. The nine stages are NOT in the correct order.

   By writing the letters **A** to **I**, put each of the stages into the correct order.

   A – the data is then sent to the printer and it is stored in a temporary memory known as a printer buffer

   B – as the sheet of paper is fed through the printer, the print head moves from side to side across the paper printing the text or image; the four ink colours are sprayed in their exact amounts to produce the desired final colour

   C – the data from the document is sent to a printer driver

   D – once the printer buffer is empty, the printer sends an interrupt to the CPU in the computer; this is a request for more data to be sent to the printer; the whole process continues until the whole of the document has been printed

   E – the printer driver ensures that the data is in a format that the chosen printer can understand

   F – at the end of each full pass of the print head, the paper is advanced very slightly to allow the next line to be printed; this continues until the whole page has been printed

   G – a check is made by the printer driver to ensure that the chosen printer is available to print (e.g. is it busy, is it off-line, is it out of ink, and so on)

   H – if there is more data in the printer buffer, then the whole process from stage 5 is repeated until the buffer is finally empty

   I – a sheet of paper is then fed into the main body of the printer; a sensor detects whether paper is available in the paper feed tray – if it is out of paper (or the paper is jammed) then an error message is sent back to the computer

3 a Explain the difference between LED screens and LCD-LED backlit screens.

   b Modern LCD screens use blue-white LEDs as backlighting. Cold cathode ray (fluorescent) tubes were used. Give three advantages of using LEDs.

4 Filipe has music stored on his computer's backing store. He wishes to listen to his music through a pair of loudspeakers. Describe how the music, which is digitally stored can be played through his two analogue loudspeakers.

▲ **Figure 3.48** Mercury thermometer

3.2.3 Sensors

Sensors are input devices which read or measure physical properties from their surroundings. Examples include temperature, pressure, acidity level and length (there are many others). Real data is analogue in nature; this means it is constantly changing and doesn't have a single discrete value. Therefore, analogue data needs some form of interpretation by the user, for example, the temperature measurement on a mercury thermometer requires the user to look at the height of the mercury column and use their best judgement (by looking at the scale) to find the temperature. There are an infinite number of values depending on how precisely the height of the mercury column is measured.

However, computers cannot make any sense of these physical quantities so the data needs to be converted into a digital format. This is usually achieved by an **analogue to digital converter (ADC)**. This device converts physical values into discrete digital values.

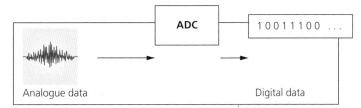

▲ **Figure 3.49** ADC

<table>
<tr><td>Link</td></tr>
<tr><td>For more on actuators see Section 3.2.2.</td></tr>
</table>

When the computer is used to control devices, such as a motor or a valve, it is necessary to use a **digital to analogue converter** (DAC) since these devices need analogue data to operate in many cases. Actuators are used in such control applications.

Sensor readings may cause the microprocessor to, for example, alter a valve or a motor that will then change the next reading taken by the sensor. So the output from the microprocessor will impact on the next input received as it attempts to bring the system within the desired parameters. This is known as **feedback**.

It is important to realise that sensors send out constant values; they don't suddenly send a reading when the parameter they are measuring changes. It is the microprocessor they are giving the input to that will analyse the incoming data and take the necessary action.

Table 3.8 shows a number of common sensors and examples of applications where the sensors might be used.

▼ **Table 3.8** Sensors

Sensor	Description of sensor	Example applications
Temperature	measures temperature of the surroundings by sending signals; these signals will change as the temperature changes	• control of a central heating system • control/monitor a chemical process • control/monitor temperature in a greenhouse
Moisture	measures water levels in, for example, soil (it is based on the electrical resistance of the sample being monitored)	• control/monitor moisture levels in soil in a greenhouse • monitor the moisture levels in a food processing factory
Humidity	this is slightly different to moisture; this measures the amount of water vapour in, for example, a sample of air (based on the fact that the conductivity of air will change depending on the amount of water present)	• monitor humidity levels in a building • monitor humidity levels in a factory manufacturing microchips • monitor/control humidity levels in the air in a greenhouse
Light	these use photoelectric cells that produce an output (in the form of an electric current) depending on the brightness of the light	• switching street lights on or off depending on light levels • switch on car headlights automatically when it gets dark
Infrared (active)	these use an invisible beam of infrared radiation picked up by a detector; if the beam is broken, then there will be a change in the amount of infrared radiation reaching the detector (sensor)	• turn on car windscreen wipers automatically when it detects rain on the windscreen • security alarm system (intruder breaks the infra-red beam)
Infrared (passive)	these sensors measure the heat radiation given off by an object, for example, the temperature of an intruder or the temperature in a fridge	• security alarm system (detects body heat) • monitor the temperature inside an industrial freezer or chiller unit
Pressure	a pressure sensor is a transducer and generates different electric currents depending on the pressure applied	• weighing of lorries at a weighing station • measure the gas pressure in a nuclear reactor
Acoustic/sound	these are basically microphones that convert detected sound into electric signals/pulses	• pick up the noise of footsteps in a security system • detect the sound of liquids dripping at a faulty pipe joint
Gas	most common ones are oxygen or carbon dioxide sensors; they use various methods to detect the gas being monitored and produce outputs that vary with the oxygen or carbon dioxide levels present	• monitor pollution levels in the air at an airport • monitor oxygen and carbon dioxide levels in a greenhouse • monitor oxygen levels in a car exhaust
pH	these measure acidity through changes in voltages in, for example, soil	• monitor/control acidity levels in the soil in a greenhouse • control acidity levels in a chemical process
Magnetic field	these sensors measure changes in magnetic fields – the signal output will depend on how the magnetic field changes	• detect magnetic field changes (for example, in mobile phones and CD players) • used in anti-lock braking systems in cars
Accelerometer	these are sensors that measure acceleration and motion of an application, i.e. the change in velocity (a piezoelectric cell is used whose output varies according to the change in velocity)	• used in cars to measure rapid deceleration and apply air bags in a crash • used by mobile phones to change between portrait and landscape mode
Proximity	these sensors detect the presence of a nearby object	• detect when a face is close to a mobile phone screen and switches off screen when held to the ear
Flow (rate)	these sensors measure the flow rate of a moving liquid or gas and produce an output based on the amount of liquid or gas passing over the sensor	• used in respiratory devices and inhalers in hospitals • measure gas flows in pipes (for example, natural gas)
Level	these sensors use ultrasonics (to detect changing liquid levels in, for example, a tank) or capacitance/conductivity (to measure static levels (for example, height of water in a river) – note, level sensors can also be optical or mechanical in nature	• monitor levels in a petrol tank in a car • in a pharmaceutical process where powder levels in tablet production need to be monitored • leak detection in refrigerant (air conditioning)

Sensors are used in both monitoring and control applications. There is a subtle difference between how these two methods work (the flowchart is a simplification of the process):

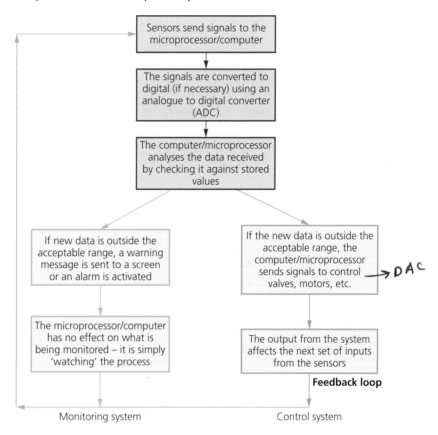

▲ **Figure 3.50** Monitoring and control systems using sensors

Examples of monitoring

» Monitoring of a patient in a hospital for vital signs such as heart rate, temperature, etc.
» Monitoring of intruders in a burglar alarm system
» Checking the temperature levels in a car engine
» Monitoring pollution levels in a river.

Examples of control

» Turning street lights on at night and turning them off again during daylight
» Controlling the temperature in a central heating/air conditioning system
» Chemical process control (for example, maintaining temperature and pH of process)

>> Operating anti-lock brakes on a car when necessary
>> Controlling the environment in a green house.

Monitoring applications

Security systems

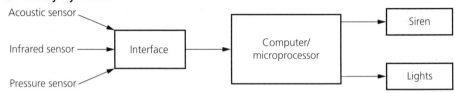

▲ **Figure 3.51** Security system

Note: compare this to Figure 3.9 (embedded systems) which shows the security system in more detail. Figure 3.51 concentrates on the sensor input.

The security monitoring system will carry out the following actions:

>> the system is activated by keying in a password on a keypad
>> the **infrared sensor** will pick up the movement of an intruder in the building
>> the **acoustic sensor** will pick up sounds such as footsteps or breaking glass
>> the **pressure sensor** will pick up the weight of an intruder coming through a door or through a window
>> the sensor data is passed through an ADC if it is in an analogue form ...
>> ... to produce digital data
>> the computer/microprocessor will sample the digital data coming from these sensors at a given frequency (e.g. every 5 seconds) ...
>> ... the data is compared with the stored values by the computer/microprocessor
>> if any of the incoming data values are outside the acceptable range, then the computer sends a signal ...
>> ... to a siren to sound the alarm, or
>> ... to a light to start flashing
>> a DAC is used if the devices need analogue values to operate them
>> the alarm continues to sound/lights continue to flash until the system is re-set with a password.

Monitoring of patients in a hospital

>> A number of sensors are attached to the patient ...
>> ... these measure vital signs such as: temperature, heart rate, breathing rate, etc.
>> these sensors are all attached to a computer system
>> the sensors constantly send data back to the computer system
>> the computer samples the data at frequent intervals
>> the range of acceptable values for each parameter is keyed into the computer
>> the computer compares the values from the sensors with those values keyed in
>> if anything is out of the acceptable range, a signal is sent by the computer ...
>> ... to sound an alarm
>> if data from the sensors is within range, the values are shown in either graphical form on a screen and/or a digital read out
>> monitoring continues until the sensors are disconnected from the patient.

Control applications

Control of street lighting

This next sequence shows how a microprocessor is used to control the operation of a street lamp. The lamp is fitted with a light sensor which constantly sends data to the microprocessor. The data value from the sensor changes according to whether it is sunny, cloudy, raining or it is night time (etc.):

» the light sensor sends data to the ADC interface
» this changes the data into digital form and sends it to the microprocessor
» the microprocessor samples the data every minute (or at some other frequency rate)

» if the data from the sensor < value stored in memory …
» … a signal is sent from the microprocessor to the street lamp …
» … and the lamp is switched on
» the lamp stays switched on for 30 minutes before the sensor readings are sampled again (this prevents the lamp flickering off and on during brief heavy cloud cover, for example)
» if the data from the sensor >= value stored in memory …
» … a signal is sent from the microprocessor to the street lamp …
» … and the lamp is switched off
» the lamp stays switched off for 30 minutes before sensor readings are sampled again (this prevents the lamp flickering off and on during heavy cloud cover for example).

▲ **Figure 3.52** Street lighting

Anti-lock braking systems (on cars)

Anti-lock braking systems (ABS) on cars use **magnetic field sensors** to stop the wheels locking up on the car if the brakes have been applied too sharply:

» when one of the car wheels rotates too slowly (i.e. it is locking up), a magnetic field sensor sends data to a microprocessor
» the microprocessor checks the rotation speed of the other three wheels
» if they are different (i.e. rotating faster), the microprocessor sends a signal to the braking system …
» … and the braking pressure to the affected wheel is reduced …
» … the wheel's rotational speed is then increased to match the other wheels
» the checking of the rotational speed using these magnetic field sensors is done several times a second …
» … and the braking pressure to all the wheels can be constantly changing to prevent any of the wheels locking up under heavy braking …
» … this is felt as a 'judder' on the brake pedal as the braking system is constantly switched off and on to equalise the rotational speed of all four wheels
» if one of the wheels is rotating too quickly, braking pressure is increased to that wheel until it matches the other three.

Central heating systems

In this example, a gas supply is used to heat water using a heater. A valve on the gas supply is controlled by a microprocessor and is opened if the heating levels need to be increased. A water pump is used to pump hot water around the central heating system whenever the temperature drops below a pre-set value:

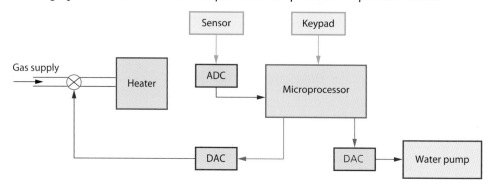

▲ **Figure 3.53** Controlling a central heating system

So how does this work?

» the required temperature is keyed in and this is stored in the microprocessor memory (this is called the <u>pre-set value</u>)
» the temperature sensor is constantly sending data readings to the microprocessor
» the sensor data is first sent to an ADC to convert the analogue data into digital data
» the digital data is sent to the microprocessor
» the microprocessor compares this data with the pre-set value
» if the temperature reading >= pre-set value then no action is taken
» if the temperature reading < pre-set value, then a signal is sent ...
» ... to an actuator (via a DAC) to open the gas valve to the heater
» ... to an actuator (via a DAC) to turn on the water pump
» the process continues until the central heating is switched off.

Chemical process control

A certain chemical process only works if the temperature is above 70°C and the pH (acidity) level is less than 3.5. Sensors are used as part of the control system. A heater is used to heat the reactor and valves are used to add acid when necessary to maintain the acidity. The following description shows how the sensors and computer are used to control this process:

» **temperature** and **pH sensors** read data from the chemical process
» this data is converted to digital using an ADC and is then sent to the computer
» the computer compares the incoming data with pre-set values stored in memory
» ... if the temperature < 70°C, a signal is sent to switch on the heater
» ... if the temperature >= 70°C, a signal is sent to switch off the heaters
» ... if the pH > 3.5, then a signal is sent to open a valve and acid is added
» ... if the pH <= 3.5, then a signal is sent to close this valve
» the computer signals will be changed into analogue signals using a DAC so that it can control the heaters and valves
» this continues as long as the computer system is activated.

Greenhouse environment control

Five different sensors could be used here to control the greenhouse environment, namely: **humidity**, **moisture**, **temperature**, **pH** and **light**. To simplify this problem the control mechanisms are shown in Figure 3.54.

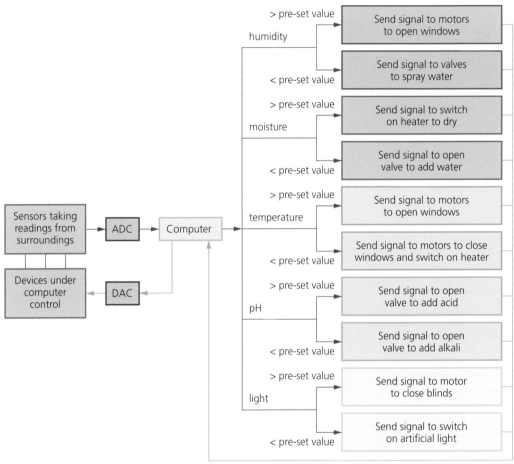

Computer processing

▲ **Figure 3.54** Control of greenhouse environment

Because of the number of sensors, this is clearly quite a complex problem. Let us consider the humidity sensor only. This sends a signal to an ADC, which then sends a digital signal to the computer. This compares the input with stored (pre-set) values and decides what action needs to be taken (follow the orange lines in Figure 3.54). If humidity is > pre-set value, the computer sends a signal to a DAC (follow the green lines in the figure) to operate the motors to open windows thus reducing the humidity. If it is < pre-set value, the computer sends a signal to open valves to spray water into the air (follow the green lines). If the reading = pre-set value, then no action is taken (this isn't shown in the diagram since it could follow either direction). The control process continues as long as the system is switched on. Similar arguments can be used for all five sensors.

Activity 3.5

1 An air conditioning unit in a car is being controlled by a microprocessor and a number of sensors.

a Describe the main differences between **control** and **monitoring** of a process.

b Describe how the sensors and microprocessor would be used to control the air conditioning unit in the car. Name at least two different sensors that might be used and explain the role of positive feedback in your description.

You might find drawing a diagram of your intended process to be helpful.

2 Look at Figure 3.54 and describe how the pH sensor would be used to control the acidity levels in the soil to optimise growing conditions in the greenhouse.

3 The diagram (Figure 3.55) below shows a nuclear reactor. Two of the sensors used in the control and monitoring of the reactor are:

» a temperature sensor to monitor the reactor temperature (if this exceeds 300°C then the water flow into the reactor is increased)

» a pressure sensor to monitor the gas pressure of carbon dioxide circulating in the reactor (if this is less 10 bar then the gas pump is opened)

» note that: ⊗ represents a gas or liquid pump

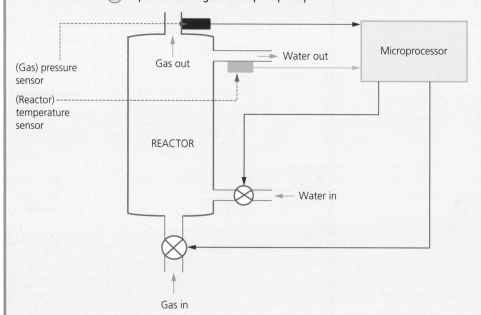

▲ **Figure 3.55**

Describe how the sensors and microprocessor are used to maintain the correct water (reactor) temperature and gas pressure in the reactor. Name any other hardware devices you think may be needed in your description.

4 The junction (Figure 3.56) is controlled by traffic lights.

Describe how sensors in the road and a microprocessor are used to control the traffic at the junction. The microprocessor is able to change the colour sequence of the lights.

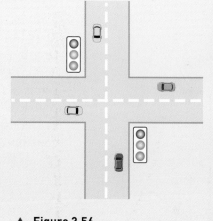

▲ **Figure 3.56**

3.3 Data storage

All computers require some form of memory and storage. Memory is usually referred to as the internal devices used to store data that the computer can access directly. This is also known as primary memory. This memory can be the user's workspace, temporary data or data that is key to running the computer.

Storage devices allow users to store applications, data and files. The user's data is stored permanently and they can change it or read it as they wish. Storage needs to be larger than internal memory since the user may wish to store large files (such as music files or videos). Storage devices can also be removable to allow data, for example, to be transferred between computers. Removable devices allow a user to store important data in a different location in case of data loss.

However, all of this removeable storage has become less important with the advent of technology such as 'data drop' (which uses Bluetooth) and cloud storage. Figure 3.57 summarises the types of memory and storage devices covered in this section.

Memory and storage devices can be split up into two distinct groups:

» primary memory
» secondary storage.

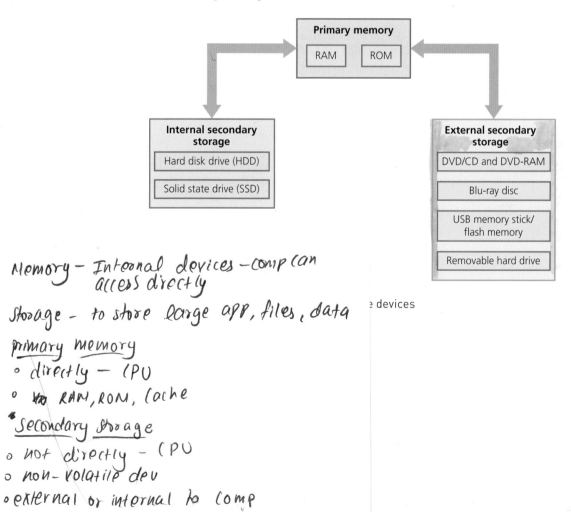

e devices

Handwritten notes:

Memory – Internal devices – comp can access directly

Storage – to store large app, files, data

primary memory
  ○ directly – CPU
  ○ RAM, ROM, cache

Secondary storage
  ○ not directly – CPU
  ○ non-volatile dev
  ○ external or internal to comp

Here is a summary of the differences between primary memory and storage devices:

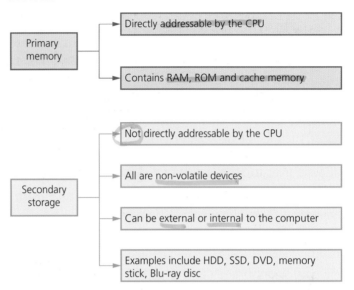

▲ **Figure 3.58** Summary of primary, secondary and off-line devices

3.3.1 Primary memory

Primary memory is the part of the computer memory which can be accessed directly from the CPU; this includes **random access memory (RAM)** and **read-only memory (ROM)** memory chips. Primary memory allows the CPU to access applications and services temporarily stored in memory locations. The structure of primary memory is shown in Figure 3.59.

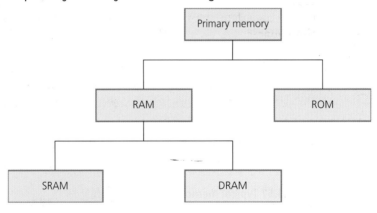

▲ **Figure 3.59** Primary memory

Random access memory (RAM)

All computer systems come with some form of RAM. These memory devices are not really random; this refers to the fact that any memory location in RAM can be accessed independent of which memory location was last used. When you run an application or program, data is retrieved from secondary storage and placed temporarily into RAM. Access time to locate data is much faster in RAM than in secondary or off-line devices. Features of RAM include:

» can be written to or read from, and the data can be changed by the user or the computer (i.e. it is a temporary memory)

of an application or part of the operating

...mory contents are lost when powering off the

In general, the larger the size of RAM the faster the computer will operate. In reality, RAM never runs out of memory; it continues to operate but just becomes slower and slower as more data is stored. As RAM becomes 'full', the CPU has to continually access the secondary data storage devices to overwrite **old** data on RAM with **new** data. By increasing the RAM size, the number of times this has to be done is considerably reduced; thus making the computer operate more quickly.

There are currently two types of RAM technology:

» dynamic RAM (DRAM)
» static RAM (SRAM).

Dynamic RAM (DRAM)

▲ **Figure 3.60** DRAM

▲ **Figure 3.61** SRAM

Each DRAM chip consists of transistors and capacitors. Each of these parts is tiny since a single RAM chip will contain millions of transistors and capacitors. The function of each part is:

» capacitor – this holds the bits of information (0 or 1)
» transistor – this acts like a switch; it allows the chip control circuitry to read the capacitor or change the capacitor's value.

This type of RAM needs to be constantly **refreshed** (that is, the capacitor needs to be re-charged every 15 microseconds otherwise it would lose its value). If it wasn't refreshed, the capacitor's charge would leak away very quickly leaving every capacitor with the value 0.

DRAMs have a number of advantages over SRAMs:

» they are much less expensive to manufacture than SRAM
» they consume less power than SRAM
» they have a higher memory capacity than SRAM.

Static RAM (SRAM)

A major difference between SRAM and DRAM is that SRAM doesn't need to be constantly refreshed.

It makes use of **flip flops**, which hold each bit of memory.

SRAM is much faster than DRAM when it comes to data access (typically, access time for SRAM is 25 nanoseconds and for DRAM is 60 nanoseconds).

DRAM is the most common type of RAM used in computers, but where absolute speed is essential, for example, in the CPU's memory cache, SRAM is the preferred technology. Memory cache is a high-speed portion of the memory; it is effective because most programs access the same data or instructions many times. By keeping as much of this information as possible in SRAM, the computer avoids having to access the slower DRAM.

Table 3.9 summarises the differences between DRAM and SRAM.

▼ **Table 3.9** Differences between DRAM and SRAM

DRAM	SRAM
consists of a number of transistors and capacitors	uses flip flops to hold each bit of memory
needs to be constantly refreshed	doesn't need to be constantly refreshed
less expensive to manufacture than SRAM	has a faster data access time than DRAM
has a higher memory capacity than SRAM	CPU memory cache makes use of SRAM
main memory is constructed from DRAM	
consumes less power than SRAM	

Read-only memory (ROM)

Another form of primary memory is read-only memory (ROM). This is similar to RAM in that it shares some of its properties, but the main difference is that it cannot be changed or written to. ROM chips have the following features:

» they are non-volatile (the contents are not lost after powering off the computer)
» they are permanent memories (the contents cannot be changed or written to by the user, the computer or any application/program)
» the contents can only be read
» they are often used to store data that the computer needs to access when powering up for the first time (the basic input/output system (BIOS)); these are known as the start-up instructions (or bootstrap)

Here is a summary of the main differences between RAM and ROM:

▼ **Table 3.10** RAM and ROM features

RAM	ROM
temporary memory device	permanent memory device
volatile memory	non-volatile memory device
can be written to and read from	data stored cannot be altered
used to store data, files, programs, part of OS **currently** in use	always used to store BIOS and other data needed at start up
can be increased in size to improve operational speed of a computer	

Example of an application

We will now consider an application, other than a computer, where both RAM and ROM chips are used:

A remote-controlled toy car has circuitry which contains both RAM and ROM chips. The remote control is a hand-held device. Explain the function of the RAM and ROM chip in this application.

We will consider the function of each type of memory independently:

ROM

» storing the factory settings such as remote control frequencies
» storing the 'start-up' routines when the toy car is first switched on
» storing of the set routines; for example, how the buttons on the hand-held device control turning left, acceleration, stopping, and so on.

RAM

» the user may wish to program in their own routines; these new instructions would be stored in the RAM chip
» the RAM chip will store the data/instructions received from the remote control unit.

Activity 3.6

1 Describe how ROM and RAM chips could be used in the following devices:
   a a microwave oven
   b a refrigerator
   c a remote-controlled model aeroplane; the movement of the aeroplane is controlled by a hand-held device.

3.3.2 Secondary and off-line storage

Secondary (and off-line) storage includes storage devices that are not directly addressable by the CPU. They are non-volatile devices that allow data to be stored as long as required by the user. This type of storage can store more data than primary memory, but data access time is considerably longer than with RAM or ROM. All applications, the operating system, device drivers and general files (for example, documents, photos and music) are stored on secondary storage. The following section discusses the various types of secondary storage that can be found on the majority of computers.

3.3.3 Magnetic, optical and solid-state storage

Secondary (and off-line) storage falls into three categories according to the technology used:

» magnetic
» solid state
» optical.

Magnetic storage

Hard Disk Drives (HDD)
Hard disk drives (HDD) are still one of the most common methods used to store data on a computer.

(handwritten margin notes)
• not directly - CPU
• non-volatile
• longer data access time

▲ **Figure 3.62** HDD

Data is stored in a digital format on the magnetic surfaces of the disks (or platters, as they are frequently called). The hard disk drive will have a number of platters that can spin at about 7000 times a second. Read-write heads consist of electromagnets that are used to read data from or write data to the platters. Platters can be made from aluminium, glass or a ceramic material. A number of read-write heads can access all of the surfaces of the platters in the disk drive. Normally each platter will have two surfaces which can be used to store data. These read-write heads can move very quickly – typically they can move from the centre of the disk to the edge of the disk (and back again) 50 times a second.

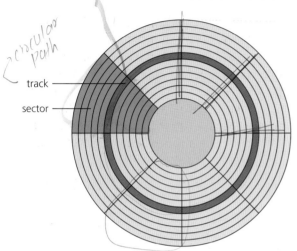

▲ **Figure 3.63** Tracks and sectors

Data is stored on the surface in sectors and tracks. A sector on a given track will contain a fixed number of bytes. Unfortunately, hard disk drives have very slow data access when compared to, for example, RAM. Many applications require the read-write heads to constantly look for the correct blocks of data; this means a large number of head movements. The effects of **latency** then become very significant. Latency is defined as the time it takes for a specific block of data on a data track to rotate around to the read-write head.

Users will sometimes notice the effect of latency when they see messages such as 'Please wait' or, at its worst, 'not responding'.

When a file or data is stored on a HDD, the required number of sectors needed to store the data will be allocated. However, the sectors allocated may not be adjacent to each other. Through time, the HDD will undergo numerous deletions and editing which leads to sectors becoming increasingly fragmented resulting in a gradual deterioration of the HDD performance (in other words, it takes longer and longer to access data). Defragmentation software can improve on this situation by 'tidying up' the disk sectors.

All data in a given sector on a HDD will be read in order (that is, sequentially); however, access to the sector itself will be by a direct read/write head movement.

Removable hard disk drives are essentially HDDs external to the computer that can be connected to the computer using one of the USB ports. In this way, they can be used as a back-up device or another way of transferring files between computers.

Solid state drives (SSD)

Latency is an issue in HDDs as described earlier. Solid state drives (SSD) remove this issue considerably since they have no moving parts and all data is retrieved at the same rate. They don't rely on magnetic properties; the most common type of solid state storage devices store data by controlling the movement of electrons within NAND or NOR chips. The data is stored as 0s and 1s in millions of tiny transistors (at each junction one transistor is called a floating gate and the other is called a control gate) within the chip. This effectively produces a non-volatile rewritable memory.

Floating gate and control gate transistors

Floating gate and control gate transistors use CMOS (complementary metal oxide semi-conductor) NAND technology. Flash memories make use of a matrix; at each

> **Link**
>
> See Section 4.1.1 for more on defragmentation.

> **Link**
>
> For more on NAND and NOR gates see Chapter 10.

intersection on the matrix there is a floating gate and a control gate arranged as follows:

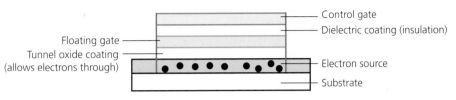

▲ **Figure 3.64** Flash memory

A dielectric coating separates the two transistors, which allows the floating gate transistor to retain its charge (which is why the memory is non-volatile). The floating gate transistor has a value of 1 when it is charged and a value of 0 when it isn't. To program one of these 'intersection cells' a voltage is applied to the control gate and electrons from the electron source are attracted to it. But due to the dielectric coating, the electrons become trapped in the floating gate. Hence, we have control over the bit value stored at each intersection. (**Note:** After about 12 months, this charge can leak away, which is why a solid state device should be used at least once a year to be certain it will retain its memory.)

The main benefits of this newer solid state technology over hard disk drives are:

» they are more reliable (no moving parts to go wrong)
» they are considerably lighter (which makes them suitable for laptops)
» they don't have to 'get up to speed' before they work properly
» they have a lower power consumption
» they run much cooler than HDDs (both these points again make them very suitable for laptop computers)
» because of no moving parts, they are very thin
» data access is considerably faster than HDD.

The main drawback of SSD is still the longevity of the technology (although this is becoming less of an issue). Most solid state storage devices are conservatively rated at only 20 GB of write operations per day over a three year period – this is known as SSD endurance. For this reason, SSD technology is still not used in all servers, for example, where a huge number of write operations take place every day. However, the durability of these solid state systems is being improved by a number of manufacturers and they are rapidly becoming more common in applications such as servers and **cloud storage** devices.

Note: It is also not possible to over-write existing data on a flash memory device; it is necessary to first erase the old data and then write the new data at the same location.

Memory sticks/flash memories

Memory sticks/flash memories (also known as pen drives) use solid state technology.

They usually connect to the computer through the USB port. Their main advantage is that they are very small, lightweight devices, which make them very suitable as a method for transferring files between computers. They can also be used as small back-up devices for music or photo files, for example.

Complex or expensive software, such as financial planning software, often uses memory sticks as a dongle. The dongle contains additional files that are needed to run the software. Without this dongle, the software won't work properly. It therefore prevents illegal or unauthorised use of the software, and also prevents copying of the software since, without the dongle, it is useless.

Optical media

CD/DVD disks

CDs and **DVDs** are described as **optical storage devices**. Laser light is used to read and write data to and from the surface of the disk.

- Laser light - Read / write
- metal alloy
- light sensitive dye

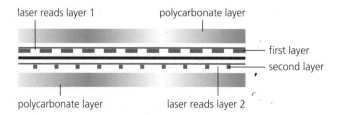

pits

lands

single spiral track runs from the centre to outer part of disk

▲ **Figure 3.65** Optical media

Both CDs and DVDs use a thin layer of metal alloy or light-sensitive organic dye to store the data. As can be seen from the diagram in Figure 3.65, both systems use a single, spiral track which runs from the centre of the disk to the edge. When a disk spins, the optical head moves to the point where the laser beam 'contacts' the disk surface and follows the spiral track from the centre outwards. As with a HDD, a CD/DVD is divided into sectors allowing direct access to data. Also, as in the case of HDD, the outer part of the disk runs faster than the inner part of the disk.

HDD & CD ① ②

The data is stored in 'pits' and 'lands' on the spiral track. A red laser is used to read and write the data. CDs and DVDs can be designated 'R' (write once only) or 'RW' (can be written to or read from many times).

DVD technology is slightly different to that used in CDs. One of the main differences is the potential for **dual-layering**, which considerably increases the storage capacity. Basically, this means that there are two individual recording layers. Two layers of a standard DVD are joined together with a transparent (polycarbonate) spacer and a very thin reflector is also sandwiched between the two layers. Reading and writing of the second layer is done by a red laser focusing at a fraction of a millimetre difference compared to the first layer.

laser reads layer 1   polycarbonate layer

first layer
second layer

polycarbonate layer   laser reads layer 2

▲ **Figure 3.66** Dual-layering on a DVD

Standard, single layer DVDs still have a larger storage capacity than CDs because the 'pit' size and track width are both smaller. This means that more data can be stored on the DVD surface. DVDs use lasers with a wavelength of 650 nanometres; CDs use lasers with a wavelength of 780 nanometres. The shorter the wavelength of the laser light, the greater the storage capacity of the medium.

↓ wavelength, ↑ storage capacity

Blu-ray discs

Blu-ray discs are another example of optical storage media. However, they are fundamentally different to DVDs in their construction and in the way they carry out read-write operations.

Note: it is probably worth mentioning why they are called Blu-ray rather than Blue-ray; the simple reason is it was impossible to copyright the word 'Blue' and hence the use of the word 'Blu'.

The main differences between DVD and Blu-ray are:

▲ **Figure 3.67** Blu-ray disc

- » a blue laser, rather than a red laser, is used to carry out read and write operations; the wavelength of blue light is only 405 nanometres (compared to 650 nm for red light)
- » using blue laser light means that the 'pits' and 'lands' can be much smaller; consequently, Blu-ray can store up to five times more data than normal DVD
- » single-layer Blu-ray discs use a 1.2 mm thick polycarbonate disk; however, dual-layer Blu-ray and normal DVDs both use a sandwich of two 0.6 mm thick disks (i.e. 1.2 mm thick)
- » Blu-ray disks automatically come with a secure encryption system that helps to prevent piracy and copyright infringement
- » the data transfer rate for a DVD is 10 Mbps and for a Blu-ray disc it is 36 Mbps (this equates to 1.5 hours to transfer 25 GiB of data).

Since Blu-ray discs can come in single layer or dual-layer format (unlike DVD, which is always dual-layer), it is probably worth also comparing the differences in capacity and interactivity of the two technologies.

Comparison of the capacity and interactivity of DVDs and Blu-ray discs

- » A standard dual-layer DVD has a storage capacity of 4.7 GB (enough to store a 2-hour standard definition movie)
- » A single-layer Blu-ray disc has a storage capacity of 27 GB (enough to store a 2-hour high definition movie or 13 hours of standard definition movies)
- » A dual-layer Blu-ray disc has a storage capacity of 50 GB (enough to store 4.5 hours of high definition movies or 20 hours of standard definition movies).

Blu-ray allows greater interactivity than DVDs. For example, with Blu-ray, it is possible to:

- » record high definition television programs
- » skip quickly to any part of the disc
- » create playlists of recorded movies and television programmes
- » edit or re-order programmes recorded on the disc
- » automatically search for empty space on the disc to avoid over-recording
- » access websites and download subtitles and other interesting features.

Finally, Table 3.11 summarises the main differences between CDs, DVDs and Blu-ray.

All these optical storage media are used as back-up systems (for photos, music and multimedia files). This also means that CDs and DVDs can be used to transfer files between computers. Manufacturers sometimes supply their software (e.g. printer drivers) using CDs and DVDs. When the software is supplied in this way, the disk is usually in a read-only format.

▼ **Table 3.11** Comparison of CD, DVD and Blu-ray (Note: nm = 10^{-9} metres and μm = 10^{-6} metres)

Disk type	Laser colour	Wavelength of laser light	Disk construction	Track pitch (distance between tracks)
CD	Red	780 nm	single 1.2 mm polycarbonate layer	1.60 μm
DVD (dual-layer)	Red	650 nm	two 0.6 mm polycarbonate layers	0.74 μm
Blu-ray (single layer)	Blue	405 mm	single 1.2 mm polycarbonate layer	0.30 μm
Blu-ray (dual-layer)	Blue	405 nm	two 0.6 mm polycarbonate layers	0.30 μm

The most common use of DVD and Blu-ray is the supply of movies or games. The memory capacity of CDs isn't big enough to store most movies (see earlier comparison notes).

3.3.4 Virtual memory

One of the problems associated with memory management is the case when processes run out of RAM. If the amount of available RAM is exceeded due to multiple programs running, it is likely to cause a system crash. This can be solved by utilising the hard disk drive (or SSD) if we need more memory. This is the basis behind **virtual memory**. Essentially RAM is the ***physical memory***, while ***virtual memory*** is RAM + swap space on the hard disk or SSD.

To execute a program, data is loaded into memory from HDD (or SSD) whenever required. It is possible to show the differences between using normal memory management and virtual memory management in two simple diagrams.

Without virtual memory

Suppose we have five programs (numbered 0 to 4) that are in memory, all requiring access to RAM. The first diagram shows what would happen without virtual memory being used (i.e. the computer would run out of RAM memory space):

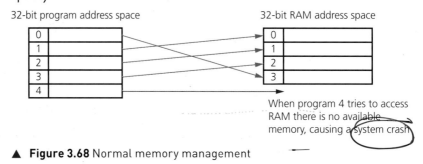

▲ **Figure 3.68** Normal memory management

[handwritten note in margin] ✗ A memory management system that accesses sec storage or software to compensate for shortage of physical memory

With virtual memory

We will now consider what happens if the CPU uses virtual memory to allow all five programs to access RAM as required. This will require moving data out of RAM into HDD/SSD and then allowing other data to be moved out of HDD/SSD into RAM:

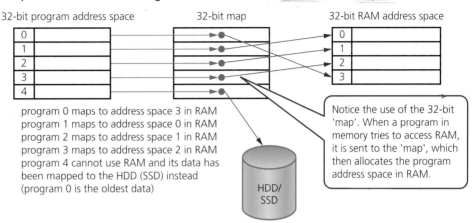

program 0 maps to address space 3 in RAM
program 1 maps to address space 0 in RAM
program 2 maps to address space 1 in RAM
program 3 maps to address space 2 in RAM
program 4 cannot use RAM and its data has been mapped to the HDD (SSD) instead (program 0 is the oldest data)

Notice the use of the 32-bit 'map'. When a program in memory tries to access RAM, it is sent to the 'map', which then allocates the program address space in RAM.

▲ **Figure 3.69** Status just before program 4 is given RAM space

Virtual memory now moves the oldest data out of RAM into the HDD/SSD to allow program 4 to gain access to RAM. The 32-bit 'map' is now updated to reflect this new situation:

» data from program 0 (which was using RAM address space 3 – the oldest data) is now mapped to the HDD/SSD instead, leaving address space 3 free for use by program 4

» program 4 now maps to address space 3 in RAM, which means program 4 now has access to RAM.

Our diagram now changes to:

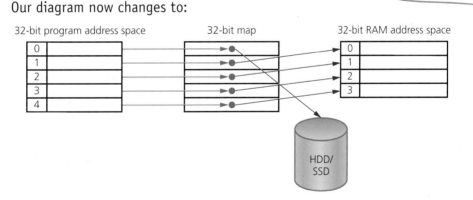

▲ **Figure 3.70** Status with program 0 now mapped to HDD and program 4 has access to RAM

All of this will continue to occur until RAM is no longer being over-utilised by the competing programs running in memory. Virtual memory gives the illusion of unlimited memory being available. Even though RAM is full, data can be moved in and out of the HDD/SSD to give the illusion that there is still memory available. In computer operating systems, **paging** is used by memory management to store and retrieve data from HDD/SSD and copy it into RAM. A **page** is a fixed-length consecutive (or contiguous) block of data utilised in virtual memory systems.

This is a key part of how virtual memory works allowing **data blocks** (pages) to be moved in and out of a HDD/SSD. However, accessing data in virtual memory is slower so, as mentioned earlier on in this chapter, the larger the RAM the faster the CPU can operate. This is one of the benefits of increasing RAM size as far as possible.

The main benefits of virtual memory are:

» programs can be larger than physical memory and still be executed
» there is no need to waste memory with data that isn't being used (e.g. during error handling)
» it reduces the need to buy and install more expensive RAM memory (although as mentioned earlier there are limits to the value of doing this).

When using HDD for virtual memory the main drawback is **disk thrashing**. As main memory fills, more and more data needs to be swapped in and out of virtual memory leading to a very high rate of hard disk read/write head movements; this is known as disk thrashing. If more and more time is spent on moving data in and out of memory than actually doing any processing, then the processing speed of the computer will be considerably reduced. A point can be reached when the execution of a process comes to a halt since the system is so busy moving data in and out of memory rather than doing any actual execution – this is known as the **thrash point**. Due to large numbers of head movements, this can also lead to premature failure of a hard disk drive. Thrashing can be reduced by installing more RAM, reducing the number of programs running at a time or reducing the size of the swap file. Another way of reducing this problem is to make use of a solid state drive (SSD) rather than using HDD.

3.3.5 Cloud storage

Public and private cloud computing

Cloud storage is a method of data storage where data is stored on remote servers. The same data is stored on more than one server in case of maintenance or repair, allowing clients to access data at any time. This is known as **data redundancy.** The physical environment is owned and managed by a hosting company and may include hundreds of servers in many locations.

There are three common systems:

» Public cloud – this is a storage environment where the customer/client and cloud storage provider are different companies
» Private cloud – this is storage provided by a dedicated environment behind a company firewall; customer/client and cloud storage provider are integrated and operate as a single entity
» Hybrid cloud – this is a combination of the two above environments; some data resides in the private cloud and less sensitive/less commercial data can be accessed from a public cloud storage provider.

Instead of saving data on a local hard disk or other storage device, a user can save their data 'in the cloud'. The benefits and drawbacks of using cloud storage are shown in Table 3.12.

▼ **Table 3.12** Benefits and drawbacks of cloud storage

Benefits of using cloud storage	Drawbacks of using cloud storage
customer/client files stored on the cloud can be accessed at any time from any device anywhere in the world provided internet access is available	if the customer/client has a slow or unstable internet connection, they would have many problems accessing or downloading their data/files
there is no need for a customer/client to carry an external storage device with them, or even use the same computer to store and retrieve information	costs can be high if large storage capacity is required; it can also be expensive to pay for high download/upload data transfer limits with the customer/client internet service provider (ISP)
the cloud provides the user with remote back-up of data with obvious benefits to alleviate data loss/disaster recovery	the potential failure of the cloud storage company is always possible – this poses a risk of loss of all back-up data
if a customer/client has a failure of their hard disk or back-up device, cloud storage will allow recovery of their data	
the cloud system offers almost unlimited storage capacity	

Data security when using cloud storage

Companies that transfer vast amounts of confidential data from their own systems to a cloud service provider are effectively relinquishing control of their own data security. This raises a number of questions:

» what physical security exists regarding the building where the data is housed?
» how good is the cloud service provider's resistance to natural disasters or power cuts?
» what safeguards exist regarding personnel who work for the cloud service company; can they use their authorisation codes to access confidential data for monetary purposes?

Potential data loss when using cloud storage

There is a risk that important and irreplaceable data could be lost from the cloud storage facilities. Actions from hackers (gaining access to accounts or pharming attacks, for example) could lead to loss or corruption of data. Users need to be certain that sufficient safeguards exist to overcome these risks.

The following breaches of security involving some of the largest cloud service providers suggest why some people are nervous of using cloud storage for important files:

» The XEN security threat, which forced several cloud operators to reboot all their cloud servers, was caused by a problem in the XEN hypervisor (a hypervisor is a piece of computer software, firmware or hardware that creates and runs virtual machines).
» A large cloud service provider permanently lost data during a routine back-up procedure.
» The celebrity photos cloud hacking scandal, in which more than 100 private photos of celebrities were leaked. Hackers had gained access to a number of cloud accounts, which enabled them to publish the photos on social networks and sell them to publishing companies.
» In 2016, the National Electoral Institute of Mexico suffered a cloud security breach in which 93 million voter registrations, stored on a central database, were compromised and became publicly available to everyone. To make matters worse, much of the information on this database also linked to a cloud server outside Mexico.

Activity 3.7

1 Name two types of memory used in a mobile phone. For each named memory, describe its purpose in the mobile phone.

2 a Explain what is meant by *virtual memory*.

b Five programs are currently being run in a computer. Program 1 is using 10 GiB of RAM, program 2 is using 5 GiB of RAM, program 3 is using 12 GiB of RAM and program 4 is using 4 GiB of RAM. The programs are at the stage where program 5 now needs to access RAM, but RAM is presently full (RAM has a 32 GiB maximum capacity). Explain how virtual memory could be used to allow program 5 to access RAM without any of the data from the other four programs being lost.

3 Five descriptions of computer terms are shown on the left and five terms are shown on the right. Draw lines to connect each description to the correct computer term.

storage environment where the client and remote storage provider are different companies	thrashing
high rate of HDD read/write operations causing large amount of head movement	swap space
space on HDD or SSD reserved for data used in virtual memory management	cloud storage
situation where a HDD is so busy doing read/write operations that execution of a process is halted	thrash point
method of data storage where the data is stored on hundreds of off-site servers	public cloud

4 a Give four differences between RAM and ROM chips.

b Give an example of the use of each type of memory.

5 a Use the following words to complete the paragraph below which describes how solid state memories work (each word may be used once, more than once or not at all).

Word list:	control gate	NAND
	electrons	negative
	floating gate	positive
	intersection	transistor
	matrix	volatile

Solid state devices control the movement of .... within a .... chip. The device is made up of a .... and at each .... there is a .... and a .... transistor. .... are attracted towards .... when a voltage is applied.

b Give three advantages of using SSD, rather than HDD, which make SSD technology particularly suitable for use in laptop computers.

c Describe one disadvantage of solid state technology.

3.4 Network hardware

3.4.1 Network interface card (NIC)

A **network interface card (NIC)** is needed to allow a device to connect to a network (such as the internet). It is usually part of the device hardware and contains the **Media Access Control (MAC)** address generated at the manufacturing stage.

Wireless network interface cards/controllers (WNICs) are the same as NICs in that they are used to connect devices to the internet or other networks. However, they use wireless connectivity utilising an antenna to communicate with networks via microwaves. They would normally plug into the USB port or be part of an internal integrated circuit.

3.4.2 Media Access Control (MAC)

A MAC address is made up of 48 bits which are shown as six groups of hexadecimal digits with the general format:

NN – NN – NN – DD – DD – DD

manufacturer's code   device serial number

For example, 00 – 1C – B3 – 4F – 25 – FF where the first six hex digits identify the device as made by, for example, Apple and the second set of six hex digits are the serial number of the device itself (this is unique). If the NIC card is replaced, the MAC address will also change.

Types of MAC address

It should finally be pointed out that there are two types of MAC address: the **Universally Administered MAC Address (UAA)** and the **Locally Administered MAC Address (LAA)**.

The UAA is by far the most common type of MAC address and this is the one set by the manufacturer at the factory. It is rare for a user to want to change this MAC address.

However, there are some occasions when a user or organisation wishes to change their MAC address. This is a relatively easy task to carry out, but it will cause big problems if the changed address isn't unique.

There are a few reasons why the MAC address needs to be changed using LAA:

» certain software used on mainframe systems need all the MAC addresses of devices to fall into a strict format; because of this, it may be necessary to change the MAC address of some devices to ensure they follow the correct format
» it may be necessary to bypass a MAC address filter on a router or a firewall; only MAC addresses with a certain format are allowed through, otherwise the devices will be blocked if their MAC address doesn't adhere to the correct format
» to get past certain types of network restrictions it may be necessary to emulate unrestricted MAC addresses; hence it may require the MAC address to be changed on certain devices connected to the network.

3.4.3 Internet protocol (IP) address

When a device connects to a private network, a router assigns a private IP address to it. That IP address is unique on that network, but might be the same as an IP address on a separate network. However, when a router connects to the internet it is given a unique public IP address. This is usually supplied by the internet service provider (ISP). No other device on the internet has the same public IP address. All the devices connected to that router have the same public IP address as the router but each have their own different private IP addresses on that network. Because the operation of the internet is based on a set of protocols (rules), it is necessary to supply an IP address. Protocols define the rules that must be agreed by senders and receivers of data communicating through the internet.

There are two versions of IP: IPv4 and IPv6. IPv4 is based on 32 bits and the address is written as four groups of eight bits (shown in denary format); for example,

254.25.28.77

Because the use of only 32 bits considerably reduces the potential number of devices and routers used on the internet at any one time, a newer version called IPv6 is now used. This uses 128-bit addresses that take the form of eight groups of hex digits; for example,

A8FB:7A88:FFF0:0FFF:3D21:2085:66FB:F0FA

Link

For more on packet routes see Section 2.1.1.

Note the use of colons (:) and hexadecimal numbering. IPv6 has been designed to allow the internet to grow in terms of the number of hosts and potential increase in the amount of data traffic. The main advantages of IPv6 compared to IPv4 are:

» removes the risk of IP address collisions
» has built-in authentication checks
» allows for more efficient packet routes.

Table 3.13 compares the features of MAC addresses and IP addresses:

▼ **Table 3.13** MAC addresses and IP addresses

MAC addresses	IP addresses
identifies the physical address of a device on the network	identifies the global address on the internet
unique for device on the network	may not necessarily be unique
assigned by the manufacturer of the device and is part of the NIC	dynamic IP addresses are assigned by ISP using DHCP each time the device connects to the internet (see later)
they can be universal or local	dynamic IP addresses change every time a device connects to the internet; static IP addresses don't change
when a packet of data is sent and received, the MAC address is used to identify the sender's and recipient's devices	used in routing operations as they specifically identify where the device is connected to the internet
use 48 bits	use either 32 bits (IPv4) or 128 bits (IPv6)
can be UAA or LAA	can be static or dynamic

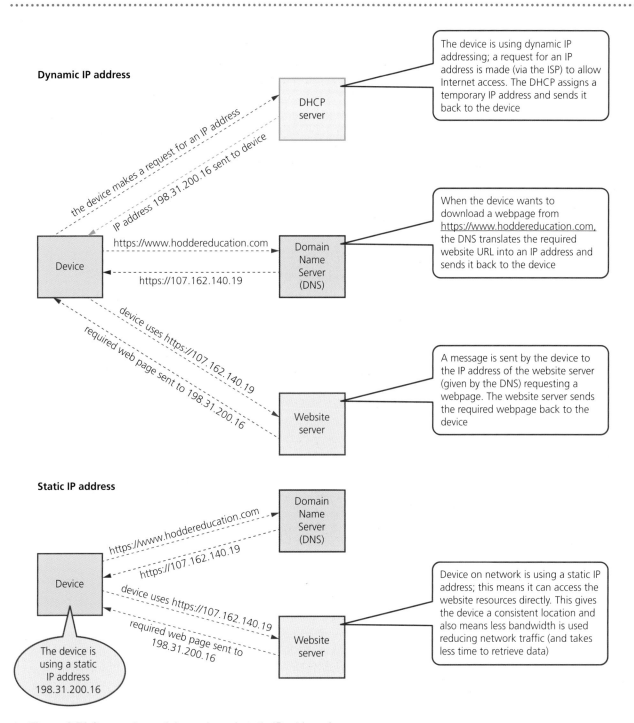

Dynamic IP address

The device is using dynamic IP addressing; a request for an IP address is made (via the ISP) to allow Internet access. The DHCP assigns a temporary IP address and sends it back to the device

the device makes a request for an IP address

IP address 198.31.200.16 sent to device

DHCP server

Device

https://www.hoddereducation.com

https://107.162.140.19

Domain Name Server (DNS)

When the device wants to download a webpage from https://www.hoddereducation.com, the DNS translates the required website URL into an IP address and sends it back to the device

device uses https://107.162.140.19

required web page sent to 198.31.200.16

Website server

A message is sent by the device to the IP address of the website server (given by the DNS) requesting a webpage. The website server sends the required webpage back to the device

Static IP address

https://www.hoddereducation.com

https://107.162.140.19

Domain Name Server (DNS)

Device

The device is using a static IP address 198.31.200.16

device uses https://107.162.140.19

required web page sent to 198.31.200.16

Website server

Device on network is using a static IP address; this means it can access the website resources directly. This gives the device a consistent location and also means less bandwidth is used reducing network traffic (and takes less time to retrieve data)

▲ **Figure 3.71** Comparison of dynamic and static IP addressing

Static and dynamic IP addresses

IP addresses can be either **static** (don't change) or **dynamic** (change every time a device connects to the internet).

Static

Static IP addresses are permanently assigned to a device by the internet service provider (ISP); they don't change each time a device logs onto the internet. Static IP addresses are usually assigned to:

>> remote servers which are hosting a website
>> an online database
>> a File Transfer Protocol (FTP) server. FTP servers are used when files need to be transferred to various computers throughout the network.

Dynamic

Dynamic IP addresses are assigned by the ISP each time a device logs onto the internet. This is done using **Dynamic Host Configuration Protocol (DHCP)**. A computer on the internet, configured as a DHCP server, is used by the ISP to automatically assign an IP address to a device. As the name suggests, a dynamic IP address could be different every time a device connects to the internet.

Table 3.14 compares static and dynamic IP addresses:

▼ **Table 3.14** Dynamic and static IP addresses

Dynamic IP addresses	Static IP addresses
greater privacy since they change each time a user logs on	since static IP addresses don't change, they allow each device to be fully traceable
dynamic IP addresses can be an issue when using, for example, VoIP since this type of addressing is less reliable as it can disconnect and change the IP address causing the VoIP connection to fail	allow for faster upload and download speeds (see Figure 3.71)
	more expensive to maintain since the device must be constantly running so that information is always available

Figure 3.71 shows the sequence of events when either a dynamic IP address or static IP address is assigned to a device using the internet. The diagram shows how a device contacts web servers that are also connected to the internet. A DHCP server supplies a dynamic IP address to the device, a DNS server looks up the domain name of the desired website into an IP address and a website server contains the web pages of the desired website.

3.4.4 Routers

Routers enable data packets to be routed between different networks, for example, to join a LAN to a WAN. The router takes data transmitted in one format from a network (which is using a particular protocol) and converts the data to a protocol and format understood by another network, thereby allowing them to communicate. A router would typically have an internet cable plugged into it and several cables connecting to computers and other devices on the LAN.

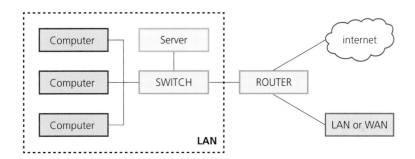

▲ **Figure 3.72** Router flow diagram

Broadband routers sit behind a firewall. The firewall protects the computers on a network. The router's main function is to transmit internet and transmission protocols between two networks and also allow private networks to be connected together.

Routers inspect the data package sent to it from any computer on any of the networks connected to it. Since every computer on the same network has the same part of an internet protocol (IP) address, the router is able to send the data packet to the appropriate switch, and the data will then be delivered to the correct device using the MAC destination address. If the MAC address doesn't match any device connected to the switch, it passes on to another switch on the same network until the appropriate device is found. Routers can be wired or wireless devices.

Activity 3.8

1 Explain each of the following terms:
   a Network interface card (NIC)
   b MAC address
   c IP address
   d Router
   e DHCP server.
2 a Give two features of dynamic IP addresses.
   b Give two features of static IP addresses.
   c Explain why we need both types of IP address.
3 Describe three differences between MAC addresses and IP addresses.

► Extension

For those students considering the study of this subject at A Level, the following section gives some insight into further study of computer hardware and wireless networks.

Topic 1: Computer ports

Input and output devices are connected to a computer via ports. The interaction of the ports with connected input and output is controlled by the control unit. Here we will summarise some of the more common types of ports found on modern computers:

USB ports

The **Universal Serial Bus (USB)** is an **asynchronous serial** data transmission method. It has quickly become the standard method for transferring data between a computer and a number of devices. Essentially, the USB cable consists of:

» a 4-wired shielded cable
» 2 of the wires are used for power and the earth
» 2 of the wires are used in the data transmission.

When a device is plugged into a computer, using one of the USB ports, the computer:
» automatically detects that a device is present (this is due to a small change in the voltage level on the data signal wires in the cable)
» the device is automatically recognised, and the appropriate device driver is loaded up so that computer and device can communicate effectively
» if a new device is detected, the computer will look for the device driver which matches the device; if this is not available, the user is prompted to download the appropriate software.

Even though the USB system has become the industrial standard, there are still a number of benefits (✔) and drawbacks (**X**) to using this system:

✔	X
devices plugged into the computer are automatically detected; device drivers are automatically loaded up	the present transmission rate is limited to less than 500 megabits per second
the connectors can only fit one way; this prevents incorrect connections being made	the maximum cable length is presently about 5 metres
USB has become the industry standard; this means that considerable support is available to users	the older USB standard (1.1) may not still be supported in the near future
several different data transmission rates are supported	
newer USB standards are backward compatible with older USB standards	

High-definition Multimedia Interface (HDMI)

High-definition Multimedia Interface (HDMI) ports allow output (both audio and visual) from a computer to an HDMI-enabled monitor or other device. It will support high definition signals (enhanced or standard). HDMI was introduced as a digital replacement for the older VGA analogue system. Modern HD (high definition) televisions have the following features which are making VGA a redundant technology:
» they use a widescreen format (16:9 aspect ratio)
» the screens use a greater number of pixels (typically 1920 ×1080)
» the screens have a faster refresh rate (e.g. 120 Hz or 120 frames a second)

» the range of colours is extremely large (some companies claim up to 4 million different colour variations!).

This all means that modern HD televisions require more data and this data has to be received at a much faster rate than with older televisions (e.g. 10 gigabits per second). HDMI increases the bandwidth making it possible to supply the necessary data to produce high quality sound and visual effects.

Topic 2: Wired and wireless networks

Wireless

Wi-Fi and Bluetooth

Both Wi-Fi and Bluetooth offer wireless communication between devices. They both use electromagnetic radiation as the carrier of data transmission.

Bluetooth sends and receives radio waves in a band of 79 different frequencies (known as channels). These are all centred on a 2.45 GHz frequency. Devices using Bluetooth automatically detect and connect to each other; but they don't interfere with other devices since each communicating pair uses a different channel (from the 79 options).

When a device wants to communicate, it picks one of the 79 channels at random. If the channel is already being used, it randomly picks another channel. This is known as spread-spectrum frequency hopping. To further minimise the risks of interference with other devices, the communication pairs constantly change the frequencies (channels) they are using (several times a second). Bluetooth creates a secure wireless personal area network (WPAN) based on key encryption.

Essentially, Bluetooth is useful:

» when transferring data between two or more devices which are very close together (<30 metres distance)
» when the speed of data transmission is not critical
» for low bandwidth applications (e.g. when sending music files from a mobile phone to a headset).

Wi-Fi is best suited to operating full-scale networks since it offers much faster data transfer rates, better range and better security than Bluetooth. A Wi-Fi-enabled device (such as a computer or smartphone) can access the internet wirelessly at any wireless access point (WAP) or 'hot spot' up to 100 metres away.

As mentioned above, wireless connectivity uses electromagnetic radiation: radio waves, microwaves or infrared. The scale of frequency and wavelength of magnetic radiation can be seen in the table below:

	Radio waves	Microwaves	Infrared	Visible light	Ultra violet	X-rays	Gamma rays
Wave length (m)	102	10^{-1}	10^{-5}	10^{-5}	10^{-7}	10^{-9}	10^{-11}
← -							
Frequency (Hz)	3 MHz	3 GHz	300 GHz	30 THz	3 PHz	300 PHz	30 EHz

Wired

There are three main types of cable used in wired networks:

» twisted pair
» coaxial
» fibre optic.

copper wire   insulation   copper mesh   outside insulation

Coaxial cable

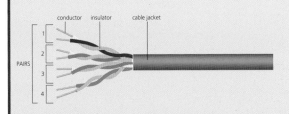

Twisted pair cable

Fibre optic cable

Wired versus wireless

When deciding whether a network should use wired or wireless connectivity, the following factors should be considered:

Wireless networking	Wired networking
it is easier to expand the networks and it isn't necessary to connect the devices using cables	using cables produces a more reliable and stable network; wireless connectivity is often subject to interference
this gives devices increased mobility provided they are within range of the WAPs	data transfer rates tend to be faster and there won't be any 'dead spots'
there is an increased chance of interference from external sources	setting up cabled networks tends to be cheaper overall in spite of the need to buy and install cable
data is less secure than with wired systems; it is easier to intercept radio waves and microwaves than cables; it is essential to protect data transmissions using encryption (e.g. WEP, WPA2)	however, cabled networks lose the ability for devices to be mobile; they must be close enough to allow for cable connections
the data transmission rate is still slower than for cabled networks although it continues to improve	having lots of wires can lead to a number of hazards such as tripping hazards, overheating of connections (leading to potential fire risk) and disconnection of cables during routine office cleaning
it is possible for signals to be stopped by thick walls (e.g. in old houses) and there may be areas of variable signal strength leading to 'drop out'	

In this chapter, you have learnt about:
- ✔ the role of a CPU/microprocessor
- ✔ von Neumann architecture
- ✔ the Fetch–Decode–Execute cycle
- ✔ the function of a cache, (system) clock and multi-core core CPUs
- ✔ instruction sets
- ✔ embedded systems
- ✔ the operation of a number of input devices
- ✔ the operation of a number of output devices
- ✔ the use of sensors in a number of control and monitoring applications
- ✔ primary storage
- ✔ secondary storage (magnetic, optical and solid state)
- ✔ virtual memories
- ✔ cloud storage
- ✔ network interface card (NIC)
- ✔ MAC and IP addressing
- ✔ routers in networks.

Key terms used throughout this chapter

central processing unit (CPU) – responsible for the execution or processing of all the instructions and data in a computer

integrated circuit – usually a chip made from a semi-conductor material which carries out the same tasks as a larger circuit made from individual components

von Neumann architecture – a type of computer architecture which introduced the concept of the stored program in the 1940s

Arithmetic & Logic Unit (ALU) – the component of the CPU that carries out all arithmetic and logical operations

accumulator (ACC) – temporary general-purpose register that stores numerical values at any part of a given operation

memory address register (MAR) – a register that stores the address of the memory location currently being read from or written to

current instruction register (CIR) – a register that stores the current instruction being decoded and executed

memory data register (MDR) – a register that stores data that has just been read from memory or data that is about to be written to memory

program counter (PC) – a register that stores the address where the next instruction to be read can be found

control unit – the component of a computer's CPU that ensures synchronisation of data flow and programs throughout the computer by sending out control signals along the control bus

system clock – produces timing signals on the control bus to ensure synchronisation takes place

clock cycle – clock speeds are measured in terms of GHz; this is the vibrational frequency of the system clock which sends out pulses along the control bus; for example, a 3.5 GHZ clock cycle means 3.5 billion clock cycles a second

immediate access store (IAS) – memory that holds all data and programs needed to be accessed by the control unit

backing store – a secondary storage device (such as HDD or SSD) used to store data permanently even when the computer is powered down

cache – is temporary memory using static RAM to hold frequently used data/instructions by the CPU thereby increasing CPU performance. More generally, cache means any area of storage used to quickly access frequently-used data - other examples include web cache, database cache, DNS cache

register – a temporary component in the CPU which can be general or specific in its use; it holds data or instructions as part of the Fetch–Decode–Execute cycle

address – a label for a memory location used by the CPU to track data

memory location – a numbered place in memory where values can be stored

system buses – a connection between major components in a computer that can carry data, addresses or control signals

address bus – the system bus that carries the addresses throughout the computer system

data bus – the system bus that allows data to be carried from CPU to memory (and vice versa) or to and from input/output devices

control bus – the system bus that carries signals from control unit to all other computer components

unidirectional – can travel in one direction only; used to describe data

bidirectional – can travel in both directions; used to describe data

word – a group of bits used by a computer to represent a single unit; for example, modern computers often use 64-bit word lengths

overclocking – changing the clock speed of a system clock to a value higher than the factory/recommended setting

core – a unit on a CPU made up of an ALU, control unit and registers; a CPU may contain a number of cores

dual core – a CPU containing two cores

quad core – a CPU containing four cores

Fetch–Execute–Decode – a cycle in which instructions and data are fetched from memory, decoded and finally executed

Basic Input/Output System (BIOS) – a suite of programs on firmware that are used to perform the initialisation of a computer system during the boot-up process

opcode – part of a machine code instruction that identifies what action the CPU has to perform

operand – part of a machine code instruction that identifies what data is to be used

instruction set – the complete set of machine code instructions used a particular microprocessor

embedded system – a combination of hardware and software designed to carry out a specific set of functions

barcode – a series of dark and light lines of varying thickness used to represent data; the code has to be scanned using laser or LED light source

key field – the field that uniquely identifies a record in a file

quick response (QR) code – a matrix of dark and light squares which represent data; the pattern can be read and interpreted using a smartphone camera and QR app

frame QR code – a type of QR code that includes a space for advertising

DAC (digital to analogue converter) – device that converts digital data into electric currents that can drive motors, actuators and relays, for example

ADC (analogue to digital converter) – a device that converts analogue data (for example, data read from sensors) into a form understood by a computer

charge couple device (CCD) – a light sensitive cell made up of millions of tiny sensors acting as photodiodes

virtual keyboard – an onscreen keyboard which uses the features of the touch screen to emulate a physical keyboard

touch screen – a screen that allows the user to select or manipulate a screen image using the touch of a finger or stylus; touch screens most frequently use capacitive, infra-red or resistive technology

repetitive strain injury (RSI) – pain felt in the muscles, nerves and tendons caused by a repetitive action (for example, excessive clicking of a mouse button over a period of time)

optical mouse – a pointing device that uses a red LED to track the movement of the device and then relays its coordinates to a computer

pointing device – an input device that allows the user to control the movement of an onscreen cursor or to allow onscreen selection by clicking a button on the device

complementary metal oxide semi-conductor (CMOS) – a chip that generates an electric current (or pulses) when light falls on its surface

digital signal processor (DSP) – a processor that calculates, for example, the coordinates of a pointing device based on the pulses of electricity received

optical character recognition – technology that can convert hard copy text or images into a digital format to be stored in a computer memory

computer sided design (CAD) – software used to create drawings (for example, to send to a 3D printer or to produce blue-prints of a microprocessor design)

computed tomographic (CT) scanner – technology that can create a 3D image of a solid object by slicing up the object into thin layers (tomography)

capacitive touch screen – a type of touch screen that uses the change in the screen's capacitance (the ability to store an electrical charge) when it is touched by a finger or stylus

infra-red touch screen – a type of touch screen that uses infra-red beams and sensors to detect where the screen has been touched

resistive touch screen – a type of touch screen that uses two conductive layers which make contact where the screen has been touched

actuator – an output device that converts electrical energy into mechanical movement

digital micromirror device (DMD) – a chip that uses millions of tiny mirrors on its surface to create a video display

thermal bubble – inkjet printer technology whereby tiny resistors create heat and form an ink bubble which is ejected onto paper in an inkjet printer

piezoelectric crystal – a crystal located in an ink reservoir within an inkjet printer; the crystal vibrates and forces ink out onto paper

direct 3D printing – a 3D printing technique in which the print head moves in the x, y and z directions

binder 3D printing – a 3D printing method that uses a two-stage pass; the first stage uses dry powder and second stage uses a binding agent

cathode – a negative electrode

snode – a positive electrode

organic LED (OLED) – a light-emitting diode that uses the movement of electrons between a cathode and an anode to produce an on-screen image; it generates its own light so no backlighting is required

loudspeaker – an output device that converts electric current into sound

memory – the devices within the computer that are directly accessible by the CPU; there are two types of memory – RAM and ROM; memory is different to hard disk drives, for example, which are known as storage devices

random access memory (RAM) – primary memory that can be written to or read from

read only memory (ROM) – primary memory that cannot be written to (changed) and can only be read

dynamic RAM (DRAM) – a type of RAM chip that needs to be constantly refreshed

static RAM (SRAM) – a type of RAM chip that uses flip flops and doesn't need to be constantly refreshed

volatile – describes memory that loses its contents when the power is turned off

refresh – recharge every few seconds in order to maintain charge; for example with a device such as a capacitor

flip flop – electronic circuit with only two stable conditions

latency – the lag in a system; for example, the time it takes to find a track on a hard disk, which depends on the time it takes for the disk to rotate around to its read-write head

SSD endurance – the total guaranteed number of times data can be written to or read from a solid state drive (SSD) in its usable life cycle

optical storage – a type of storage that uses laser light to read and write data, and includes CDs, DVDs and Blu-ray discs

dual layering – using two recording layers in storage media such as DVDs and some Blu-rays

virtual memory – a memory management system that makes use of secondary storage and software to enable a computer to compensate for the shortage of actual physical RAM memory

disk thrashing (HDD) – a problem in a hard disk drive (HDD) caused by excessive swapping in and out of data causing a high rate of head movements during virtual memory operations

thrash point – the point at which the execution of a program comes to a halt because the system is so busy moving data in and out of memory rather than actually executing the program

data redundancy – the unnecessary storing of the same data on several storage devices at the same time

cloud storage – a method of data storage where data is stored on offsite servers; the physical storage may be on hundreds of servers in many locations

network interface card (NIC) – a hardware component (circuit board or chip) that is required to allow a device to connect to a network, such as the internet

router – a device that enables data packets to be moved between different networks, for example, to join a LAN to a WAN

static IP address – an IP address that doesn't change

MAC address – a unique identifier which acts as a network address for a device; it takes the form NN-NN-NN-DD-DD-DD, where NN is the manufacturer code and DD is the device code

dynamic IP address – a temporary IP address assigned to a device each time it logs onto a network

dynamic host configuration protocol (DHCP) – a server that automatically provides and assigns an IP address

Exam-style questions

1 a Many mobile phone and tablet manufacturers are moving to OLED screen technology. Give **three** reasons why this is happening. [3]

b A television manufacturer makes the following advertising claim:
"Our OLED screens allow the user to enjoy over 1 million vivid colours in true-to-life vision"
Comment on the validity of this claim by the manufacturer. [4]

2 a A company is developing a new games console. The console games will be stored on a ROM chip once the program to run the new game has been fully tested and developed.
   i Give **two** advantages of putting the game's program on a ROM chip.
   ii The manufacturers are also using RAM chips on the internal circuit board. Why have they done this?
   iii The games console will have four USB ports. Apart from the need to attach games controllers, give reasons why USB ports are incorporated. [8]

b During development of the games console the plastic parts are being made by a 3D printer. Give **two** reasons why the manufacturer would use 3D printers. [2]

3 An air conditioning unit in a car is being controlled by a microprocessor and a number of sensors.
a Describe the main differences between **control** and **monitoring** of a process. [2]
b Describe how the sensors and microprocessor would be used to control the air conditioning unit in the car. Name at least **two** different sensors that might be used and explain the role of positive feedback in your description.
You might find drawing a diagram of your intended process to be helpful. [6]

4 a Describe the differences between a static IP address and a dynamic IP address. Include in your explanation, why both types of IP addressing are used. [4]
b What is meant by a MAC address? Describe the **two** different types of MAC address. [4]

5 a Five statements about two types of RAM memory (DRAM and SRAM) are
       shown below.
       By drawing lines, link each statement to the correct type of RAM.

| the data has to be refreshed constantly in order to retain data |

| this type has the more complex circuitry |

DRAM

| it does not need to be refreshed as long as the power supply is still on |

SRAM

| it requires higher power consumption which is significant when installed in battery-powered devices, such as a laptop |

| it is mostly used in the cache memory of the CPU where operational speed is important |

                                                                          [5]
   b Describe **three** of the differences between RAM and ROM.   [3]
   c Compare the two optical storage devices: DVD and Blu-ray. Your answer
      should include:
      » technology differences
      » capacity differences
      » other features of the two types of storage.   [6]

6 a Name **two** types of touchscreen technology used on mobile phones.
      For each named technology, describe how the position of
      where a finger touched the screen can be identified.   [6]
   b Organic LED (OLED) screens are now becoming increasingly common.
      i   Briefly describe the technology behind OLED screens.
      ii Give **three** advantages of OLED screens when compared to
          LED/LCD screens.   [3]

7 A zoo has an information point.
      » Visitors use a menu to select information about animals.
      » The menu includes 500 different animals.
      » The information is provided only using high definition video with an
        audio track.
   a State **one** input device that could be used for the information point. [1]
   b The output is shown on a monitor.
      State **one** other output device that could be used for the information
      point.   [1]
   c The video files are stored at the information point.
      State **one** secondary storage device that could be used.   [1]

d The zoo decides to introduce Quick Response codes in different places in the zoo. These provide further information about the animals.
Describe how customers obtain the information from the Quick Response codes. [4]

Cambridge IGCSE Computer Science 0478, Paper 11 Q4, Oct/Nov 2019

8 Anna has a farm that grows fruit.
She has a system that monitors the conditions for growing the fruit. Sensors are used in this system.
a Explain what is meant by the term **sensor**. [2]
b State **two** sensors that could be used in this system and describe how they could be used. [6]

Cambridge O Level Computer Science 2210, Paper 12 Q9, Oct/Nov 2017

9 The diagram shows **five** output devices and **five** descriptions.
Draw a line between each output device and its description. [4]

Output device	Description
Inkjet printer	Flat panel display that uses the light modulating properties of liquid crystals.
LCD screen	Flat panel display that uses an array of light emitting diodes as pixels.
2D cutter	Droplets of ink are propelled onto paper.
LED screen	Electrically charged powdered ink is transferred onto paper.
Laser printer	2D High-powered laser that uses the X-Y plane. cutter

Cambridge O Level Computer Science 0478, Paper 12 Q3, May/June 2017

Software

In this chapter you will learn about some of the key software used in computer systems. The chapter will consider essential software (such as an operating system) all the way through to application software (such as word processors). The first part of the chapter will cover how the software is used, while the second part will cover how software is translated so that a computer can carry out the software's instructions.

4.1 Types of software and interrupts

4.1.1 System software and application software

All computers begin life as a group of connected hardware items. Without software, the hardware items would be useless. This section considers the link between hardware and software. Figure 4.1 summarises the hierarchy of software and hardware.

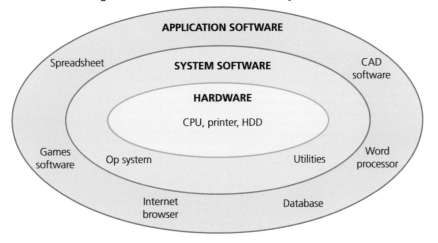

▲ **Figure 4.1** Software and hardware hierarchy

You will notice from Figure 4.1 that there are two types of software: system software and application software:

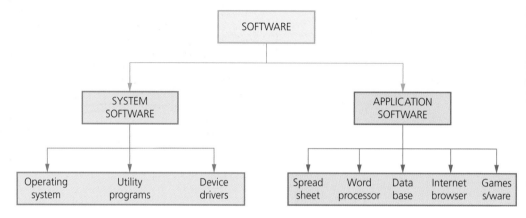

▲ **Figure 4.2** Software types

General features of system software

›› set of programs to control and manage the operation of computer hardware
›› provides a platform on which other software can run
›› required to allow hardware and software to run without problems
›› provides a human computer interface (HCI)
›› controls the allocation and usage of hardware resources.

General features of application software

›› used to perform various applications (apps) on a computer
›› allows a user to perform specific tasks using the computer's resources
›› may be a single program (for example, NotePad) or a suite of programs (for example, Microsoft Office)
›› user can execute the software as and when they require.

Examples of typical application software

WORD PROCESSOR:
Word processing software is used to manipulate a text document, such as an essay or a report. Text is entered using a keyboard and the software provides tools for copying, deleting and various types of formatting. Some of the functions of word processing software include:
- creating, editing, saving and manipulating text
- copy and paste functions
- spell checkers and thesaurus
- import photos/images into a structured page format
- translation into a foreign language.

SPREADSHEET:
Spreadsheet software is used to organise and manipulate numerical data (in the form of integer, real, date, and so on). Numbers are organised on a grid of lettered columns and numbered rows. The grid itself is made up of cells, and each cell is identified using a unique combination of columns and rows, for example, B6. Some of the functions of spreadsheets include:
- use of formulas to carry out calculations
- ability to produce graphs
- ability to do modelling and "what if" calculations.

DATABASE:
Database software is used to organise, manipulate and analyse data. A typical database is made up of one or more tables. Tables consist of rows and columns. Each row is called a 'record' and each column is called a 'field.' This provides the basic structure for the organisation of the data within the database. Some of the functions include:
- ability to carry out queries on database data and produce a report
- add, delete and modify data in a table.

CONTROL AND MEASURING SOFTWARE:
Control and measuring software is designed to allow a computer or microprocessor to interface with sensors so that it is possible to:
- measure physical quantities in the real world (such as temperatures)
- to control applications (such as a chemical process) by comparing sensor data with stored data and sending out signals to alter process parameters (e.g. open a valve to add acid and change the pH).

APPLICATION SOFTWARE:
these are programs that allow the user to do specific tasks.

Examples include:

APPS:
Apps is short for applications – a type of software. They normally refer to software which runs on mobile phones or tablets. They are normally downloaded from an "App Store" and range from games to sophisticated software such as phone banking. Common examples of apps include:
- video and music streaming
- GPS (global positioning systems – help you find your way to a chosen location)
- camera facility (taking photos and storing/manipulating the images taken).

PHOTO EDITING SOFTWARE:
Photo editing software allows a user to manipulate digital photographs stored on a computer; for example, change brightness, change contrast, alter colour saturation or remove "red eye". They also allow for very complex manipulation of photos (e.g. change the features of a face, combine photos, alter the images to give interesting effects and so on). They allow a photographer to remove unwanted items and generally "touch up" a photo to make it as perfect as possible.

VIDEO EDITING SOFTWARE:
Video editing software is the ability to manipulate videos to produce a new video. It enables the addition of titles, colour correction and altering/adding sound to the original video. Essentially it includes:
- rearranging, adding and/or removing sections of video clips and/or audio clips
- applying colour correction, filters and other video enhancements
- creating transitions between clips in the video footage.

GRAPHICS MANIPULATION SOFTWARE:
Graphics manipulation software allows bitmap and vector images to be changed. Bitmap images are made up of pixels which contain information about image brightness and colour. Bitmap graphics editors can change the pixels to produce a different image. Vector graphic editors operate in a different way and don't use pixels – instead they manipulate lines, curves and text to alter the stored image as required. Both types of editing software might be chosen depending on the format of the original image.

▲ **Figure 4.3** Application software

Examples of typical system software

COMPILERS:
A compiler is a computer program that translates a program written in a high-level language (HLL) into machine code (code which is understood by the computer) so that it can be directly used by a computer to perform a required task. The original program is called the *source code* and the code after compilation is called the *object code*. Once a program is compiled, the machine code can be used again and again to perform the same task without re-compilation. Examples of high-level languages include: Java, Python, Visual Basic, Fortran, C++ and Algol.

LINKERS:
A linker (or link editor) is a computer program that takes one or more object file produced by a compiler and combines them into a single program which can be run on a computer. For example, many programming languages allow programmers to write different pieces of code, called modules, separately. This simplifies the programming task since it allows the program to be broken up into small, more manageable sub-tasks. However, at some point, it will be necessary to put all the modules together to form the final program. This is the job of the linker.

DEVICE DRIVERS:
A device driver is the name given to software that enables one or more hardware devices to communicate with the computer's operating system. Without drivers, a hardware device (for example, a computer printer) would be unable to work with the computer. All hardware devices connected to a computer have associated drivers. As soon as a device is plugged into the USB port of a computer, the operating system looks for the appropriate driver. An error message will be produced if it can't be found. Examples of drivers include: printers, memory sticks, mouse, CD drivers, and so on.

OPERATING SYSTEMS (O/S):
The operating system (OS) is essentially software running in the background of a computer system. It manages many of the basic functions. Without the OS, most computers would be very user-unfriendly and the majority of users would find it almost impossible to work with computers on a day-to-day basis.
For example, operating systems allow:
• input/output operations
• users to communicate with the computer (e.g. *Windows*)
• error handling to take place
• the loading and running of programs to occur
• managing of security (e.g. user accounts, log on passwords).

SYSTEM SOFTWARE:
these are programs that allow the hardware to run properly and allow the user to communicate with the computer

Examples include:

UTILITIES:
Utility programs are software that are designed to carry out specific tasks on a computer. Essentially, they are programs that help to manage, maintain and control computer resources. Examples include:
• anti-virus (virus checkers)
• anti-spyware
• back-up of files
• disk repair and analysis
• file management and compression
• security
• screensavers
• disk defragmenter/ defragmentation software.

▲ **Figure 4.4** System software

Link

Refer to Section 4.1.3 on the running of apps on a computer.

The remainder of this section considers the role of the operating system, utility programs and device drivers in much more depth. Compilers and linkers will be considered later on in this book.

Utility software (utilities)

Computer users are provided with a number of utility programs (often simply referred to as utilities) that are part of the system software.

Utility programs are often initiated by the user, but some, notably virus checkers, often just run in the background without the need for any user input. Utility programs offered by most computer system software include:

>> virus checkers
>> defragmentation software
>> disk contents analysis and repair
>> file compression and file management
>> back-up software
>> security
>> screensavers.

Virus checkers (anti-virus software)
Any computer (including mobile phones and tablets) can be subject to a virus attack. Operating systems offer virus checkers, but these must be kept thoroughly up to date and should run in the background to maintain their ability to guard against being infected by such **malware**. There are many ways to help prevent viruses (such as being careful when downloading material from the internet, not opening files or websites given in emails from unknown senders or by not using non-original software). However, virus checkers still afford the best defence against such malware.

Running **anti-virus software** in the background on a computer will constantly check for virus attacks. Although various types of anti-virus software work in different ways they all have the following common features:

>> they check software or files before they are run or loaded on a computer
>> anti-virus software compares a possible virus against a database of known viruses
>> they carry out **heuristic checking** – this is the checking of software for types of behaviour that could indicate a possible virus; this is useful if software is infected by a virus not yet on the database
>> any possible files or programs which are infected are put into **quarantine** which:
  – allows the virus to be automatically deleted, or
  – allows the user to make the decision about deletion (it is possible that the user knows that the file or program is not infected by a virus – this is known as a **false positive** and is one of the drawbacks of anti-virus software)
>> anti-virus software needs to be kept up to date since new viruses are constantly being discovered
>> full system checks need to be carried out once a week, for example, since some viruses lie dormant and would only be picked up by this full system scan.

Defragmentation software
As a HDD becomes full, blocks used for files will become scattered all over the disk surface (in potentially different sectors and tracks as well as different surfaces). This will happen because files will become deleted, partially-deleted, extended and so on over time. The consequence of this is slower data access time; the HDD read-write head will now require several movements just to find and retrieve the data making up the required file.

It would obviously be advantageous if files could be stored in **contiguous** sectors considerably reducing HDD head movements. (Note that due to the different operation of SSDs when accessing data, this is not a problem when using solid state devices.)

Link

See Section 5.3 for more on computer viruses.

Link

Refer to Chapter 3 for more detail on how data is stored on a hard disk drive (HDD).

contiguous means 'next to each other'

Consider the following scenario using a disk with 12 (numbered 0 to 11) sectors per surface:

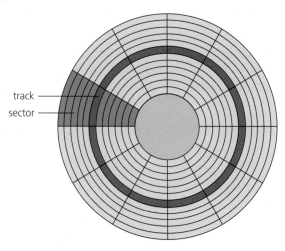

track

sector

▲ **Figure 4.5** Hard disk drive tracks and sectors

In this example we have three files (1, 2 and 3) stored on track 8 of a disk surface covering all 12 sectors:

sectors:	0	1	2	3	4	5	6	7	8	9	10	11
track: 8		File 1			File 2				File 3			

Now file 2 is deleted by the user and file 1 has data added to it; however, the file 2 sectors which become vacant are not filled up straight away by new file 1 data since this would require 'too much effort' for the HDD resources; we now get the following (file 1 is now stored in sectors 0, 1, 2, 3, 10 and 11):

sectors:	0	1	2	3	4	5	6	7	8	9	10	11
track 8:		File 1							File 3		File 1	

File 1 has now been extended to write data is sectors 10 and 11; now suppose file 3 is extended with the equivalent of 3 blocks of data; this now requires filling up sector 9 and then finding some empty sectors to write the remainder of the data – suppose the next free sectors are on track 11:

sectors:	0	1	2	3	4	5	6	7	8	9	10	11
track 8:		File 1							File 3		File 1	

sectors:	0	1	2	3	4	5	6	7	8	9	10	11
track 11:		File 3										

If this continues, the files just become more and more scattered throughout the disk surfaces. It is possible for sectors 4, 5 and 6 (on track 8) to eventually become used if the disk starts to fill up and it has to use up whatever space is available. A **disk defragmenter** will rearrange the blocks of data to store files in **contiguous** sectors wherever possible. After defragmentation Track 8 would now become:

sectors:	0	1	2	3	4	5	6	7	8	9	10	11
track 8:			File 1					File 3				

This obviously allows for much faster data access and retrieval since the HDD will now require fewer read-write head movements to access and read files 1 and 3. Track 11 would be empty after the defragmentation process.

Back-up software

While it is sensible to take manual back-ups using, for example, a memory stick or portable HDD, it is also good practice to use the operating system **back-up utility**. This utility will:

>> allow a schedule for backing up files to be made
>> only carry out a back-up procedure if there have been any changes made to a file.

For total security there should be three versions of a file:

1 the current (working) version stored on the internal HDD or SSD
2 a locally backed up copy of the file (stored on a portable SSD, for example)
3 a remote back-up version stored well away from the computer (for example, using cloud storage).

The Microsoft Windows environment offers the following facilities using the back-up utility:

>> restore data, files or the computer from the back-up (useful if there has been a problem and files have been lost and need to be recovered)
>> create a restore point (this is basically a kind of 'time machine' where your computer can be restored to its state at this earlier point in time; this can be very useful if a very important file has been deleted and can't be recovered by any of the other utilities)
>> options of where to save back-up files; this can be set up from the utility to ensure files are automatically backed up to a chosen device.

Windows uses File History, which takes snapshots of files and stores them on an external HDD at regular intervals. Over a period of time, File History builds up a vast library of past versions of files – this allows a user to choose which version of the file they want to use. File History defaults to backing up every hour and retains past versions of files for ever unless the user changes the settings.

Mac OS offers the Time Machine back-up utility. This erases the contents of a selected drive and replaces them with the contents from the back-up. To use this facility, it is necessary to have an external HDD or SSD (connected via USB port) and ensure that the Time Machine utility is installed and activated on the selected computer. Time machine will automatically:

>> back-up every hour
>> do daily back-ups for the past month, and
>> weekly back-ups for all the previous months.

(Note: once the back-up HDD or SSD is almost full, the oldest back-ups are deleted and replaced with the newest back-up data.) The following screen shows the Time Machine message:

▲ **Figure 4.6** Time machine message on Mac OS

Security software
Security software is an over-arching utility that:

>> manages access control and user accounts (using user IDs and passwords)
>> links into other utility software, such as virus checkers and spyware checkers
>> protects network interfaces (for example, through the use of firewalls)
>> uses encryption and decryption to ensure any intercepted data is meaningless without a decryption key
>> oversees the updating of software (does the update request come from a legitimate source, for example).

Screensavers
Screensavers are programs that supply moving and still images on the monitor screen after a period of inactivity by the computer. They were originally developed to protect older CRT (cathode ray tube) monitors which would suffer from 'phosphor burn' if the same screen image remained for any length of time. With modern LCD and OLED screens, this problem no longer exists; consequently, screensavers are now mostly just a way of customising a device. However, many screensavers are also used as part of the computer's security system. If a computer is unused for five minutes, for example, and hasn't been logged out, this will trigger the screensaver to be loaded. The computer user will then be automatically logged out and a screensaver will indicate that the computer is now locked. This gives an extra layer of security for computers used in an office environment, for example.

Some screensavers are often used to activate useful background tasks that can only go on when the computer is in an 'idle' state. For example:

>> virus scans
>> distributed computing applications – these allow apps to use the computer's resources only when it is idle (for example, an online gaming app).

Device drivers
Device drivers are software that communicate with the operating system and translate data into a format understood by a hardware peripheral device. Without device drivers, a hardware device would be unable to work with a computer – a message such as 'device not recognised' would appear on the screen. As soon as a device is plugged into a USB port (for example, a memory stick, printer or camera), the operating system looks for the appropriate device driver.

> **Link**
>
> Refer back to Section 2.3 for more information on encryption and decryption.

All USB device drivers contain a collection of information about devices called **descriptors**; this allows the USB bus to ask a newly connected device what it is. Descriptors include vendor id (VID), product id (PID) and unique serial numbers. If a device has no serial number associated with it, the operating system will treat the device as new every time it is plugged into a USB port. Serial numbers must be unique since this could prove rather interesting if two different devices with the same serial number were plugged into a computer at the same time.

4.1.2 Operating systems

To enable computer systems to function correctly and allow users to communicate with computer systems, software known as an **operating system** needs to be installed. An operating system provides both the environment in which applications can be run and a useable interface between humans and computer. An operating system also disguises the complexity of computer software and hardware. Common examples of operating systems include: Microsoft Windows, Apple Mac OS, Google Android and Apple IOS (the latter two being used primarily on tablets and smartphones).

Most computers store the operating system on a hard disk drive (HDD) or solid state drive (SSD) since they tend to be very large programs. Mobile phones and tablets store the operating system on a solid state device since they are too small to accommodate an HDD.

Figure 4.7 summarises some of the functions in a typical operating system.

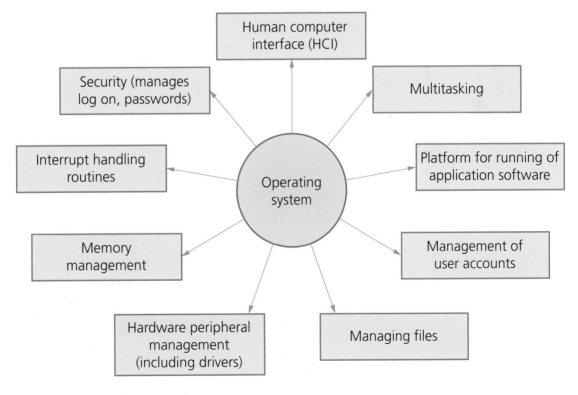

▲ **Figure 4.7** Operating system functions

The next section describes each of the nine functions shown in Figure 4.7.

Human computer interface (HCI)

The **human computer interface (HCI)** is in the form of a **Command Line Interface (CLI)** or a **Graphical User Interface (GUI)**.

A CLI requires a user to type in instructions in order to choose options from menus, open software, etc. There are often a number of commands that need to be typed in, for example, to save or load a file. The user has to therefore learn a number of commands just to carry out basic operations. It is also slow having to key in these commands every time an operation has to be carried out. However, the advantage of CLI is that the user is in direct communication with the computer and is not restricted to a number of pre-determined options.

A GUI allows the user to interact with a computer (or MP3 player, gaming device, mobile phone, etc.) using pictures or symbols (icons) rather than having to type in a number of commands. Figure 4.8 shows a mobile screen with a number of GUI icons.

▲ **Figure 4.8** GUI icons on a mobile phone

Simply selecting any of the icons from the screen would automatically load the application into the phone ready to be used. There is no need to type in anything.

GUIs use various technologies and devices to provide the user interface. One of the most common is **WIMP (windows icons menu and pointing device)**, which was developed for use on personal computers (PC). Here a mouse is used to control a cursor and icons are selected to open/run windows. Each window contains an application and modern computer systems allow several windows to be open at the same time. An example is shown below (here a number of icons can be seen on the left-hand side and on the bottom):

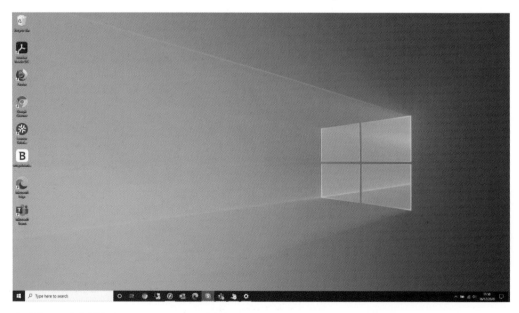

▲ **Figure 4.9** Windows screen showing icons

A windows manager looks after the interaction between windows, the applications, the pointing devices and the cursor's position.

More recently, devices such as mobile phones and tablets increasingly use touch screens and use **post-WIMP** interactions. With this system, fingers are in contact with the screen allowing actions such as pinching and rotating, which would be difficult to do using a single pointer and a device such as a mouse.

▼ **Table 4.1** Differences between GUI and CLI interfaces

Interface	Advantages	Disadvantages
command line interface (CLI)	the user is in direct communication with the computer the user is not restricted to a number of pre-determined options it is possible to alter computer configuration settings uses a small amount of computer memory	the user needs to learn a number of commands to carry out basic operations all commands need to be typed in which takes time and can be error-prone each command must be typed in using the correct format, spelling, and so on
graphical user interface (GUI)	the user doesn't need to learn any commands it is more user-friendly; icons are used to represent applications a pointing device (such as a mouse) is used to click on an icon to launch the application – this is simpler than typing in commands or a touch screen can be used where applications are chosen by simply touching the icon on the screen	this type of interface uses up considerably more computer memory than a CLI interface the user is limited to the icons provided on the screen needs an operating system, such as Windows, to operate, which uses up considerable memory

Who would use each type of interface?

» CLI: a programmer, analyst or technician; basically somebody who needs to have a direct communication with a computer to develop new software, locate errors and remove them, initiate memory dumps (contents of the computer memory at some moment in time), and so on
» GUI: the end-user who doesn't have or doesn't need to have any great knowledge of how the computer works; a person who uses the computer to run software or play games or stores/manipulates photographs, for example.

Memory management

Memory management carries out the following functions:

» manages the primary storage (RAM) and allows data to be moved between RAM and HDD/SSD during the execution of programs
» keeps track of all the memory locations
» carries out memory protection to ensure that two competing applications cannot use the same memory locations at the same time. If this wasn't done the following might happen:
   – data would probably be lost
   – applications could produce incorrect results (based on the wrong data being in memory locations)
   – potential security issues (if data is placed in the wrong location, it might make it accessible to other software, which would be a major security issue)
   – in extreme cases, the computer could crash.

Security management

Security management is another part of a typical operating system; the function of security management is to ensure the integrity, confidentiality and availability of data. This can be achieved as follows (many of these features are covered in more depth elsewhere in this book):

>> by carrying out operating system updates as and when they become available
>> ensuring that anti virus software (and other security software) is always up to date, preserving the integrity, security and privacy of data
>> by communicating with, for example, a firewall to check all traffic to and from the computer
>> by making use of privileges to prevent users entering 'private areas' on a computer that permits multi-user activity (this is done by setting up user accounts and making use of passwords and user IDs); this helps to ensure the privacy of data
>> by maintaining access rights for all users
>> by offering the ability for the recovery of data (and system restore) when it has been lost or corrupted
>> by helping to prevent illegal intrusion into the computer system (also ensuring the privacy of data).

> **Link**
>
> See Section 5.3 for more on cyber security.

 Find out more

By checking out the remainder of this chapter and Chapter 5, find out the methods available to ensure the security, privacy and integrity of data and how these link into the operating system security management. It is important to distinguish between what constitutes security, privacy and integrity of data.

Hardware peripheral management

Hardware management involves all input and output peripheral devices. Hardware management:

>> communicates with all input and output devices using device drivers
>> uses a device driver to take data from a file (defined by the operating system) and translates it into a format that the input/output device can understand
>> ensures each hardware resource has a priority so that they can be used and released as required
>> manages input/output devices by controlling queues and **buffers**; consider the role of the printer management when printing out a document:
  – first of all, the printer driver is located and loaded into memory
  – then the data is sent to a printer buffer ready for printing
  – if the printer is busy (or the printing job has a low priority) then the data is sent to a printer queue before it can be sent to the printer buffer
  – it will send various control commands to the printer throughout the printing process
  – it receives and handles error messages and interrupts from the printer.

> **Link**
>
> See Section 4.1.1 for more information on drivers.

Find out more

Find out about the tasks carried out by a Keyboard Manager when a user is typing in the text to a word processor. Consider the use of buffers and queues in your answer.

You may need to do some research throughout this book to find out how the Keyboard Manager works.

File management

The main tasks of **file management** include:

>> file naming conventions which can be used i.e. filename.docx
(where the extension can be .bat, .htm, .dbf, .txt, .xls, etc.)
>> performing specific tasks (for example, create, open, close, delete, rename, copy, and move)
>> maintaining the directory structures
>> ensuring access control mechanisms are maintained (for example, access rights to files, password protection, or making files available for editing or locking them)
>> ensuring memory allocation for a file by reading it from the HDD/SSD and loading it into memory.

Interrupts

Please refer to Section 4.1.4 for a discussion on interrupts.

Platform for running of application software

Please refer to Section 4.1.3 for a discussion on the running of application software.

Multitasking

Multitasking allows computers to carry out more than one task (i.e. a process) at a time. Each of the processes will share the hardware resources under the control of the operating system software. To make sure that multitasking operates correctly (in other words, the processes don't clash with each other), the operating system needs to constantly monitor the status of each of the processes under its control:

>> resources are allocated to a process for a specific time limit
>> the process can be interrupted while it is running
>> the process is given a priority so it can have resources according to its priority (the risk here is that a low priority process could be starved of resources).

these three bullet points are called pre-emptive multitasking

Using multitasking management, main memory, HDD/SSD and virtual memory are better managed making the most effective use of CPU time.

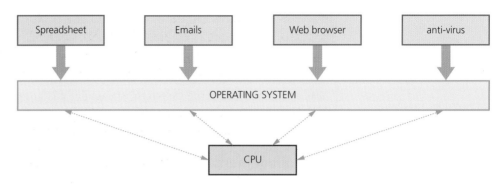

▲ **Figure 4.10** Multitasking diagram

Management of user accounts

Computers allow more than one user to log onto the system. It is therefore important that users' data is stored in separate parts of the memory for security reasons (also refer to security management earlier in this section). Each person logging onto the computer will be given a user account protected by a user name and password. The operating system is given the task of managing these different user accounts. This allows each user to:

›› customise their screen layout and other settings
›› use separate folders and files and to manage these themselves.

Very often an **administrator** oversees the management of these user accounts. The administrator can create accounts, delete user accounts and restrict user account activity. On large university or industrial computers, part of the operating system's tasks will be to oversee several users' accounts, since a complex multi-user system may be in place. The operating system has to maintain accounts for several users, managing data that may range from personal data and technical research work down to the ordering of stationery. Multi-access levels permit this control to take place. For example, a clerk in the office may have access to ordering stationery but can't have access to any personal data.

4.1.3 Running of applications

This section will bring together some of the topics covered in Section 4.1.2. As mentioned earlier, application software requires the operating system to provide a platform on which the software can run successfully.

When a computer starts up, part of the operating system needs to be loaded into RAM – this is known as **booting up** the computer (or a **bootstrap loader**). The start-up of the computer's motherboard is handled by the basic input/output system (BIOS). The BIOS tells the computer where the storage device that holds the operating system can be found; it then loads the part of the operating system that is needed and executes it.

The BIOS is often referred to as **firmware**. Firmware is defined as a program that provides low level control for devices.

Advice

EEPROM is included to fully explain the BIOS, but details about EEPROM go beyond the requirements of the syllabus.

The BIOS program is stored in a special type of ROM, called an **EEPROM** (Electrically Erasable Programmable ROM). EEPROM is a flash memory chip, which means its contents remain even when the computer is powered down. However, it also means the BIOS can be rewritten, updated or even deleted by a user.

However, while the BIOS is stored on an EEPROM, the BIOS **settings** are stored on a CMOS chip (Complementary Metal Oxide Semi-conductor). The CMOS is powered up at all times via a rechargeable battery on the motherboard. Therefore, the BIOS settings would be reset if the battery was removed or disconnected for some reason. Once the CMOS is re-started, it will access the same BIOS program from EEPROM, but the settings will now be the default factory settings. Consequently, if a user has changed the BIOS settings (for example, the clock speed), the settings will revert to those settings made at the factory once power is restored to the CMOS.

▲ **Figure 4.11** Firmware interface between OS and hardware

The application software will be under the control of the operating system and will need to access system software such as the device drivers while it is running. Different parts of the operating system may need to be loaded in and out of RAM as the software runs.

4.1.4 Interrupts

An **interrupt** is a signal sent from a device or from software to the microprocessor. This will cause the microprocessor to temporarily stop what it is doing so that it can service the interrupt. Interrupts can be caused by:

» a timing signal
» an input/output process (for example, a disk drive or printer requiring more data)
» a hardware fault (for example, a paper jam in the printer)
» user interaction (for example, the user presses a key (or keys) on a keyboard, such as <CTRL><ALT><BREAK>, which causes the system to be interrupted)
» software errors that cause a problem (for example, an .exe file that cannot be found to initiate the execution of a program, two processes trying to access the same memory location, or an attempt to divide by zero).

Once the interrupt signal is received, the microprocessor either carries on with what it was doing or stops to service the device or program that caused the interrupt. The computer needs to identify the interrupt type and also establish the level of **interrupt priority.**

Interrupts allow computers to carry out many tasks or to have several windows open at the same time. An example would be downloading a file from the internet at the same time as listening to some music from a library. Interrupts allow these two functions to co-exist and the user has the impression that both functions are being carried out simultaneously. In reality, data is being passed in and out of memory very rapidly allowing both functions to be serviced. This can all be achieved by using an area in memory known as a **buffer.** A buffer is a memory area that stores data temporarily (see Figure 4.12). For example, buffers are used when downloading a movie from the internet to compensate for the difference between download speeds and the data requirements of the receiving device. The data transmission rate of the movie file from the web server to the buffer must be greater than the rate at which data is transmitted from buffer to media player. Without buffers, the movie would frequently 'freeze'.

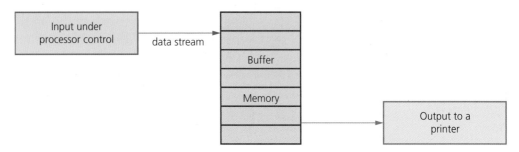

▲ **Figure 4.12** Use of a buffer when sending data to a printer (buffer used to store data temporarily since printer speed is much slower than microprocessor speed)

 Find out more

Find out how buffers are used to stream movies from the internet to a device (such as a tablet).

Whenever an interrupt is received it needs to be **serviced**. The status of the current task being run first needs to be saved. The contents of the Program Counter (PC) and other registers are saved. Then the **interrupt service routine (ISR)** is executed by loading the start address into the Program Counter (PC). Once the interrupt has been fully serviced, the status of the interrupted task is reinstated (the contents of all the saved registers are then retrieved) and the process continues.

Buffers and interrupts are often used together to allow standard computer functions to be carried out. These functions are often taken for granted by users of modern computer systems. For example, the following diagram (Figure 4.13) shows how buffers and interrupts are used when a document is sent from memory to a printer. The important thing to remember here is the time taken to print out a document is *much* longer than the time it takes for the microprocessor to send data to the printer. Without buffers and interrupts, the microprocessor would remain idle waiting for a document to be printed. This would be an incredible waste of microprocessor time; the buffers and interrupts allow the microprocessor to carry on with other tasks while the document is being printed thus maximising its processing power and speed.

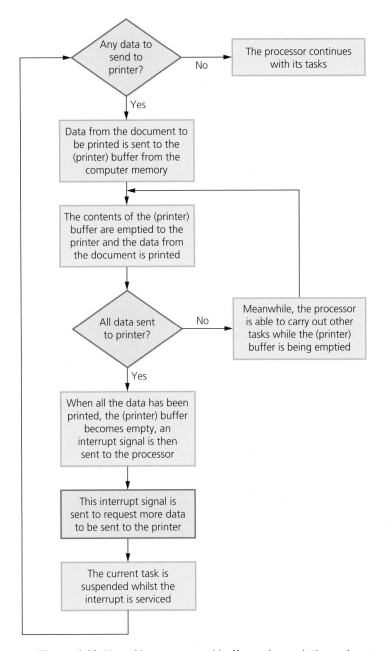

▲ **Figure 4.13** Use of interrupts and buffers when printing a document

 Find out more

Try to produce a flow chart (similar to Figure 4.13) that shows the role of buffers and interrupts when the memory sends data to a disk drive for storage.

Remember that the time to write data to disk is much longer than the time it takes for the microprocessor to carry out its tasks.

Activity 4.1

1 Tick (✓) the appropriate column in the following table to indicate whether the named software is system software or application software.

Software	System software	Application software
screensaver		
anti-virus software		
control and measurement software		
printer driver		
video editing software		
compiler		
QR code reader		
on-screen calculator		
operating system software		

2 Mike is downloading a video from the internet to his laptop. The speed of data transfer from the internet is slower than the speed at which data is being sent to the media player.

a What could be used to stop the video constantly freezing while Mike is watching it on his laptop?

b While watching the video, Mike is meanwhile printing a 160-page document on his inkjet printer. Describe how interrupts could be used to allow him to watch his movie at the same time as the printing is being done. The printer memory can store up to 20 pages at a time.

c Describe what happens if the inkjet printer runs out of black ink during the printing process.

3 Choose four features of an operating system and describe their function.

4 What is meant by a **descriptor** in a device driver? What role does the descriptor play when a new memory stick, for example, is plugged into a USB port of a computer for the first time?

5 a Describe what is meant by a *BIOS* and state its function. What is the task of a BIOS when a computer is first powered up?

b BIOS software and BIOS settings are different. Describe the different types of memory needs for both the software and its settings. In your explanation state why both types of memory are used.

6 Seven descriptions are shown on the left and seven computer terms are shown on the right. Draw lines to connect each description to the correct computer term.

when a computer starts up, OS is loaded into RAM	firmware
software that communicates with the OS and translates data into a format that can be understood by an I/O device	printer driver
computer carrying out many different processes at the same time	bootstrap loader
program that provides low level control for devices including embedded systems	interrupt
program that supplies static or moving images on a monitor when a computer has been idle for a period of time	screensaver
signal from a device or software sent to a microprocessor to temporarily halt the process currently being carried out	buffer
memory area used to hold data temporarily	multitasking

4.2 Types of programming language, translators and integrated development environments (IDEs)

People use many different languages to communicate with each other. In order for two people to understand each other they need to speak the same language or another person, an interpreter, is needed to translate from one language to the other language.

Programmers use many different programming languages to communicate with computers. Computers only 'understand' their own language, called **machine code**. A program needs to be translated into machine code before it can be 'understood' by a computer.

Programs are our way of telling a computer what to do, how to do it and when to do it. This enables a single computer to perform many different types of task. A computer can be used to stream videos, write reports, provide weather forecasts and many, many other jobs.

Here is an example of a simple task that can be performed by a computer:

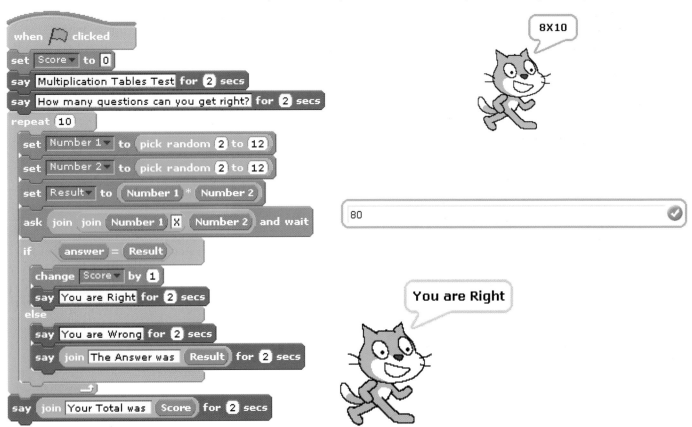

▲ **Figure 4.14** A Scratch multiplication table test program

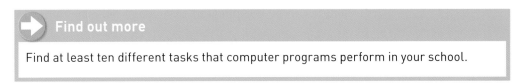

Find out more

Find at least ten different tasks that computer programs perform in your school.

A **computer program** is a list of instructions that enable a computer to perform a specific task. Computer programs can be written in **high-level languages** and **low-level languages** depending on the task to be performed and the computer to be used. Most programmers write programs in high-level languages.

4.2.1 High-level languages and low-level languages

High-level languages

Link

For more on instruction sets, see Section 3.1.4.

High-level languages enable a programmer to focus on the problem to be solved and require no knowledge of the hardware and instruction set of the computer that will use the program. Many high-level programming languages are portable and can be used on different types of computer.

High-level languages are designed with programmers in mind; programming statements are easier to understand than those written in a low-level language. This means that programs written in a high-level language are easier to:

» read and understand as the language used is closer to English
» write in a shorter time
» debug at the development stage
» maintain once in use.

The following snippet of program to add two numbers together is a single program statement written in a typical high-level language. It shows how easy it is to understand what is happening in a high-level language program:

```
Sum := FirstNumber + SecondNumber
```

There are many different high-level programming languages in use today including C++, Delphi, Java, Pascal, Python, Visual Basic and many more. Once a programmer has learned the techniques of programming in any high-level language, these can be transferred to writing programs in other high-level languages.

 Find out more

High-level programming languages are said to be 'problem oriented'. What type of problems are the languages named above used for? Find out about five more high-level languages. Name each programming language and find out what it is used for.

Low-level languages

Low-level languages relate to the specific architecture and hardware of a particular type of computer. Low-level languages can refer to **machine code**, the binary instructions that a computer understands, or **assembly language** that needs to be translated into machine code.

Machine code
Programmers do not usually write in machine code as it is difficult to understand, and it can be complicated to manage data manipulation and storage.

Link

For more on hexadecimal see Section 1.1.2.

The following snippet of program to add two numbers together is written in typical machine code, shown in both hexadecimal and binary, and consists of three statements:

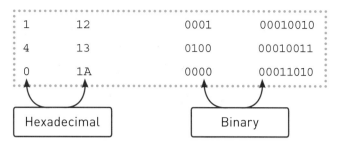

```
1       12              0001    00010010
4       13              0100    00010011
0       1A              0000    00011010
```

Hexadecimal   Binary

As you can see, this is not easy to understand in binary! Machine code is usually shown in hexadecimal.

 Find out more

Find out about two different types of machine code. Name each chip set the machine code is used for and find the codes for load, add and store.

▼ **Table 4.2** Differences between high-level and low-level languages

Language	Advantages	Disadvantages
High-level	independent of the type of computer being used easier to read, write and understand programs quicker to write programs programs are easier and quicker to debug easier to maintain programs in use	programs can be larger programs can take longer to execute programs may not be able make use of special hardware
Low-level	can make use of special hardware includes special machine-dependent instructions can write code that doesn't take up much space in primary memory can write code that performs a task very quickly	it takes a longer time to write and debug programs programs are more difficult to understand

4.2.2 Assembly languages

Fewer programmers write programs in an assembly language. Those programmers who do, do so for the following reasons:

» to make use of special hardware
» to make use of special machine-dependent instructions
» to write code that doesn't take up much space in primary memory
» to write code that performs a task very quickly.

The following snippet of program to add two numbers together is written in a typical assembly language and consists of three statements:

```
LDA         First
ADD         Second
STO         Sum
```

In order to understand this program, the programmer needs to know that:

» `LDA` means load value of the variable (in this case, First) into the accumulator
» `ADD` means add value of variable (in this case, Second) to the value stored in the accumulator
» `STO` replace the value of the variable (in this case, Sum) by the value stored in the accumulator

Assembly language needs to be translated into machine code using an assembler in order to run. See the next section for more details.

 Find out more

Find out about two assembly languages. Name each assembly language and find out what type of computer it is used for.

4.2.3 Translators

Computer programs can exist in several forms.

Programs are written by humans in a form that people who are trained as computer programmers can understand. In order to be used by a computer, programs need to be translated into the binary instructions, machine code, that the computer understands. Humans find it very difficult to read binary, but computers can only perform operations written in binary.

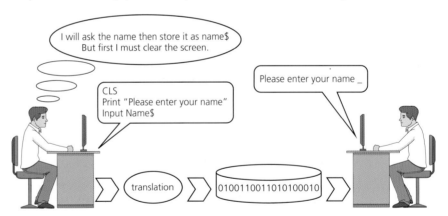

▲ **Figure 4.15** Translation

A program must be translated into binary before a computer can use it; this is done by a utility program called a **translator**. There are several types of translator program in use; each one performs a different task.

Compilers

A **compiler** is a computer program that translates an entire program written in a high-level language (HLL) into machine code all in one go so that it can be directly used by a computer to perform a required task. Once a program is compiled the machine code can be used again and again to perform the same task without re-compilation. If errors are detected, then an error report is produced instead of a compiled program.

The high-level program statement:

```
Sum := FirstNumber + SecondNumber
```

becomes the following machine code instructions when translated:

```
0001          00010010
0100          00010011
0000          00011010
```

Interpreters

An **interpreter** is a computer program that reads a statement from a program written in a high-level language, translates it, performs the action specified and then does the same with the next statement and so on. If there is an error in the statement then execution ceases and an error message is output, sometimes with a suggested correction.

A program needs to be interpreted again each time it is run.

Assemblers

An **assembler** is a computer program that translates a program written in an assembly language into machine code so that it can be directly used by a computer to perform a required task. Once a program is assembled the machine code can be used again and again to perform the same task without re-assembly.

The assembly language program statements:

```
LDA          First
ADD          Second
STO          Sum
```

become the following machine code instructions when translated:

```
0001          00010010
0100          00010011
0000          00011010
```

▼ **Table 4.3** Translation programs summary

Compiler	Interpreter	Assembler
Translates a high-level language program into machine code.	Executes a high-level language program one statement at a time.	Translates a low level assembly language program into machine code.
An executable file of machine code is produced.	No executable file of machine code is produced.	An executable file of machine code is produced.
One high-level language statement can be translated into several machine code instructions.	One high-level language program statement may require several machine code instructions to be executed.	One low-level language statement is usually translated into one machine code instruction.
Compiled programs are run without the compiler.	Interpreted programs cannot be run without the interpreter.	Assembled programs are used without the assembler.
A compiled program is usually distributed for general use.	An interpreter is often used when a program is being developed.	An assembled program is usually distributed for general use.

4.2.4 Advantages and disadvantages of compilers and interpreters

The advantages and disadvantages of compilers and interpreters are compared in Table 4.4.

▼ **Table 4.4** Comparing translators

Translators	Advantages	Disadvantages
Interpreter	easier and quicker to debug and test programs during development easier to edit programs during development	programs cannot be run without the interpreter programs can take longer to execute
Compiler	a compiled program can be stored ready for use a compiled program can be executed without the compiler a compiled program takes up less space in memory when it is executed a compiled program is executed in a shorter time	it takes a longer time to write, test and debug programs during development

4.2.5 Integrated Development Environment (IDE)

An Integrated Development Environment (IDE) is used by programmers to aid the writing and development of programs. There are many different IDEs available; some just support one programming language, others can be used for several different programming languages. You may be using PyCharm (for Python), Visual Studio (for Visual Basic) or BlueJ (for Java) as your IDE.

 Find out more

Find out which programming language and IDE you are using in school and see if there are any other IDEs available for your programming language.

IDEs usually have these features:

» code editors
» a translator
» a runtime environment with a debugger
» error diagnostics
» auto-completion
» auto-correction
» an auto-documenter and prettyprinting.

Let's look at each of these features in turn and see how they help the development process.

Code editor

A code editor allows a program to be written and edited without the need to use a separate text editor. This speeds up the program development process, as editing can be done without changing to a different piece of software each time the program needs correcting or adding to.

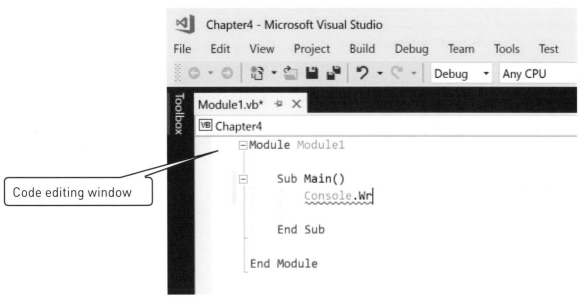

▲ **Figure 4.16** Visual Studio code editor

Translator

Most IDEs usually provide a translator, this can be a compiler and/or an interpreter, to enable the program to be executed. The interpreter is often used for developing the program and the compiler to produce the final version of the program to be used.

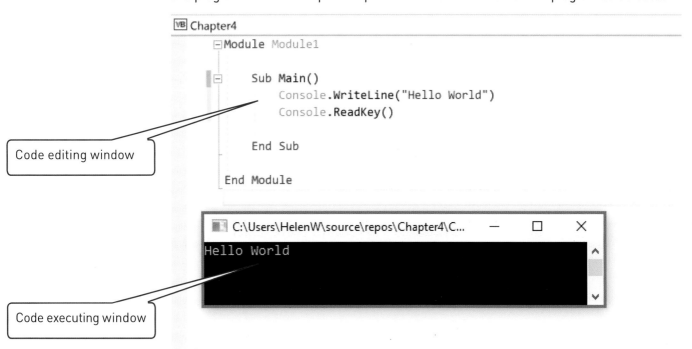

▲ **Figure 4.17** Visual Studio code editor and program running

A runtime environment with a debugger

A debugger is a program that runs the program under development and allows the programmer to step through the program a line at a time (single stepping) or to set a breakpoint to stop the execution of the program at a certain point in the source code. A report window then shows the contents of the variables and expressions evaluated at that point in the program. This allows the programmer to see if there are any logic errors in the program and check that the program works as intended.

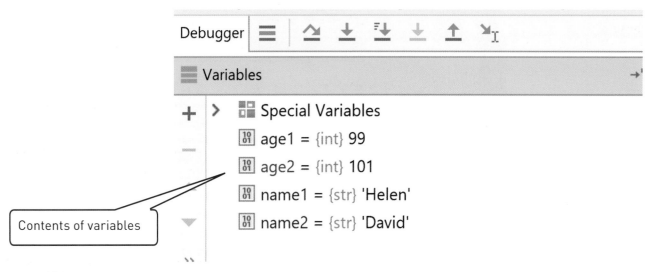

▲ **Figure 4.18** PyCharm debugger

Error diagnostics and auto-correction

Dynamic error checking finds possible errors as the program code is being typed, alerts the programmer at the time and provides a suggested correction. Many errors can therefore be found and corrected during program writing and editing before the program is run.

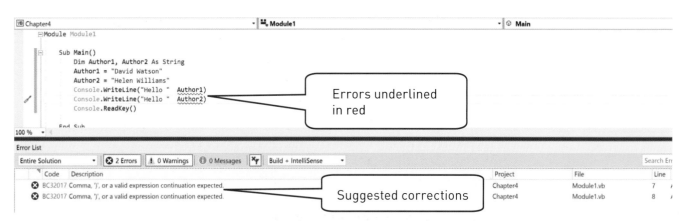

▲ **Figure 4.19** Visual Studio error list with suggested corrections

Auto-completion

Code editors can offer context-sensitive prompts with text completion for variable names and reserved words.

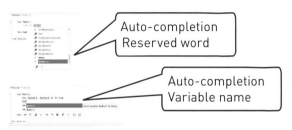

Auto-completion
Reserved word

Auto-completion
Variable name

Auto-documenter
explaining the
purpose of
Console.WriteLine

▲ **Figure 4.20** Visual Studio showing auto-completion

▲ **Figure 4.21** Visual Studio auto-documenter

Auto-documenter and prettyprinting

IDEs can provide an auto-documenter to explain the function and purpose of programming code.

Most code editors colour code the words in the program and lay out the program in a meaningful way – this is called **prettyprinting**.

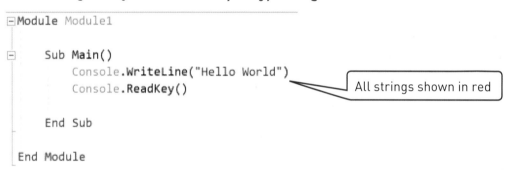

```
Module Module1

    Sub Main()
        Console.WriteLine("Hello World")
        Console.ReadKey()

    End Sub

End Module
```

All strings shown in red

▲ **Figure 4.22** Visual Studio code editor showing prettyprinting

Find out more

Find out which of these features are available in the IDE you are using in school.

Activity 4.2

1 Tick (✓) the appropriate column in the following table to indicate whether the statement about the translator is True or False.

	True	False
An assembler translates a high-level language program.		
It is more difficult to write a program in a low-level language.		
Java is an assembly language.		
It is quicker to develop a program using a high-level language.		
You always need a compiler to run a compiled program.		
A program that is interpreted takes a longer time to run than a compiled program.		
Low-level languages are machine dependent.		

2 a Suki is writing a program in a high-level language. Describe three features of an IDE that she would find helpful.

   b Describe the difference between a compiler and an interpreter.

   c Explain why a programmer would choose to write a program in assembly language.

> ## Extension

For those students considering the study of this subject at A Level, the following shows how interrupts are used in the Fetch–(Decode)–Execute cycle.

Use of interrupts in the Fetch–Execute cycle

The following figure shows a general overview of how a computer uses interrupts to allow it to operate efficiently and to allow it, for example, to carry out multi-tasking functions. Just before we discuss interrupts in this general fashion, the following notes explain how interrupts are specifically used in the Fetch–Execute cycle.

A special register called the interrupt register is used in the Fetch–Execute cycle. While the CPU is in the middle of carrying out this cycle, an interrupt could occur that will cause one of the bits in the interrupt register to change its status. For example, the initial status might be 0000 0000 and a fault might occur while writing data to the hard drive; this would cause the register to change to 0000 **1**000. The following sequence now takes place:

» at the next Fetch–Execute cycle, the interrupt register is checked bit by bit
» the contents 0000 1000 would indicate an interrupt occurred during a previous cycle and it still needs servicing; the CPU would now service this interrupt or 'ignore' it for now depending on its priority
» once the interrupt is serviced by the CPU, it stops its current task and stores the contents of its registers
» control is now transferred to the interrupt handler (or interrupt service routine, ISR)
» once the interrupt is fully serviced, the register is reset and the contents of registers are restored.

The following flow diagram summarises the interrupt process during the Fetch–Execute cycle:

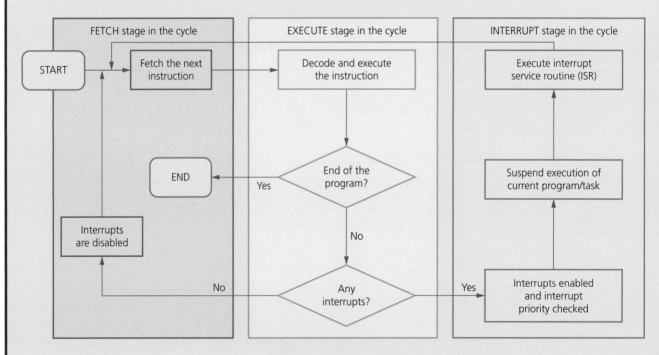

▲ **Figure 4.23** The interrupt process in the Fetch–Execute cycle

In this chapter, you have learnt about:
- ✔ system software
- ✔ application software
- ✔ utility programs
- ✔ the role and the function of an operating system
- ✔ how hardware, firmware and operating systems are used to run application software
- ✔ the role and operation of interrupts
- ✔ types of programming language – high-level and low-level
- ✔ translation software – compilers, translators and assemblers
- ✔ an Integrated Development Environment (IDE).

Key terms used throughout this chapter

utility programs (utilities) – part of an operating system which carries out certain functions such as virus checking, defragmentation and screensaver

malware – programs (such as viruses, worms and Trojan horses) that are installed on a user's computer with the aim of deleting, corrupting or manipulating data illegally

anti-virus software – software that quarantines and deletes files or programs infected by a computer virus; the software can run in the background or be initiated by the user

heuristic checking – checking software for behaviour that could indicate a possible virus

quarantine – to isolate (in order to later delete) a file or program identified by anti-virus software as being infected by a virus

defragmentation – a process that reorganises sectors on an HDD by rearranging blocks of data so that they are contiguous

contiguous – next to each other

back-up – make copies of files onto another storage media in case the original file becomes corrupted or is deleted

screensaver – software that supplies a still or moving image on a monitor if a computer has been inactive for a period of time

device driver – software that communicates with the operating system and translates data into a format understood by the device

descriptor – a collection of information about a device plugged into a USB port; this can be vendor ID (VID), product ID (PID) or serial number

operating system – software that provides an environment in which applications can run and also provides an interface between computer and human operator

boot up/bootstrap loader – a small program that is used to load other programs to correctly 'start-up' a computer system

EEPROM – stands for electronically erasable programmable ROM

human computer interface (HCI) – an interface supplied by the operating system to 'hide' the complexities of the software and hardware from the human user

command line interface (CLI) – an interface which allows communication with the computer by typing in commands using a keyboard

graphical user interface (GUI) – an interface that uses icons to represent apps and tasks which the user can select/launch by clicking on a mouse or using a touch screen

windows icons menu and pointing device (WIMP) – an interface that uses a pointing device such as a mouse to select options from screen icons or a menu

post-WIMP – a modern touch screen interface system that allows actions such as pinching and rotating

memory management – the part of an operating system that controls main memory

security management – the part of an operating system that ensures the integrity, confidentiality and availability of data

hardware management – the part of an operating system that controls all input and output devices; it is made up of sub-systems such as printer management

buffer – a memory area used to store data temporarily

file management – part of an operating system that manages files in a computer (for example, the ability to create, delete, copy, open, close and rename files)

interrupt – a signal sent from a device or software to a microprocessor requesting its attention; the microprocessor suspends all operations until the interrupt has been serviced

multitasking – a function that allows a computer to process more than one task/process at a time

administrator – a person responsible for the upkeep and maintenance of a computer system that involves multi-user function

user account – an agreement that allows an individual to use a computer; the user needs a user name and password to enter the user's area

error handling routine – a routine in a program or operating system that recognises and recovers a system from abnormal inputs or hardware faults (for example, recovery from an attempt to divide by zero)

firmware – a program that provides low level control for devices

interrupt priority – the priority assigned to an interrupt are given a priority so that the microprocessor knows which one needs to be serviced first and which interrupts are to be dealt with quickly

service (an interrupt) – when an interrupt is received, some action needs to be taken by the processor depending on what caused the interrupt; until this is resolved (that is, it is serviced), the interrupt cannot be removed to allow the processor to continue

interrupt service routine (ISR) – software that handles interrupt requests (for example, when the printer out of paper) and sends a request to the CPU for processing

machine code – a binary programming language, a program written in machine code can be loaded and executed without translation

high-level language (HLL) – a programming language that is independent of computer hardware, a program written in a HLL needs to be translated into machine code before it is executed.

low-level language (LLL) – a programming language that is dependent on computer hardware, both machine code and assembly language are LLLs

assembly language – a programming language that is dependent on computer hardware, a program written in an assembly language program needs to be translated into machine code before it is executed

assembler – a computer program that translates programming code written in assembly language into machine code

compiler – a computer program that translates a source program written in a high-level language to machine code

translator – converts a program written in a high-level language program into machine code

interpreter – a computer program that analyses and executes a program written in a high-level language line by line

Integrated Development Environment (IDE) – a suite of programs used to write and test a computer program written in a high-level language

debugging – finding errors in a computer program by running or tracing the program

prettyprinting – displaying source code using different colours and formatting, which make the code easier to read and understand

report window – a separate window in the runtime environment of an IDE that shows the contents of variables during the execution of a program

Exam-style questions

1 There are five types of software on the left and four items of hardware on the right.

Draw lines to connect each software item to the hardware item where the software will reside; each hardware item may be used once, more than once or not at all.

part of a program or OS currently in use		CMOS
the actual BIOS settings		flash memory
the actual BIOS software		hard disk drive (HDD)
operating system software		random access memory (RAM)
virus scanner software		

[5]

2 Which utility programs are being described below?
  a Software that runs in the background and checks for malware; suspect programs are quarantined and deleted if necessary
  b Software that rearranges data on a hard disk drive (HDD) to reduce the scattering of the data stored on the HDD
  c Software that manages access control and user accounts and also protects network interfaces
  d Program that supplies static or moving images on a monitor when the computer has been idle for a period of time
  e Software that communicates with the operating system and translates data into a format understood by an input/output device [5]

3 a Describe the purpose of an *operating system*.
  b What is meant by *virtual memory*?
  c What is meant by *disk thrashing* and why does it occur?
  d What is meant by *multitasking*?
  e Describe what an *interrupt* is. [10]

4 a Explain the differences between a *Graphical User Interface (GUI)* and a *Command Line Interface (CLI)*. [3]
  b Give **one** advantage and **one** disadvantage of using a GUI interface. [2]
  c Give **one** advantage and **one** disadvantage of using a CLI interface. [2]

5 In this question you will be given a statement followed by four possible answers. Select which of the four answers you think is correct.

a What is meant by the term *buffer*?

A	part of the RAM which is used to store the operating system in use
B	unused areas on a hard disk drive
C	an area in memory that temporarily holds data
D	an example of firmware

b What is the function of a printer driver?

A	area of memory that holds data waiting to be printed out
B	software that communicates with the operating system and translates data into a format which can be printed out
C	an area in memory that temporarily holds data
D	an example of firmware used to interface with the printer

c Which of these options describes a task carried out by the operating system?

A	preventing unauthorised access to a computer system
B	handling the HTTPS requests from a website
C	allocating memory to competing applications running on a computer system
D	booting up the computer motherboard when the computer is powered up

d Which of these is the correct name for the operating system function that allows many programs to run simultaneously?

A	utility program
B	application package
C	embedded system
D	multitasking

e Which of these is the name of a type of interface that allows the user to type in commands on a keyboard which gives the computer instructions?

A	command line interface (CLI)
B	graphical user interface (GUI)
C	touchscreen interface
D	drop down menu interface

f Which of these descriptions is the main purpose of a GUI?

A	allows a user to directly carry out very complex tasks on a computer
B	the apps will run faster in a GUI environment
C	a GUI interface makes it much easier to use the computer
D	it is a type of app that allows a user to create drawings and images on the screen

g Which of the following will produce a signal which is sent to the CPU to suspend its current operation?

A	bootstrap
B	buffer
C	interrupt
D	quarantine

h On which one of the following memories are the BIOS *settings* stored?

A	ROM
B	RAM
C	EEPROM
D	CMOS

i Which one of the following statements is TRUE?

A	any device plugged into the USB port of a computer must have a unique serial number
B	the BIOS settings are stored in ROM so that they cannot be altered at any time by the user
C	interrupts from software always have a higher priority than an app currently being run on a computer
D	user accounts allow users to share resources, such as printers

j Which one of the following statements is FALSE?

A	security management is part of a typical operating system
B	post-WIMP interfaces make use of the more modern optical mouse to select icons
C	logical errors include errors such as 'division by zero'
D	printers use interrupts when they need more data to continue a printing job

[10]

6 a Describe the differences between a *compiler* and an *interpreter*. [4]
  b Give **one** advantage and **one** disadvantage of using a compiler. [2]
  c Give **one** advantage and **one** disadvantage of using an interpreter. [2]

7 Describe the differences between a *compiler* and an *assembler*. [4]

8 An Integrated Development Environment contains these features:
  – **Auto-completion**
  – **Auto-correction**
  – **Prettyprinting**
  a Explain what is meant by the term *IDE*. [2]
  b Describe each of the features given. Include a suitable example with each description. [6]
  c Identify **two** other features that should be included in an IDE. Give a reason why each feature is necessary. [4]

9 Pedro has written a program in a high-level language to do some calculations for a friend. His friend needs to use the program immediately on his laptop. Pedro does not know what software is available on the laptop. Also, his friend's internet connection is very slow. Explain which type of translator Pedro should use for his program. Give reasons why this is the best choice in this case. [6]

The internet and its uses

In this chapter you will learn about:
★ the internet and the World Wide Web
  – the differences between the internet and the World Wide Web
  – what is meant by a uniform resource locator (URL)
  – the purpose and operation of hypertext transfer protocols (HTTP and HTTPS)
  – the purpose and function of a web browser
  – how web pages are located, retrieved and displayed
  – cookies (including session and persistent cookies)
★ digital currency
  – digital currencies and how they are used
  – the process of blockchaining and how it is used to track digital currency transactions
★ cyber security
  – cyber security threats
  – solutions to keep data safe from security threats.

The internet is probably one of the greatest inventions of the twentieth century; it has changed the way the world works and communicates for ever. It is a great source of good, but has also spawned new types of crime which can be just as devastating as physical crime. This chapter will investigate many of the features of the internet but, in particular, will concentrate on cyber security threats, how we can recognise such threats and take the necessary action to stay safe.

5.1 The internet and the World Wide Web (WWW)

5.1.1 The differences between the internet and the World Wide Web (WWW)

Link
....
See Section 3.4 for more on network hardware and devices.

The word **internet** comes from INTERconnected NETwork, since it is basically a worldwide collection of interconnected networks. The internet is actually a concept rather than something tangible (that is, something we can touch). It relies on a physical infrastructure that allows networks and individual devices to connect to other networks and devices.

In contrast, the **World Wide Web (WWW)** is only a part of the internet that users can access using web browser software. The World Wide Web consists of a massive collection of web pages, and is based on the hypertext transfer protocol – see Section 5.1.3. Therefore, the World Wide Web is a way of accessing information using the internet; so the internet and the World Wide Web are actually quite different. In summary:

▼ **Table 5.1** Summary of differences between the internet and the World Wide Web

Internet	World Wide Web (WWW)
• users can send and receive emails	• it is a collection of multimedia web pages and other information on websites
• allows online chatting (via text, audio and video)	• http(s) protocols are written using hypertext mark-up language (HTML)
• makes use of transmission protocols (TCP) and internet protocols (IP)	• uniform resource locators (URLs) are used to specify the location of web pages
• it is a worldwide collection of interconnected networks and devices	• web resources are accessed by web browsers
	• uses the internet to access information from web servers

5.1.2 Uniform resource locators (URLs)

Web browsers are software that allow users to access and display web pages on their device screens. Browsers interpret **hypertext mark-up language (HTML)** sent from websites and produce the results on the user's device. **Uniform resource locators (URLs)** are text addresses used to access websites. A URL is typed into a browser address bar using the following format:

> Web browsers are usually just referred to as browsers

protocol://website address/path/file name

The protocol is usually either http or https.

The website address is:

» domain host (www),
» domain name (website name),
» domain type (.com, .org, .net, .gov, for example),
» and sometimes country code (.uk, .de, .cy, for example).

The path is the web page, but is often omitted and it then becomes the root directory of the website (see example below).

The file name is the item on the web page. For example:

https://www.hoddereducation.co.uk/ict

5.1.3 HTTP and HTTPS

Hypertext transfer protocol (http) is a set of rules that must be obeyed when transferring files across the internet. When some form of security (for example, SSL or TLS) is used, then this changes to https (you will often see the green padlock 🔒 in the status bar as well). The 's' stands for secure, and indicates a more secure way of sending and receiving data across a network (for example, the internet).

5.1.4 Web browsers

As mentioned earlier, browsers are software that allow a user to access and display web pages on their device screens. Browsers interpret (translate) the HTML from websites and show the result of the translation; for example, videos, images/text and audio. Most browsers have the following features:

» they have a home page
» they can store a user's favourite websites/web pages (referred to as bookmarks)
» they keep a history of websites visited by the user (user history)
» they have the ability to allow the user to navigate forwards and backwards through websites/web pages already opened
» many web pages can be open at the same time by using multiple tabs
» they make use of cookies (see Section 5.1.6)
» they make use of hyperlinks that allow navigation between websites and web pages; links can be opened in one of two ways:

either open in a new tab by using <ctrl> + <click>

or open in the same tab by simply clicking on the link

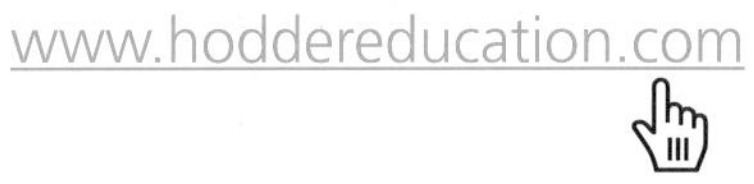

www.hoddereducation.com

▲ **Figure 5.1**

» data is stored as a cache (see Section 5.1.5)
» make use of JavaScript
» they use an address bar; for example:

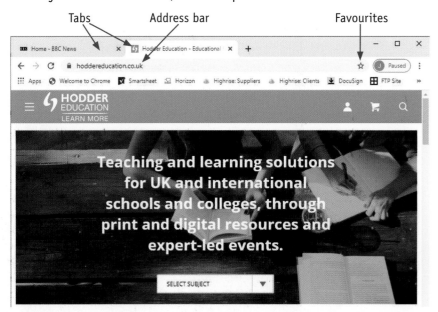

▲ **Figure 5.2** Browser address bar

5.1.5 Retrieval and location of web pages

HTML (HyperText Markup Language) is a language used to display content on browsers. All websites are written in HTML and hosted on a web server that has its own IP address. To retrieve pages from a website your browser needs to know this IP address. The **Domain Name Server (DNS)** (also known as domain name system) is a system for finding IP addresses for a domain name given in a URL. URLs and domain name servers eliminate the need for a user to memorise IP addresses. The DNS process involves converting a URL (such as www.hoddereducation.co.uk) into an IP address the computer can understand (such as 107.162.140.19). The DNS process involves more than one server.

DNS servers contain a database of URLs with the matching IP addresses. Figure 5.3 shows how a web page can be located and then sent back to the user's computer. The DNS plays a vital role in this process:

> ### Link
> For more on IP addresses see Section 3.4.

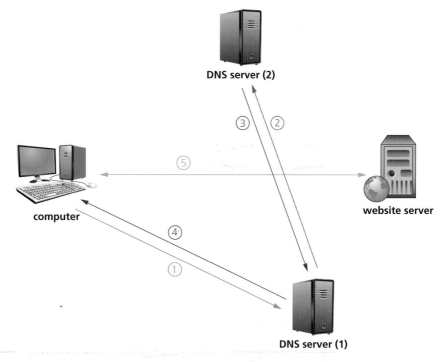

▲ **Figure 5.3** How DNS is used to locate and retrieve a web page

(1) The user opens their browser and types in the URL (www.hoddereducation.co.uk) and the browser asks the DNS server (1) for the IP address of the website.

(2) In this case, let's assume the DNS server can't find www.hoddereducation.co.uk in its database or its cache, so it sends out a request to a DNS server (2).

(3) The DNS server (2) finds the URL and can map it to 107.162.140.19; this IP address is sent back to the DNS server (1) which now puts this IP address and associated URL into its cache/database.

(4) This IP address is then sent back to the user's computer.

(5) The computer now sets up a communication with the website server and the required pages are downloaded. HTML files are sent from the website server to the computer. The browser interprets the HTML, which is used to structure content, and then displays the information on the user's computer.

(Note: in this case, the IP address was found on the second DNS server.)

5.1.6 Cookies

> this tracks data about users, such as IP addresses and browsing activity

Cookies are small files or code stored on a user's computer. They are sent by a web server to a browser on a user's computer. Each cookie is effectively a small look-up table containing pairs of (key, data) values, for example, (surname, Jones) (music, rock). Every time a user visits a website, it checks if it has set cookies on their browser before. If so, the browser reads the cookie which holds key information on the user's preferences such as language, currency and previous browsing activity. Cookies allow user tracking and maintain user preferences. Collected data can also be used to customise the web page for each individual user. For example, if a user buys a book online, the cookies remember the type of book chosen by the user and the web page will then show a message such as *"Customers who bought Hodder IGCSE ICT also bought Hodder IGCSE Computer Science"*.

There are two types of cookie:

» session cookie
» persistent (or permanent) cookie.

If a cookie doesn't have an expiry date associated with it, it is always considered to be a session cookie. So what are the basic differences?

Session cookies

Session cookies are used, for example, when making online purchases. They keep a user's items in a **virtual shopping basket**. This type of cookie is stored in temporary memory on the computer, doesn't actually collect any information from the user's computer and doesn't personally identify a user. Hence, session cookies cease to exist on a user's computer once the browser is closed or the website session is terminated.

Persistent (permanent) cookies

Persistent cookies remember a user's log in details (so that they can authenticate the user's browser). They are stored on the hard drive of a user's computer until the expiry date is reached or the user deletes it. These cookies remain in operation on the user's computer even after the browser is closed or the website session is terminated. Their advantage is that they remove the need to type in login details every time a certain website is visited. Some websites use cookies to store more personal information or user preferences. However, this can only be done if the user has provided the website with certain personal information and agrees to it being stored. Legitimate websites will always encrypt any personal information stored in the cookie to prevent unauthorised use by a third party that has access to your cookie folder. Many countries have introduced laws to protect users and these cookies are supposed to become deactivated after six months (even if the expiry date has not yet been reached).

Persistent cookies are a very efficient way of carrying data from one website session to another, or even between sessions on related websites; they remove the need to store massive amounts of data on the web server itself. Storing the data on the web server without using cookies would also make it very difficult to retrieve a user's data without requiring the user to log in every time they visit the website.

Figures 5.4 and 5.5 summarise what happens when a website is first visited and then what happens in subsequent visits:

1 First time the user logs in to website:

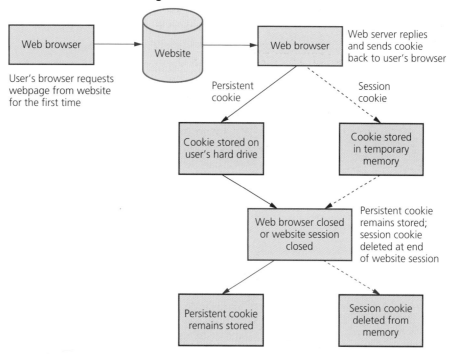

▲ **Figure 5.4** Cookies (first login)

2 User logs in to website again

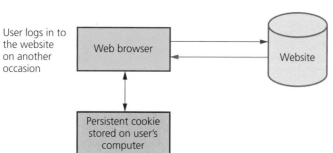

▲ **Figure 5.5** Cookies (subsequent logins)

Summary of the uses of (persistent) cookies:

» allow the website to remember users' passwords, email addresses and invoice details, so they won't have to insert all of this information every time they visit or every time they purchase something from that website

» serve as a memory, enabling the website to recognise users every time they visit it

» save users' items in a virtual shopping basket/cart

» track internet habits and users' website histories or favourites/bookmarks

» target users with advertising that matches their previous buying or surfing habits

» store users' preferences (for example, recognise customised web pages)

» are used in online financial transactions
» allow progress in online games and quizzes to be stored
» allow social networking sites to recognise certain preferences and browsing histories
» allow different languages to be used on the web pages automatically as soon as users log on.

Activity 5.1

1 A URL being entered is: **http://www.urlexample.co.ie/sample_page**
   Identify:
   a the domain name
   b the domain type
   c the file name
   d which protocol is being used.

2 a Give two differences between session cookies and persistent cookies.

   b Describe three uses of cookies.

3 The following table shows five features of the internet and the World Wide Web. Tick (✓) the appropriate box to indicate which feature refers to the internet and which feature refers to the World Wide Web:

Feature	Internet	World Wide Web
it is possible to send and receive emails		
makes use of http protocols		
uses URLs to specify the locations of websites and web pages		
resources can be accessed by using web browsers		
makes use of TCP and IP		

4 Why do you think persistent cookies are sometimes referred to as *tracking cookies*? Give at least two pieces of evidence to support your answer.

5.2 Digital currency

5.2.1 What is digital currency?

Digital currency exists purely in a digital format. It has no physical form unlike conventional **fiat currency** (for example, $, £, €, and ¥).

(Note: Fiat is a Latin word meaning 'let it be done'; since conventional currency is backed by governments and banks rather than being linked to gold or silver reserves, it is referred to as fiat currency.)

Digital currency is an accepted form of payment to pay for goods or services. As with cash or credit/debit cards, digital currency can be transferred between various accounts when carrying out transactions. It has made it possible to bank online (for example, using *PayPal*) or via a smartphone app (for example,

Apple Pay). This is all possible because money only exists as data on a computer system, but it can be transferred into physical cash if we need it.

Digital currency relies on a **central banking system**. For example, suppose Nick wishes to send Irina some money; Nick uses bank 'X' and Irina uses bank 'Y':

▲ **Figure 5.6** Digital currency

The problem with centralisation is maintaining confidentiality and security; these have always been issues with digital currency systems. However, one example of digital currency, known as cryptocurrency, has essentially overcome these issues by introducing decentralisation:

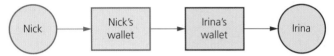

▲ **Figure 5.7** Cryptocurrency and decentralisation

» Cryptocurrency uses **cryptography** to track transactions; it was created to address the problems associated with the centralisation of digital currency.
» Traditional digital currencies are regulated by central banks and governments (in much the same way as fiat currencies). This means all transactions and exchange rates are determined by these two bodies. Cryptocurrency has no state control and all the rules are set by the cryptocurrency community itself.
» Unlike existing digital currencies, cryptocurrency transactions are publicly available and therefore all transactions can be tracked and the amount of money in the system is monitored.
» The cryptocurrency system works by being within a **blockchain** network which means it is much more secure.

5.2.2 Blockchaining

Blockchain is a decentralised database. All the transactions of networked members are stored on this database. Essentially, the blockchain consists of a number of interconnected computers but they are **not connected** to a central server. All transaction data is stored on **all** computers in the blockchain network.

Whenever a new transaction takes place, all the networked computers get a copy of the transaction; therefore **it cannot be changed without the consent** of **all** the network members. This effectively removes the risk of security issues such as hacking. Blockchain is used in many areas, such as:

» cryptocurrency (digital currency) exchanges
» smart contracts
» research (particularly within pharmaceutical companies)
» politics
» education.

How blockchain works

Whenever a new transaction takes place, a new **block** is created:

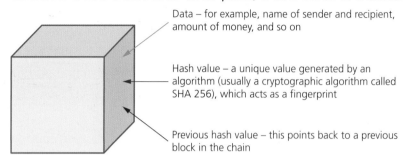

Data – for example, name of sender and recipient, amount of money, and so on

Hash value – a unique value generated by an algorithm (usually a cryptographic algorithm called SHA 256), which acts as a fingerprint

Previous hash value – this points back to a previous block in the chain

▲ **Figure 5.8** Block description

A new hash value is created each time a new block is created. This hash value is unique to each block and includes a **timestamp**, which identifies when an event actually takes place. We will now consider what happens when a chain of blocks is created. Figure 5.9 shows part of a typical blockchain:

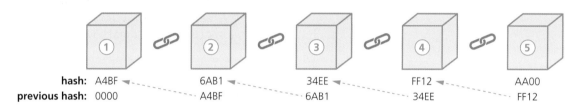

hash: A4BF	6AB1	34EE	FF12	AA00
previous hash: 0000	A4BF	6AB1	34EE	FF12

▲ **Figure 5.9** Part of blockchain (showing 5 blocks)

It is clear from Figure 5.9 how these blocks are connected. Block '1' is known as the *genesis block* since it doesn't point to any previous block. Now suppose block '2' is changed in some way. Any changes to the data within block '2' will cause the value of the hash to change (it will no longer have the value 6AB1). This means that block '3' and beyond will now be invalid since the chain was broken between block '2' and '3' (previous hash 6AB1 in block '3' is no longer valid).

This will prevent tampering (for example, by a hacker). However, it may be crossing your mind that computers are now so fast that it should be possible to quickly create a whole new string of blocks, and therefore recreate a new chain before the problem has been discovered. This is prevented by **proof-of-work**, which makes sure it takes ten minutes to determine the necessary proof-of-work for *each* block **before** it can be added to the chain. This is 'policed' by **miners**, which are special network users that get a commission for each new block created. Thus, the whole process of creating new blocks is slowed down which foils hackers and also means that the currency is regulated by all the network computers.

Consequently, this makes it almost impossible to hack into the blockchain since it would be necessary to attack every single block in the chain at the same time. It only takes one block to break the link for any transaction to be terminated. When a new block is created, it is sent to each computer in the blockchain and is checked for correctness before being added to the blockchain. If a new network user is created, they get a copy of everything in the whole blockchain system.

5.3 Cyber security

5.3.1 Cyber security threats

Keeping data safe is extremely important for many reasons. It may be **personal data** that you want to keep within your family or close friends, or it may be commercial data, such as passwords and bank details.

Data can be corrupted or deleted either through accidental damage or malicious acts. There are also many ways data can be intercepted leading to cyber security threats. The following list shows the cyber threats which will be considered in this section:

» brute force attacks
» data interception
» distributed denial of service (DDoS) attacks
» hacking
» malware (viruses, worms, Trojan horse, spyware, adware and ransomware)
» phishing
» pharming
» social engineering.

Brute force attacks

If a hacker wants to 'crack' your password, they can systematically try all the different combinations of letters, numbers and other symbols until eventually they find your password. This is known as a **brute force attack** and there isn't a lot of sophistication in the technique.

One way to reduce the number of attempts needed to crack a password is to first go through a series of logical steps:

1 Check if the password is one of the ***most*** common ones used (the five most common are: 123456, password, qwerty, 111111 and abc123); since these simple passwords are seen so many times it's a good place for the hacker to start.
2 If it isn't in the common password list, the next thing to do is to start with a **strong word list** (this is a text file containing a collection of words that can be used in a brute force attack); some programs will generate a word list containing a million words. Nonetheless this is still a faster way of cracking a password than just total trial and error.

Clearly method (2) would still take several hours until the password was found. The **longer** a password is and the **greater the variation** of characters used, the harder it will be to crack (also refer to the notes on the use of passwords in authentication).

Data interception

Data interception is a form of stealing data by **tapping** into a wired or wireless communication link. The intent is to compromise privacy or to obtain confidential information.

Interception can be carried out using a **packet sniffer**, which examines data packets being sent over a network. The intercepted data is sent back to the hacker. This is a common method when wired networks are used.

Wi-Fi (wireless) data interception can be carried out using **wardriving** (or sometimes called **Access Point Mapping**). Using this method, data can be intercepted using a laptop or smartphone, antenna and a GPS device (together with some software) outside a building or somebody's house. The intercepted Wi-Fi signal can then reveal personal data to the hacker, often without the user being aware this is happening.

Obviously, encryption of data makes life more difficult for the hacker. While it doesn't stop the data being intercepted or altered in some way, encryption will make the data incomprehensible to the hacker if they don't have access to a decryption key. Therefore, to safeguard against wardriving, the use of a **wired equivalency privacy (WEP)** encryption protocol, together with a firewall, is recommended. It is also a good idea to protect the use of the wireless router by having complex passwords. It is important not to use Wi-Fi (wireless) connectivity in public places (such as an airport) since no data encryption will exist and your data is then open to interception by anyone within the airport.

Distributed Denial of Service (DDoS) attacks

A **denial of service (DoS)** attack is an attempt at preventing users from accessing part of a network, notably an internet server. This is usually temporary but may be a very damaging act or a large breach of security. It doesn't just affect networks; an individual can also be a target for such an attack. The attacker may be able to prevent a user from:

>> accessing their emails.
>> accessing websites/web pages
>> accessing online services (such as banking).

One method of attack is to flood the network with useless **spam** traffic. How does this cause a problem?

When a user enters a website's URL in their browser, a request is sent to the web server that contains the website or web page. Obviously, the server can only handle a finite number of requests. So if it becomes overloaded by an attacker sending out thousands of requests, it won't be able to service a user's legitimate request. This is effectively a denial of service. In a **distributed denial of service (DDoS)** the spam traffic originates from many different computers, which makes it hard to block the attack.

This can happen to a user's email account, for example, by an attacker sending out many spam messages to their email account. Internet service providers (ISPs) only allow a specific data quota for each user. Consequently, if the attacker sends out thousands of emails to the user's account, it will quickly become clogged up

Link

For more on data packets refer to Chapter 2.

and the user won't be able to receive legitimate emails. An individual user or a website can guard against these attacks to some degree by:

>> using an up-to-date malware checker
>> setting up a firewall to restrict traffic to and from the web server or user's computer
>> applying email filters to filter out unwanted traffic (for example, spam).

There are certain signs a user can look out for to see if they have become a victim of a DDoS attack:

>> slow network performance (opening files or accessing certain websites)
>> inability to access certain websites
>> large amounts of spam email reaching the user's email account.

Hacking

Hacking is generally the act of gaining illegal access to a computer system without the user's permission. This can lead to identity theft or the gaining of personal information; data can be deleted, passed on, changed or corrupted. As mentioned earlier, encryption does not stop hacking; it makes the data meaningless to the hacker but it doesn't stop them from deleting, corrupting or passing on the data. Hacking can be prevented through the use of firewalls, user names and frequently changed strong passwords. Anti-hacking software and intrusion-detection software also exists in the fight against hacking.

Malicious hacking, as described above, takes place without the user's permission, and is always an illegal act. However, universities and companies now run courses in **ethical hacking**. This occurs when companies authorise paid hackers to check out their security measures and test how robust their computer systems are to hacking attacks.

Malware

Malware is one of the biggest risks to the integrity and security of data on a computer system. There are many forms of malware; this chapter will only consider the following in any detail:

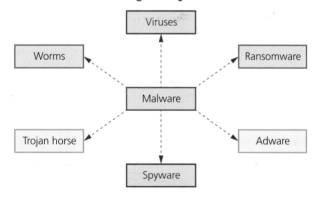

▲ **Figure 5.10** Malware types

Viruses

Viruses are programs or program code that replicate (copies themselves) with the intention of deleting or corrupting files, or causing a computer to malfunction (for example, by deleting .exe files, filling up the hard drive with 'useless' data, and so on).

Viruses need an **active host** program on the target computer or an operating system that has already been infected, before they can actually run and cause harm (that is, they need to be executed by some trigger before starting to cause any damage).

Viruses are often sent as email attachments, reside on infected websites or on infected software downloaded to the user's computer. Apart from all the usual safety actions (for example, don't open emails from unknown sources, don't install non-original software), always run an up-to-date virus scanner (refer to Chapter 4 for more details).

Find out more

Reading this chapter and other chapters throughout this book, find out the various ways viruses can be sent. Produce a wall chart showing all of these ways and the various ways to avoid receiving viruses.

Worms

Worms are a type of stand-alone malware that can self-replicate. Their intention is to spread to other computers and corrupt whole networks; unlike viruses, they don't need an active host program to be opened in order to do any damage. They remain inside applications which allows them to move throughout networks. In fact, worms replicate without targeting and infecting specific files on a computer; they rely on security failures within networks to permit them to spread unhindered.

Worms frequently arrive as message attachments and only one user opening a worm-infested email could end up infecting the whole network. As with viruses, the same safeguards should be employed, together with the running of an up-to-date anti-virus program. Worms tend to be problematic because of their ability to spread throughout a network without any action from an end-user; whereas viruses require each end-user to somehow initiate the virus.

Examples include the 'I love you' worm, which attacked nearly every email user in the world, overloaded phone systems and even brought down television networks. All of this makes them more dangerous than viruses.

Trojan horse

A **Trojan horse** is a program which is often disguised as legitimate software but with malicious instructions embedded within it. A Trojan horse replaces all or part of the legitimate software with the intent of carrying out some harm to the user's computer system.

They need to be executed by the end-user and therefore usually arrive as an email attachment or are downloaded from an infected website. For example, they could be transmitted via a fake anti-virus program that pops up on the user's screen claiming their computer is infected and action needs to be taken. The user will be invited to run fake anti-virus as part of a free trial. Once the user does this, the damage is done.

Once installed on the user's computer, the Trojan horse will give cyber criminals access to personal information on your computers, such as IP addresses, passwords and other personal data. Spyware (including key logging software) and ransomware are often installed on a user's computer via Trojan horse malware.

Because they rely on tricking end-users, firewalls and other security systems are often useless since the user can overrule them and initiate the running of the malware.

Spyware

Spyware is software that gathers information by monitoring a user's activities carried out on their computer. The gathered information is sent back to the cybercriminal who originally sent the spyware. They are primarily designed to monitor and capture web browsing and other activities and capture personal data (for example, bank account numbers, passwords and credit/debit card details). Spyware can be detected and removed by anti-spyware software. The big danger of spyware is the method it used to enter a user's system and exploit it; for example, did it come from social engineering? If spyware is found on a computer, it should set off alarm bells since a weakness in the security has been found which could be exploited by other, often more dangerous, malware.

 Find out more

Key logging software is often part of spyware.
1   How does this type of malware gather data from the user's computer?
2   Some banks use drop-down menus to overcome key logging software. Explain how using drop-down boxes to enter characters from, for example, a password can help in security.

Adware

Adware is a type of malware. At its least dangerous it will attempt to flood an end-user with unwanted advertising. For example, it could redirect a user's browser to a website that contains promotional advertising, it could appear in the form of pop-ups, or it could appear in the browser's toolbar and redirect search requests.

Although not necessarily harmful, adware can:

» highlight weaknesses in a user's security defences
» be hard to remove – it defeats most anti-malware software since it can be difficult to determine whether or not it is harmful
» hijack a browser and create its own default search requests.

Ransomware

Essentially, ransomware are programs that encrypt data on a user's computer and 'hold the data hostage'. The cybercriminal waits until the ransom money is paid and, sometimes, the decryption key is then sent to the user. It has caused considerable damage to some companies and individuals.

Imagine a situation where you log on to your computer, only to find the screen is locked and you can't unlock it until the demands of the cybercriminal have been met. This malware restricts access to the computer and encrypts all the data until a ransom is paid. It can be installed on a user's computer by way of a Trojan horse or through social engineering.

When ransomware is executed, it either encrypts files straightaway or it waits for a while to determine how much of a ransom the victim can afford. The malware can be prevented by the usual methods (for example, by avoiding phishing emails) but once it is executed, it is almost impossible to reverse the damage caused. The best way to avoid a catastrophe is to ensure regular back-ups of key files are kept and thus avoid having to pay a ransom.

Summary of malware

Table 5.2 summarises the six types of malware described in Section 5.3.1.

▼ **Table 5.2** Summary of types of malware

Viruses – programs (or program code) that can replicate/copy themselves with the intention of deleting or corrupting files, or causing the computer to malfunction. They need an active host program on the target computer or an operating system that has already been infected before they can run
Worms – these are types of standalone viruses that can replicate themselves with the intention of spreading to other computers; they often networks to search out computers with weak security that are prone to such attacks
Trojan horses – these are malicious programs often disguised as legitimate software; they replace all or part of the legitimate software with the intent of carrying out some harm to the user's computer system
Spyware – software that gathers information by monitoring, for example, all the activity on a user's computer; the gathered information is then sent back to the person who sent the software (sometimes spyware monitors key presses and is then referred to as key logging software)
Adware – software that floods a user's computer with unwanted advertising; usually in the form of pop-ups but can frequently appear in the browser address window redirecting the browser to a fake website which contains the promotional adverts
Ransomware – programs that encrypt the data on a user's computer; a decryption key is sent back to the user once they pay a sum of money (a ransom); they are often sent via a Trojan horse or by social engineering

Phishing

Phishing occurs when a cybercriminal sends out legitimate-looking emails to users. The emails may contain links or attachments that, when initiated, take the user to a fake website; or they may trick the user into responding with personal data (for example, bank account details or credit/debit card details).

The email usually appears to be genuine coming from a known bank or service provider (also refer to Section 5.3.2). The key point is that the recipient has to initiate some act before the phishing scam can cause any harm. If suspicious emails are deleted or not opened, then phishing attacks won't cause any problems.

There are numerous ways to help prevent phishing attacks:

» users need to be aware of new phishing scams; those people in industry or commerce should undergo frequent security awareness training to become aware of how to identify phishing (and pharming) scams
» it is important not to click on any emails links unless totally certain that it is safe to do so; fake emails can often be identified by 'Dear Customer ......' or 'Dear email person@gmail.com ....' and so on
» it is important to run anti-phishing toolbars on browsers (this includes tablets and mobile phones) since these will alert the user to malicious websites contained in an email
» always look out for https or the green padlock symbol 🔒 in the address bar

>> regular checks of online accounts are also advisable as well as maintaining passwords on a regular basis
>> ensure an up-to-date browser is running on the computer device (which contains all of the latest security upgrades) and run a good firewall in the background at all times; a combination of a desktop firewall (usually software) and a network firewall (usually hardware) considerably reduces the risk of hacking, pharming and phishing on network computers
>> be very wary of pop-ups and use the browser to block them; if pop-ups get through your defences, don't click on 'cancel' since this can ultimately lead to phishing or pharming sites – the best option is to select the small **✗** in the top right-hand corner of the pop-up window which closes it down.

Note: another term connected to phishing is **spear phishing**; this is where the cybercriminal targets **specific** individuals or companies to gain access to sensitive financial information or industrial espionage – regular phishing is not specific regarding who the victims are.

Pharming

Pharming is malicious code installed on a user's computer or on an infected website. The code redirects the user's browser to a fake website **without** the user's knowledge. Unlike phishing, the user doesn't actually need to take any action for it to be initiated. The creator of the malicious code can gain personal data, such as bank details, from the user. Often the website appears to come from a trusted source and can lead to fraud and identity theft.

Why does pharming pose a threat to data security?
As mentioned above, pharming redirects internet users to a fake or malicious website set up by, for example, a hacker; redirection from a legitimate website to the fake website can be done using **DNS cache poisoning**.

> Every time a user types in a URL, their browser contacts the DNS server; the IP address of the website will then be sent back to their browser. However, DNS cache poisoning changes the real IP address values to those of the fake website; consequently, the user's computer will connect to the fake website.

When a user enters a web address (URL) into a browser, the computer is sent the IP address of the website; if the IP address has been modified somehow the user's computer will be redirected to the fake website.

It is possible to mitigate against the risk of pharming:

>> Use of anti-virus software can detect unauthorised alterations to a website address and warn the user of the potential risks.
>> However, if the DNS server itself has been infected (rather than the user's computer) it is much more difficult to mitigate the risk.
>> Many modern browsers can alert users to pharming and phishing attacks.
>> It is very important to check the spelling of websites to ensure the web address used is correct.
>> As with phishing, use of https or the green padlock symbol 🔒 in the address bar is an additional form of defence.

> ## Link
>
> See Section 5.1 for more on URLs, IP addresses and DNS (Domain Name Server).

Activity 5.3

1 A company has offices in four different countries. Communication and data sharing between the offices is done via computers connecting over the internet.

a Describe **three** data security issues the company might encounter during their day-to-day communications and data sharing.

b For each issue described, explain why it could be a threat to the security of the company.

c For each issue described, describe a way to mitigate the threat that has been posed.

2 Explain the following three terms:
- worm
- ransomware
- Trojan horse.

3 John works for a car company. He maintains the database that contains all the personal data of the people working for the car company. John was born on 28th February 1990 and has two pet cats called Felix and Max.

a John needs to use a password and a user name to log onto the database. Why would the following passwords not be a very good choice:

i 280290

ii FiLix1234

iii John04

b Describe how John could improve his passwords and also how he should maintain his passwords to maximise database security.

c When John enters a password on his computer he is presented with the following question on his screen:

> Would you like to save the password on this device?

Why is it important that John always says **No** to this question?

 Find out more

Apart from malware, data can be *accidentally* lost. Find out ways that data could be recovered and ways to minimise the risk for each of the following situations:
1 Accidental data loss, such as accidental deletion of a file
2 Hardware fault, such as a head crash on a hard disk drive
3 Software fault, due to installation of software incompatible with existing software
4 Incorrect operation of the computer, such as using incorrect procedure for the removal of a memory stick from a computer.

Social engineering

Social engineering occurs when a cybercriminal creates a social situation that can lead to a potential victim dropping their guard. It involves the manipulation of people into breaking their normal security procedures and not following best practice. There are five types of threat that commonly exist:

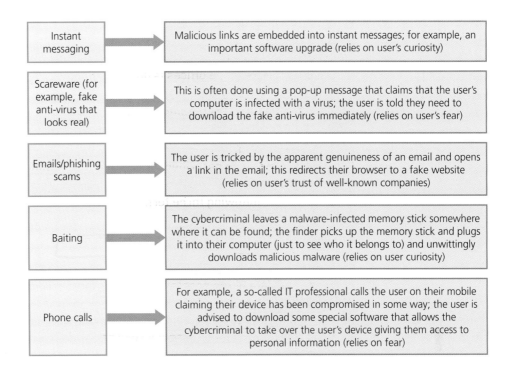

▲ **Figure 5.11** Social engineering

It is clear from the five examples that social engineering links into many other types of malware, and is an effective method of introducing malware. The whole idea is based on the exploitation of certain human emotions; the three most common ones to exploit are:

» fear – the user is panicked into believing their computer is in immediate danger and isn't given time to logically decide if the danger is genuine or not; fear is a very powerful emotion that can easily be exploited by a cybercriminal
» curiosity – the user can be tricked into believing they have won a car or they find an infected memory stick lying around; their curiosity gets the better of them and they give their details willingly to win the car (for example, credit card details to pay for delivery or road tax) or they are curious who the memory stick belongs to; without thinking clearly, their curiosity gets the better of them and the damage is done
» empathy and trust – a real belief that all genuine-sounding companies can be trusted, therefore emails or phone calls coming from such companies must be safe; a dangerous assumption that the cybercriminal can exploit fully.

There is no hacking involved, since the user is willingly allowing the cybercriminal to have access to their computer, to download malicious software or visit fake websites; the user is rushed into making rash decisions.

Figure 5.12 shows the course of action taken by a cybercriminal in targeting their victim:

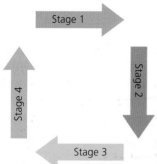

Stage 1 – The victims are identified; information about victim gathered and method of attack decided

Stage 2 – At this stage the victim is being targeted (either through email, phone call, Trojan horse and so on; it all depends on who the victim is)

Stage 3 – The attack on the victim is now executed allowing the cybercriminal to obtain the information or to cause the disruption decided on at Stage 1

Stage 4 – When the cybercriminal has decided they have what they wanted they try to remove all traces of the malware to cover their tracks

▲ **Figure 5.12** Stages in a typical social engineering scam

5.3.2 Keeping data safe from security threats

Access levels

In many computer systems, user accounts control a user's rights. This often involves having different **levels of access** for different people. For example, in a hospital it would not be appropriate for a cleaner to have access to medical data about a patient. However, a consultant would need access to this vital data. Therefore, most systems have a hierarchy of access levels depending on a person's level of security; this is usually achieved using a user name and password as shown in Figure 5.13.

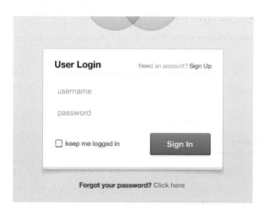

▲ **Figure 5.13** Access level log in screen

Link

See Chapter 9 for more details about databases.

When using databases, levels of access are particularly important; it is essential to determine who has the right to read, write and delete data, for example. By having different views of data tables, it is possible for different users to only have access to certain data.

Another area where access levels are very important is in social networks (such as Facebook); with this type of application, there are usually four access levels:

1 public access (this refers to the data anyone from the general public can access)
2 friends (only people identified as 'friends' by the owner of the data can see certain data)
3 custom (this allows the user to further refine what data can be seen by 'friends' allowing them to exclude certain content from selected people)
4 data owner (this is data only the owner of the data can see).

In this type of application, users are allowed to use **privacy settings** rather than passwords to decide the level of access (for more on this see later in this section).

Anti-malware

The two most common types of anti-malware are anti-virus and anti-spyware.

Anti-virus
Anti-virus has already been described in great detail in Chapter 4.

Anti-spyware
Anti-spyware software detects and removes spyware programs installed illegally on a user's computer system. The software is based on one of the following methods:

>> rules – in this case, the software looks for typical features which are usually associated with spyware thus identifying any potential security issues
>> file structures – in this case, there are certain file structures associated with potential spyware which allows them to be identified by the software.

Anti-spyware is now often part of a generic malware bundle that contains an anti-virus, anti-spyware and a personal firewall.

The general features of anti-spyware are:

>> detect and remove spyware already installed on a device
>> prevent a user from downloading spyware
>> encrypt files to make the data more secure in case it is 'spied' on
>> encryption of keyboard strokes to help remove the risk posed by the keylogging aspects of some spyware
>> blocks access to a user's webcam and microphone (the software stops the spyware taking over the control of a user's webcam and microphone which can be used to collect information without the user's knowledge)
>> scans for signs that the user's personal information has been stolen and warns the user if this has happened.

Authentication

Authentication refers to the ability of a user to prove who they are. There are three common factors used in authentication:

>> something you know (for example, a password or PIN code)
>> something you have (for example, a mobile phone or tablet)
>> something which is unique to you (for example, biometrics).

Link

For more on anti-virus software see Section 4.1.

There are a number of ways authentication can be done.

Passwords and user names

Passwords are used to restrict access to data or systems. They should be hard to crack and changed frequently to retain any real level of security. Passwords can also take the form of biometrics (for example, on a mobile phone – see later). In addition to protecting access levels to computer systems, passwords are frequently used when accessing the internet. For example:

» when accessing email accounts
» when carrying out online banking or shopping
» accessing social networking sites.

It is important that passwords are protected; some ways of doing this are described below:

» run anti-spyware software to make sure that your passwords aren't being relayed back to whoever put the spyware on your computer
» change passwords on a regular basis in case they have come into the possession of another user, illegally or accidentally
» passwords should not be easy to crack (for example, your favourite colour, name of a pet or favourite music artist); passwords are grouped as either strong (hard to crack or guess) or weak (relatively easy to crack or guess)
» strong passwords should contain:
   – at least one capital letter
   – at least one numerical value
   – at least one other keyboard character (such as @, *, &, etc.)
   – an example of a strong password would be: Sy12@#TT90kj=0
   – an example of a weak password would be: GREEN

When the password is typed in, it often shows on the screen as ******** so nobody else can see what the user has typed in. If the user's password doesn't match up with the user name then access will be denied. Many systems ask for a new password to be typed in twice as a verification check (to check for input errors). To help protect the system, users are only allowed to type in their password a finite number of times – usually three times is the maximum number of tries allowed before the system locks the user out. After that, the user will be unable to log on until they have reset their password.

When using an online company, if a user forgets their password or they need to reset it, they will be sent an email which contains a link to a web page where they can reset their password. This is done as an added precaution in case an unauthorised person has tried to change the user's password.

As mentioned above, it is usually necessary to use a user name as well as a password. This gives an additional security level since the user name and password must match up to allow a user to gain access to, for example, a bank website.

Activity 5.4

1   Which of the following are weak passwords and which are strong passwords? Explain your decision in each case.

   a 25-May-2000

   b Pas5word

   c ChapTer@06

   d AbC*N55!

   e 12345X

2   An airport uses a computer system to control security, flight bookings, passenger lists, administration and customer services.

   a Describe how it is possible to ensure the safety of the data on the system so that senior staff can see all the data, while customers can only access flight times (arrivals and departures) and duty-free offers.

   b Describe how the airport can guard against malware attacks from outside and also from customers using the airport services.

Biometrics

Biometrics can be used in much the same way as passwords as a way of identifying a user. Biometrics relies on certain unique characteristics of human beings; examples include:

>> fingerprint scans
>> retina scans
>> face recognition
>> voice recognition.

Biometrics is used in a number of applications as a security device. For example, some of the latest mobile phones use fingerprint matching before they can be operated; some pharmaceutical companies use face recognition or retina scans to allow entry to secure areas.

We will now consider fingerprint scanning and retina scans in a little more detail.

Fingerprint scans

Images of fingerprints are compared against previously scanned fingerprint images stored in a database; if they match, then a user has been correctly recognised. The system compares patterns of 'ridges' and 'valleys' that are unique. The accuracy of the scan is about around 1 in 5000. Fingerprint scanning techniques have the following benefits as a form of security:

>> fingerprints are unique, therefore this technique can improve security since it would be difficult to replicate a person's fingerprints
>> other security devices (such as magnetic cards to gain entry to a building) can be lost or even stolen which makes them less effective
>> it would be impossible to 'sign in' for somebody else since the fingerprints would match with only one person on the database
>> fingerprints can't be misplaced; a person always has them!

Link

For more on face recognition scans see Section 3.2.1.

▲ **Figure 5.14** Fingerprint scan

What are the drawbacks of fingerprint scanning?

>> it is relatively expensive to install and set up
>> if a person's fingers are damaged through an injury, this can have an effect on the scanning accuracy
>> some people may regard any biometric device as an infringement of civil liberties.

Retina scans

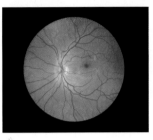

▲ **Figure 5.15** Retina scan

Retina scans use infrared light to scan the unique pattern of blood vessels in the retina (at the back of the eye); it is a rather unpleasant technique requiring a person to sit totally still for 10 to 15 seconds while the scan takes place; it is very secure since nobody has yet found a way to duplicate the blood vessels patterns. The accuracy is about 1 in 10 million.

Table 5.3 shows a comparison of the benefits and drawbacks of the four common biometric techniques:

▼ **Table 5.3** Comparison of biometric devices

Biometric technique	Benefits	Drawbacks
fingerprint scans	it is one of the most developed biometric techniques very easy to use relatively small storage requirements for the biometric data created	for some people it is very intrusive, since it is still related to criminal identification it can make mistakes if the skin is dirty or damaged (e.g. cuts)
retina scans	very high accuracy there is no known way to replicate a person's retina	it is very intrusive it can be relatively slow to verify retina scan with stored scans very expensive to install and set up
face recognition	non-intrusive method relatively inexpensive technology	it can be affected by changes in lighting, the person's hair, change in age, and if the person is wearing glasses
voice recognition	non-intrusive method verification takes less than 5 seconds relatively inexpensive technology	a person's voice can be easily recorded and used for unauthorised access low accuracy an illness such as a cold can change a person's voice, making absolute identification difficult or impossible

Biometric applications

❓ A door security system protected by retina scanner

In this example, a company uses retina scans to permit entry to their secure research laboratories.

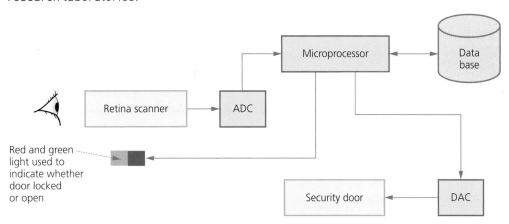

▲ **Figure 5.16** Security system controlled by retina scanners

A person stands facing the retina scanner. The scanned data is sent via an ADC (analogue-digital converter) to a microprocessor. The microprocessor compares the data received with retina scan data already stored in a database. If the two sets of data match, a signal is sent to turn a light from red to green and also unlock the security door. The door is controlled by a DAC (digital-analogue converter) and an actuator. If the retina scan data and database data don't match, then entry is denied and the light remains red.

Link

For more on actuators see Chapter 3.

➡️ Find out more

One of the most common security systems used on mobile phones is the ***capacitance fingerprint reader***. Describe how this system works.

Activity 5.5

1 In the biometric application example, retina scans were used to control entry to a secure research building.

  a Describe how the system might change if face recognition was used instead of retina scanners. The system is triggered automatically if a motion sensor detects the presence of a person.

  b Name other biometric devices which could be used to control entry to this building.

2 Many cars now use voice control as a form of security before a car can be started and it is also used to give some key commands, such as start navigation system. Describe the benefits and drawbacks of such systems in cars.

Two-step verification

Two-step verification requires two methods of authentication to verify who a user is. It is used predominantly when a user makes an online purchase using a credit/debit card as payment method.

For example, suppose Kate wishes to buy a new camera from a website. She logs into the website using her computer. This requires her to enter a user name and a password, which is step 1 of the authentication process.

To improve security, an eight-digit PIN (called a one-time pass code) is sent back to her either in an email or as a text message to her mobile phone (the mobile phone has already been registered by Kate on the website as the second stage of the authentication process). Kate now enters this eight-digit PIN into her computer and she is now authorised to buy the camera. In summary:

▲ **Figure 5.17** Two-step verification using a mobile phone

Using the definitions of authentication at the start of this section, the mobile phone is something she has and the password/PIN code is something she knows.

Automatic software updates

Automatic software updates mean software on computers and mobile phones/tablets is kept up-to-date. Sometimes this is done overnight or when you log off the device.

These updates are vital since they may contain **patches** that update the software security (to protect against malware) or improve the software performance (for example, removal of bugs and addition of new features). The only downside to this is the potential for updates to disrupt your device following installation. If this happens, the user either has to wait for another patch to put this right, or use the techniques described in Chapter 4 that reverse the clock time to an earlier date before the updates were made.

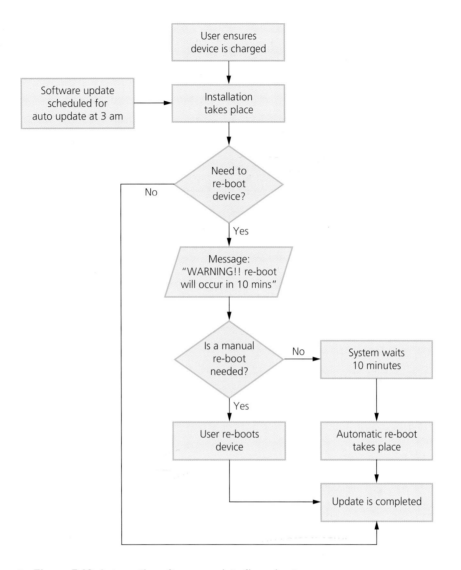

▲ **Figure 5.18** Automatic software update flow chart

Checking the spelling and tone of communication and URL links

When emails are sent to you, there are three actions you always need to take before opening them or activating any links in them.

» Check out the spellings in the email and in the links; professional, genuine organisations will not send out emails which contain spelling or major grammatical errors (for example, Amazzon.com)

» Carefully check the tone used in the email message; if it is rushing you into doing something or if the language used seems inappropriate or incorrect, then it could be a phishing email or worse.

There are five things to look out for:

1 The email address itself; no legitimate company will use an email address such as: @gmail.com
Carefully check the part of the address after the '@' symbol which should match the company's name; for example:

account-update@amazon.com

2 The tone of the email and bad spelling of words is a clear indication of a potential scam. Look at this message that claimed it came from PayPal. See if you can find the ten errors in the email that should set off alarm bells.

From: PayPal <paypal@customer-notices55.com>
To: PayPal user 551-121-998
Sent: Feb 1st 2021 @ 10:55
Subject: Compremised Account [CaseID Nr: KX-003-551-121-998]

Dear Customer

We need you help to resolve issue with account. We have temporarily stop account due to problem's.
Unusual account activity on PayPal account means action need be taken immediately. If your not sure this was you, an unauthorized user might be trying to access your accounts. Please to log in here to change your password:

LOG IN HERE

▲ **Figure 5.19** Sample scam email

Did you find all the errors? An email like this looks official but there are many clues that it didn't come from a legitimate company; such as, many spelling mistakes, grammatical errors and the domain name in the email address. An email like this should be regarded as phishing; by clicking on the 'LOG IN HERE' box, you will divulge passwords and other key information since you will be sent to a fake 'PayPal' website.

3 Misspelling of domain names in a link are very common errors found in emails sent by scammers and fraudsters. The authors of this book have seen these incorrect spellings:

www.gougle.com
www.amozon.com

This is known as **typo squatting** where names close to the genuine names are used to fool you.

4 Suspicious links; destination addresses should match the rest of the email. Look at this message that claims to be from Netflix:

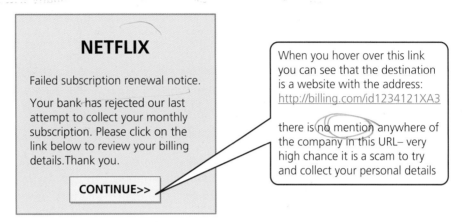

▲ **Figure 5.20** Second example of probable scam

5 Other errors to look out for are just plain spelling mistakes. Look at this address from TKMaxx; find the three errors:

http://www.tkmax.co.ie

» since the company involve online payments, it's very likely to use secure links therefore you would expect to see `https`
» the spelling of the company is incorrect
» it is more likely to see `.com` since they are a large company.

Firewalls

A **firewall** can be either software or hardware. It sits between the user's computer and an external network (for example, the internet) and filters information in and out of the computer. This allows the user to decide whether or not to allow communication with an external source and it also warns a user that an external source is trying to access their computer. Firewalls are the primary defence to any computer system to help protect it from hacking, malware (viruses and spyware), phishing and pharming.

▲ **Figure 5.21** Typical firewall set up

The main tasks carried out by a firewall include:

» to examine the 'traffic' between user's computer (or internal network) and a public network (for example, the internet)
» checks whether incoming or outgoing data meets a given set of criteria
» if the data fails the criteria, the firewall will block the 'traffic' and give the user (or network manager) a warning that there may be a security issue
» the firewall can be used to log all incoming and outgoing 'traffic' to allow later interrogation by the user (or network manager)
» criteria can be set so that the firewall prevents access to certain undesirable sites; the firewall can keep a list of all undesirable IP addresses
» it is possible for firewalls to ***help prevent*** viruses or hackers entering the user's computer (or internal network)

» the user is warned if some software on their system is trying to access an external data source (for example, automatic software upgrade); the user is given the option of allowing it to go ahead or request that such access is denied.

The firewall can be a hardware interface which is located somewhere between the computer and the internet connection. Alternatively, the firewall can be software installed on a computer; in some cases, it is part of the operating system.

However, there are certain circumstances where the firewall can't prevent potential harmful 'traffic':

» it cannot prevent individuals, on internal networks, using their own hardware devices (e.g. modems, smartphones) to bypass the firewall
» employee misconduct or carelessness cannot be controlled by firewalls (for example, control of passwords or user accounts)
» users on stand-alone computers can choose to disable the firewall, leaving their computer open to harmful 'traffic' from the internet.

All of these issues require management control or personal control (on a single computer) to ensure that the firewall is allowed to do its job effectively.

Proxy servers

Proxy servers act as an intermediate between the user and a web server:

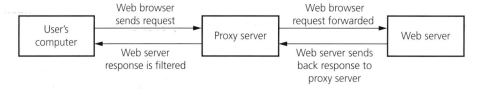

▲ **Figure 5.22** Proxy server

Features of proxy servers:

» allows internet traffic to be filtered; it is possible to block access to a website if necessary
» keeps users' IP addresses secret which improves security
» if the internet traffic is valid, access to the web server is allowed
» if the internet traffic is invalid, access to the web server is denied
» it is possible to block requests from certain IP addresses
» prevents direct access to a web server by sitting between the user and the web server
» if an attack is launched, it hits the proxy server instead – this helps to prevent hacking, DoS, and so on
» used to direct invalid traffic away from web servers which gives additional protection
» by using the feature known as a cache, it is possible to speed up access to information/data from a website; when the website is first visited, the home page is stored on the proxy server; when the user next visits the website, it now comes from the proxy server cache instead, giving much faster access
» proxy servers can also act as firewalls.

Privacy settings

Privacy settings are the controls available on web browsers, social networks and other websites that are designed to limit who can access and see a user's personal profile. They were discussed earlier in the section on access rights. Privacy settings can refer to:

» a 'do not track' setting; the intention here is to stop websites collecting and using browsing data which leads to improved security
» a check to see if payment methods have been saved on websites; this is a useful safety feature which prevents the need to type in payment details again (every time you have type in financial details, there will be a risk of data interception)
» safer browsing; an alert is given when the browser encounters a potentially dangerous website (the undesirable website will be in a 'blacklist' stored on the user's computer)
» web browser privacy options (e.g. storing browsing history, storing cookies)
» website advertising opt-outs; a website may be tracked by any number of third parties who gather information about your browsing behaviour for advertising purposes
» apps; for instance, the sharing of location data in map apps can be switched off.

Secure sockets layer (SSL)

Secure Sockets Layer (SSL) is a type of protocol – a set of rules used by computers to communicate with each other across a network. This allows data to be sent and received securely over the internet.

When a user logs onto a website, SSL encrypts the data – only the user's computer and the web server are able to make sense of what is being transmitted. A user will know if SSL is being applied when they see https or the small padlock 🔒 in the status bar at the top of the screen.

The address window in the browser when https protocol is being applied, rather than just http protocol, is quite different:

| using https: | 🔒 secure | https://www.xxxx.org/documents |
| using http: | ⓘ | http://www.yyyy.co.uk/documents |

Figure 5.23 shows what happens when a user wants to access a secure website and receive and send data to it:

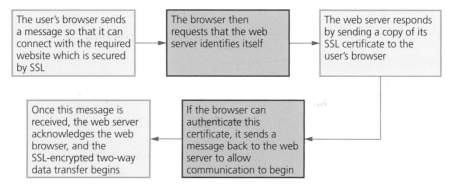

The user's browser sends a message so that it can connect with the required website which is secured by SSL → The browser then requests that the web server identifies itself → The web server responds by sending a copy of its SSL certificate to the user's browser

Once this message is received, the web server acknowledges the web browser, and the SSL-encrypted two-way data transfer begins ← If the browser can authenticate this certificate, it sends a message back to the web server to allow communication to begin

▲ **Figure 5.23** Secure sockets layer (SSL)

The term **SSL certificate** was mentioned in Figure 5.23. An SSL certificate is a form of digital certificate which is used to authenticate a website. This means any communication or data exchange between browser and website is secure provided this certificate can be authenticated.

Examples of where SSL would be used:

>> online banking and all online financial transactions
>> online shopping/commerce
>> when sending software out to a restricted list of users
>> sending and receiving emails
>> using cloud storage facilities
>> intranets and extranets (as well as the internet)
>> Voice over Internet Protocols (VoIP) when carrying out video chatting and/or audio chatting over the internet
>> used in instant messaging
>> when making use of a social networking site.

Activity 5.6

1   Which computer terms (used in this chapter) are being described below?

a   a user is granted access only after successfully presenting two pieces of evidence to verify or identify who they are

b   uses a cache to speed up access to web pages from a website

c   controls that are used on social networks and other websites to allow users to limit who can access data from their stored profile

d   protocol that is used to allow data to be sent securely over a network, such as the internet

e   software or hardware that sits between a computer and an external network which monitors and filters out all incoming and outgoing traffic

f   supplies domain names for internet hosts and is used to find IP addresses of domain names

g   use of unique human characteristics to identify a user as a form of authentication

h   made up of three types of identification:
    –   something you know
    –   something you have
    –   something you are

i   manipulation of people into breaking normal security procedures and best practices to gain illegal access to a user's computer system

j   malicious code stored on a user's hard drive or web server used to redirect a browser to a fake website without their knowledge

2   Describe how SSL and TLS certificates are used to ensure that secure sharing of data between a browser and website takes place.

3   a   Describe three things you should look out for when deciding whether or not an email is a potential phishing scam.

    b   Identify at least three potentials problems with this email from a company called Watson, Williams and Co:

> **From:** WW and Co <accounts@customer nr 012305555>
> **To:** customer 012305555
> **Sent:** February 15th 2021 @ 13:45
> **Subject:** Payment of January 2021 account
>
> Dear WW & Co customer
>
> We not able to take payments for account 012305555 on January 30th Please re-submit account details immediatly to the following address:
>
> **Customer accounts link**

▶ Extension

For those students considering the study of this subject at A Level, the following extension to SSL may be of interest.

Transport Layer Security (TLS)

Transport Layer Security (TLS) is a more modern and more secure version of SSL. It is a form of protocol that ensures the security and privacy of data between devices and users when communicating over a network (for example, the internet). It is essentially designed to provide encryption, authentication and data integrity in a more effective way than its predecessor, SSL. When a website and client communicate over the internet, TLS is designed to prevent third party eavesdropping which could cause a breach of security. TLS is comprised of two main layers:

» record protocol – this part of the communication can be used with or without encryption (it contains the data being transmitted over the network/internet)

» handshake protocol – this permits the web server and client to authenticate each other and to make use of encryption algorithms (a secure session between client and server is then established).

Only the most recent web browsers support both SSL and TLS which is why the older, less secure, SSL is still used in many cases (although very soon SSL won't be supported and users will have to adopt the newer TLS protocol if they wish to access the internet using a browser). The main differences between SSL and TLS can be summarised as follows:

» it is possible to extend TLS by adding new authentication methods (unlike SSL)

» TLS can make use of session caching which improves the overall performance of the communication when compared to SSL (see below)

» TLS separates the handshaking process from the record protocol (layer) where all the data is held.

Session caching

When opening a TLS session, it requires considerable computer time (due mainly to complex cryptographic processes taking place). The use of session caching can avoid the need to utilise as much computer time for each connection. TLS can either establish a new session or attempt to resume an existing session; using the latter can considerably boost the system performance.

Summary

As already indicated, two of the main functions of SSL/TLS are:

» encryption of data

» identifying client and server to ensure each knows 'who they are communicating with'.

We will now consider how this is done:

Stage 1

Once the client types the URL into the browser and hits the <enter> key, several steps will occur before any actual encrypted data is sent; this is known as the handshaking stage.

Stage 2

The client's browser now requests secure pages (https) from the web server.

Stage 3

The web server sends back the TLS digital certificate (which also contains the public key) – the certificate is digitally signed by a third party called the Certificate Authority (CA).

Stage 4

Once the client's browser receives the digital certificate it checks:

» the digital signature of the CA (is it one of those in the browser's trusted store – a list of trusted CAs is part of the browser which the client downloads to their computer)

» that the start and end dates shown on the certificate are still valid

» that the domain listed in the certificate is an exact match with the domain requested by the client in the first place

Stage 5

Once the browser trusts the digital certificate, the public key (which forms part of the digital certificate) is used by the browser to generate a temporary session key with the web server; this session key is then sent back to the web server.

Stage 6

The web server uses its private key to decrypt the session key and then sends back an acknowledgement that is encrypted using the same session key).

Stage 7

The browser and web server can now encrypt all the data/traffic sent over the connection using this session key; a secure communication can now take place.

In this chapter, you have learnt about:

✔ the difference between the internet and the World Wide Web
✔ what is meant by a URL
✔ the purpose of hypertext transfer protocols (http and https)
✔ the purpose and function of a (web) browser
✔ how to locate and retrieve web pages from a website
✔ session and persistent cookies
✔ digital currency and blockchaining
✔ cyber security threats (brute force attacks, data interception, DDoS, hacking and social engineering)
✔ malware (viruses, worms, Trojan horses, spyware, adware and ransomware)
✔ phishing and pharming
✔ ways of alleviating cyber security threats (anti-malware, access levels, authentication, firewalls, proxy servers and SSL)
✔ improving security using automatic software updates, privacy settings and looking for security clues in emails and URL links.

Key terms used throughout this chapter

internet – the world-wide interconnection of networks; the internet makes use of TCP and IP protocols

World Wide Web – a massive collection of web pages and is based on hypertext transfer protocols (http and https)

(web) browser – software that connects to a domain name server (DNS) to locate IP addresses; a browser interprets HTML web pages sent to a user's computer so that the user can read documents and watch multimedia

hypertext mark-up language (HTML) – the language used to design, display and format web pages, and to write http(s) protocols

uniform resource locator (URL) – a text-based address for a web page

hypertext transfer protocol secure (https) – http with extra security (such as SSL) applied

hyperlink – highlighted text or an image that is activated by clicking and links to further text, images, a web page or a website

domain name server (DNS) – a server that looks up domain names for websites (for example, www.hoddereducation.com) in order to find the IP addresses that a computer needs to locate the web servers (for example, 107.162.140.19)

cookie – a text file sent from a website to a user's browser; it is used to remember user preferences each time they visit the website

user preferences – settings or options stored in cookies that can remember customised web pages or indicate browsing history to target adverts

session cookie – a cookie that is stored temporarily on a computer; it is deleted when the browser is closed or the website session ends

persistent cookies – a cookie that is stored on the user's hard drive and only deleted when the expiry date is reached or the cookie is deleted by the user

virtual shopping basket – an area of memory in a website where items a user wishes to purchase are temporarily stored; items remain in the basket until payment is made or the session has ended

digital currency – currency (a system of money) that exists in electronic form only; it has no physical form and is essentially data on a database

cryptocurrency – a form of digital currency that uses a chain of decentralised computers to control and monitor transactions

cryptography – the protection of data/information by use of coding; it usually involves encryption and decryption

blockchain – a decentralised database where all transactions are stored; it consists of a number of interconnected computers but not a central server

timestamp – a digital record of the date and time that a data block is created in blockchain networks

proof-of-work – the algorithm used in blockchain networks to confirm a transaction and to produce new blocks to add to the chain; special users called miners complete and monitor transactions on the network for a reward

brute force attack – a 'trial and error' method used by cybercriminals to crack passwords by finding all possible combinations of letters, numbers and symbols until the password is found

word list – a text file containing a collection of words used in a brute force attack

data interception – an attempt to eavesdrop on a wired or wireless network transmission; cybercriminal often use packet sniffing or access point mapping / wardriving to intercept data

packet sniffing – a method used by a cybercriminal to examine data packets being sent over a network and to find the contents of a data packet, which are sent back to the cybercriminal

wardriving – using a laptop, antenna, GPS device and software to intercept Wi-Fi signals and illegally obtain data; sometimes called Access Point Mapping

wired equivalency privacy (WEP) encryption protocol security – an algorithm for wireless networks to protect them against data interception

denial of service (DoS) attack – a cyberattack in which cybercriminals seek to disrupt the normal operation of a website by flooding it with requests; also used to clog up a user's mailbox by sending out thousands of spam emails

distributed denial of service (DDoS) attack – a denial of service (DoS) attack in which the fake requests come from many different computers, which makes it harder to stop

spam – unsolicited emails sent to a user's mailbox

hacking – the act of gaining illegal access to a computer system without the owner's permission

malware – programs (such as viruses, worms and Trojan horses) installed on a user's computer with the aim of deleting, corrupting or manipulating data illegally

virus – a program or program code that replicates itself with the intention of deleting or corrupting files or by causing the computer system to malfunction

active host – functioning software that a virus can affect by attaching itself to the code or by altering the code to allow the virus to carry out its attack

worm – a stand-alone type of malware that can self-replicate; unlike viruses, worms don't need an active host; they can spread throughout a network without the need for any action by an end-user

Trojan horse – a type of malware that is designed to look like legitimate software but contains malicious code that can cause damage to a computer system

spyware – a type of malware that gathers information by monitoring a user's activities on a computer and sends the gathered information back to the cybercriminal who sent out the spyware

adware – a type of malware that attempts to flood the end-user with unwanted advertising

ransomware – a type of malware that encrypts data on a user's computer and 'holds the data hostage' until a ransom is paid

phishing – sending out legitimate-looking emails designed to trick the recipients into giving their personal details to the sender of the email

spear phishing – similar to phishing but targeting specific people or organisations rather than carrying out a blanket attack

pharming – redirecting a user to a fake website in order to illegally obtain personal data about the user without their knowledge; unlike phishing, pharming is initiated without needing any action by the user

DNS cache poisoning – altering IP addresses on a domain name server (DNS) with the intention of redirecting a user's browser to a fake website; carried out by a pharmer (see pharming) or hacker (see hacking)

social engineering – manipulating people into breaking normal security procedures (such as giving away their password) in order to gain illegal access to computer systems or to place malware on their computer

access levels – different levels of access in a computer system allowing a hierarchy of access levels depending on user's level of security

anti-spyware – software that detects and removes spyware programs installed on a system; the software is based on typical spyware rules or known file structures

authentication – the process of proving a user's identity by using something they know, something they have or something unique to them

biometrics – type of authentication that uses a unique human characteristic, such as fingerprints, voice or retina blood vessel pattern

two-step verification – a type of authentication that requires two methods of verification to prove the identity of a user

patch – an update for software that is developed to improve the software and/or to remove any bugs

typo squatting – the use by cybercriminals of subtle spelling errors in website addresses used to trick users into visiting their fake websites

firewall – software or hardware that sits between a computer and an external network (for example, the internet); the firewall monitors and filters all incoming and outgoing traffic

proxy server – a server that acts as an intermediary server through which internet requests are processed; it often makes use of cache memory to speed up web page access

privacy settings – controls available on social networking and other websites which allow users to limit who can access their profile or what they are allowed to see

secure sockets layer (SSL) – a security protocol used when sending data over a network (such as the internet)

SSL certificate – a form of digital certificate which is used to authenticate a website; providing the SSL certificate can be authenticated, any communication or data exchange between browser and website is secure

Exam-style questions

1 a i What is meant by a *cookie*? [1]

   ii Describe the difference between a *session cookie* and a *persistent cookie*. [2]

   iii Give **three** uses of persistent cookies. [3]

2 A company has several offices. It uses the Internet to transfer data between offices. The company also makes payments to staff and suppliers using online banking.

The company are concerned about spyware and other security aspects of using the Internet.

a Explain what is meant by spyware **and** how it is used to obtain data. [3]

b The company uses a web page to log on to the online bank.
Identify **one** method that could be used by the online bank to reduce the impact of spyware when logging on.
State **how** the method prevents the use of spyware. [2]

c The company has installed a firewall as part of its data security.
Describe how a firewall can help protect against unauthorised access to data. [4]

d State **two** other methods the company could use to help prevent unauthorised access to data.
Method 1
Method 2 [2]

3 Six statements are shown on the left and six computer terms are shown on the right.
By drawing lines, connect each statement correct term. [6]

set of rules that must be obeyed when transferring files and data across the internet	cookie
software used to access, translate and display web pages on a user's screen	World Wide Web (WWW)
collection of multimedia web pages and other information on websites; these resources are accessed by a browser	digital currency
worldwide collection of interconnected network computers that make use of TCP and IP protocols	hypertext transfer protocol (http)
small file or program downloaded when user visits a website; it remembers user preferences and other data	internet
financial system which allows the transfer of funds and purchasing items electronically	web browser

4 a John uses two step verification when purchasing some items from a website. There are five stages in the process. These stages are listed below but are not in the correct order.
Place the five stages into their correct order.
A – user takes note of the one-time authentication code
B – user enters the one-time authentication code into the original device
C – user enters website user name and password into device
D – user is authenticated and allowed access to website to order items
E – one-time authentication code sent to user's email address [4]

b One form of authentication is fingerprint recognition. A school is using fingerprints to uniquely identify each student. The system is used to act as a register instead of the existing manual system. Describe how fingerprint recognition can be used so that the school knows exactly which students are presently attending. [5]

5 a Describe four ways cybercriminals can use to trick a user into downloading malicious code onto their computers using social engineering. [4]

b There are four stages in the course of action when a cybercriminal targets an individual using social engineering. Describe each of the four stages in the diagram below which depicts these stages.

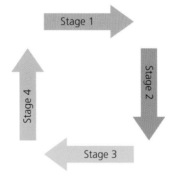

[4]

c Some cybercriminals have decided to hack into a company's financial system.
Customers buy goods using digital currency.
i How does digital currency vary from traditional fiat currency? [2]
ii Explain how blockchaining could protect the company and the customers from hackers. [4]

6 HTML can be used to create the structure and the presentation of web pages.

   a Describe what is meant by HTML structure. [2]

   b Gloria writes a paragraph as an answer to an examination question about accessing a website.

      Use the list given to complete Gloria's answer by inserting the correct **four** missing terms. Not all terms will be used.

      – browser
      – cookies
      – Hypertext Markup Language (HTML)
      – hypertext transfer protocol (http)
      – hypertext transfer protocol secure (https)
      – Internet Protocol address (IP address)
      – Media Access Control address (MAC address)
      – web server

      The user enters the URL of the website. The _____ uses the DNS server to look up the _____ of the website.

      The browser sends a request to the _____ to obtain the website files. The website files are sent as _____ that is interpreted by the browser. [4]

Cambridge IGCSE Computer Science 0478, Paper 11 Q9, Oct/Nov 2019

7 An art gallery has a website that is used to display and sell art.

   a The gallery uses Secure Socket Layer (SSL) to provide a secure connection when selling art.

      Describe the process of SSL and how it provides a secure connection. [6]

   b The art gallery also uses a firewall.

      Six statements are given about firewalls.

      Tick (✔) to show if the statement is **True** or **False**.

Statement	True (✔)	False (✔)
Firewalls are only available as hardware devices		
Firewalls allow a user to set rules for network traffic		
Firewalls will automatically stop all malicious traffic		
Firewalls only examine traffic entering a network		
Firewalls encrypt all data that is transmitted around a network		
Firewalls can be used to block access to certain websites		

[6]

Cambridge IGCSE Computer Science 0478, Paper 11 Q8, May/June 2019

Automated and emerging technologies

Whether it's robots welding cars in a factory, autonomous grass cutters or smart road signs, the effects of automated systems can be seen all around us. These automated systems are becoming increasingly sophisticated and complex. This chapter will consider examples of automated systems, robotics and artificial intelligence (AI) and how they affect our everyday lives. This is by no means an exhaustive list and the reader is advised to try to keep up to date with all the latest developments.

6.1 Automated systems

6.1.1 Sensors, microprocessors and actuators

An **automated system** is a combination of software and hardware (for example, sensors, microprocessors and actuators) that is designed and programmed to work automatically without the need of any human intervention. However, such systems often involve human monitoring.

The role of sensors, microprocessors and actuators was discussed at great length in Section 3.2. It may be worth the reader revisiting this part of the book before continuing with this chapter; you should remember that:

Link

See Section 3.2 for more details on sensors, microprocessors and actuators.

» Sensors are input devices that take readings from their surroundings and send this data to a microprocessor or computer. If the data is analogue, it is first converted into a digital format by an analogue-digital converter (ADC).
» The microprocessor will process the data and take the necessary action based on programming.
» This will involve some form of output, usually involving signals sent to actuators to control motors, wheels, solenoids, and so on.

Advice

» On first sight, all of the examples in 6.1 will appear very complicated.
» However, you will not learn any of the industrial or scientific processes described fully in this chapter. Any processes used in any questions will be fully described to you (possibly including a diagram).
» You basically need to go through each example carefully and understand the processes taking place. In other words, what is the interaction between the sensors, actuators and microprocessor/computer to allow the process to take place.
» On completion of Section 6.1 the important learning process is to understand the sensor, actuator and microprocessor interaction; to this end, you need to do two things:
  – for each example, complete a table as follows:

Example	Which sensors are used?	What is the function of the actuators?	What is the function of the computer?	Additional notes

  – then try the activities 6.1 to 6.7 to make sure you fully understand the processes going on.
  You will then find out that the examples were much easier than they appeared at first.

6.1.2 Advantages and disadvantages of automated systems

In this section, a number of examples will be used to show the advantages and disadvantages of using automated systems. This list is by no means exhaustive, and simply intends to show the role of sensors, microprocessors (or computers) and actuators in the following application areas:

» industrial
» transport
» agriculture
» weather
» gaming
» lighting
» science.

Industrial applications

Automated systems are used in a number of industrial applications. Many of the automated systems involve robotics, which is covered in more depth in Section 6.2.

In recent years, the focus on increased automation has led to improved quality and flexibility. For example, in the manufacture of car engines, when done manually, the installation of pistons into the engine had an error-rate of ~1.5%; with automated systems, the error-rate has fallen to 0.00001%.

We will now consider two very different industrial applications.

❓ Example 1: A nuclear power station

A key use of automated systems is in the control and monitoring of a nuclear power station. This is a good example, since automation gives increased safety both in the process itself and to the workforce. At the centre of the system is a **distributed control system (DCS)**. DCS is essentially a powerful computer that has been programmed to monitor and control the whole process with no human interaction required:

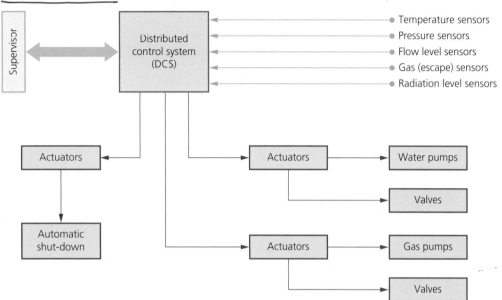

▲ **Figure 6.1** Nuclear power station (automated system)

Data from a number of sensors is sent to a DCS (computer) – if the data is analogue, it must first be converted into digital format using an ADC. The DCS will have access to a large database containing operational data and parameters. If any action needs to be taken, then signals will be sent to the appropriate actuators to operate pumps, valves or even an emergency shutdown system. The key here is that the system is fully automated. A human operator (the supervisor) will sit in a remote control room where a schematic of the process will show on a large screen. While the process is fully automatic, the supervisor can still override the DCS and shut down the process.

The main advantages of this automated system are:
» much faster than a human operator to take any necessary action
» much safer (an automated system is more likely to make timely interventions than a human; it also keeps humans away from a dangerous environment)
» the process is more likely to run under optimum conditions since any small changes needed can be identified very quickly and action taken
» in the long run, it is less expensive (an automatic system replaces most of the workforce who would need to monitor the process 24 hours a day).

The main disadvantages of this automated system are:
» expensive to set up in the first place and needs considerable testing
» always possible for a set of conditions to occur that were never considered during testing which could have safety implications (hence the need for a supervisor)
» any computerised system is subject to cyberattacks no matter how good the system (one way round this is to have no external links to the DCS; although the weak link could potentially be the connection to the supervisor)
» automated systems always need enhanced maintenance which can be expensive.

? Example 2: Manufacture of paracetamol

= Actuators

= Sensors

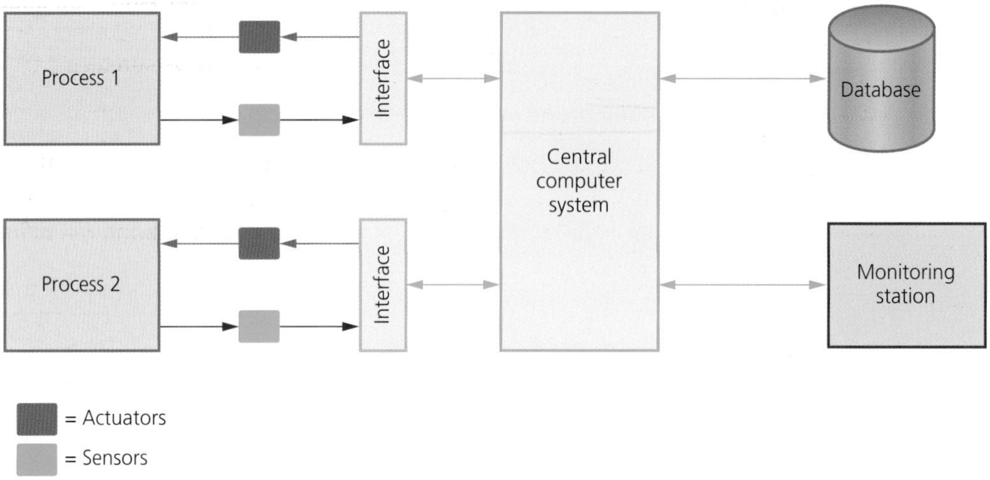

▲ **Figure 6.2** Manufacture of paracetamol (automated system)

This automated system also depends on sensors, a computer, actuators and software. Process 1 is the manufacture of the paracetamol. Process 2 is the making of the solid tablets. Both processes are monitored by a number of sensors that send their data back to a central computer. The computer consults its database to ensure both processes are operating within correct parameters. Any necessary action is taken by the computer, sending signals to the appropriate actuator to operate pumps, valves, heaters, stirrers or pistons to ensure both processes can operate without any human intervention. Again, this system uses a remote monitoring station manned by an operator. The system is fully automated, but the operator can override the central computer system if necessary.

The main advantages of this automated system are:
>> much faster than a human operator to take any necessary action
>> much safer (an automated system is more likely to make timely interventions than a human if necessary; it also keeps humans away from a potentially dangerous environment)
>> the process is more likely to run under optimum conditions since any small changes needed can be identified very quickly and action taken
>> in the long run, it is less expensive (an automatic system replaces most of the workforce who would need to monitor the process 24 hours a day)
>> more efficient use of materials
>> higher productivity
>> more consistent results.

The main disadvantages of this automated system are:
>> expensive to set up in the first place and needs considerable testing
>> always possible for a set of conditions to occur that were never considered during testing which could have safety implications (hence the need for a monitoring station)
>> automated systems always need enhanced maintenance which can be expensive
>> any computerised system is subject to cyberattacks no matter how good the system.

There are many other examples; the above two examples can be applied to many other industrial processes.

Activity 6.1

A company manufactures fizzy drinks that are then labelled and bottled:

The system is fully automatic. Sensors are used to ensure the correct amount of each ingredient is added. A stirrer is activated whenever ingredients are added. The bottling plant is again monitored by sensors to ensure the correct amount of drink is added to each bottle, and that the right amount of carbon dioxide gas is added to each bottle. The whole process is computer-controlled and is totally automatic.

a   Describe how the sensors, actuators and central computer would be used to monitor and control this bottling plant automatically. You may wish to add/show sensors and actuators in the diagram given above.

b   Finally, describe the advantages and disadvantages of fully automating this bottling plant (you can assume that none of the ingredients used in making the drink are harmful).

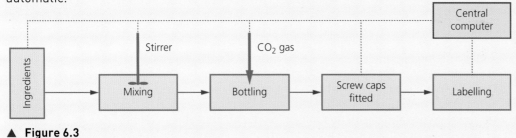

▲ **Figure 6.3**

> **Find out more**

Find out:
i   which sensors are used in modern aircraft when using auto pilot
ii   how sensors and actuators are used to control the flaps, throttle and rudder
iii   why airplanes use the 'three computer system'.

Transport

As with industrial processes, many of the automated systems in transport refer to robotic systems (for example, autonomous buses/cars, autonomous trains and unpiloted aircraft). These will be considered in Section 6.2.

But automated systems are still used in manually controlled transport, which includes cars, buses/lorries, trains and aircraft. (Examples 3 and 4 which follow, will use cars as the application.)

For example, modern trains will use an automatic signal control system. If the driver of the train goes through a red (stop) light, then the computer will automatically stop the train. This will make use of sensors at the side of the track sending signals to the on-board computer; actuators will be used to apply the brakes. Airplanes extensively use automatic pilots, which control the wing flaps, throttle and rudder to maintain the correct height, speed and direction.

? Example 3: Self-parking cars

Step 1

Step 2

▲ **Figure 6.4** Self-parking cars

The driver goes along the row of parked cars. On-board sensors and cameras gauge the size of any parking spaces, and the on-board computer warns the driver if a suitable space has been found. The driver then selects auto-parking and the on-board computer takes over. Actuators are used to operate the steering rack, brakes and throttle under the full control of the computer. This allows the car in Figure 6.4 to go from Step 1 to Step 2 automatically and complete the parking manoeuvre with no driver intervention.

Sensors in the bumpers of the car are both transmitters and receivers. The sensors transmit signals that bounce off objects and are reflected back. The car's on-board computer uses the amount of time it takes for the signal to return to the sensor to calculate the position of any objects. The sensors give the computer a 3D image of its surroundings. This allows the car to fit into its parking space automatically with no driver intervention. (Note: cheaper and older self-parking systems are not fully automatic; they require the driver to operate the brakes and throttle manually and only control the steering.)

The main advantages of this automated system are:
» allows the same number of cars to use fewer parking spaces
» avoids traffic disruption in cities (a manually controlled car takes several seconds to fit into a parking space)
» cars can fit into smaller spaces
» fewer dents and scratches to cars (reduced insurance claims)
» safer system since sensors monitor all objects, including young children (the car's manoeuvre will be stopped if any new object is encountered)
» very consistent results.

The main disadvantages of this automated system are:
» over-reliance on automated systems by the driver (loss of skills)
» faulty/dirty sensors or cameras can send false data/images to the on-board computer which could lead to a malfunction
» kerbing of wheels is a common problem since the sensors may not pick-up low kerbs
» expensive option that doesn't really save the driver any money
» requires additional maintenance to ensure it functions correctly at all times.

Activity 6.2

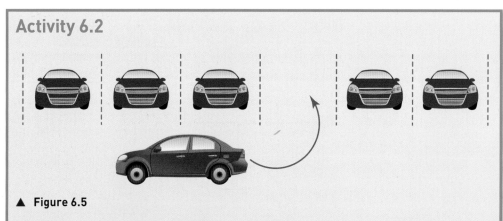

▲ **Figure 6.5**

This time the driver needs to reverse in between two other cars and park at 90° to the direction of travel.

Describe what additional information is needed to allow the car to park between two cars within the parallel lines.

What extra sensor device(s) might be needed to give this additional information?

❓ Example 4: Adaptive cruise control

▲ **Figure 6.6** Adaptive cruise control

Adaptive cruise control makes use of sensors, an on-board computer and actuators to allow a car to remain a safe distance from another vehicle.

The driver will set a cruising speed (for example, 100 kph) on his touch screen in the car. Lasers (set into the bumpers of the car) are used to send out signals constantly. The lasers bounce off the vehicle in front of the car and are reflected back to the car's sensors. The time taken for the signal to bounce back is used by the on-board computer to calculate the distance between the two vehicles. If the car is getting too close to the vehicle in front, the computer will send signals to slow the car down. This is done by actuators applying the brakes and/or reducing the throttle. If the distance between vehicles is greater than the safe distance, the computer will check to see if the current speed equals the value set by the driver. If the speed is different to the set speed, the computer sends signals to the actuators to increase or decrease the throttle.

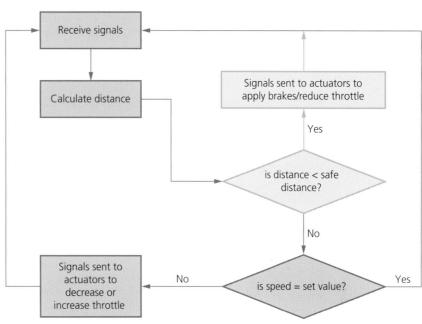

▲ **Figure 6.7** Flowchart showing how adaptive cruise control works

Activity 6.3

Assuming the following stopping distances:

Car's speed (kph)	Stopping distance (metres)
40	17
50	24
60	32
70	42
80	53
90	64
100	77
110	92
120	107

Using figure 6.7 and the data in the table above, explain how the on-board computer would calculate if a car was too close to the vehicle in front and apply the brakes if necessary. (It is not necessary to show all the maths, it is sufficient to explain what would need to be done. However, this could be a class exercise using a spreadsheet or small computer program).

Agriculture

There are many examples of the use of automated systems in agriculture. Again, many of the systems involve robotics, which is fully described in Section 6.2. We will now consider one important example that is being used in Brazil to irrigate crops automatically.

? Example 5: Automated system used in the Brazil irrigation system

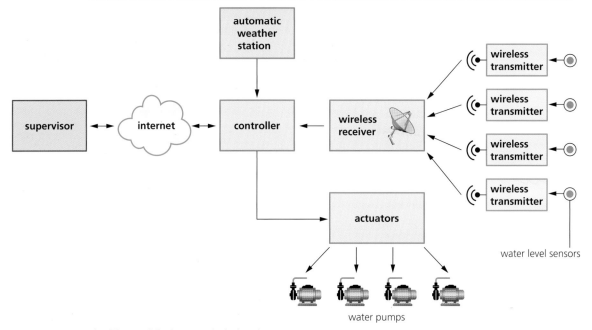

▲ **Figure 6.8** Automatic irrigation system

The watering of crops (irrigation) is fully automatic and also involves considerable amounts of wireless transmission. This allows the system to be used in very remote areas that are vast in size – some of the fields are more than 10 km² in area.

Data from an automatic weather station (see next example) is received by the **controller** (a computer system) every ten minutes. This is particularly important if very wet or very dry conditions are being predicted or detected by the weather station. Ultrasonic water level sensors are used in the crop fields that measure the amount of water in the irrigation channels. The sensors send their data back via wireless transmitters. This data is then picked up by the wireless receiver, which sends the data back to the controller. The controller then uses this data, together with the data from the weather station, to decide whether it is necessary to stop or start a series of water pumps. This is done by sending signals to actuators, which operate the pumps. Although the whole system is fully automatic, a supervisor still monitors the process remotely. Using a schematic of a number of processes on a computer screen and via internet links to the controllers, the supervisor can oversee several irrigation processes from one central point. If the supervisor wishes to further increase or reduce the water supply in any of the irrigation systems, they can override the controller if necessary.

The main advantages of this automated system are:
» reduced labour costs since the system only needs a supervisor to monitor vast areas (if any maintenance is needed, then a dedicated team can cover all of the irrigation systems rather than having a separate team for each system)
» better and more efficient control of the irrigation process
» better control of precious resources, such as water

>> faster response than a human having to manually check many kilometres of irrigation channels
>> safer (temperatures in the fields could be 40°C and other risks could exist)
>> different crops may require different irrigation requirements (for example, rice crops need flooding conditions, whereas orange trees like dry conditions); it is possible to program the controllers so that different growing conditions can be maintained simultaneously.

The main disadvantages of this automated system are:
>> expensive to set up initially (expensive equipment needs to be bought)
>> very high maintenance costs are associated with automated systems (also require specialist technicians if a fault occurs, which could be a problem in some remote areas of the world)
>> increased need to maintain the water channels to ensure the system works correctly at all times (a blocked or collapsed channel wouldn't be picked up by the automated system, which could result in some areas being over-watered and some areas being starved of water).

Weather (stations)

Automated weather stations are designed to save labour and to gather information from remote regions or where constant weather data is a requirement. Automated weather stations require a microprocessor, storage (database), battery (usually with solar-powered charging) and a range of sensors:

>> thermometer (to measure temperature)
>> anemometer (to measure wind speed)
>> hygrometer (to measure humidity)
>> barometer (to measure air pressure)
>> level sensor (to measure rain fall)
>> light sensor (to measure hours of daylight).

The data from sensors is all sent to a microprocessor; any calculations are then done (for example, calculate hours of daylight, actual rainfall and wind direction). The data from the sensors and the calculated values are then stored on a central database. Some automated weather stations are sited near airports, where reports are sent out automatically every five minutes to pilots in the vicinity of the airport.

The only part of the weather station that needs to use actuators is the 'tipping bucket rain gauge'. At a pre-determined time interval, a signal is sent from the microprocessor to an actuator to operate a piston, which tips a bucket that was collecting rain water. The water is tipped into a vessel where level sensors are then used to measure the amount of rainfall that fell during the required time interval.

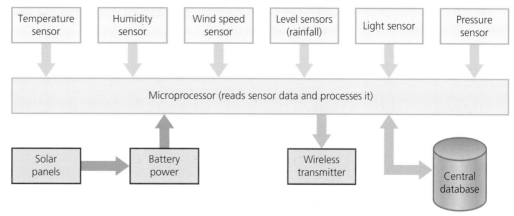

▲ **Figure 6.9** Automated weather station

Activity 6.4

Find out all of the advantages and disadvantages of using automated weather stations.

Gather all the results from the whole class, and put your results into a table as follows:

Advantages	Disadvantages

Activity 6.5

1 Describe how automated weather stations can be used in the fight against climate change.

2 A large greenhouse is being used to grow tomatoes under controlled conditions.

For optimum growth, the tomatoes require the right lighting levels, correct temperature and regular watering. Describe how automated systems could be used to ensure the correct growing conditions are maintained. The only human involvement would be as a remote supervisor.

(You might find it useful to draw a diagram of your automated system showing sensors, microprocessor and any actuators.)

3 A new car being developed utilises many automated systems. In particular:

i the ability to recognise road signs

ii the ability to predict when to change to the correct gear for the road condition.

Describe how sensors, actuators and an on-board computer allow the car to take the necessary action automatically if:

– it encounters road works with a speed limit of 60 kph so that the car maintains the correct speed

– the car is on a very twisty road where the correct gear is needed for optimum performance.

4 One example of an automated system is the control of entry and exit to a car park. Cameras take a photograph of a car's number plate on entry before opening a barrier. At the exit, another camera captures a car's number plate before raising the barrier. Describe how sensors, cameras, actuators and a microprocessor can be used to:

i control the raising and lowering of the entry and exit barriers

ii ensure that the car exiting the car park has paid the correct parking fee before it can exit

iii describe the advantages and disadvantages of this car parking system.

Gaming

Gaming devices involve sensors to give a degree of realism to games:

» **accelerometers** (these measure acceleration and deceleration and therefore measure and respond to tilting the gaming device forward/backward and side to side)

» **proximity** sensors (used in smart touch pads; here electrodes are embedded in touch pads that can detect hand/finger position thus increasing user awareness).

Embedded accelerometers and proximity sensors (together with a microcontroller) in games consoles allow increased human interaction with the game. This allows players to take actions that simulate real events happening, giving a more immersive games experience.

Activity 6.6

What are the advantages and disadvantages of using these immersive games consoles?

Are any other sensors used in games consoles other than accelerometers and proximity sensors?

Lighting

Microprocessor-controlled lighting was discussed in Section 3.1.5 (Embedded systems). The example used in Chapter 3 was the control of lighting in an office using:

» light sensors (to automatically switch lights on or off depending on the ambient lighting)
» motion sensors (to automatically turn lights on in a room when somebody enters)
» infrared sensors (to be used either as a motion detector or as part of the security system).

? Example 6: Lighting system in a house

The example we will consider here is used in a house:
» where lights in the garden are turned on automatically when someone enters the garden or it turns dark
» where a lighting show is part of a microprocessor-controlled water fountain display; the lighting only comes on when it becomes dark.

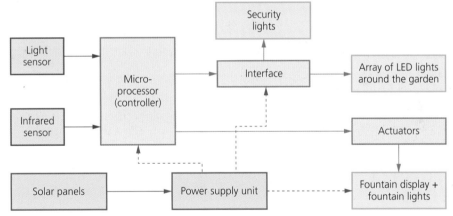

▲ **Figure 6.10** Automatic lighting system

As it becomes dark, the light sensor value will change, and the microprocessor will send signals to the interface to control the array of LED lights around the garden. Data from the infrared sensor would also be used (during day and night) as a security device whenever the house is unoccupied.

Also, as it becomes dark, the lighting show in the fountain could also be initiated. This could involve a pre-programmed display involving changing colours under the control of the microprocessor. The fountain display itself will also be under microprocessor control with signals being sent to actuators to turn water pumps on and off according to the installed program. The whole system will be fully automated.

The main advantages of this automated system are:
» it is possible to control light sources automatically
» a reduced energy consumption (since lights are only turned on when necessary)
» wireless connections can be chosen which are much safer (no trailing wires)
» longer bulb life (due to dimming or switching off when not in use)
» possible to program new light displays for various occasions.

The main disadvantages of this automated system are:
» expensive to set the system up in the first place
» if wireless connections chosen (for safety reasons), they can be less reliable than wired systems
» to ensure consistent performance, the automated system will require more maintenance (which can be expensive).

Science

Automated systems in scientific research are widely used. There are literally thousands of possible applications. The example we will use here is the automatic control of a laboratory experiment which requires accuracy and repeatability.

? Example 7: Chemical process in a laboratory

Imagine an experiment in a pharmaceutical laboratory where two chemicals are reacted together in a vessel. One of the chemicals is being added from a piece of equipment ('A') known as a **burette** (which has a tap to control the flow of liquid; the tap is operated automatically using a small actuator) to a reaction vessel ('B'). Once the reaction is complete, it turns a bright orange colour (see Figure 6.11). The whole process is under microprocessor control:

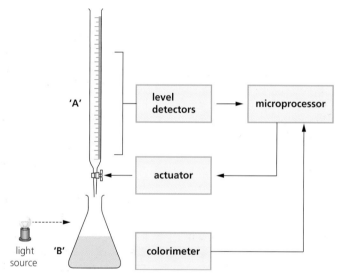

▲ **Figure 6.11** Pharmaceutical laboratory experiment

The level sensors measure how much liquid is being added from 'A'; this data is sent to a microprocessor. Readings are also sent to the microprocessor from a colorimeter next to vessel 'B' (this instrument checks the colour of the chemical produced). The microprocessor controls the opening and closing of the tap in 'A'; this is done by sending signals to an actuator that operates the tap. This means the microprocessor has automatic control of the experiment with no human interaction needed. This type of automated system is of great benefit to pharmaceutical companies when developing new drugs and vaccines (several experiments can be carried out at the same time with only one person needed to monitor the system).

The main advantages of this automated system are:
» more consistent (repeatable) results
» less dangerous (especially if the chemicals used are hazardous)
» faster results (several different experiments can be done simultaneously)
» automatic analysis of the results is possible
» fewer highly trained staff needed for each experiment
» results/experiments can be monitored anywhere in the world in real time.

The main disadvantages of this automated system are:
>> less flexible than when using human technicians
>> security risks are always present if the data is being shared globally
>> equipment can be expensive to buy and set up in the first place.

Finally, there are many automated systems being used in both industry and scientific research that incorporate artificial intelligence (AI). It is therefore worth considering the generic advantages of using AI in these automated systems (also refer to Section 6.3):

>> ability to access and store vast amounts of facts (very important in research)
>> they are able to learn from huge amounts of available data that would overwhelm humans (or at the very least take them many months/years to do the same analysis)
>> they are able to see patterns in results that could be missed by humans.

While all of this is positive, there are a few disadvantages in this approach:

>> a change in skills set (is it the human or the AI that controls the research?)
>> AI is dependent on the data which trains it.

Activity 6.7

1 a Name suitable sensors for each of the following automated systems.

   i   Manufacture of a new vaccine that requires the mixing of four liquids in the ratio 1:2:3:4 as a single batch. The four liquids must be totally mixed and the temperature must be maintained at 35°C (+/- 1°C) which is a critical temperature.

   ii A lighting display has been set up in one room of an art gallery. A random sequence of different coloured lights is under microprocessor control. The display in the room only switches on when visitors walk into the room; at the same time, the room lights are also dimmed to give the most dramatic effect of the light display.

   iii A train uses automatic twin-doors. Both doors open automatically when the train stops. Both doors close again when no-one is still boarding or leaving the train. The doors have a safety mechanism so that a passenger cannot become trapped between the two closing doors. The train can only move off when every door on the train has been safely closed.

   b For **each** application in **part a**, give **two** advantages and **two** disadvantages of using automated systems.

2 The eight statements on the left-hand side of the table are either true or false. Tick (✓) the appropriate box to indicate which statements are true and which statements are false.

Statement	True	False
automated systems lead to less consistent results or less consistent products		
automated systems are more expensive to set up than traditional manual systems		
automated systems would be quickly overwhelmed by the amount of data presented to it		
automated systems are inherently less safe than manual systems		
automated systems generally require enhanced maintenance when compared to manual systems		
automated systems allow processes to run at optimum conditions at all times		
software failures, due to unforeseen conditions, are unlikely to impact on an automated system		
automated systems will react more quickly to unusual process conditions		

6.2 Robotics

6.2.1 What is robotics?

The word **robot** comes from the Czech word ***robota*** (which means 'forced labour') and the term was first used in the 1920s play 'Rossum's Universal Robots'. The concept of the robot has fired the imagination of science fiction writers for countless years; indeed Isaac Asimov even composed his ***three laws of robotics***:

» a robot may not injure a human through action or inaction
» a robot must obey orders given by humans, unless it comes into conflict with law 1
» a robot must protect itself, unless this conflicts with law 1.

So what is a robot in the real world? **Robotics** is a branch of (computer) science that brings together the design, construction and operation of robots. Robots can be found in:

▲ **Figure 6.12** Robot welder

» in the home
  – **autonomous** floor sweepers (see Figure 6.13)
  – autonomous lawn mower
  – ironing robots (for example, 'dressman')
  – pool cleaning
  – automatic window cleaners
  – entertainment ('friend' robots)

» factories
  – welding parts together
  – spray-painting panels on a car
  – fitting windscreens to cars
  – cutting out metal parts to a high precision
  – bottling and labelling plants
  – warehouses (automatic location of items)

▲ **Figure 6.13** Robot carpet sweeper

» drones
  – unmanned aerial vehicles (UAVs) are drones that are either remotely controlled or totally autonomous using embedded systems
  – can be used in reconnaissance (for example, taking aerial photographs)
  – can be used to make parcel deliveries (for example, Amazon).

▲ **Figure 6.14** Reconnaissance drone

6.2.2 Characteristics of a robot

To be correctly called a robot, they need to have the following characteristics:

1 Ability to sense their surroundings:
   - this is done via sensors (such as light, pressure, temperature, acoustic, and so on)
   - sensors allow a robot to recognise its immediate environment and gives it the ability to determine things like size, shape or weight of an object, detect if something is hot or cold, and so on; all sensor data is sent to a microprocessor or computer.

2 Have a degree of movement:
   - they can make use of wheels, cogs, pistons, gears (etc.) to carry out functions such as turning, twisting, moving backwards/forwards, gripping or lifting
   - they are **mechanical structures** made up of many parts (for example, motors, hydraulic pipes, actuators and circuit boards)
   - they contain many **electrical components** to allow them to function
   - can make use of **end effectors** (different attachments to allow them to carry out specific tasks such as welding, spraying, cutting or lifting).

3 Programmable:
   - they have a 'brain' known as a **controller** that determines the action to be taken to perform a certain task (the controller relies on data sent from sensors or cameras, for example)
   - controllers are **programmable** to allow the robots to do certain tasks.

It is important to realise that robotics and artificial intelligence (AI) are almost two entirely different fields:

TWO IMPORTANT NOTES:

1 Many robots don't possess artificial intelligence (AI) since they tend to do repetitive tasks rather than requiring adaptive human characteristics.
2 It is important not to confuse *physical robots* with *software robots* such as:
   - search engine *bots* or *WebCrawlers* (these 'robots' roam the internet scanning websites, categorising them for search purposes)
   - chat bots (these are programs that *pop up* on websites that seem to enter some form of conversation with the web user – see Section 6.3)

According to our definition above, software robots are not true robots.

Physical robots can be classified as **independent** or **dependent**:

» Independent robots:
   - have no direct human control (they are said to be **autonomous**, for example, an **autonomous** vehicle)
   - can replace the human activity totally (no human interaction is required for the robot to function fully).
» Dependent robots:
   - have a human who is interfacing directly with the robot (the human interface may be a computer or a control panel)
   - can supplement, rather than totally replace, the human activity (for example, in a car assembly plant where both humans and robots work together to produce a car).

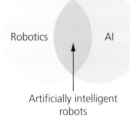

Robotics — AI

Artificially intelligent robots

▲ **Figure 6.15** Robots and AI

▲ **Figure 6.16** Independent robot

▲ **Figure 6.17** Dependent robot

6.2.3 The role of robots and their advantages and disadvantages

We will now consider the use of robots in a number of areas, together with the advantages and disadvantages of using robots in each of these areas:

» industry
» transport
» agriculture
» medicine
» domestic (home) use
» entertainment.

Industry

Robots are used in many areas of industry, from heavy lifting work right through to delicate procedures. Examples include: paint spraying of car bodies, welding bodywork on cars, manufacturing of microchips, manufacturing electrical goods and automatic warehouses.

Control of robots is either through embedded (built-in) microprocessors or directly linked to a computer system. Programming of the robot to do a series of tasks is generally done in two ways:

1 The robot is programmed with a sequence of instructions which allow it to carry out the series of tasks (for example, spraying a car body with paint).
2 Alternatively, a human operator manually carries out the series of tasks; this can be done in two ways. In our example, we will assume an object is being painted using a robot arm.
Figure 6.18 shows a robot arm equipped with a spray gun end-effector. Different **end-effectors** allow the robot arm to carry out many different tasks:
  i the robot arm is guided manually by a worker when spraying the object; each movement of the arm is stored as an instruction on the computer; **or**
  ii the worker straps sensors to his own arm and sprays the object; each movement is stored as a set of instructions on a computer; the sensors send back information such as position relative to the object, arm rotation and so on – this information forms part of the instructions stored on the computer.

▲ **Figure 6.18** Robot with spray gun end-effector

Whichever method is used, once the instructions have been saved, each series of tasks can then be carried out by a robot arm automatically. Each instruction will be carried out identically every time (for example, assembling parts in a television) giving a consistent product.

Robots are equipped with sensors so they can gather important information about their surroundings and also preventing them from doing 'stupid things'; for example, stopping a robot spraying a car if no car is present, or stop the spraying operation if the supply of paint has run out, and so on.

Robots are very good at repetitive tasks. However, if there are specialist tasks that require 'thinking' to cope with variable circumstances, (for example, making specialist glassware for some scientific work) then it is often better to still use human operators.

Table 6.1 shows the relevant advantages and disadvantages of using robots in industrial applications:

▼ **Table 6.1** Advantages and disadvantages of using robots

Advantages	Disadvantages
robots are capable of working in conditions that may be hazardous to humans	robots can find it difficult to do 'non-standard' tasks (for example, windscreen being fitted to a car is cracked)
robots work 24/7 without the need to stop	
robots are less expensive in the long run (since there will be fewer salaries to pay)	robots can lead to higher unemployment amongst manual labour tasks
robots are more productive than humans (higher productivity)	there is a risk of deskilling when robots take over certain tasks (for example, welding and paint spraying)
although not necessarily more accurate, robots are more consistent	
robots are better suited to boring, repetitive tasks than humans (therefore less likely to make mistakes)	factories can now be moved to anywhere in the world where operation costs are lower (leading again to unemployment in some countries)
there will be less cost in heating and lighting (robots don't need good light or warmth)	robots are expensive to buy and set up in the first place

Transport

Driverless vehicles are increasing in number every year. These are very complex robots, but the big problem is not really the technology (since problems will be ironed out through time), it is human perception. It will take a large leap of faith for humans to ride in a driverless car or an airplane with no pilot. We are already used to autonomous trains since these are used in many cities throughout the world. These systems have been generally accepted; but that is probably because trains don't overtake other trains and have a very specific track to follow (see notes later).

Autonomous cars and buses

In this section, we will consider autonomous cars as our example. Autonomous cars use sensors, cameras, actuators and microprocessors (together with very complex algorithms) to carry out their actions safely. Sensors (radar and ultrasonics) and cameras allow the control systems in cars to perform critical functions by sensing the dynamic conditions on a road. They act as the 'eyes' and 'ears' of the car.

Microprocessors process the data received from cameras and sensors and send signals to actuators to perform physical actions, such as:

>> change gear
>> apply the brakes
>> turn the steering wheel.

Cameras catch visual data from the surroundings, while radar and ultrasonics allow the vehicle to build up a 3D image of its surroundings (very important when visibility is poor, such as heavy rain, fog or at night). Suppose an autonomous car is approaching a set of traffic lights that are showing red. The first thing is the control system in the car needs to recognise the road sign and then check its database as to what action to take. Since the traffic light shows red, the microprocessor must send signals to actuators to apply brakes and put the gear into 'park'. Constant monitoring must take place until the light changes to green. When this happens, the microprocessor will again instruct actuators to put the car into first gear, release the brakes and operate the throttle (accelerator). This is a very complex set of operations since the microprocessor must constantly check all sensors and cameras to ensure moving off is safe (for example, has the car in front of it broken down or has a pedestrian started to cross the road, and so on). To go any further is outside the scope of this book.

Let us now consider some of the advantages and disadvantages specific to autonomous vehicles:

▼ **Table 6.2** Advantages and disadvantages of autonomous vehicles

Advantages of autonomous vehicles	Disadvantages of autonomous vehicles
safer since human error is removed leading to fewer accidents	very expensive system to set up in the first place (high technology requirements)
better for the environment since vehicles will operate more efficiently	the ever-present fear of hacking into the vehicle's control system
reduced traffic congestion (humans cause 'stop-and-go' traffic known as **'the phantom traffic jam'**, autonomous vehicles will be better at smoothing out traffic flow reducing congestion in cities)	security and safety issues (software glitches could be catastrophic; software updates would need to be carefully controlled to avoid potential disasters)
increased lane capacity (research shows autonomous vehicles will increase lane capacity by 100% and increase average speeds by 20%, due to better braking and acceleration responses together with optimized distance between vehicles)	the need to make sure the system is well-maintained at all times; cameras need to be kept clean so that they don't give false results; sensors could fail to function in heavy snowfall or blizzard conditions (radar or ultrasonic signals could be deflected by heavy snow particles)
reduced travel times (for the reasons above) therefore less commuting time	driver and passenger reluctance to use the new technology
stress-free parking for motorists (the car will find car parking on its own and then self-park)	reduction in the need for taxis could lead to unemployment (imagine New York without its famous yellow cabs!)

Autonomous trains

As mentioned earlier, autonomous (driverless) trains have been around for a number of years in a number of large cities. As with other autonomous vehicles, driverless trains make considerable use of sensors, cameras, actuators and on-board computers/microprocessors. Autonomous trains make use of a system called **LiDaR** (Light Detection and Ranging); LiDaR uses lasers which build up a 3D image of the surroundings. Other sensors (such as proximity sensors on train doors) and cameras (including infrared cameras) are all used for various purposes to help control the train and maintain safety. The control system in the train also makes use of global positioning satellite (GPS) technology, which allows accurate changes in speed and direction to be calculated. Again, actuators pay a huge role here in controlling the train's speed, braking and the opening and closing of the train doors.

▲ **Figure 6.19** Autonomous train (London Transport)

Let us now consider some of the advantages and disadvantages specific to autonomous trains:

▼ **Table 6.3** Advantages and disadvantages of autonomous trains

Advantages of autonomous trains	Disadvantages of autonomous trains
this improves the punctuality of the trains	the ever-present fear of hacking into the vehicle's control system
reduced running costs (fewer staff are required)	system doesn't work well with very busy services (at the moment)
improves safety since human error is removed	high capital costs and operational costs initially (that is, buying the trains, expensive signalling and control equipment and the need to train staff)
minimises energy consumption since there is better control of speed and an optimum service requires less energy (trains stuck in stations still use energy)	ensuring passenger behaviour is acceptable particularly during busy times (for example, jamming doors open on trains, standing too near the edge of platforms and so on)
it is possible to increase the frequency of trains (automated systems allow for shorter times between trains)	passenger reluctance to use the new technology
it is easier to change train scheduling (for example, more trains during busier times)	no drivers mean there will be a need for CCTV to monitor railway stations

Autonomous (unpiloted) airplanes

Airplanes have used auto-pilots for many years to control flights. Human pilots only take over during take-off and landing. Autonomous (pilotless) airplanes would make even more extensive use of sensors, actuators and microprocessors to control all stages of the flight. Some of the main features of a control system on a pilotless airplane would include:

» sensors to detect turbulence to ensure smooth flights
» an increase in self-testing of all circuits and systems
» sensors that would automatically detect depressurisation in the cabin; thus allowing for quick stabilisation of the airplane
» use of GPS for navigation and speed calculations
» use of actuators to control, for example, throttle, flaps (on the wings) and the rudder.

Let us now consider some of the advantages and disadvantages specific to pilotless airplanes:

▼ **Table 6.4** Advantages and disadvantages of pilotless airplanes

Advantages of pilotless airplanes	Disadvantages of pilotless airplanes
improvement in passenger comfort (reasons given earlier)	security aspects if no pilots on-board (for example, handling terrorist attacks)
reduced running costs (fewer staff are required)	emergency situations during the flight may be difficult to deal with
improved safety (most crashes of airplanes have been attributed to pilot-induced errors)	hacking into the system (it might be possible to access flight controls)
improved aerodynamics at the front of the airplane since there would no longer be the need to include a cockpit for the pilots	passenger reluctance to use the new technology
	software glitches (recent software issues with modern airplanes have highlighted that software glitches can have devastating results)

Agriculture

With the world's population predicted to reach nine billion by the year 2050, more efficient agriculture via increased use of robotics is inevitable. Robots could replace slow, repetitive and dull tasks allowing farmers to concentrate on improving production yields. We will consider the following five areas where robotics could play a big role:

» harvesting/picking of vegetables and fruit
» weed control
» phenotyping (plant growth and health)
» seed-planting and fertiliser distribution
» autonomous labour-saving devices.

Harvesting and picking

» robots have been designed to do this labour-intensive work; they are more accurate (only pick ripe fruit, for example) and much faster at harvesting
» for the reasons above, this leads to higher yields and reduces waste (for example, **vegebot** (Cambridge University) uses cameras to scan, for example, a lettuce and decide whether or not it is ready to be harvested
» a second camera in **vegebot** (near the cutting blades) guides an arm to remove the lettuce from its stalk with no damage.

Weed control

» weed management robots can distinguish between a weed and crop using AI (see Section 6.3)
» examples of weed control robots are being used in France (by Mouton-Rothschild) to remove weeds between grape vines in their vineyards; this saves considerably on labour costs and improves vine growth
» weed control robots use GPS tracking to stay on course to move along the rows of vines and remove the weeds; a weed removal blade is operated by an actuator under the control of the controller (microprocessor) in the robot

>> very often a **drone** (flying robot) is used first to do an aerial view of the vineyard, so that a programmed course of action can be produced, which is then sent to the weed control robot's memory.

Phenotyping

>> **phenotyping** is the process of observing physical characteristics of a plant in order to assess its health and growth
>> robots designed to do phenotyping are equipped with sensors (including spectral sensors and thermal cameras) that can create a 3D image/model of the plant, thus allowing it to be monitored for health and growth
>> machine learning (see Section 6.3) is used to recognise any issues with leaves (for example, if they have a blight or have the wrong colour) so that the robot can convey this back to the farmer
>> these robots are much more accurate and faster at predicting problems than when done manually.

Seed-planting drones and fertiliser distribution

>> drones (flying robots) can produce an aerial image of a farm sending back a 'bird's eye view' of the crops and land
>> they allow seed-planting to be done far more accurately
>> they also allow for more efficient fertiliser-spreading to reduce waste and improve coverage (this is much more efficient than conventional crop spraying)
>> drones can also be used in cloud seeding where the drone can add silver iodide crystals to a cloud forcing it to give up its rainwater
>> the drones use a very complex camera system to target seeding and allow fertiliser spraying.

Autonomous agriculture devices
Several of the devices described above could be referred to as autonomous. The following list summarises some of the devices that can work independently of humans:

>> grass mowers/cutters
>> weeding, pruning and harvesting robots
>> seeding robots
>> fertiliser spraying
>> all of these devices use sensors and cameras to go around obstacles, or they can even be programmed to 'go to sleep' if the weather turns bad.

Activity 6.8
Look through all the notes on use of robots in agriculture, and make a table showing all the advantages and disadvantages of using robots.

Activity 6.9

1 Describe three areas where robots can be used in agriculture to increase efficiency and reduce labour requirements.

For each example, write down the advantages and disadvantages of using robots.

2 Five statements are shown on the left and five computer terms are shown on the right.

By drawing lines, connect each description to its correct computer term.

no direct human control and has the ability to carry out human activity totally on its own	dependent robot
machine that requires human interface to operate and allow it to supplement human activities	actuator
branch of computer science that brings together the design, construction and operation of 'intelligent' mechanical machines	end-effector
devices attached to a robotic arm which allows it to carry out various tasks	autonomous
device, under the control of a microprocessor, which allows it to operate pumps, wheels, motors and pistons, for example	robotics

Medicine

» robots are used in surgical procedures, which makes the operation safer and also makes the procedures quicker and less costly
» robots can be used from monitoring patients to doing actual minor surgery
» the disinfecting of rooms and operating theatres can all be done by autonomous robots (similar to the types described in agriculture)
» robots can take blood samples from patients:
  – less painful to patients since the robot is better at determining a 'good vein'
  – safer to doctors and nurses if the patient has an infectious disease
  – doctors and nurses can be freed up to do more skilled work
» microbots can be used in target therapy:
  – these use microscopic mechanical components (including microprocessor) to localise a drug or other therapy to target a specific site causing less damage to surrounding tissue
» prosthetic limbs are now mini robots in their own right (since they meet the three characterisations of what defines a robot)
  – bionic skins and neural implants that interface with the human nervous system (of the damaged limb) giving feedback to allow for better control of the prosthetic limb (again sensors and actuators are used to give human-like responses, such as grip).

Domestic robots

Robots used around the house vary from devices to carry out household chores through to devices used to entertain people. For example:

» autonomous vacuum cleaners:
  – these use proximity sensors and cameras to avoid bumping into obstacles and allows them to cover a whole room automatically

▲ **Figure 6.20** Vector robot (personal assistant)

- – these robots have a microprocessor to control the overall operation of the device; this also allows the user to program the device
- – actuators are used to control motors which allow movement forward/ backward and from side to side
- ›› autonomous grass cutters (mowers):
  - – these use the same type of sensor, camera, microprocessor and actuator set up as vacuum cleaners
- ›› personal assistants (such as 'Vector')
  - – this is a robot controlled by a micro-processor that also uses cloud connectivity to connect to the internet
  - – it understands voice commands (using a microphone) and will answer any questions it is asked
  - – it also makes use of an HD camera, utilising computer vision, allowing it to recognise somebody's face as well as navigate a room (using proximity sensors and actuators) to steer around objects in its way.

Robots used in entertainment

The use of robots in the entertainment industry is increasing. They are now found in areas such as:
- ›› entertainment parks and arenas/venues
- ›› the film and TV industry.

The following examples indicate where robots are being used in the world of entertainment. The reader is advised to research the ever-increasing number of examples.
- ›› theme parks are now using autonomous robots to entertain visitors to the park; these robots (often dressed as cartoon characters) can interact with visitors to allow them to engage safely with the theme park attractions and make the whole experience 'more realistic'
- ›› music festivals are much more immersive for the audience; robotic methods are used to control lighting (including laser displays), visual effects and animation (e.g. superimposing an actor's image onto a robotic caricature and synchronising mouth movements); the visual performances can be fully synchronised with the music
- ›› use of robots to control cameras; for example, keeping them steady and auto-focusing when moving around a scene; the movie *Gravity* used many robots to operate cameras, props and the actors (for example, to give an actor the appearance of moving around in the vacuum of space uncontrollably, robot arms were used to simulate human behaviour and produce life-like moving images)
- ›› humanoid robots (either remote-controlled or pre-programmed) can perform 'stunt' action in movies/ television by performing tasks impossible for a human to do; they use CGI (computer-generated imagery) and image capture techniques to generate special effects
- ›› robots are capable of producing special effects with a precision, speed and coordination which is beyond human capabilities; actions and special effects can be synchronised to within a millisecond and produce fully coordinated/ synchronised sound effects (e.g. movement of the mouth to match the sounds produced in a realistic manner).

Activity 6.10

Research five robots used as entertainment.

a Give the names of these five robots.

b Write down the advantages and disadvantages of the five robots you chose.

Activity 6.11

1 Write down **four** advantages and **four** disadvantages of using robots in the manufacturing industry.

2 To be referred to as a robot, it needs to be demonstrated that it has the following three characteristics:
   - ability to sense its surroundings
   - ability to move in some way
   - a perceived intelligence.

   For **each** of these **three** characteristics, describe **two** features you could use to demonstrate that a device could be called a robot.

3 Choose suitable words/phrases from the following list to correctly complete the paragraph that follows:

   Word list:
activators	lasers
actuators	light detection and ranging
autonomous	primary vision
cameras	radar and ultrasonics
lane assist	sensors

   Driverless cars are described as ....; these vehicles use ...., ..., microprocessors, software and .... to allow them to function. A 3D image of the surroundings is produced by using .... Parking and nose to tail driving is achieved by using .... in the bumpers.

4 Choose suitable words/phrases from the following list to correctly complete the paragraph that follows:

   Word list:
actuators	environment	programs
adaptive	intelligence	repetitive
controller	microprocessor	sensors
end-effectors	physical	system

   Robots can collect data from their surroundings by using .... The data is then sent to a .... to allow the robot to build up an image of its .... Robots can perform various tasks by using different .... The 'brain' of the robot is often called a .... which contains .... to allow it carry out various tasks automatically. Many robots are not (artificially) intelligent, since they only do .... tasks rather than requiring .... human characteristics.

5 Autonomous robots are used in space exploration and in undersea exploration. These robots have to either work in the near vacuum of space or the very high-water pressures under the oceans. They need to be equipped with many sensors and cameras to carry out their remote tasks.

   a Undersea robots are being used to investigate shipwrecks. Describe how the sensors and cameras could be used to photograph the shipwrecks. Also describe the role of the microprocessor and actuators in taking photographs and any samples needed from the shipwreck for further investigation.

   b A space exploration robot has been sent on a mission to Mars. The robot needs to move around the surface of the planet safely

taking photographs and also taking soil/rock samples for later analysis.
  i   Describe how sensors, actuators and a microprocessor can be used to take samples from the planet's surface.
  ii Describe three uses of the cameras on this autonomous robot.
c Describe the advantages and disadvantages of using autonomous robots in both undersea and outer space exploration.
d Give two other examples of where autonomous robots could be used.

6.3 Artificial intelligence (AI)

6.3.1 Introduction

Artificial intelligence (AI) is a branch of computer science dealing with the simulation of intelligent human behaviour by a computer. This is often referred to as the cognitive functions of the human brain (that is, the mental process of acquiring knowledge and understanding through thought, experience and the five senses). All of these cognitive functions can be replicated in a machine, and they can be measured against human benchmarks such as reasoning, speech and sight.

6.3.2 Characteristics of AI

Essentially, AI is really just a collection of rules and data, and the ability to reason, learn and adapt to external stimuli. AI can be split into three categories:

>> narrow AI – this occurs when a machine has superior performance to a human when doing one specific task
>> general AI – this occurs when a machine is similar (not superior) in its performance to a human doing a specific task
>> strong AI – this occurs when a machine has superior performance to a human in many tasks.

Reasoning is the ability to draw reasoned conclusions based on given data/situations. Deductive reasoning is where a number of correct facts are built up to form a set of rules which can then be applied to other problems (for example, if AI is used to produce the perfect cup of tea based on a number of facts, the machine will learn from the experience and apply its new rules in the making of a cup of coffee, hot chocolate, and so on – modifying its methodology where necessary). By carrying out a sequence of steps, the AI machine can learn, and next time it will know how to do the task more effectively and even apply it to a novel/new situation. Thus the AI system is capable of learning and adapting to its surroundings. AI can very quickly discern patterns (which in some cases, humans cannot) and then make predictions by adapting to the new data. How all this is done is beyond the scope of this book (interested readers can find out more about this topic by consulting *Cambridge International AS and A Level Computer Science*, ISBN: 9781510457584).

Examples of AI include:

>> news generation based on live news feeds
>> smart home devices (such as Amazon Alexa, Google Now, Apple Siri and Microsoft Cortana):
    – the AI device interacts with a human by recognising verbal commands
    – it learns from its environment and the data it receives

- the device becomes increasingly sophisticated in its responses, thus showing the ability to use automated repetitive learning

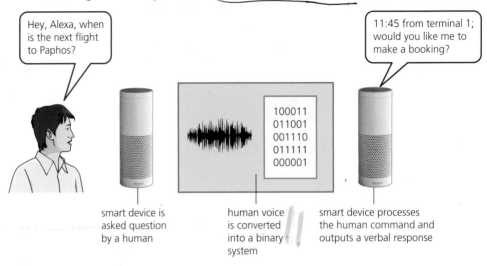

▲ **Figure 6.21** Smart home devices

» use of **chatbots** that interact through instant messaging, artificially replicating patterns of human interactions using AI to respond to typed or voice messages; when a question is asked, the chatbot responds using the information known at the time:

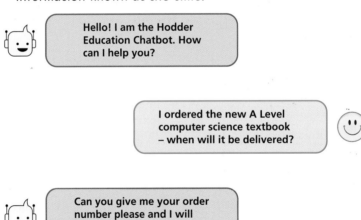

▲ **Figure 6.22** Chatbots

» autonomous cars (see Section 6.2)
» facial expression recognition
  - algorithms identify key facial landmarks such as the corners of the eyebrows, corners of the mouth, and so on
  - a combination of these landmarks can be used to map emotions (such as anger, fear, joy and surprise).

Find out more

The Turing Test is a method to test a machine's ability to match human intelligence levels. Find out how the **Turing Test** is used.

6.3.3 AI systems

This section considers two types of AI system:

» expert system – a computer system that mimics the decision-making ability of a human; expert systems use AI to simulate the judgement and behaviour of a human or organisation that has expert knowledge and experience

» machine learning – this is the science of training computers with sample data so that they can go on to make predictions about new unseen data, without the need to specifically program them for the new data.

Expert systems

Expert systems are a form of AI that has been developed to mimic human knowledge and experiences. They use knowledge and inference to solve problems or answer questions that would normally require a human expert.

For example, suppose the user was investigating a series of symptoms in a patient. The expert system would ask a series of questions, and the answers would lead to its diagnosis. The expert system would explain its reasoning with a statement such as *'impaired vision, lack of coordination, weak muscles, slurred speech and the patient used to work in a paint factory – the diagnosis is mercury poisoning'* – the user could then probe deeper if necessary.

The expert system will supply a conclusion and any suggested actions to take and it will also give the percentage probability of the accuracy of its conclusions (for example, the following statement could be made *'Based on the information given to me, the probability of finding oil bearing rocks in location 123AD21G is about 21%'*).

There are many applications that use expert systems:

» oil and mineral prospecting
» diagnosis of a patient's illness
» fault diagnostics in mechanical and electronic equipment
» tax and financial calculations
» strategy games, such as chess
» logistics (efficient routing of parcel deliveries)
» identification of plants, animals and chemical/biological compounds.

Expert systems have many advantages:

» they offer a high level of expertise
» they offer high accuracy
» the results are consistent
» they have the ability to store vast amounts of ideas and facts
» they can make traceable logical solutions and diagnostics
» it is possible for an expert system to have multiple expertise
» they have very fast response times (much quicker than a human expert)
» they provide unbiased reporting and analysis of the facts
» they indicate the probability of any suggested solution being correct.

Expert systems also have disadvantages:

» users of the expert system need considerable training in its use to ensure the system is being used correctly

>> the set up and maintenance costs are very high
>> they tend to give very 'cold' responses that may not be appropriate in certain medical situations
>> they are only as good as the information/facts entered into the system
>> users sometimes make the very dangerous assumption that they are infallible.

So what makes up an expert system? Figure 6.23 shows the typical structure of an expert system:

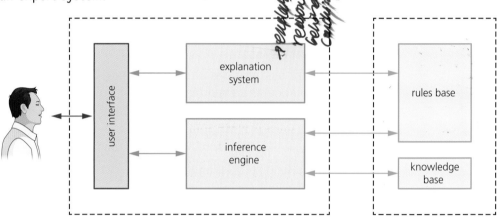

Expert System Shell

▲ **Figure 6.23** Expert system structure

Advice

Explanation systems are not explicitly covered in the syllabus (Figure 6.23).

Find out more

Using Figure 6.23, find out how the explanation system works and why it is included in a typical expert system.

User interface

>> method by which the expert system interacts with a user
>> interaction can be through dialogue boxes, command prompts or other input methods
>> the questions being asked usually only have Yes/No answers and are based on the responses to previous questions.

Inference engine

>> this is the main processing element of the expert system
>> the **inference engine** acts like a **search engine** examining the **knowledge base** for information/data that matches the queries
>> it is responsible for gathering information from the user by asking a series of questions and applying responses where necessary; each question being asked is based on the previous responses
>> the inference engine is the problem-solving part of the expert system that makes use of **inference rules** in the **rules base**
>> since the knowledge base is a collection of **objects** and **attributes**, the inference engine attempts to use information gathered from the user to find an object that matches (making use of the rules base to find a match)

Knowledge base

>> the knowledge base is a repository of facts
>> it stores all the knowledge about an area of expertise obtained from a number of expert resources

>> it is basically a collection of **objects** and their **attributes**; for example:

Object	Attribute 1	Attribute 2	Attribute 3	Attribute 4	Attribute 5	Attribute 6
dog	mammal	can be a pet	lives on land	makes bark sounds	body is covered in fur	walks on 4 legs
whale	mammal	not a pet	lives in water	makes sonic sound	body covered in skin	swims; no legs
duck	bird	not a pet	lives in water	makes quack sounds	body covered in feathers	swims; has two legs

>> so if we had a series of questions:
- is it a mammal?   YES
- can it be a pet?   NO
- does it live in water?   YES
- does it make sonic sounds?   YES
- is its body covered in skin?   YES
- does it have any legs?   NO

conclusion: it is a WHALE.

Rules base

>> the rules base is a set of inference rules
>> inference rules are used by the inference engine to draw conclusions (the methods used closely follow human reasoning)
>> they follow logical thinking like the example above; usually involving a series of 'IF' statements, for example:

IF continent = "South America" AND language = "Portuguese" THEN country = "Brazil"

Setting up an expert system

>> information needs to be gathered from human experts or from written sources such as textbooks, research papers or the internet
>> information gathered is used to populate the knowledge base that needs to be first created
>> a rules base needs to be created; this is made up of a series of inference rules so that the inference engine can draw conclusions
>> the inference engine itself needs to be set up; it is a complex system since it is the main processing element making reasoned conclusions from data in the knowledge base
>> the user interface needs to be developed to allow the user and the expert system to communicate
>> once the system is set up, it needs to be fully tested; this is done by running the system with known outcomes so that results can be compared and any changes to the expert system made.

Example use of an expert system (medical diagnosis)

Input screen

- First of all an interactive screen is presented to the user
- The system asks a series of questions about the patient's illness
- The user answers the questions asked (either as multiple choice or YES/NO questions)
- A series of questions are asked based on the user's responses to previous questions

Expert system

- The inference engine compares the symptoms entered with those in the knowledge base looking for matches
- The rules base (inference rules) is used in the matching process
- Once a match is found, the system suggests the probability of the patient's illness being identified accurately
- The expert system also suggests possible solutions and remedies to cure the patient or recommendations on what to do next
- The explanation system will give reasons for its diagnosis so that the user can determine the validity of the diagnosis or suggested treatment

Output screen

- The diagnosis can be in the form of text or it may show images of the human anatomy to indicate where the problem may be
- The user can request further information from the expert system to narrow down even further the possible illness and its treatment

▲ **Figure 6.24** Use of an expert system

Activity 6.12

Which computer terms, connected to AI, are being described below?

a a repository of facts made up of a collection of objects and their attributes

b informs the user of the reasoning behind the expert system's conclusions and recommended actions

c made up of user interface and inference engine

d a sub-set of AI where machines mimic human activities and can manipulate objects using end-effectors all the way through to autonomous vehicles

e contains a set of inference rules.

Machine learning

Recall the AI 'family' as shown in Figure 6.25.

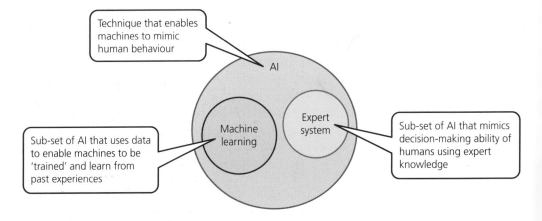

▲ **Figure 6.25** AI family

Machine learning is a sub-set of artificial intelligence (AI), in which algorithms are 'trained' and learn from their past experiences and examples. It is possible for the system to make predictions or even take decisions based on previous scenarios. They can offer fast and accurate outcomes due to very powerful processing capability. One of the key factors is the ability to manage and analyse considerable volumes of complex data; some of the tasks would take humans years to complete without the help of machine learning techniques. One example that uses machine learning are the most sophisticated **search engines**:

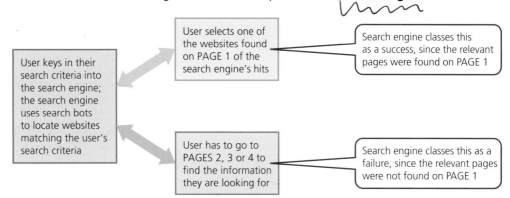

▲ **Figure 6.26** Search engine success or failure

The search engine will learn from its past performance, meaning its ability to carry out searches becomes more and more sophisticated and accurate.

Differences between AI and machine learning

▼ **Table 6.5** Difference between AI and machine learning

AI	Machine learning
represents simulated intelligence in machines	this is the practice of getting machines to make decisions without being programmed to do so
the aim is to build machines that are capable of thinking like humans	the aim is to make machines that learn through data acquisition, so that they can solve new problems

Examples of machine learning

Example 1: Categorising email as spam

Consider email messages such as *'You have won $2 million in the National Lottery'*; how can machine learning determine that this email should be put into your spam folder?

» A machine learning algorithm collects data about emails, such as email content, headers, senders name/email address and so on.
» It carries out a 'cleaning' process by removing **stop words** (for example, the, and, a) and punctuation, leaving only the relevant data.
» Certain words/phrases are frequently used in spam (for example, lottery, earn, full-refund) and indicate that the incoming email is very likely to be spam.
» The machine learning model is built and a 'training data set' is used to train the model and make it learn using past email known to be spam.
» Once it is evaluated, the model is fine-tuned and tested live.

❓ Example 2: Recognising user buying history

When you visit an online retailer, such as Amazon, you might receive the message *'customers who bought Hodder Education IGCSE ICT textbook also bought Hodder Education IGCSE Computer Science textbook'*. How is machine learning used to establish a user's buying characteristics?

» This comes from **collaboration filtering**, which is the process of comparing customers who have similar shopping behaviour to a new customer who has similar shopping behaviour.

» Suppose customer 'A' is very interested in playing football and they also bought a jazz CD, a book on Roman history and some health food.

» Two weeks later, customer 'B' who likes to go cycling also bought a similar jazz CD and a book on ancient Roman history.

» The machine learning algorithms will then recommend that customer 'B' might like to buy some health food due to the similarities between 'A' and 'B's shopping behaviour.

» This technique is particularly popular when asking your mobile phone to generate a playlist from your music library based on a few criteria you might select.

❓ Example 3: Detection of fraudulent activity

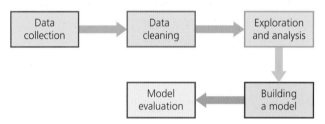

▲ **Figure 6.27** Machine learning model development

» Data is gathered by a survey or **web scraping**; for example, to detect credit card fraud, information about customers is gathered, such as types of transactions (does the customer buy designer clothes?), shopping habits and certain personal data.

» Redundant data is then removed; this needs to be carefully done to remove the possibility of wrong predictions.

» The most important machine learning step: the algorithm is trained through real examples of customer purchasing behaviour.

» A model is built based on learning from the training data, and the machine learning algorithm can now be used to detect fraud (for example, if a customer spends an unusual amount on a piece of jewellery, there is a high chance a fraudulent activity has taken place).

» The machine learning model is then fully tested with known data and known outcomes; the system is modified if it hasn't met its criteria to detect fraudulent activity.

Activity 6.13

1 Use words/phrases from the following list to complete the paragraph below:
  Word list:

artificial intelligence	expert systems	machine learning
attributes	explanation system	robotics
cognitive	inference engine	rules base
database	inference rules	search engine

.... is a branch of computer science where the .... function of the human brain is studied. .... are a branch of AI which mimic the knowledge and experience of humans. The application uses an .... to explain its reasoning and logic to the user. The main element of this application is an .... which acts like a .... by applying .... to a knowledge base.

2 John has bought an expert system to help him find faults in computer systems. John has been asked to look at a computer that won't play music through some external speakers, attached to a computer using a USB port.
  » The music is stored in a file on the solid state drive (SSD).
  » The computer uses a sound card to output sound.
  » The external loud speaker is plugged into a USB port.

  a The expert system asks John a series of questions. Each question is dependent on his response to a previous question.

  For example:

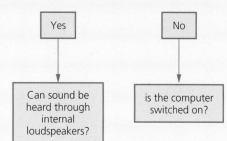

▲ Figure 6.28

  Write a further series of questions that helps John identify that there is actually a fault in the external loud speaker plugged into his computer.

  b Describe three other uses of expert systems.

3 a Define the term **machine learning**.
  b Explain how **machine learning** and **artificial intelligence (AI)** differ.
  c Describe how a search engine might use machine learning to determine the most appropriate results based on a user's search criteria.

4 Six statements are shown on the left and nine computer terms on the right. Draw lines to link each statement with its correct computer term.

branch of computer science where cognitive behaviour of the human brain is studied	rules base
when a machine shows superior performance to a human in many tasks	search engine
application that uses knowledge and inference to solve problems that would require human expertise	strong AI
repository of facts that is a collection of objects and their attributes	artificial intelligence
contains the inference rules used to determine any matches between input data and stored data	machine learning
sub-set of AI in which the algorithms are 'trained' and learn from past experience and examples	robotics
	expert system
	knowledge base
	user interface

Extension

For those students considering the study of this subject at A Level, the following section gives some insight into further study on a sub-set of machine learning called deep learning

Deep learning

Deep learning structures algorithms in layers (input layer, output layer and hidden layer(s)) to create an artificial neural network made up of 'units' or 'nodes', which is essentially based on the human brain (i.e. its interconnections between neurons). Neural network systems are able to process more like a human and their performance improves when trained with more and more data. The hidden layers are where data from the input layer is processed into something that can be sent to the output layer. Artificial neural networks are excellent at tasks that computers normally find hard. For example, they can be used in face recognition:

The following diagram shows an artificial neural network (with two hidden layers) – each circle, called a unit or node, is like an 'artificial neuron':

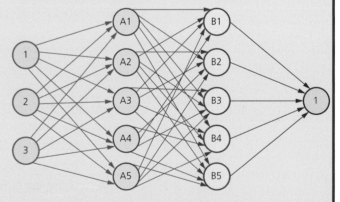

Neural networks are effective at complex visual processing such as recognising birds, for example, by their shape and colour. There are many different sizes, colours and types of bird, and machine learning algorithms struggle to successfully recognise such a wide variety of complex objects. But the hidden layers in an artificial neural network allow a deep learning algorithm to do so.

A deep learning system can perform visual processing by analysing pixel densities of camera images of objects. Consider the following small section of an image, where each pixel on the left is represented by its RGB value in hexadecimal:

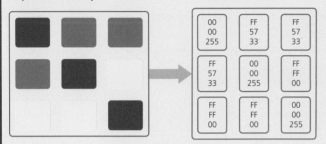

00 00 255	FF 57 33	FF 57 33
FF 57 33	00 00 255	FF FF 00
FF FF 00	FF FF 00	00 00 255

Link

For more on representing pixels in hexadecimal see Section 1.2.

Deep learning using artificial neural networks can be used to recognise objects by looking at the binary codes of each pixel, thus building up a picture of the object. For example, the following image shows a close up of part of a face where each pixel can be assigned its binary value; patterns of binary codes can be recognised by deep learning algorithms as a person's face.

Example showing how deep learning works:

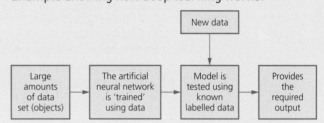

Large amounts of data are input into the model. One of the methods of object recognition, using pixel densities, was described above. The nodes in the artificial neural networks learn certain parameters, based on the training data. Once this has been done, labelled data is entered (this is data which has already been defined and is therefore recognised) into the model to make sure it gives the correct responses. If the output isn't sufficiently accurate, then the model is refined until it gives satisfactory results – this might mean changing the number of nodes or number of layers. The refinement process may take several 'adjustments' until it provides reliable and consistent outputs.

Comparison between machine learning and deep learning

Machine learning	Deep learning
uses algorithms to enable machines to make decisions on their own based on past data	uses algorithms arranged as an artificial neural network to enable machines to make decisions
tends to need less data than deep learning – though this can still mean large amounts of data are required to carry out the training	the system needs large amounts of data during the training stages
is very good at certain classification tasks such as spam email	is very good at very complex non-linear tasks such as visual processing
a modular approach is taken to solve a given problem/task; each module is then combined to produce the final model	the problem is solved from beginning to end as a single entity
does not always need a large amount of computing power – however for complex problems machine learning can still require a lot of computing power	deep learning requires a large amount of computing power
testing of the system takes a long time to carry out	testing of the system takes much less time to carry out
there are clear rules which explain why each stage in the model was made	since the system makes decisions based on its own logic, the reasoning behind those decisions may be very difficult to understand (hence why they are often referred to as a **black box**)

In this chapter, you have learnt about:
- ✔ use of sensors, microprocessors and actuators in automated systems
- ✔ the advantages and disadvantages of automated systems in a number of key areas
- ✔ what is meant by robotics
- ✔ what characterises a robot
- ✔ the role of robots in a number of areas
- ✔ the advantages and disadvantages of robots in these areas
- ✔ the concept of artificial learning (AI)
- ✔ the main characteristics of AI
- ✔ expert systems
- ✔ machine learning.

Key terms used throughout this chapter

automated system – a combination of software and hardware designed and programmed to work automatically without the need for any human intervention

distributed control system (DCS) – a powerful computer system programmed to monitor and control a complex process without the need for human interaction

adaptive cruise control – the use of sensors, actuators and microprocessors to ensure that a vehicle keeps a safe distance behind another vehicle

accelerometer – a sensor that measures acceleration and deceleration and that can detect, for example, the orientation of a device

robotics – the branch of (computer) science that encompasses the design, construction and operation of robots

robot – a mechanical device that can carry out tasks normally done by humans

autonomous – able to operate independently without any human input

controller – a microprocessor that is in control of a process

WebCrawler/search bot – a software robot that roams the internet scanning websites and categorising them; often used by search engines

chatbots – a pop-up robot on a website that appears to enter into a meaningful conversation with a web user

end-effector – an attachment to a robot arm that allows it to carry out a specific task, such as spray painting

LiDaR – a contraction of light detection and ranging; the use of lasers to build up a 3D image of the surroundings

drone – a flying robot that can be autonomous or operated using remote control; a drone can be used for reconnaissance or deliveries

phenotyping – the process of observing the physical characteristics of a plant to assess its health and growth

cognitive – relating to the mental processes of the human brain involved in acquiring knowledge and understanding through thought, experiences and input from the five senses

artificial intelligence (AI) – a collection of rules and data which gives a computer system the ability to reason, learn and adapt to external stimuli

expert system – a form of AI that has been developed to mimic a human's knowledge and expertise

explanation system – part of an expert system which informs the user of the reasoning behind its conclusions and recommendations

inference engine – a kind of search engine used in an expert system which examines the knowledge base for information that matches the queries

inference rules – rules used by the inference engine and in expert systems to draw conclusions using IF statements

knowledge base – a repository of facts which is a collection of objects and attributes

object – an item stored in the knowledge base

attribute – something that defines the objects stored in a knowledge base

rules base – a collection of inference rules used to draw conclusions

machine learning – a sub-set of AI in which algorithms are trained and learn from past experiences and examples

web scraping – a method of obtaining data from websites

Exam-style questions

1 A distribution company has decided to automate its packaging and dispensing of items to online customers. The system is totally automated, where each required item is identified using barcodes. Once found, the item is packaged, an address label applied and then placed in a delivery van.

    a Describe the advantages and disadvantages to the company of using robots to automatically find, package and load parcels. [5]

    b Some humans will still have to be present in the building to carry out special tasks. Describe what safety systems need to be part of the robot to prevent any risks to the humans when walking around the building. [3]

2 A company is developing a new game for a hand-held console:

The console is moved in various directions to control movement and speed of a racing car on a television screen. Gear changes can be done using the LCD screen on the device itself.

Name and describe which sensors would need to be used for the game to be as realistic as possible. [5]

3 A robot is being used to deliver the post around the headquarters of a large company, which is housed in a 20-storey building.
The robot moves around the corridors picking up the post and delivering the post throughout the building. If a person comes close to the robot, it stops and waits until the person is out of range.

    a Proximity sensors are used to detect how close to a person the robot is. Describe how the microprocessor (which is built into the robot) would ensure the robot stops when it encounters a person. [4]

    b The lighting throughout the building is controlled by sensors and a computer.

       i Describe how the lighting in the corridors and offices are controlled by sensors and the computer.

      ii Describe the advantages and disadvantages of using an automated system to control the building lights. [4]

4 A computer has been designed to do a number of different tasks:

    » control a process
    » monitor a process (by taking data samples only)
    » run an expert system.

    a The table below shows eight tasks which the computer could be carrying out. Tick (✓) the appropriate box to show if the task is an example of control, monitor or an expert system:

Task	Control	Monitor	Expert system
automatic control of the atmosphere in a large greenhouse (to ensure ideal growing conditions)			
self-parking system in a car			
playing a strategy game, such as chess			
an automatic weather station sending data to pilots flying near an airport			
a 24/7 check on patients in an intensive care unit of a hospital			
automatic system used to diagnose the illness of a patient			
automatic closing and opening of the doors on a train			
fault identification in electronic devices together with suggested actions to rectify the fault			

[8]

b Name and describe the function of four of the components that make up an expert system. [4]

5 The following schematic shows how sensors, actuators and a computer can be used to control the opening and closing of doors in a train.

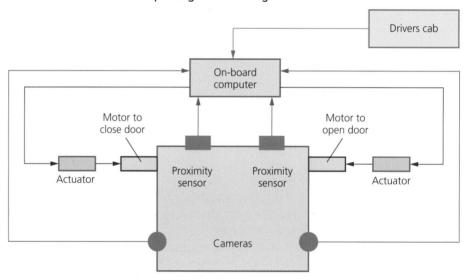

As the train approaches a station and stops, the system automatically opens the doors. Passengers can then get on and off the train.

After 30 seconds the computer automatically sounds an alarm and starts to close the doors. But if someone is still trying to get on or off the train at this point, then the doors automatically re-open and then try to close again. This is all done under the control of the computer. Cameras and sensors are used to send data back to the computer. The driver of the train is able to monitor the camera images from his cab and take any additional action if necessary.

a Describe how the sensors, cameras, actuators and computer are all used to safely operate the doors on the train. Name any sensors that you think would be needed. [6]

b Explain the advantages and disadvantages of using this computer-controlled system. [4]

c Explain why you think camera images are still sent to the driver in the cab. [2]

d The train company are slowly upgrading all their trains to be autonomous.
  i Explain the term *autonomous*. [1]
  ii Describe what additional sensors and actuators may be needed to allow the trains to be upgraded to autonomous operation. [4]
  iii Describe two advantages and two disadvantages of making this upgrade. [4]

6 a Give **three** characteristics needed to define a machine as a robot. [3]

b Robots can be described as *dependent* or *independent*. Explain what is meant by the two types of robot. [4]

7 Six descriptions are shown on the left and six computer terms are shown on the right.

By drawing lines, connect each description to its correct computer term. [6]

a form of AI which has been developed to mimic human knowledge and expertise	knowledge base
a repository of facts and expertise in the form of a collection of objects and their attributes	autonomous
a sub-set of AI in which the algorithms are trained and can learn from their past experience and examples	artificial intelligence
simulated intelligence in machines; building of machines capable of thinking like a human	expert system
branch of (computer) science that brings together the design, construction and operation of 'intelligent' mechanical machines	robotics
devices which can move between point 'A' and point 'B' without the need for any input from a driver or a pilot	machine learning

8 Which computer terms are being described below?
  a Attachment to a robot arm which allows it to carry out a specific task, such as spray painting.
  b A kind of search engine used in an expert system which examines the knowledge base for information that matches the queries.
  c General name of any robotic device that can operate independently without any human input.
  d A sub-set of AI in which algorithms are trained and learn from past experiences and examples.

e A combination of software and hardware designed and programmed to work automatically without the need for any human intervention.

f A collection of rules and data which leads to the ability to reason, learn and adapt to external stimuli.

g Pop-up robots found on websites that appear to enter into a meaningful conversation with a web user.

h Robots that roam the internet scanning all websites and categorising them for search purposes.

i A branch of (computer) science that brings together the design, construction and operation of intelligent mechanical devices.

j The mental process of the human brain whereby it acquires knowledge and understanding through thought, experiences and the five senses.

k Something that defines the objects stored in a knowledge base.

l A repository of facts which is a collection of objects and attributes.

m A flying robot that can be autonomous or under remote control; used for reconnaissance or deliveries.

n The name essentially given to a microprocessor which is in control of a process.

o Used by the inference engine to draw conclusions using IF statements.

[15]

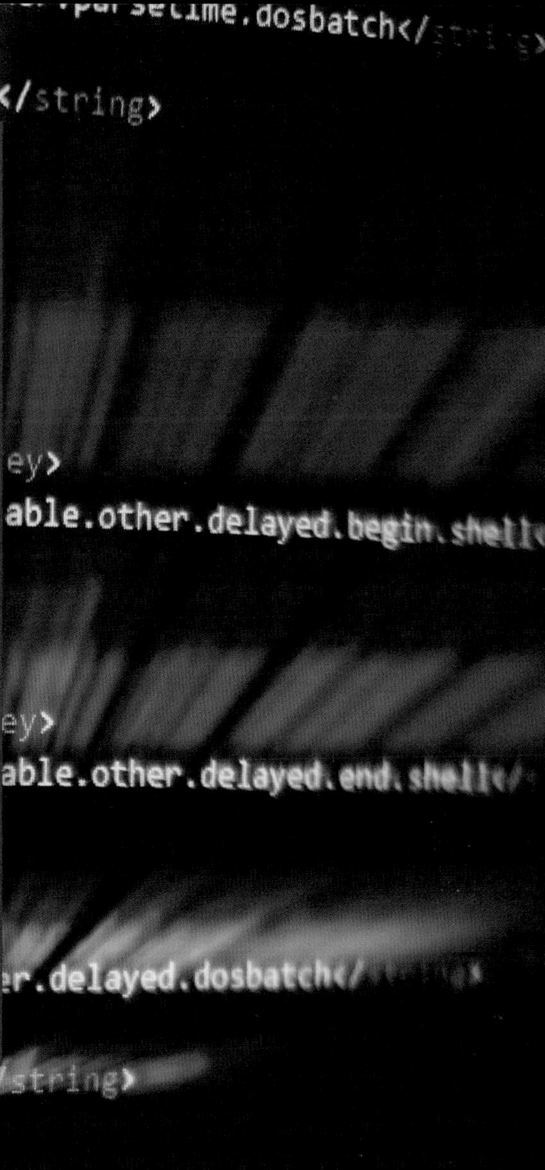

SECTION 2

Algorithms, programming and logic

Chapters

7 Algorithm design and problem solving

> **In this chapter, you will learn about:**
> ★ the stages in the program development cycle:
>   - analysis
>   - design
>   - coding
>   - testing
> ★ computer systems and sub-systems
> ★ problem decomposition into component parts
> ★ methods used to design and construct solutions to problems
> ★ the purpose of an algorithm and the processes involved in it
> ★ standard methods of solution:
>   - linear search
>   - bubble sort
>   - totalling
>   - counting
>   - finding average, maximum, minimum
> ★ validation checks when data is input
> ★ verification checks when data is input
> ★ use of different types of test data including:
>   - documentation of a dry run using a trace table
> ★ writing, amending, identifying, and correcting errors in:
>   - flowcharts
>   - programs
>   - pseudocode.

7.1 The program development life cycle

The program development life cycle is divided into five stages: analysis, design, coding, testing and maintenance. This chapter and Chapter 8 will discuss the four stages listed below:

>> **analysis**
>> **design**
>> **coding**
>> **testing**

7.1.1 Analysis

Before any problem can be solved, it needs to be clearly defined and set out so anyone working on the solution understands what is needed. This is called the 'requirements specification' for the program. The analysis stage uses **abstraction** and **decomposition** tools to identify exactly what is required from the program.

Abstraction keeps the key elements required for the solution to the problem and discards any unnecessary details and information that is not required. For example, a map only shows what is required for travelling from one place to another. Different methods of transport will require different types of map.

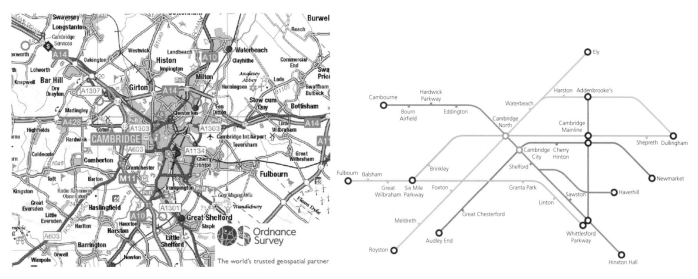

▲ **Figure 7.1** Road map and rail map

Decomposition breaks down a complex problem into smaller parts, which can then be subdivided into even smaller parts, that can be solved easily. Any daily task can be divided into its constituent parts.

For example, getting dressed:

>> Select items to wear
>> Remove any clothes being worn
>> Put selected items on in order.

Find out more

Decompose getting dressed further, it can get quite complicated to show all the details required.

7.1.2 Design

The program specification from the analysis stage is used to show to how the program should be developed. When the design stage is complete, the programmer should know what is to be done, i.e. all the tasks that need to be completed, how each task is to be performed and how the tasks work together. This can be formally documented using **structure charts**, **flowcharts** and **pseudocode** – see Section 7.2.

7.1.3 Coding and iterative testing

The program or set of programs is developed. Each module of the program is written using a suitable programming language and then tested to see if it works. **Iterative testing** means that modular tests are conducted, code amended, and tests repeated until the module performs as required.

7.1.4 Testing

The completed program or set of programs is run many times with different sets of test data. This ensures that all the tasks completed work together as specified in the program design.

7.2 Computer systems, sub-systems and decomposition

A **computer system** is made up of software, data, hardware, communications and people; each computer system can be divided up into a set of sub-systems. Each sub-system can be further divided into sub-systems and so on until each sub-system just performs a single action.

Computer systems can be very large, very small or any size in between; most people interact with many different computer systems during their daily life without realising it.

For example, when you wake up in the morning, you might use an app on your smartphone for your alarm, then you might check the weather forecast on your computer before driving to work.

The alarm program is a very small computer system but when you check the weather forecast, you obtain the information you need from one of the largest computer systems in the world.

Find out more

Find at least **five** computer systems you frequently use in your daily life; see if you can decide the size of each system.

7.2.1 The computer system and its sub-systems

In order to understand how a computer system is built up and how it works it is often divided up into sub-systems. This division can be shown using top-down design to produce structure diagrams that demonstrate the modular construction of the system. Each sub-system can be developed by a programmer as a sub-routine. How each sub-routine works can be shown by using **flowcharts** or **pseudocode**.

Top-down design is the decomposition of a computer system into a set of sub-systems, then breaking each sub-system down into a set of smaller sub-systems, until each sub-system just performs a single action. This is an effective way of designing a computer system to provide a solution to a problem, since each part of the problem is broken down into smaller more manageable problems. The process of breaking down into smaller sub-systems is called stepwise refinement.

This structured approach works for the development of both large and small computer systems. When larger computer systems are being developed this means that several programmers can work independently to develop and test different sub-systems for the same system at the same time. This reduces the development and testing time.

7.2.2 Decomposing a problem

Any problem that uses a computer system for its solution needs to be decomposed into its component parts. The component parts of any computer system are:

- » **inputs** – the data used by the system that needs to be entered while the system is active
- » **processes** – the tasks that need to be performed using the input data and any other previously stored data
- » **outputs** – information that needs to be displayed or printed for the users of the system
- » **storage** – data that needs to be stored in files on an appropriate medium for use in the future.

? Example 1: An alarm app

For example, the alarm app can be decomposed into:
» inputs – time to set the alarm, remove a previously set alarm time, switch an alarm off, press snooze button
» processes – continuously check if the current time matches an alarm time that has been set, storage and removal of alarm times, management of snooze
» outputs – continuous sound/tune (at alarm time or after snooze time expired)
» storage – time(s) for alarms set.

Activity 7.1

Using one of the computer systems that you identified, decompose it into its component parts of inputs, processes, outputs and storage.

7.2.3 Methods used to design and construct a solution to a problem

Solutions to problems need to be designed and developed rigorously. The use of formal methods enables the process to be clearly shown for others to understand the proposed solution. The following methods need to be used by IGCSE Computer Science students:

» structure diagrams
» flowcharts
» pseudocode.

Structure diagrams

Structure diagrams can be used to show top-down design in a diagrammatic form. **Structure diagrams** are hierarchical, showing how a computer system solution can be divided into sub-systems with each level giving a more detailed breakdown. If necessary, each sub-system can be further divided.

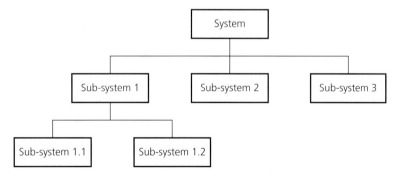

▲ **Figure 7.2** Basic structure diagram

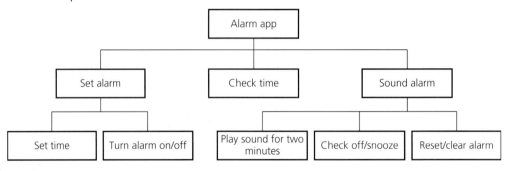

Example 2: Alarm app for a smart phone

Consider the alarm app computer system for a smart phone; this could be divided into three sub-systems, setting the alarm, checking for the alarm time, sounding the alarm. These sub-systems could then be further sub-divided; a structure diagram makes the process clearer.

 Find out more

Draw a structure diagram for cleaning your teeth. If you are brave enough ask another student to try out the system to see if it works.

▲ **Figure 7.3** Structure diagram for alarm app

Activity 7.2

Break down the 'Check time' sub-system from the smart phone alarm app into further sub-systems.

Flowcharts

A **flowchart** shows diagrammatically the steps required to complete a task and the order that they are to be performed. These steps, together with the order, are called an **algorithm.** Flowcharts are an effective way to communicate how the algorithm that makes up a system or sub-system works.

Example 3: Checking for the alarm time

Have a look at a flowchart showing how the checking for the alarm time sub-system works.

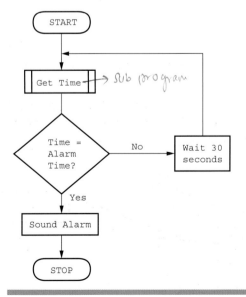

◀ **Figure 7.4** Flowchart for check time sub-system

Flowcharts are drawn using standard flowchart symbols.

Begin/End

Terminator flowchart symbols are used at the beginning and end of each flowchart.

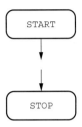

▲ **Figure 7.5** Terminator symbols

Process

Process flowchart symbols are used to show actions, for example, when values are assigned to variables. If a process has been defined elsewhere then the name of that process is shown.

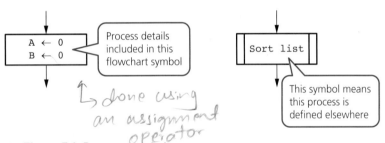

↳ done using an assignment operator

▲ **Figure 7.6** Process symbols

Input and output

The same flowchart symbol is used to show the input of data and output of information.

Parallelogram 4 Input and output

▲ **Figure 7.7** Symbol used to show input and symbol used to show output

Decision

Decision flowchart symbols are used to decide which action is to be taken next; these can be used for selection and repetition/iteration. There are always two outputs from a decision flowchart symbol.

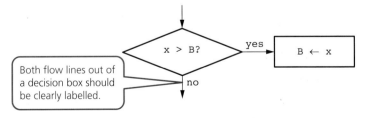

▲ **Figure 7.8** Decision symbol

▲ **Figure 7.9** Flow line

Flow lines

Flowchart flow lines use arrows to show the direction of flow, which is usually, but not always, top to bottom and left to right.

❓ Example 4: Concert ticket sales

Tickets are sold for a concert at $20 each, if 10 tickets are bought then the discount is 10%, if 20 tickets are bought the discount is 20%. No more than 25 tickets can be bought in a single transaction.

This is flowchart showing an algorithm to calculate the cost of buying a given number of tickets:

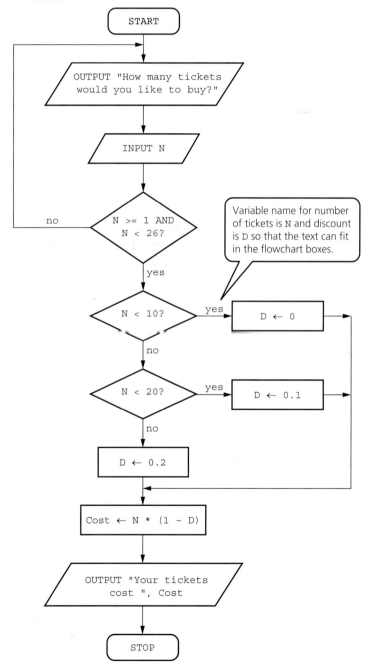

▲ **Figure 7.10** Flowchart for ticket cost calculator

Pseudocode

Pseudocode is a simple method of showing an algorithm. It describes what the algorithm does by using English key words that are very similar to those used in a high-level programming language. Data items to be processed by the algorithm are given meaningful names in the same way that variables and constants are in a high-level programming language. However, pseudocode is not bound by the strict syntax rules of a programming language. It does what its name says, it pretends to be programming code!

To ensure that pseudocode is easily understandable by others it is useful to be consistent in the way that it is written.

The pseudocode in this book is written in the following way to match the pseudocode given in the IGCSE Computer Science syllabus and to help you understand the algorithms more easily:

» a non-proportional font is used throughout
» all keywords (words used to describe a specific action e.g. INPUT) are written in capital letters
» all names given to data items and subroutines start with a capital letter
» where conditional and loop statements are used, repeated or selected statements are indented by two spaces.

The pseudocode for an assignment statement

A value is assigned to an item/variable using the ← operator. The variable on the left of the ← is assigned the value of the expression on the right. The expression on the right can be a single value or several values combined with any of the following mathematical operators.

▼ **Table 7.1** Mathematical operators

Operator	Action
+	Add
−	Subtract
*	Multiply
/	Divide
^	Raise to the power
( )	Group

Examples of pseudocode assignment statements:

`Cost ← 10`	**Cost** has the value 10
`Price ← Cost * 2`	**Price** has the value 20
`Tax ← Price * 0.12`	**Tax** has the value 2.4
`SellingPrice ← Price + Tax`	**SellingPrice** has the value 22.4
`Gender ← "M"`	**Gender** has the value **M**
`Chosen ← False`	**Chosen** has the value **False**

Activity 7.3

What values will the following variables have after the assignments have been completed?

```
Amount ← 100

TotalPrice ← Amount * 3.5

Discount ← 0.2

FinalPrice ← TotalPrice - TotalPrice * Discount

Name ← "Nikki"

Message ← "Hello " + Name
```

The pseudocode for conditional statements

When different actions are performed by an algorithm according to the values of the variables, conditional statements can be used to decide which action should be taken.

There are two types of conditional statement:

1 a condition that can be true or false such as: **IF ... THEN ... ELSE ... ENDIF**

```
IF Age < 18

  THEN

    OUTPUT "Child"

  ELSE

    OUTPUT "Adult"

ENDIF
```

2 a choice between several different values, such as: **CASE OF ... OTHERWISE ... ENDCASE**

```
CASE OF Grade

  "A" : OUTPUT "Excellent"

  "B" : OUTPUT "Good"

  "C" : OUTPUT "Average"

  OTHERWISE OUTPUT "Improvement is needed"

ENDCASE
```

IF ... THEN ... ELSE ... ENDIF

For an **IF** condition the **THEN** path is followed if the condition is true and the **ELSE** path is followed if the condition is false. There may or may not be an **ELSE** path. The end of the statement is shown by **ENDIF**.

There are different ways that an **IF** condition can be set up:

» use of a Boolean variable that can have the value **TRUE** or **FALSE** (see Chapter 8 for details of Boolean variables). For example:

```
IF Found

   THEN

      OUTPUT "Your search was successful"

   ELSE

      OUTPUT "Your search was unsuccessful"

ENDIF
```

» comparisons made by using comparison operators, where comparisons are made from left to right, for example: **A > B** means 'A is greater than B' Comparisons can be simple or more complicated, for example:

```
IF ((Height > 1) OR (Weight > 20)) AND (Age < 70) AND
   (Age > 5)

   THEN

      OUTPUT "You can ride"

   ELSE

      OUTPUT "Too small, too young or too old"

ENDIF
```

▼ **Table 7.2** Comparison operators

Operator	Comparison
>	Greater than
<	Less than
=	Equal
>=	Greater than or equal
<=	Less than or equal
<>	Not equal
AND	Both
OR	Either
NOT	Not

Have a look at the algorithm below that checks if a percentage mark is valid and whether it is a pass or a fail. This makes use of two **IF** statements; the second **IF** statement is part of the first **ELSE** path. This is called a **nested IF**.

Find out more

Programming is covered in Chapter 8. When you have started your programming, write and test a program for this algorithm.

```
OUTPUT "Please enter a mark "
INPUT PercentageMark
IF PercentageMark < 0 OR PercentageMark > 100
  THEN
     OUTPUT "Invalid Mark"
  ELSE
     IF PercentageMark > 49
       THEN
          OUTPUT "Pass"
       ELSE
          OUTPUT "Fail"
     ENDIF
ENDIF
```

A rejected percentage mark must be either less than zero or greater than 100

This is a nested IF statement, shown clearly by the use of a second level of indentation. The percentage mark is only tested if it is in the correct range

Activity 7.4

Re-write the algorithm to check for a mark between 0 and 20 and a pass mark of 10.

CASE OF ... OTHERWISE ... ENDCASE

For a **CASE** statement the value of the variable decides the path to be taken. Several values are usually specified. **OTHERWISE** is the path taken for all other values. The end of the statement is shown by **ENDCASE**.

Have a look at the algorithm below that specifies what happens if the value of **Choice** is **1**, **2**, **3** or **4**.

```
CASE OF Choice
   1 : Answer ← Num1 + Num2
   2 : Answer ← Num1 - Num2
   3 : Answer ← Num1 * Num2
   4 : Answer ← Num1 / Num2
   OTHERWISE OUTPUT "Please enter a valid choice"
ENDCASE
```

Activity 7.5

Use a **CASE** statement to display the day of the week if the variable **DAY** has a whole number value between **1** and **7** inclusive and an error message otherwise.

The pseudocode for iteration

When some actions performed as part of an algorithm need repeating this is called iteration. Loop structures are used to perform the iteration.

Pseudocode includes these three different types of loop structure:

A set number of repetitions	`FOR … TO … NEXT`
A repetition, where the number of repeats is not known, that is completed at least once:	`REPEAT … UNTIL`
A repetition, where the number of repeats is not known, that may never be completed:	`WHILE … DO … ENDWHILE`

All types of loops can all perform the same task, for example displaying ten stars:

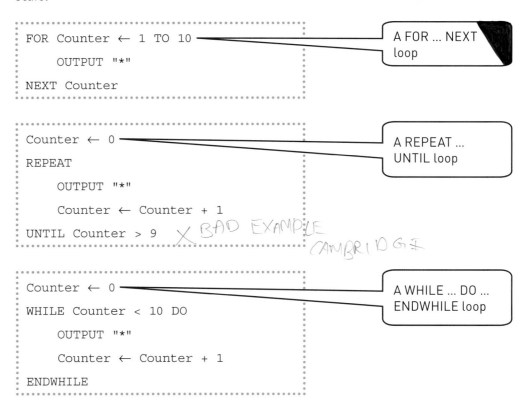

```
FOR Counter ← 1 TO 10
    OUTPUT "*"
NEXT Counter
```
A FOR … NEXT loop

```
Counter ← 0
REPEAT
    OUTPUT "*"
    Counter ← Counter + 1
UNTIL Counter > 9
```
A REPEAT … UNTIL loop

✗ BAD EXAMPLE CAMBRIDGE

```
Counter ← 0
WHILE Counter < 10 DO
    OUTPUT "*"
    Counter ← Counter + 1
ENDWHILE
```
A WHILE … DO … ENDWHILE loop

As you can see, the **FOR … TO … NEXT** loop is the most efficient way for a programmer to write this type of task as the loop counter is automatically managed.

FOR … TO … NEXT loops

A variable is set up, with a start value and an end value, this variable is incremented in steps of one until the end value is reached and the iteration finishes. The variable can be used within the loop so long as its value is not changed. This type of loop is very useful for reading values into lists with a known length.

Link

For more on arrays see Chapter 8.

```
FOR Counter ← 1 TO 10
    OUTPUT "Enter Name of Student "
    INPUT StudentName[Counter]
NEXT
```
Counter starts at 1 and finishes at 10

Array (see Chapter 8) items `StudentName[1]` to `StudentName[10]` have data input

REPEAT ... UNTIL loop

This loop structure is used when the number of repetitions/iterations is not known and the actions are repeated **UNTIL** a given condition becomes true. The actions in this loop are always completed at least once. This is a post-condition loop as the test for exiting the loop is at the end of the loop.

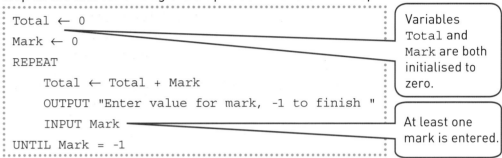

```
Total ← 0
Mark ← 0
REPEAT
    Total ← Total + Mark
    OUTPUT "Enter value for mark, -1 to finish "
    INPUT Mark
UNTIL Mark = -1
```

Variables Total and Mark are both initialised to zero.

At least one mark is entered.

WHILE ... DO ... ENDWHILE loop

This loop structure is used when the number of repetitions/iterations is not known and the actions are only repeated **WHILE** a given condition is true. If the **WHILE** condition is untrue then the actions in this loop are never performed. This is a pre-condition loop as the test for exiting the loop is at the beginning of the loop.

```
Total ← 0
OUTPUT "Enter value for mark, -1 to finish "
INPUT Mark
WHILE Mark <> -1 DO
    Total ← Total + Mark
    OUTPUT "Enter value for mark, -1 to finish"
    INPUT Mark
ENDWHILE
```

Only the variable Total is initialised to zero

Condition tested at start of loop

The pseudocode for input and output statements

INPUT and **OUTPUT** are used for the entry of data and display of information. Sometimes **READ** can be used instead of **INPUT** but this is usually used for reading from files – see Chapter 8. Also, **PRINT** can be used instead of **OUTPUT** if a hard copy is required.

INPUT is used for data entry; it is usually followed by a variable where the data input is stored, for example:

```
INPUT Name
```

```
INPUT StudentMark
```

OUTPUT is used to display information either on a screen or printed on paper; it is usually followed by a single value that is a string or a variable, or a list of values separated by commas, for example:

```
OUTPUT Name
```

```
OUTPUT "Your name is ", Name
```

```
OUTPUT Name1, "Ali", Name3
```

7.3 Explaining the purpose of an algorithm

An algorithm sets out the steps to complete a given task. This is usually shown as a flowchart or pseudocode, so that the purpose of the task and the processes needed to complete it are clear to those who study it.

You will be able to practise this skill as you become more familiar with writing and finding and correcting errors in algorithms.

? Example 1: Output an alarm sound

The purpose of the following pseudocode is to output the alarm sound at the appropriate time. The processes are: waiting 10 seconds, getting the current time, checking the current time with the alarm time, and outputting the alarm sound when the times match.

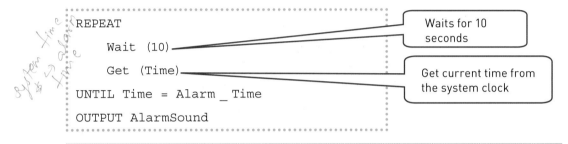

```
REPEAT
        Wait (10)                    ┌─── Waits for 10 seconds
        Get (Time)                   ├─── Get current time from the system clock
UNTIL Time = Alarm _ Time
OUTPUT AlarmSound
```

Activity 7.6

Have a look at the flowchart and pseudocode below:
» identify the purpose of the algorithm that they both represent
» identify the processes included in the algorithm.

What would be output if the numbers 7 and 18 were input?

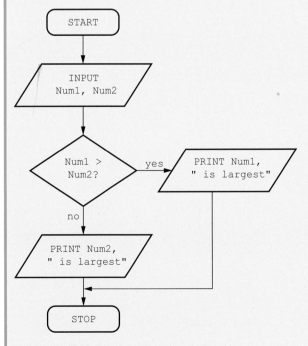

```
INPUT Num1, Num2

IF Num1 > Num2

    THEN PRINT NUM1, " is largest"

    ELSE PRINT NUM2, " is largest"

ENDIF
```

▲ **Figure 7.11** Flowchart and pseudocode

7.4 Standard methods of solution

The ability to repeat existing methods is very important in the design of algorithms; when an algorithm is turned into a program the same methods may be repeated many thousands of times.

You need to be able to use and understand these standard methods used in algorithms:

» Totalling
» Counting
» Finding maximum, minimum, and average (mean) values
» Searching using a linear search
» Sorting using a bubble sort.

All the standard methods of solution are shown as pseudocode algorithms and will be used to practise program writing in the next chapter.

7.4.1 Totalling

Totalling means keeping a total that values are added to. For example, keeping a running total of the marks awarded to each student in a class.

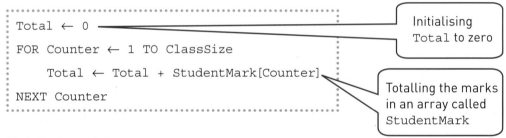

```
Total ← 0

FOR Counter ← 1 TO ClassSize

    Total ← Total + StudentMark[Counter]

NEXT Counter
```

Initialising Total to zero

Totalling the marks in an array called StudentMark

7.4.2 Counting

Keeping a count of the number of times an action is performed is another standard method. For example, counting the number of students that were awarded a pass mark:

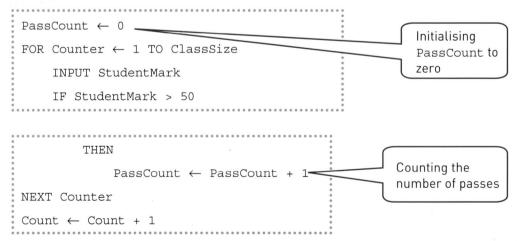

```
PassCount ← 0

FOR Counter ← 1 TO ClassSize

    INPUT StudentMark

    IF StudentMark > 50
```

Initialising PassCount to zero

```
        THEN

            PassCount ← PassCount + 1

NEXT Counter

Count ← Count + 1
```

Counting the number of passes

Counting is also used to count down until a certain value is reached, for example, checking the number of items in stock in a supermarket:

```
    :
NumberInStock ← NumberInStock - 1
IF NumberInStock < 20
    THEN
        CALL Reorder()
    :
```

> Counting down items in stock

7.4.3 Maximum, minimum and average

Finding the largest and smallest values in a list are two standard methods that are frequently found in algorithms, for example, finding the highest and lowest mark awarded to a class of students.

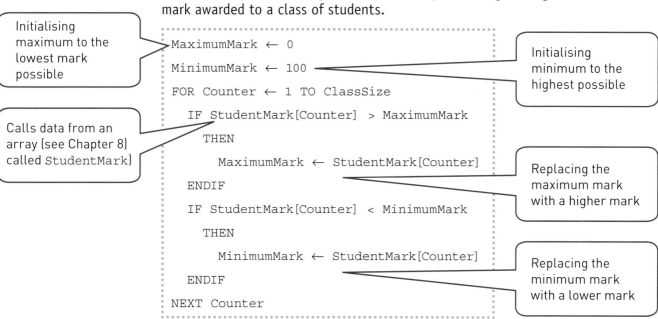

> Initialising maximum to the lowest mark possible

> Calls data from an array (see Chapter 8) called StudentMark

> Initialising minimum to the highest possible

> Replacing the maximum mark with a higher mark

> Replacing the minimum mark with a lower mark

```
MaximumMark ← 0
MinimumMark ← 100
FOR Counter ← 1 TO ClassSize
  IF StudentMark[Counter] > MaximumMark
    THEN
      MaximumMark ← StudentMark[Counter]
  ENDIF
  IF StudentMark[Counter] < MinimumMark
    THEN
      MinimumMark ← StudentMark[Counter]
  ENDIF
NEXT Counter
```

If the largest and smallest values are not known, an alternative method is to set the maximum and minimum values to the first item in the list.

For example, using this method to find the highest and lowest mark awarded to a class of students.

```
MaximumMark ← StudentMark[1]
MinimumMark ← StudentMark[1]
FOR Counter ← 2 TO ClassSize
  IF StudentMark[Counter] > MaximumMark
    THEN
      MaximumMark ← StudentMark[Counter]
  ENDIF
  IF StudentMark[Counter] < MinimumMark
    THEN
      MinimumMark ← StudentMark[Counter]
  ENDIF
NEXT Counter
```

> Initialising minimum and maximum to the first mark

> Starting the loop at the second position in the list.

Calculating the average (mean) of all the values in a list is an extension of the totalling method, for example, calculating the average mark for a class of students.

```
Total ← 0
FOR Counter ← 1 TO ClassSize
  Total ← Total + StudentMark[Counter]
NEXT Counter
Average ← Total / ClassSize
```

> Calculating the average from the total after the loop has been completed

7.4.4 Linear search

A search is used to check if a value is stored in a list, performed by systematically working through the items in the list. There are several standard search methods, but you only need to understand one method for IGCSE Computer Science. This is called a **linear search**, which inspects each item in a list in turn to see if the item matches the value searched for.

For example, searching for a name in a class list of student names, where all the names stored are different:

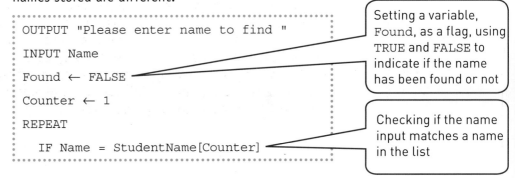

```
OUTPUT "Please enter name to find "
INPUT Name
Found ← FALSE
Counter ← 1
REPEAT
  IF Name = StudentName[Counter]
```

> Setting a variable, Found, as a flag, using TRUE and FALSE to indicate if the name has been found or not

> Checking if the name input matches a name in the list

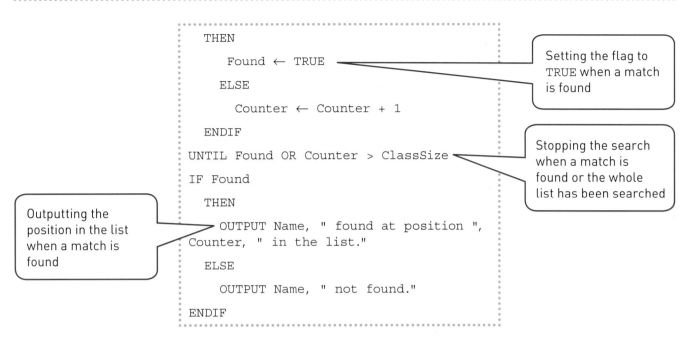

```
   THEN
      Found ← TRUE
   ELSE
      Counter ← Counter + 1
   ENDIF
UNTIL Found OR Counter > ClassSize
IF Found
   THEN
      OUTPUT Name, " found at position ",
Counter, " in the list."
   ELSE
      OUTPUT Name, " not found."
ENDIF
```

Setting the flag to TRUE when a match is found

Stopping the search when a match is found or the whole list has been searched

Outputting the position in the list when a match is found

In this example, the search checks how many people chose ice cream as their favourite dessert, where several values in the list can be the same.

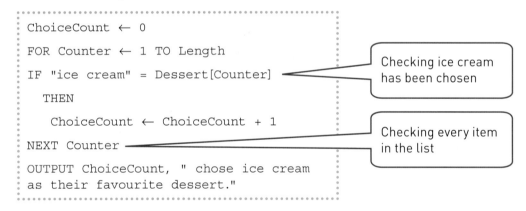

```
ChoiceCount ← 0
FOR Counter ← 1 TO Length
IF "ice cream" = Dessert[Counter]
   THEN
      ChoiceCount ← ChoiceCount + 1
NEXT Counter
OUTPUT ChoiceCount, " chose ice cream
as their favourite dessert."
```

Checking ice cream has been chosen

Checking every item in the list

7.4.5 Bubble sort

Lists can be more useful if the items are sorted in a meaningful order. For example, names could be sorted in alphabetical order, or temperatures could be sorted in ascending or descending order. There are several standard sorting methods available, but you only need to understand one method for IGCSE Computer Science.

This method of sorting is called a **bubble sort.** Each element is compared with the next element and swapped if the elements are in the wrong order, starting from the first element and finishing with next-to-last element. Once it reaches the end of the list, we can be sure that the last element is now in the correct place. However, other items in the list may still be out of order. Each element in the list is compared again apart from the last one because we know the final element is in the correct place. This continues to repeat until there is only one element left to check or no swaps are made.

For example, the bubble sort algorithm can be used to sort a list of ten temperatures stored in the array, **Temperature[]**, into ascending order. It could be written in pseudocode as:

```
First ← 1
Last ← 10
REPEAT
  Swap ← FALSE
  FOR Index ← First TO Last - 1
    IF Temperature[Index] > temperature[Index + 1]
      THEN
        Temp ← Temperature[Index]
        Temperature[Index] ← Temperature[Index + 1]
        Temperature[Index + 1] ← Temp
        Swap ← TRUE
    ENDIF
  NEXT Index
  Last ← Last - 1
UNTIL (NOT Swap) OR Last = 1
```

The IF..THEN condition checks if temperatures are in ascending order and swaps them if they are not, using the Temp variable (short for temporary)

7.5 Validation and verification

In order for computer systems to only accept data inputs that are reasonable and accurate, every item of data needs to be examined before it is accepted by the system.

Two different methods, with very similar sounding names, are used. For data entry, validation ensures that only data that is reasonable is accepted. Verification is used to check that the data does not change as it is being entered.

7.5.1 Validation

Validation is the automated checking by a program that data is reasonable before it is accepted into a computer system. When data is validated by a computer system, if the data is rejected a message should be output explaining why the data was rejected and another opportunity given to enter the data.

There are many different types of validation checks including:

>> **range checks**
>> **length checks**
>> **type checks**
>> **presence checks**
>> **format checks**
>> **check digits.**

Different types of check may be used on the same piece of data; for example, an examination mark could be checked for reasonableness by using a range check, a type check and a presence check.

Range check

A **range check** checks that the value of a number is between an upper value and a lower value. For example, checking that percentage marks are between 0 and 100 inclusive:

```
OUTPUT "Please enter the student's mark "

REPEAT

INPUT StudentMark

IF StudentMark < 0 OR StudentMark > 100

   THEN

      OUTPUT "The student's mark should be in the range
                0 to 100, please re-enter the mark "

ENDIF

UNTIL StudentMark >= 0 AND StudentMark <= 100
```

Length check

A **length check** checks *either*:

>> that data contains an exact number of characters, for example that a password must be exactly eight characters in length so that passwords with seven or fewer characters or nine or more characters would be rejected, for instance:

> Password has a data type of string and LENGTH is the pseudocode operation that returns a whole number showing the number of characters in the string

```
OUTPUT "Please enter your password of eight
characters "

REPEAT

   INPUT Password

   IF LENGTH(Password) <> 8

      THEN

         OUTPUT "Your password must be exactly eight
                 characters, please re-enter "

      ENDIF

UNTIL LENGTH(Password) = 8
```

>> *or* that the data entered is a reasonable number of characters, for example, a family name could be between two and thirty characters inclusive so that names with one character or thirty-one or more characters would be rejected.

> FamilyName has a data type of string and LENGTH is the pseudocode operation that returns a whole number showing the number of characters in the string

```
OUTPUT "Please enter your family name "
REPEAT
  INPUT FamilyName
  IF LENGTH(FamilyName) > 30 OR LENGTH(FamilyName) < 2
    THEN
      OUTPUT "Too short or too long,
      please re-enter "
  ENDIF
UNTIL LENGTH(FamilyName) <= 30 AND LENGTH(FamilyName) >= 2
```

Link

To understand some of the concepts and commands in this code, such as **DIV**, see Chapter 8.

 Find out more

Programming is covered in Chapter 8. When you have started your programming, find out how you could test for a whole number and write and test a program for this validation rule.

Type check

A type check checks that the data entered is of a given data type, for example, that the number of brothers or sisters would be an integer (whole number).

```
OUTPUT "How many brothers do you have? "
REPEAT
INPUT NumberOfBrothers
IF NumberOfBrothers <> DIV(NumberOfBrothers, 1)
  THEN
    OUTPUT "This must be a whole number, please re-enter"
ENDIF
UNTIL NumberOfBrothers = DIV(NumberOfBrothers, 1)
```

Presence check

A **presence check** checks to ensure that some data has been entered and the value has not been left blank, for example, an email address for an online transaction must be completed.

```
OUTPUT "Please enter your email address "
REPEAT
INPUT EmailAddress
IF EmailAddress = ""
  THEN
    OUTPUT "*=Required "
ENDIF
UNTIL EmailAddress <> ""
```

▲ **Figure 7.12** Presence check error message

Format check and check digit

A **format check** checks that the characters entered conform to a pre-defined pattern, for example, in Chapter 9 the cub number must be in the form CUB9999. The pseudocode for this example will be given in the string handling section of Chapter 9.

A **check digit** is the final digit included in a code; it is calculated from all the other digits in the code. Check digits are used for barcodes, product codes, International Standard Book Numbers (ISBN) and Vehicle Identification Numbers (VIN).

Check digits are used to identify errors in data entry caused by mis-typing or mis-scanning a barcode. They can usually detect the following types of error:

>> an incorrect digit entered, for example, 5327 entered instead of 5307
>> transposition errors where two numbers have changed order for example 5037 instead of 5307
>> omitted or extra digits, for example, 537 instead of 5307 or 53107 instead of 5307
>> phonetic errors, for example, 13, thirteen, instead of 30, thirty.

> ### Link
>
> ISBN and modulo-11 check digit calculations are covered in Chapter 2.

▲ **Figure 7.13** ISBN 13 code with check digit

 Find out more

1   Find an ISBN, then show that its check digit is correct.
    Working in pairs find two ISBNs each, copy one down with a transposition error and the other one correctly.
    Swap your ISBNs and see if you can find the one with the error.
    Look at a correct ISBN, can you think of an error that this system will not identify and explain with an example why this is the case?
2   Find out how limit checks and consistency checks are used.

Activity 7.7

1 State, with reasons, which validation checks you could use for the following inputs.

 You may decide that more than one validation check is required.
 - Entering a telephone number
 - Entering a pupil's name
 - Entering a part number in the form XXX999, when X must be a letter and 9 must be a digit.

2 Write an algorithm using pseudocode to check the age and height of a child who wants to go on a fairground ride. The age must be over 7 and under 12, the height must be over 110 centimetres and under 150 centimetres.

3 Write an algorithm using pseudocode to check that the length of a password is between 8 and 12 characters inclusive.

7.5.2 Verification

Verification is checking that data has been accurately copied from one source to another – for instance, input into a computer or transferred from one part of a computer system to another.

Verification methods for input data include:

» Double entry
» Screen/visual check.

For **double entry** the data is entered twice, sometimes by different operators. The computer system compares both entries and if they are different outputs an error message requesting that the data is entered again.

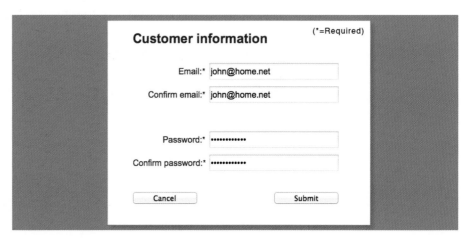

Customer information   (*=Required)

Email:* john@home.net

Confirm email:* john@home.net

Password:* ••••••••••••

Confirm password:* ••••••••••••

Cancel   Submit

▲ **Figure 7.14** Double entry

Link

Parity checks and checksums are used when data is transferred from one part of a computer system to another, or across a network, and are discussed in Chapter 2.

A **screen/visual check** is a manual check completed by the user who is entering the data. When the data entry is complete the data is displayed on the screen and the user is asked to confirm that it is correct before continuing. The user either checks the data on the screen against a paper document that is being used as an input form or, confirms whether it is correct from their own knowledge.

7.6 Test data

7.6.1 How to suggest and apply suitable test data

In order to determine whether a solution is working as it should, it needs to be tested. Usually before a whole system is tested each sub-system is tested separately.

Algorithms written in pseudocode or as flowcharts can be tested by a person working through them using any data that is required and seeing what the result is. Computer programs can be tested by running them on a computer using any data that is required and seeing what result is output. However, in order to test a solution thoroughly it may need to be worked through several times with different sets of test data.

A **set of test data** is all the items of data required to work through a solution. For instance, the set of test data used for Activity 7.6 was 7 and 18.

In order to prove that program or algorithm solutions do what they are supposed to do, a set of test data should be used that the program would normally be expected to work with, together with the result(s) that are expected from that data. The type of test data used to do this is called **normal data**. Normal data should be used to work through the solution to find the actual result(s) and see if they are the same as the expected result(s).

For example, consider an algorithm that records the percentage marks, entered in whole numbers, from ten end-of-term examinations for a pupil, and then finds the average mark. A set of normal test data for this purpose could be:

Normal test data: 50, 50, 50, 50, 50, 50 50, 50, 50, 50

Expected result: 50

Solutions also need to be tested to prove that they do **not** do what they are supposed not to do. In order to do this, test data should be chosen that would be rejected by the solution as not suitable, if the solution is working properly. This type of test data is called **abnormal test data**. (It is also sometimes called **erroneous test data**.)

For example, erroneous/abnormal data for our algorithm to find the average percentage marks from ten end of term examinations could be:

Erroneous/abnormal data: -12, eleven

Expected results: both of these values should be rejected

Activity 7.10

Provide some more erroneous/abnormal data and its expected results.

When testing algorithms with numerical values, sometimes only a given range of values should be allowed. For example, percentage marks should only be in the range 0 to 100. Our algorithm above should be tested with **extreme data**. Extreme data are the largest and smallest values that normal data can take. In this case:

Extreme data: 0, 100

Expected results: these values should be accepted

There is another type of test data called **boundary data**. This is used to establish where the largest and smallest values occur. At each boundary two values are required: one value is accepted and the other value is rejected. For example, for percentage marks in the range 0 to 100, the algorithm should be tested with the following **boundary data**:

Boundary data for 0 is: -1, 0

Expected results: -1 is rejected, 0 is accepted

Activity 7.11

1 Provide boundary data for the upper end of the range; assume that the percentage marks are always whole numbers.

2 The end of term examinations are now marked out of twenty. Provide the following:
   - Two sets of normal data and their expected results
   - Some erroneous/abnormal data and their expected results
   - Two sets of boundary data and their expected results.

7.7 Trace tables to document dry runs of algorithms

A thorough structured approach is required to find out the purpose of an algorithm. This involves recording and studying the results from each step in the algorithm and requires the use of test data.

? **Worked example**

Consider the algorithm represented by the following flowchart:

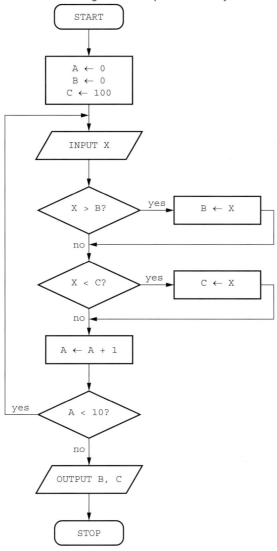

▲ **Figure 7.15** Flowchart to trace

A **trace table** can be used to record the results from each step in an algorithm; it is used to record the value of an item (variable) each time that it changes. The manual exercise of working through an algorithm step by step is called a **dry run**.

A trace table is set up with a column for each variable and a column for any output. For example:

▼ **Table 7.3** Trace table

A	B	C	X	OUTPUT
0	0	100		

Test data is then used to dry run the flowchart and record the results on the trace table. During a dry run:

» every time the value of a variable is changed, the new value is entered in that column of the trace table

» every time a value is output, the value is shown in the output column.

Test data: 9, 7, 3, 12, 6, 4, 15, 2, 8, 5

▼ **Table 7.4** Completed trace table for flowchart

A	B	C	X	OUTPUT
0	0	100		
1	9	9	9	
2		7	7	
3		3	3	
4	12		12	
5			6	
6			4	
7	15		15	
8		2	2	
9			8	
10			5	
				15 2

> The values 15 and 2 without the comma

Activity 7.12

Use a trace table and the test data 400, 800, 190, 170, 300, 110, 600, 150, 130, 900 to record another dry run of the highest and lowest number flowchart from Section 7.7.

It can be seen from the output that the algorithm selects the largest and the smallest numbers from a list of ten positive numbers. The same trace table could have been used if the algorithm had been shown using pseudocode:

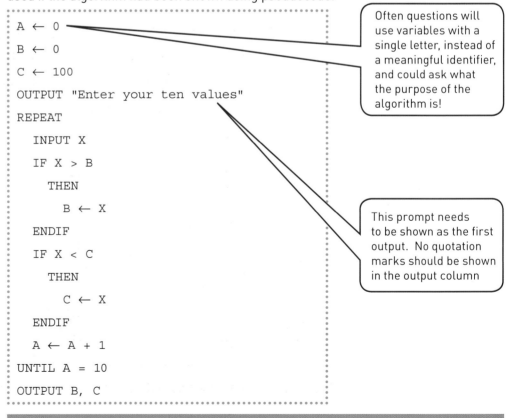

```
A ← 0
B ← 0
C ← 100
OUTPUT "Enter your ten values"
REPEAT
    INPUT X
    IF X > B
        THEN
            B ← X
    ENDIF
    IF X < C
        THEN
            C ← X
    ENDIF
    A ← A + 1
UNTIL A = 10
OUTPUT B, C
```

> Often questions will use variables with a single letter, instead of a meaningful identifier, and could ask what the purpose of the algorithm is!

> This prompt needs to be shown as the first output. No quotation marks should be shown in the output column

Activity 7.13

Use the trace table below and the test data 4, 8, 19, 17, 3, 11, 6, 1, 13, 9 to record a dry run of the pseudocode.

▼ **Table 7.5** Trace table to complete for the pseudocode

A	B	C	X	OUTPUT
0	0	100		10

Activity 7.14

Draw a trace table for the bubble sort algorithm on page 276 and use the test data 35, 31, 32, 36, 39, 37, 42, 38 to record a dry run of the pseudocode.

7.8 Identifying errors in algorithms

Trace tables and test data can be used to identify and correct errors.

Your completed trace table for Activity 7.14 should look like this:

▼ **Table 7.6** Completed trace table for flowchart

A	B	C	X	OUTPUT
0	0	100		
1	400		400	
2	800		800	
3			190	
4			170	
5			300	
6			110	
7			600	
8			150	
9			130	
10	900		900	
				900 100

There is an error as the smallest number, 110, has not been identified.

Activity 7.15

Use a trace table and some negative test data to record another dry run of the pseudocode or flowchart. What error have you found?

As this algorithm only works for numbers between 0 and 100; a better algorithm could look like this:

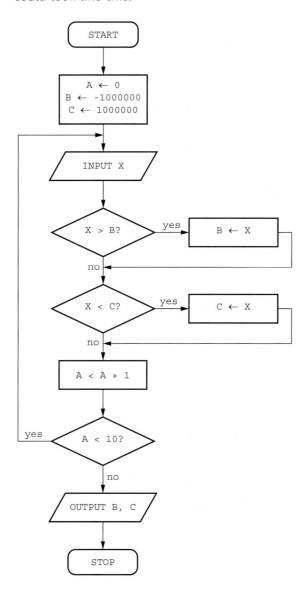

▲ **Figure 7.16** A better algorithm

This algorithm is very similar and works for a much larger range of numbers, but it still does not work for every set of numbers.

Activity 7.16

Identify two numbers where the algorithm will still fail.

In order to work for any set of numbers, the algorithm needs to be re-written to allow the largest and smallest numbers to be tested against numbers that appear in any list provided. The provisional values set at the start of the algorithm need to be chosen from the list. A standard method is to set both these provisional values to the value of the first item input.

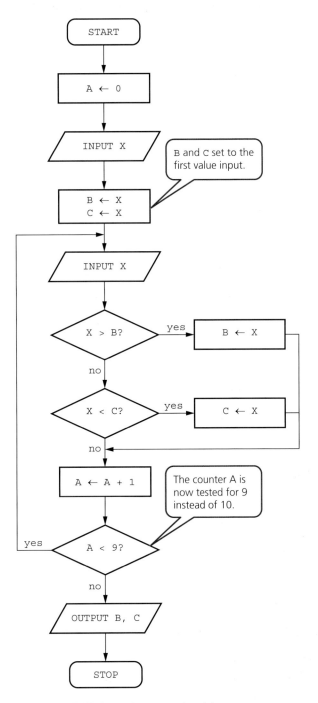

▲ **Figure 7.17** A much better algorithm

> **Activity 7.17**
> Rewrite the pseudocode so it works for every set of numbers like the flowchart above.
> Test your pseudocode algorithm with this set of test data:
> -97, 12390, 0, 77, 359, -2, -89, 5000, 21, 67

7.9 Writing and amending algorithms

There are a number of stages when producing an algorithm for a given problem:

1 Make sure that the problem is clearly specified – the purpose of the algorithm and the tasks to be completed by the algorithm.

2 Break the problem down in to sub-problems; if it is complex, you may want to consider writing an algorithm for each sub-problem. Most problems, even the simplest ones can be divided into:
   - Set up processes
   - Input
   - Processing of data
   - Permanent storage of data (if required)
   - Output of results.

3 Decide on how any data is to be obtained and stored, what is going to happen to the data and how any results are going to be displayed.

4 Design the structure of your algorithm using a structure diagram.

5 Decide on how you are going to construct your algorithm, either using a flowchart or pseudocode. If you are told how to construct your algorithm, then follow the guidance.

6 Construct your algorithm, making sure that it can be easily read and understood by someone else. Precision is required when writing algorithms, just as it is when writing program code. This involves setting it out clearly and using meaningful names for any data stores. Take particular care with conditions used for loops and selection, for example 'Counter >= 10' rather than 'Counter ten or over'. The algorithms that you have looked at so far in this chapter were not designed with readability in mind because you needed to work out what the problem being solved was.

7 Use several sets of test data (Normal, Abnormal and Boundary) to dry run your algorithm and show the results in trace tables, to enable you to find any errors.

8 If any errors are found, correct them and repeat the process until you think that your algorithm works perfectly.

Have a look at this structure diagram and flowchart for the algorithm to select the largest, Max, and smallest, Min, numbers from a list of ten numbers. This time the flowchart is more easily readable than the structure chart:

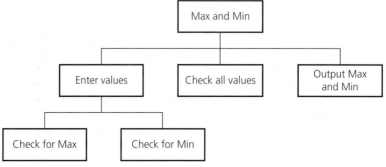

▲ **Figure 7.18** Structure chart for Max and Min

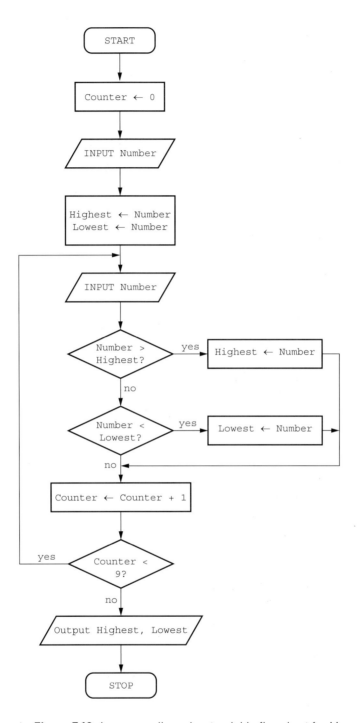

▲ **Figure 7.19** A more easily understandable flowchart for Max and Min

❓ Example 1: Writing algorithms in pseudocode

Tickets are sold for a concert at $20 each. If 10 tickets are bought then the discount is 10%, if 20 tickets are bought the discount is 20%. No more than 25 tickets can be bought in a single transaction.

a Use pseudocode to write the algorithm to calculate the cost of buying a given number of tickets.

b   Explain how you would test your algorithm.

a
```
REPEAT
   OUTPUT "How many tickets would you like to buy? "
   INPUT NumberOfTickets
UNTIL NumberOfTickets > 0 AND NumberOfTickets < 26
IF NumberOfTickets < 10
   THEN
      Discount ← 0
   ELSE
      IF NumberOfTickets < 20
         THEN
            Discount ← 0.1
         ELSE
            Discount ← 0.2
      ENDIF
ENDIF
Cost ← NumberOfTickets * 20 * (1 - Discount)
PRINT "Your tickets cost ", Cost
```

b   I would use test data with values of:

0, 26,	Expected results rejected
1, 25,	Expected results **20, 400**
9, 10,	Expected results **180, 180**
19, 20,	Expected results **342, 320**

Activity 7.18

For the test data given in Example 1, identify the type of test data used and suggest some more test data and dry run the algorithm.

? Example 2: Writing algorithms in pseudocode

A school with 600 students wants to produce some information from the results of the four standard tests in Maths, Science, English and IT. Each test is out of 100 marks. The information output should be the highest, lowest and average mark for each test and the highest, lowest and average mark overall. All the marks need to be input.

a   Use pseudocode to write the algorithm to complete this task.
b   Explain how you would test your algorithm.

a

> Comments are used to make the algorithm more understandable

```
// initialisation of overall counters
OverallHighest ← 0
OverallLowest ← 100
OverallTotal ← 0
FOR Test ← 1 TO 4   // outer loop for the tests
```

```
// initialisation of subject counters
   SubjectHighest ← 0
   SubjectLowest ← 100
   SubjectTotal ← 0
   CASE OF Test
      1 : SubjectName ← "Maths"
      2 : SubjectName ← "Science"
      3 : SubjectName ← "English"
      4 : SubjectName ← "IT"
   ENDCASE
   FOR StudentNumber ← 1 TO 600  // inner loop for the
students
      REPEAT
         OUTPUT "Enter Student", StudentNumber, "'s mark for
", SubjectName
         INPUT Mark
      UNTIL Mark < 101 AND Mark > -1
      IF Mark < OverallLowest THEN OverallLowest ← Mark
      IF Mark < SubjectLowest THEN SubjectLowest ← Mark
      IF Mark > OverallHighest THEN OverallHighest ← Mark
      IF Mark > SubjectHighest THEN SubjectHighest ← Mark
      OverallTotal ← OverallTotal + Mark
      SubjectTotal ← SubjectTotal + Mark
   NEXT StudentNumber
   SubjectAverage ← SubjectTotal / 600
   OUTPUT SubjectName
   OUTPUT "Average mark is ", SubjectAverage
   OUTPUT "Highest Mark is ", SubjectHighest
   OUTPUT "Lowest Mark is ", SubjectLowest
NEXT Test
OverallAverage ← OverallTotal / 2400
OUTPUT "Overall Average is ", OverallAverage
OUTPUT "Overall Highest Mark is ", OverallHighest
OUTPUT "Overall Lowest Mark is ", OverallLowest
```

Find out more

Programming is covered in Chapter 8. When you have started your programming, write and test programs for Examples 1 and 2.

More practice on writing algorithms will be given in Chapter 8.

b   For the algorithm to be tested by dry running, I would reduce the number of students to 5 and the number of subjects to 2.

Activity 7.19

1 Identify the changes you would need to make to the algorithm in Example 2 to reduce the number of students to 5 and the number of subjects to 2.

  Identify the test data needed to test Example 2 with the reduced number of students and subjects.

2 With the set of test data you have chosen set up, complete a trace table so that you can compare your expected results with the actual results when you dry run the algorithm.

Activity 7.20

1 Write pseudocode to input ten positive numbers and find the total and the average.

2 Write pseudocode to input any number of positive numbers and find the total and the average. The user should enter '-1' when they have finished entering their list of positive numbers.

3 Explain why you chose the loop structure for each task.

▶ Extension

For those students interested in studying computer science at A Level, the following section is an introduction to the use of Abstract Data Types (ADTs) to store data in stacks and queues.

An **ADT** is a collection of data and a set of operations on that data. For example, a stack includes the items held on the stack and the operations to add an item to the stack (push) or remove an item from the stack (pop):

» **stack** – a list containing several items operating on the Last In First Out (LIFO) principle. Items can be added to the stack (push) and removed from the stack (pop). The first item added to a stack is the last item to be removed from the stack.

» **queue** – a list containing several items operating on the First In First Out (FIFO) principle. Items can be added to the queue (enqueue) and removed from the queue (dequeue). The first item added to a queue is the first item to be removed from the queue.

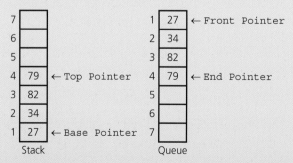

▲ **Figure 7.20** In both of these examples 27 was the first item added and 79 the last item added

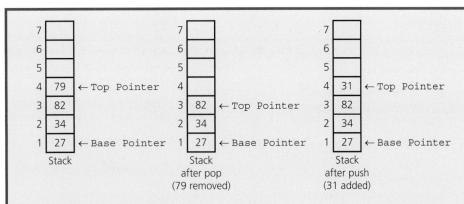

▲ **Figure 7.21** Stack operations

The value of the **Base Pointer** always remains the same during stack operations.

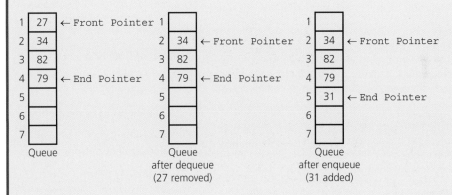

▲ **Figure 7.22** Queue operations

The values of both the **Front Pointer** and the **End Pointer** change during queue operations.

Extension activity

Show a stack and pointers after a pop operation. Show a queue and pointers after a dequeue operation.

In this chapter, you have learnt about:

✔ the program development life cycle
✔ decomposition of systems and problems in sub-systems and sub-problems
✔ design and construction of algorithms to solve problems using structure diagrams, flowcharts, and pseudocode
✔ explaining the purpose of an algorithm
✔ standard methods of solution
✔ the need and purpose of validation and verification checks on input data
✔ suggesting and applying suitable test data
✔ trace tables and dry runs
✔ writing, amending and identifying errors in algorithms.

Key terms used throughout this chapter

analysis – part of the program development life cycle; a process of investigation, leading to the specification of what a program is required to do

design – part of the program development life cycle; uses the program specification from the analysis stage to show to how the program should be developed

coding – part of the program development life cycle; the writing of the program or suite of programs

testing – part of the program development life cycle; systematic checks done on a program to make sure that it works under all conditions

abstraction – a method used in the analysis stage of the program development life cycle; the key elements required for the solution to the problem are kept and any unnecessary details and information that are not required are discarded

decomposition – a method used in the analysis stage of the program development life cycle; a complex problem is broken down into smaller parts, which can then be sub divided into even smaller parts that can be solved more easily

top-down design – the breaking down of a computer system into a set of sub-systems, then breaking each sub-system down into a set of smaller sub-systems, until each sub-system just performs a single action

inputs – the data used by the system that needs to be entered while the system is active

processes – the tasks that need to be performed by a program using the input data and any other previously stored data

output – information that needs to be displayed or printed for the users of the system

storage – data that needs to be stored in files on an appropriate media for use in the future

structure diagram – a diagram that shows the design of a computer system in a hierarchical way, with each level giving a more detailed breakdown of the system into sub-systems

flowchart – a diagram that shows the steps required for a task (sub-system) and the order in which the steps are to be performed

algorithm – an ordered set of steps to solve a problem

pseudocode – a simple method of showing an algorithm; it describes what the algorithm does by using English key words that are very similar to those used in a high-level programming language but without the strict syntax rules

linear search – an algorithm that inspects each item in a list in turn to see if the item matches the value searched for

bubble sort – an algorithm that makes multiple passes through a list comparing each element with the next element and swapping them. This continues until there is a pass where no more swaps are made

validation – automated checks carried out by a program that data is reasonable before it is accepted into a computer system

verification – checking that data has been accurately copied from another source and input into a computer or transferred from one part of a computer system to another

set of test data – all the items of data required to work through a solution

normal data – data that is accepted by a program

abnormal data – data that is rejected by a program

extreme data – the largest/smallest data value that is accepted by a program

boundary data – the largest/smallest data value that is accepted by a program and the corresponding smallest/largest rejected data value

range check – a check that the value of a number is between an upper value and a lower value

length check – a method used to check that the data entered is a specific number of characters long or that the number of characters is between an upper value and a lower value

type check – a check that the data entered is of a specific type

presence check – a check that a data item has been entered

format check – a check that the characters entered conform to a pre-defined pattern

check digit – an additional digit appended to a number to check if the entered number is error-free; check digit is a data entry check and not a data transmission check

Exam-style questions

1 A solution to a problem is decomposed into its component parts.
Name and describe the component parts. [8]

2 A computer system is to be developed to provide a modulo 11 check digit for numbers from 4 to 20 digits in length. Provide a structure diagram for this computer system. [6]

3 A phone app is being developed to split the cost of a restaurant bill between a given number of people. It is being designed to work for up to 12 diners and for bills from $10 to $500.

   a What validation checks should be used for the number of diners and the size of the bill? [2]

   b Provide two sets of normal data and their expected results. [4]

   c Provide some abnormal/erroneous data. [1]

   d Identify the boundary data required and the expected results. [4]

4 Explain what is meant by validation and verification. [4]

5 The following data is to be entered onto an online form:
  – Name
  – Date of birth
  – Password
  – Phone number.

For each item state, with reasons, the validation and verification checks that should be used on the input data. [8]

6 The following algorithm, shown as a flowchart, checks the size of a consignment of ten parcels. The dimensions of each parcel are input in centimetres.

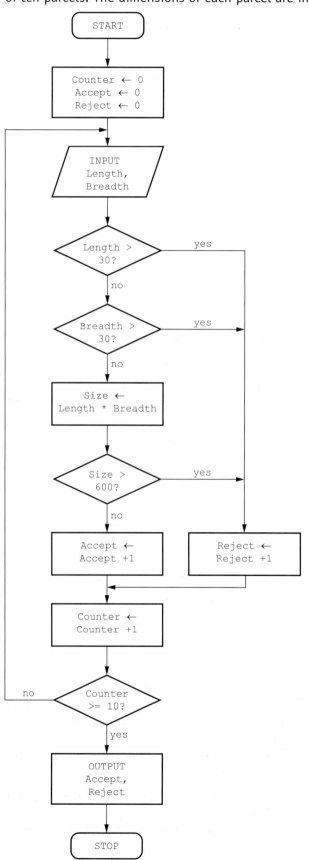

a Use this data and the following trace table to dry run the algorithm:
15, 10, 20, 17, 32, 10, 30, 35, 30, 15, 30, 28, 25, 25, 20, 15, 40, 20, 12, 10

Counter	Length	Breadth	Volume	OUTPUT

[5]

b State the processes included in this algorithm. [3]

c Identify the rules required to accept a parcel. [3]

7 The following algorithm written in pseudocode adds up 10 positive numbers and outputs the total. It contains several errors.

```
Counter ← 1
FOR Counter ← 1 TO 10
  REPEAT
    OUTPUT "Enter a positive whole number "
    INPUT Number
  UNTIL Number < 0
  Total ← Total + Counter
  Counter ← Counter + 1
  OUTPUT Total
NEXT Number
```

a Identify all the errors in the algorithm. [5]

b Rewrite the algorithm so that it is effective and error free. [4]

c Set up a trace table and some test data to dry run your rewritten algorithm. [4]

d Identify which items of your test data are normal, erroneous and extreme. [3]

8 This pseudocode algorithm inputs two non-zero numbers and a sign, and then performs the calculation shown by the sign. An input of zero for the first number terminates the process.

```
INPUT Number1, Number2, Sign

WHILE Number <> 0

    IF Sign = '+' THEN Answer ← Number1 + Number2 ENDIF

    IF Sign = '-' THEN Answer ← Number1 - Number2 ENDIF

    IF Sign = '*' THEN Answer ← Number1 * Number2 ENDIF

    IF Sign = '/' THEN Answer ← Number1 / Number2 ENDIF

    IF Sign <> '/' AND Sign <> '*' AND Sign <> '-' AND Sign <>
'+'

      THEN Answer ← 0

    ENDIF

    IF Answer <> 0 THEN OUTPUT Answer ENDIF

    INPUT Number1, Number2, Sign

ENDWHILE
```

a Complete the trace table for the input data:
5, 7, +, 6, 2, -, 4, 3, *, 7, 8, ?, 0, 0, /

Number1	Number2	Sign	Answer	OUTPUT

[3]

b Show how you could improve the algorithm written in pseudocode by writing an alternative type of conditional statement in pseudocode. [3]

Cambridge IGCSE Computer Science (0478) Paper 22 Q3, June 2018

9 A programmer has written a routine to store the name, email address and password of a contributor to a website's discussion group.
  a The programmer has chosen to verify the name, email address and password.
  Explain why verification was chosen and describe how the programmer would verify this data. [4]
  b The programmer has also decided to validate the email address and the password.
  Describe validation checks that could be used. [2]

Cambridge IGCSE Computer Science (0478) Paper 22 Q4, June 2018

8 Programming

In this chapter, you will learn about:
★ programming concepts:
  - use of variables and constants
  - input and output
  - sequence
  - selection including nesting
  - iteration
  - totalling and counting
  - string handling
  - operators – arithmetic, logical and Boolean
  - procedures and functions including the use of:
    - parameters
    - local and global variables
  - library routines
  - creating a maintainable program
★ arrays: including one- and two-dimensional arrays, use of indexes, use of iteration for reading from and writing to arrays
★ file handling: including opening, closing, reading from and writing to data and text files.

The previous chapter enabled you to develop your computational thinking by writing algorithms to perform various tasks. This chapter will show you how to put your computational thinking to the ultimate test by writing computer programs to perform tasks.

So far you have tested your algorithms by dry-running. Once you have written a program for your algorithm, and when there are no syntax errors (see Chapter 4), you will now use a computer to run the program to complete the task you have specified. The computer will perform the task exactly as you have written it; you may need to make some changes before it works exactly as you intend it to.

In Chapter 4 you learned that programs could be written in high- or low-level languages then translated and run. This chapter will introduce you to the programming concepts required for practical use of a high-level language. This chapter shows the concepts behind such programming languages but should be used in conjunction with learning the syntax of an appropriate programming language.

There are many high-level programming languages to choose from. For IGCSE Computer Science the high-level programming languages recommended are Python, Visual Basic or Java. The use of one of these languages is also required for A Level Computer Science.

Many programming languages need an interactive development environment (IDE) to write and run code. IDEs are free to download and use.

Programs developed in this chapter will be illustrated using the following freely available languages:

» `Python` a general purpose, open source programming language that promotes rapid program development and readable code. The IDE used for screenshots in this chapter is called `IDLE`.
» `Visual Basic`, a widely used programming language for Windows. The IDE used for screenshots in this chapter is called `Visual Studio`.
» `Java`, a commercial language used by many developers. The IDE used for screenshots in this chapter is called `BlueJ`.

The traditional introduction to programming in any language is to display the words 'Hello World' on a computer screen. The programs look very different, but the output is the same:

Python

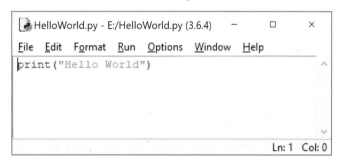

▲ **Figure 8.1** The editing window for Python

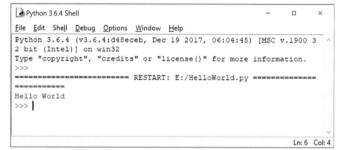

▲ **Figure 8.2** The runtime window for Python

Visual Basic

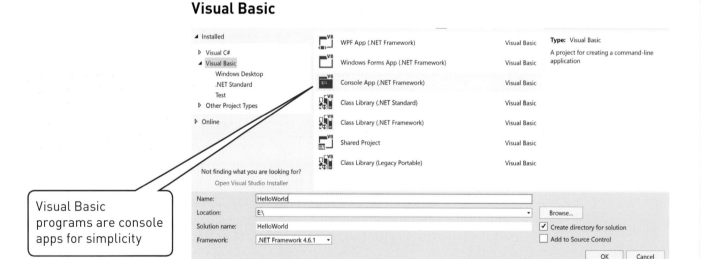

Visual Basic programs are console apps for simplicity

▲ **Figure 8.3** The Visual Basic program will run in a command line window

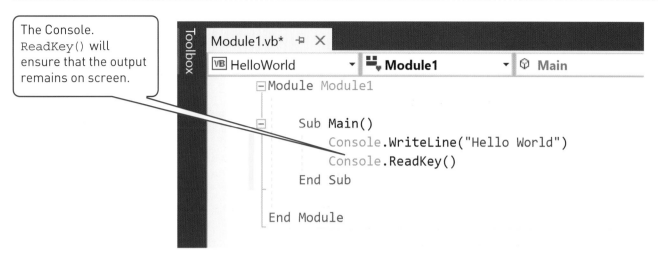

The Console.ReadKey() will ensure that the output remains on screen.

▲ **Figure 8.4** The editing window for Visual Basic

▲ **Figure 8.5** The runtime window for Visual Basic

Java

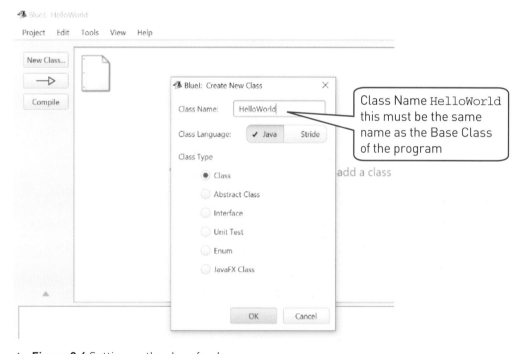

Class Name HelloWorld this must be the same name as the Base Class of the program

▲ **Figure 8.6** Setting up the class for Java

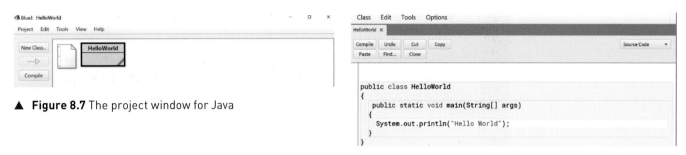

▲ **Figure 8.7** The project window for Java

▲ **Figure 8.8** The editing window for Java

Hello World

▲ **Figure 8.9** The terminal window to show the output from the program Java

---

Activity 8.1
Write and test the Hello World program in your chosen programming language.

 Find out more

Find out more about each of the three programming languages Python, Visual Basic and Java. Decide, with the help of your teacher, which programming language will be best to use for your IGCSE work.

Programming is a skill that takes time and practice to develop. In the next sections of this chapter, after you have decided which programming language you are going to use, you can just consider the examples for your chosen language.

8.1 Programming concepts
There are five basic constructs to use and understand when developing a program:

» data use – variables, constants and arrays
» sequence – order of steps in a task
» selection – choosing a path through a program
» iteration – repetition of a sequence of steps in a program
» operator use – arithmetic for calculations, logical and Boolean for decisions.

8.1.1 Variables and constants
In a program, any data used can have a fixed value that does not change while the program is running.

A **variable** in a computer program is a named data store than contains a value that may change during the execution of a program. In order to make programs understandable to others, variables should be given meaningful names.

A **constant** in a computer program is a named data store than contains a value that does not change during the execution of a program. As with variables, in order to make programs understandable to others, constants should also be given meaningful names.

Not all programming languages explicitly differentiate between constants and variables, but programmers should be clear which data stores can be changed and which cannot be changed. There are several ways of highlighting a constant, for example:

| Use of capital letters | `PI = 3.142` |
| Meaningful names that begin with Const | `ConstPi = 3.142` |

It is considered good practice to **declare** the constants and variables to be used in that program. Some languages require explicit declarations, which specifically state what type of data the variable or constant will hold. Other languages require implicit declarations, where the data type is based on the value assigned. Declarations can be at the start of a program or just before the data is used for the first time.

Here are some sample declaration statements in pseudocode and programming code – just look at the sections for pseudocode and the programming language you are using.

▼ **Table 8.1** How to declare variables and constants

Declarations of constants and variables	Language

`DECLARE FirstVar : INTEGER`
`DECLARE SecondVar : INTEGER`
`CONSTANT FirstConst ← 500`
`CONSTANT SecondConst ← 100`
	Pseudocode declarations, variables are explicit but constants are implicit.

`FirstVar = 20`
`SecondVar = 30`
`FIRSTCONST = 500`
`SECONDCONST = 100`
or
`FirstVar, SecondVar = 20, 30`
`FirstConst, SecondConst = 500,100`
	Python does not require any separate declarations and does not differentiate between constants and variables.
	
	Programmers need to keep track of and manage these differences instead.

`Dim FirstVar As Integer`
`Dim SecondVar As Integer`
`Const FirstConst As Integer = 500`
`Const SecondConst As Integer = 500`
or
`Dim FirstVar, SecondVar As Integer`
`Const First, Second As Integer = 500, 100`
	In Visual Basic variables are explicitly declared as particular data types before use. Declarations can be single statements or multiple declarations in a single statement. Constants can be explicitly typed as shown or implicitly typed, for example:
	`Const First = 500`
	… which implicitly defines the constant as an integer.

`int FirstVar;`
`int SecondVar;`
`final int FIRSTCONST = 500;`
`final int SECONDCONST = 100;`
	In Java constant values are declared as variables with a final value so no changes can be made. These final variable names are usually capitalised to show they cannot be changed.
	
	Variables are often declared as they are used rather than at the start of the code.

8.1.2 Basic data types

In order for a computer system to process and store data effectively, different kinds of data are formally given different types. This enables:

» data to be stored in an appropriate way, for example, as numbers or as characters
» data to be manipulated effectively, for example, numbers with mathematical operators and characters with concatenation
» automatic validation in some cases.

The basic data types you will need to use for IGCSE Computer Science are:

» integer – a positive or negative whole number that can be used with mathematical operators
» real – a positive or negative number with a fractional part. Real numbers can be used with mathematical operators
» char – a variable or constant that is a single character
» string – a variable or constant that is several characters in length. Strings vary in length and may even have no characters (known as an empty string); the characters can be letters and/or digits and/or any other printable symbol (If a number is stored as a string then it cannot be used in calculations.)
» Boolean – a variable or constant that can have only two values TRUE or FALSE.

▼ **Table 8.2** Examples of data types

Pseudocode	Python	Visual Basic	Java
`INTEGER`	`FirstInteger = 25`	`Dim FirstInt As Integer`	`int FirstInt;` or `byte FirstInt;`
`REAL`	`FirstReal = 25.0`	`Dim FirstReal As Decimal`	`float FirstReal;` or `double FirstReal;`
`CHAR`	`Female = 'F'` or `Female = "F"`	`Dim Female As Char`	`char Female;`
`STRING`	`FirstName = 'Emma'` or `FirstName = "Emma"`	`Dim FirstName As String`	`String FirstName;`
`BOOLEAN`	`Flag = True`	`Dim Flag As Boolean`	`boolean Flag;`

Activity 8.2

In pseudocode and the high-level programming language that your school has chosen to use, declare the variables and constants you would use in an algorithm to find the volume of a cylinder.

8.1.3 Input and output

In order to be able to enter data and output results, programs need to use input and output statements. For IGCSE Computer Science you need to be able to write algorithms and programs that take input from a keyboard and output to a screen.

For a program to be useful, the user needs to know what they are expected to input, so each input needs to be accompanied by a **prompt** stating the input required.

Here are examples of inputs in programming code – pseudocode was considered in Chapter 7. Just look at the section for the programming language you are using.

In a programming language the data type of the input must match the required data type of the variable where the input data is to be stored. All inputs default as strings, so if the input should be an integer or real number, commands are also used to change the data type of the input (for instance, in Python these are `int()` or `float()`).

▼ **Table 8.3** Examples of input statements with prompts

Input statements	Language
`radius = float(input("Please enter the radius of the cylinder "))`	Python combines the prompt with the input statement.

`Console.Write("Please enter the radius of the cylinder ")`
 	
`radius = Decimal.Parse(Console.ReadLine())`
	Visual Basic uses a separate prompt and input. The input specifies the type of data expected.

`import java.util.Scanner;`
 	
`Scanner myObj = new Scanner(System.in);`
 	
`System.out.println("Please enter the radius of the cylinder ");`
 	
`double radius = myObj.nextDouble();`
	In Java the input library has to be imported at the start of the program and an input object is set up. Java uses a separate prompt and input. The input specifies the type and declares the variable of the same type.

Find out more

These input statements use a programming technique called casting, which converts variables from one data type to another. Find out more about the use of casting in the programming language that you have decided to use.

Activity 8.2a

In the high-level programming language that your school has chosen to use, write expressions that would store user inputs as the data types represented by the following:
- 12
- 12.00
- X
- X marks the spot
- TRUE.

For a program to be useful, the user needs to know what results are being output, so each output needs to be accompanied by a **message** explaining the result. If there are several parts to an output statement, then each part is separated by a separator character.

Here are examples of outputs in programming code – pseudocode was considered in Chapter 7. Just look at the section for the programming language you are using.

▼ **Table 8.4** Examples of output statements with messages

Output the results	Language
`print("Volume of the cylinder is ", volume)`	Python uses a comma
`Console.WriteLine("Volume of the cylinder is " & volume)`	VB uses &
`System.out.println("Volume of the cylinder is " + volume);`	Java uses +

Activity 8.3

In the high-level programming language that your school has chosen to use, write and run your own program that calculates and displays the volume of a cylinder.

Examples of the complete programs are shown below:

Python

```
CONSTPI = 3.142
Radius = float(input("Please enter the radius of the cylinder "))
Length = float(input("Please enter the length of the cylinder "))
Volume = Radius * Radius * Length * CONSTPI
print("Volume of the cylinder is ", Volume)
```

Visual Basic

Every console program in VB must contain a Main module. These statements are shown in red.

```
Module Module1
    Public Sub Main()
        Dim Radius As Decimal
        Dim Length As Decimal
        Dim Volume As Decimal
        Const PI As Decimal = 3.142
        Console.Write("Please enter the radius of the cylinder ")
        Radius = Decimal.Parse(Console.ReadLine())
        Console.Write("Please enter the length of the cylinder ")
        Length = Decimal.Parse(Console.ReadLine())
        Volume = Radius * Radius * Length * PI
        Console.WriteLine("Volume of cylinder is " & volume)
        Console.ReadKey()
    End Sub
End Module
```

Java

```java
import java.util.Scanner;
class Cylinder
{
    public static void main(String args[])
    {
        Scanner myObj = new Scanner(System.in);
        final double PI = 3.142;
        double Radius;
        double Length;
        System.out.println("Please enter the radius of the cylinder ");
        Radius = myObj.nextDouble();
        System.out.println("Please enter the length of the sphere ");
        Length = myObj.nextDouble();
        double Volume = Radius * Radius * Length * PI;
    System.out.println("Volume of cylinder is " + volume);
    }
}
```

Every console program in Java must contain a class with the file name and a main procedure. These statements are shown in red.

Every statement in Java must have a semi-colon ; at the end.

8.1.4 Basic concepts

When writing the steps required to solve a problem, the following concepts need to be used and understood:

» sequence
» selection
» iteration
» counting and totalling
» string handling
» use of operators.

8.1.4(a) Sequence

The ordering of the steps in an algorithm is very important. An incorrect order can lead to incorrect results and/or extra steps that are not required by the task.

Link

For more on
REPEAT...UNTIL
loops in pseudocode
see Section 7.2.3.

❓ Worked example

For example, the following pseudocode algorithm uses a **REPEAT...UNTIL** loop to calculate and output total marks, average marks and the number of marks entered.

```
DECLARE, Total, Average : REAL
DECLARE Mark, Counter : INTEGER
Total ← 0
Mark ← 0
Counter ← 0
OUTPUT "Enter marks, 999 to finish "
REPEAT
   INPUT Mark
   Total ← Total + Mark
   IF Mark = 999
      THEN
         Average ← Total / Counter
   ENDIF
   Counter ← Counter + 1
UNTIL Mark = 999
OUTPUT "The total mark is ", Total
OUTPUT "The average mark is ", Average
OUTPUT "The number of marks is ", Counter
```

A trace table is completed using this test data:

25, 27, 23, 999

▼ **Table 8.5** Trace table of dry run for algorithm with an incorrect sequence

Total	Average	Counter	Mark	OUTPUT
0	0	0		Enter marks, 999 to finish
25		1	25	
52		2	27	
75		3	23	
1074	358	4	999	
				The total mark is 1074
				The average mark is 358
				The number of marks is 4

As you can see all the outputs are incorrect.

However if the order of the steps is changed, and the unnecessary test removed, the algorithm now works.

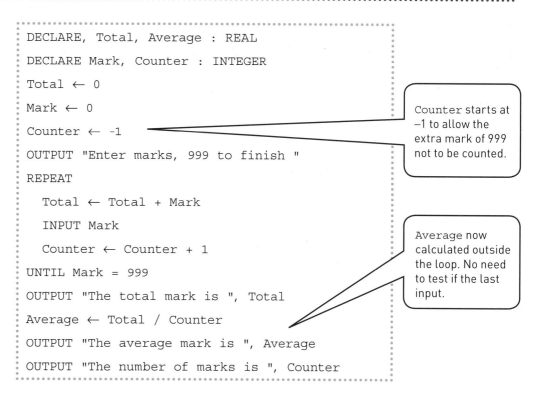

```
DECLARE, Total, Average : REAL
DECLARE Mark, Counter : INTEGER
Total ← 0
Mark ← 0
Counter ← -1
OUTPUT "Enter marks, 999 to finish "
REPEAT
  Total ← Total + Mark
  INPUT Mark
  Counter ← Counter + 1
UNTIL Mark = 999
OUTPUT "The total mark is ", Total
Average ← Total / Counter
OUTPUT "The average mark is ", Average
OUTPUT "The number of marks is ", Counter
```

> Counter starts at −1 to allow the extra mark of 999 not to be counted.

> Average now calculated outside the loop. No need to test if the last input.

A trace table is completed using the same test data:

> 25, 27, 23, 999

▼ **Table 8.6** Trace table of dry run for algorithm with a correct sequence

Total	Average	Counter	Mark	OUTPUT
0	0	−1		`Enter marks, 999 to finish`
25		0	25	
52		1	27	
75		2	23	
		3	999	
				`The total mark is 75`
	25			`The average mark is 25`
				`The number of marks is 3`

As you can see all the outputs are now correct.

 Find out more

Write and test a program, in the high-level programming language that your school has chosen to use, including similar steps to the corrected pseudocode algorithm.

8.1.4(b) Selection

Selection is a very useful technique, allowing different routes through the steps of a program. For example, data items can be picked out according to given criteria, such as: selecting the largest value or smallest value, selecting items over a certain price, selecting everyone who is male.

Selection was demonstrated in pseudocode with the use of **IF** and **CASE** statements in Chapter 7.

 Find out more

Using the high-level programming language that your school has chosen, find out about the structure of **IF…THEN…ELSE** and **CASE** statements. Not all programming languages include the use of a **CASE** statement.

IF statements

Look at some of the different types of **IF** statements available in your programming language.

▼ **Table 8.7** IF statements single choice

IF statement single choice example	Language

`IF Age > 17`
`    THEN`
`        OUTPUT "You are an adult"`
`ENDIF`
	Pseudocode

`if Age > 17:` `        print ("You are an adult")`	Python does not use **THEN** or **ENDIF** just a colon : and indentation

`If Age > 17 Then`
`    Console.WriteLine("You are an adult")`
`End If`
	Visual Basic uses Then and End If

`If (Age > 17) {`
`    System.out.println ("You are an adult");`
`}`
	Java uses curly brackets, {, instead of **THEN** and uses } instead of **ENDIF**.

▼ **Table 8.8** IF statements single choice with alternative

IF statement single choice with alternative example	Language

`IF Age > 17`
`    THEN`
`        OUTPUT "You are an adult"`
`    ELSE`
`        OUTPUT "You are a child"`
`ENDIF`
	Pseudocode

▼ **Table 8.8** (*Continued*)

```if Age > 17:`       `print ("You are an adult")`  `else:`       `print ("You are a child")```	Python uses else with a colon, : and indentation.
```If Age > 17 Then`    `Console.WriteLine("You are an adult")` `Else`    `Console.WriteLine("You are a child")` `End If```	Visual Basic uses Else and End If
```If (Age > 17) {`   `System.out.println ("You are an adult");` `} else {`   `System.out.println ("You are a child");` `}```	Java uses else and curly brackets, {, and uses } instead of ENDIF.

Activity 8.4

In the high-level programming language that your school has chosen to use, write and run a short program to test if a number input is greater than or equal to 100 or less than 100.

Case statements

Case statements are used when there are multiple choices to be made. Different programming languages provide different types of statement to do this. Have a look at the method your programming language uses.

▼ **Table 8.9** CASE statements multiple choice

Case statement examples	Language
```CASE OF OpValue`   `"+" : Answer ← Number1 + Number2`   `"-" : Answer ← Number1 - Number2`   `"*" : Answer ← Number1 * Number2`   `"/" : Answer ← Number1 / Number2`   `OTHERWISE OUTPUT "Please enter a valid choice"` `ENDCASE```	Pseudocode
```if OpValue == "+":`     `Answer = Number1 + Number2` `elif OpValue == "-":`     `Answer = Number1 - Number2` `elif OpValue == "*":`     `Answer = Number1 * Number2` `elif OpValue == "/":`     `Answer = Number1 - Number2` `else: print("invalid operator")```	Python uses elif for multiple tests

▼ **Table 8.9** (*Continued*)

```Select Case OpValue`       `Case "+"`         `Answer = Number1 + Number2`       `Case "-"`         `Answer = Number1 - Number2`       `Case "*"`         `Answer = Number1 * Number2`       `Case "/"`         `Answer = Number1 / Number2`       `Case Else`         `Console.WriteLine("invalid operator")`     `End Select```	Visual Basic uses `Select Case` and `Case Else` instead of `CASE` and `OTHERWISE`

```
Select Case OpValue
        Case "+"
          Answer = Number1 + Number2
        Case "-"
          Answer = Number1 - Number2
        Case "*"
          Answer = Number1 * Number2
        Case "/"
          Answer = Number1 / Number2
        Case Else
          Console.WriteLine("invalid operator")
        End Select
```
Visual Basic uses `Select Case` and `Case Else` instead of `CASE` and `OTHERWISE`

```
switch (OpValue) {
        case "+":
        Answer = Number1 + Number2;
        break;
        case "-":
        Answer = Number1 - Number2;
        break;
        case "*":
        Answer = Number1 * Number2;
        break;
        case "/":
        Answer = Number1 / Number2;
        break;
        default:
        System.out.println("invalid operator");
}
```
Java uses `default` instead of `OTHERWISE` and uses `break` to pass control to the end of the code block when a section is finished.

Activity 8.5

In the high-level programming language that your school has chosen to use, write and run a short program to input a number and check if that number is equal to 1, 2, 3 or 4 using the **CASE** construct (or alternative where appropriate).

8.1.4(c) Iteration

As stated in Chapter 7, there are three types of loop structures available to perform iterations so that a section of programming code can be repeated under certain conditions.

These are:

» Count-controlled loops (for a set number of iterations)
» Pre-condition loops – may have no iterations
» Post-condition loops – always has at least one iteration.

Find out more

Find out about the loop structures available in the high-level programming language that your school has chosen to use.

Count-controlled loops

FOR loops are used when a set number of iterations are required. Look at some of the different types of **FOR** statements with a counter starting at one, finishing at ten and increments by two for every iteration.

▼ **Table 8.10** FOR loops

For statement examples	Language

```for Counter in range (1,11,2):```
 	
    ```print(Counter)```
	Python uses the **range** function, a colon to show the start of the **for** loop and indentation of all statements in the **for** loop.

```For Counter = 1 To 10 Step 2```
 	
    ```Console.WriteLine(Counter)```
 	
```Next```
	Visual Basic uses `Step` and `Next`

```for (int Counter = 1; Counter <= 10;```
```Counter = Counter + 2)```
 	
```{```
 	
    ```System.out.println(Counter);```
 	
```}```
	Java uses {} to show the start and end of the `for` loop.

Condition-controlled loops

When the number of iterations is not known, there are two options:

➤ pre-condition loops which may have no iterations
➤ post-condition loops which always have at least one iteration.

Look at some of the different pre- and post-condition loops used in your programming language.

▼ **Table 8.11** Pre-condition loops

Pre-condition loops	Language

```while TotalWeight < 100:```
 	
  ```TotalWeight = TotalWeight + Weight```
	Python uses a colon to show the start of the **while** loop and indentation to show which statements are in the **while** loop.

```While TotalWeight < 100```
 	
  ```TotalWeight = TotalWeight + Weight```
 	
```End While```
	Visual Basic uses `While` and `End While`

```while (TotalWeight < 100)```
 	
```{```
 	
  ```TotalWeight = TotalWeight + Weight;```
 	
```}```
	Java uses {} to show the start and end of the `while` loop.

▼ **Table 8.12** Post-condition loops

Post-condition loops	Language
	Python only uses pre-condition loops.

`Do`
 	
  `NumberOfItems = NumberOfItems + 1`
 	
`Loop Until NumberOfItems > 19`
	Visual Basic uses `Do` and `Loop Until`

`Do`
 	
`{`
 	
  `NumberOfItems ++;`
 	
`}`
 	
`while (NumberOfItems <= 20);`
	Java uses **do** and **while** so the condition is the opposite of the **until** condition used in Visual Basic. Look at the code carefully to see the difference. Java uses {} to show the start and end of the loop.

Activity 8.6

In the high-level programming language that your school has chosen to use, write and run two short programs, one using a count-controlled loop and the other a condition-controlled loop. They should each repeat ten times, incrementing the loop counter by three and outputting the value for each iteration.

8.1.4(d) Totalling and counting

Totalling and **counting** were introduced in Chapter 7 as standard methods. Take a look at how these methods are implemented in your programming language.

Totalling is very similar in all three languages.

▼ **Table 8.13** Totalling

Totalling	Language
`TotalWeight = TotalWeight + Weight`	Python
`TotalWeight = TotalWeight + Weight`	Visual Basic
`TotalWeight = TotalWeight + Weight;`	Java

Counting is also similar in Python and Visual Basic, but Java uses a different type of statement.

▼ **Table 8.14** Counting

Counting	Language

`NumberOfItems = NumberOfItems + 1`
 	
`NumberOfItems +=1`
	Python

`NumberOfItems = NumberOfItems + 1`
 	
`NumberOfItems +=1`
	Visual Basic

`NumberOfItems ++;`
 	
`NumberOfItems = NumberOfItems + 1;`
	Java

Activity 8.7

In the high-level programming language that your school has chosen to use, write and run a short program using a condition-controlled loop to allow the user to input the weight of sacks of rice and to count the number of sacks the user has input. When the user types in '-1' this should stop the process and the program should then output the number of sacks entered and the total weight.

8.1.4(e) String Handling

Strings are used to store text. Every string contains a number of characters, from an empty string, which has no characters stored, to a maximum number specified by the programming language. The characters in a string can be labelled by position number. The first character in a string can be in position zero or position one, depending on the language.

 Find out more

Find the maximum number of characters that the high-level programming language that your school has chosen can store in a string.

Find out the position number of the first character defined by this programming language.

String handling is an important part of programming. As an IGCSE Computer Science student, you will need to write algorithms and programs for these methods:

» **length** – finding the number of characters in the string. For example, the length of the string **"Computer Science"** is 16 characters as spaces are counted as a character.
» **substring** – extracting part of a string. For example, the substring **"Science"** could be extracted from **"Computer Science"**.
» **upper** – converting all the letters in a string to uppercase. For example, the string **"Computer Science"** would become **"COMPUTER SCIENCE"**.
» **lower** – converting all the letters in a string to lowercase. For example, the string **"Computer Science"** would become **"computer science"**.

These string manipulation methods are usually provided in programming languages by **library routines**, see later in this chapter for further use of library routines.

Most programming languages support many different string handling methods. Have a look at how your programming language would complete each of the four methods you need to be able to use.

▼ **Table 8.15** Find the length of a string

Length	Language	Notes
`LENGTH("Computer Science")` `LENGTH(MyString)`	Pseudocode	Text in quotes can be used or a variable with data type string.
`len("Computer Science")` `len(MyString)`	Python	Text in quotes can be used or a variable with data type string.
`"Computer Science".Length()` `MyString.Length()`	Visual Basic	Text in quotes can be used or a variable with data type string.
`"Computer Science".length();` `MyString.length();`	Java	Text in quotes can be used or a variable with data type string.

▼ **Table 8.16** Extracting a substring from a string

Substring – to extract the word 'Science'	Language	Notes

`SUBSTRING("Computer Science", 10, 7)`
 	
`SUBSTRING(MyString, 10, 7)`
	Pseudocode	Text in quotes can be used or a variable with data type string. First parameter is the string, second parameter is the position of the start character, third parameter is the length of the required substring.
		
		Pseudocode strings start at position one.

`"Computer Science"[9:16]`
 	
`MyString[9:16]`
	Python	Text in quotes can be used or a variable with data type string. Strings are treated as lists of characters in Python. First index is the start position of the substring. Second index is the end position of the substring.
		
		Python strings start at position zero.

`"Computer Science".Substring(9, 7)`
 	
`MyString.Substring(9, 7)`
	Visual Basic	Text in quotes can be used or a variable with data type string. First parameter is the start position of the substring, second parameter is the length of the substring.
		
		Visual Basic strings start at position zero.

`"Computer Science".substring(9,17);`
 	
`MyString.substring(9,17);`
	Java	Text in quotes can be used or a variable with data type string. First parameter is the start position of the substring, second parameter is the exclusive end position of the substring. 'Exclusive' means the position after the last character, i.e. in this example the substring is made from characters 9 to 16.
		
		Java strings start at position zero.

▼ **Table 8.17** Converting a string to upper case

Upper	Language	Notes
`UCASE("Computer Science")` `UCASE(MyString)`	Pseudocode	Text in quotes can be used or a variable with data type string.
`"Computer Science".upper()` `MyString.upper()`	Python	Text in quotes can be used or a variable with data type string.
`UCase("Computer Science")` `UCase(MyString)`	Visual Basic	Text in quotes can be used or a variable with data type string.
`"Computer Science".toUpperCase();` `MyString.toUpperCase();`	Java	Text in quotes can be used or a variable with data type string.

▼ **Table 8.18** Converting a string to lower case

Lower	Language	Notes
`LCASE("Computer Science")` `LCASE(MyString)`	Pseudocode	Text in quotes can be used or a variable with data type string.
`"Computer Science".lower()` `MyString.lower()`	Python	Text in quotes can be used or a variable with data type string.
`LCase("Computer Science")` `LCase(MyString)`	Visual Basic	Text in quotes can be used or a variable with data type string.
`"Computer Science".toLowerCase();` `MyString.toLowerCase();`	Java	Text in quotes can be used or a variable with data type string.

Find out more

Find four more string handling methods that your programming language makes use of.

Activity 8.8

In the high-level programming language that your school has chosen, write and run a short program to input your full name into a variable, **MyName**, find the length of your name, extract the first three characters of your name and display your name in upper case and in lower case.

8.1.4(f) Arithmetic, logical and Boolean operators

Arithmetic operators

All programming languages make use of arithmetic operators to perform calculations. Here are the ones you must be able to use for IGCSE Computer Science.

▼ **Table 8.19** Mathematical operators

Operator	Action	Python	Visual Basic	Java
+	Add	+	+	+
-	Subtract	-	-	-
*	Multiply	*	*	*
/	Divide	/	/	/
^	Raise to the power of	**	^	import java.lang.Math; Math.pow(x, y)
MOD	Remainder division	For more on these see Section 8.1.7 Library routines.		
DIV	Integer division			

Advice

Expressions using operators can also be grouped together using brackets, for instance: ((x + y) * 3) / PI

Activity 8.9

In the high-level programming language that your school has chosen to use, write and test a short program to perform all these mathematical operations and output the results:

» Input two numbers, **Number1** and **Number2**
» Calculate **Number1 + Number2**
» Calculate **Number1 - Number2**
» Calculate **Number1 * Number2**
» Calculate **Number1 / Number2**
» Calculate **Number1 ^ Number2**
» Input an integer **Number3**
» Calculate **Number3 * (Number1 + Number2)**
» Calculate **Number3 * (Number1 - Number2)**
» Calculate **(Number1 + Number2) ^ Number3**.

Logical operators

All programming languages make use of logical operators to decide which path to take through a program. Here are the ones you must be able to use for IGCSE Computer Science.

▼ **Table 8.20** Logical operators

Operator	Comparison	Python	Visual Basic	Java
>	Greater than	>	>	>
<	Less than	<	<	<
=	Equal	==	=	==
>=	Greater than or equal	>=	>=	>=
<=	Less than or equal	<=	<=	<=
<>	Not equal	!=	<>	!=

Boolean operators

All programming languages make use of Boolean operators to decide whether an expression is true or false. Here are the ones you must be able to use for IGCSE Computer Science.

▼ **Table 8.21** Boolean operators

Operator	Description	Python	Visual Basic	Java
AND	Both True	and	And	&&
OR	Either True	or	Or	||
NOT	Not True	not	Not	!

Activity 8.10

In the high-level programming language that your school has chosen to use, write and test a short program to perform all these comparisons and output the results.

» Input two numbers, **Number1** and **Number2**
» Compare **Number1** and **Number2**:
  - Output with a suitable message if both numbers are not equal
  - Output with a suitable message identifying which number is largest
  - Output with a suitable message identifying which number is smallest
  - Output with a suitable message if both numbers are equal
» Input another number **Number3**
  - Output with a suitable message if all three numbers are not equal
  - Output with a suitable message identifying which number is largest
  - Output with a suitable message identifying which number is smallest
  - Output with a suitable message if all numbers are equal.

8.1.5 Use of nested statements

Selection and iteration statements can be nested one inside the other. This powerful method reduces the amount of code that needs to be written and makes it simpler for a programmer to test their programs.

One type of construct can be nested within another – for example, selection can be nested within a condition-controlled loop, or one loop can be nested within another loop.

? Worked example

For example, the following pseudocode algorithm uses nested loops to provide a solution for the problem set out here:

» calculate and output highest, lowest, and average marks awarded for a class of twenty students
» calculate and output largest, highest, lowest, and average marks awarded for each student
» calculate and output largest, highest, lowest, and average marks for each of the six subjects studied by the student; each subject has five tests.
» assume that all marks input are whole numbers between 0 and 100.

```
// Declarations of the variables needed
DECLARE ClassAverage, StudentAverage, SubjectAverage : REAL
DECLARE Student, Subject, Test : INTEGER
DECLARE ClassHigh, ClassLow, ClassTotal : INTEGER
DECLARE StudentHigh, StudentLow, StudentTotal : INTEGER
DECLARE SubjectHigh, SubjectLow, SubjectTotal : INTEGER
ClassHigh ← 0
ClassLow ← 100
ClassTotal ← 0
// Use of constants enables you to easily change the values for testing
CONSTANT NumberOfTests = 5
CONSTANT NumberOfSubjects = 6
CONSTANT ClassSize = 20
FOR Student ← 1 TO ClassSize
    StudentHigh ← 0
    StudentLow ← 100
    StudentTotal ← 0
    FOR Subject ← 1 TO NumberOfSubjects
        SubjectHigh ← 0
        SubjectLow ← 100
        SubjectTotal ← 0
        FOR Test ← 1 TO NumberOfTests
            OUTPUT "Please enter mark "
            INPUT Mark
            IF Mark > SubjectHigh
            THEN
                SubjectHigh ← Mark
            ENDIF
            IF Mark < SubjectLow
              THEN
                SubjectLow ← Mark
```

> You will need to set up these values to use in your middle loop.

> You will need to set up these values to use in your inner loop.

```
              ENDIF
              SubjectTotal ← SubjectTotal + Mark
         NEXT Test
         SubjectAverage ← SubjectTotal / NumberOfTests
         OUTPUT "Average mark for Subject ", Subject, " is ", SubjectAverage
         OUTPUT "Highest mark for Subject ", Subject, " is ", SubjectHigh
         OUTPUT "Lowest mark for Subject ", Subject, " is ", SubjectLow
         IF SubjectHigh > StudentHigh
            THEN
               StudentHigh ← SubjectHigh
         ENDIF
         IF SubjectLow < StudentLow
            THEN
               StudentLow ← SubjectLow
         ENDIF
         StudentTotal ← StudentTotal + SubjectTotal
      NEXT Subject
      StudentAverage ← StudentTotal / (NumberOfTests * NumberOfSubjects
      OUTPUT "Average mark for Student ", Student, " is ", StudentAverage
      OUTPUT "Highest mark for Student ", Student, " is ", StudentHigh
      OUTPUT "Lowest mark for Student ", Student, " is ", StudentLow
      IF StudentHigh > ClassHigh
         THEN
            ClassHigh = StudentHigh
      ENDIF
      IF StudentLow < ClassLow
         THEN
            ClassLow ← StudentLow
      ENDIF
      ClassTotal ← ClassTotal + StudentTotal
   NEXT Student
   ClassAverage ← ClassTotal / (NumberOfTests * NumberOfSubjects * ClassSize)
   OUTPUT "Average mark for Class is ", ClassAverage
   OUTPUT "Highest mark for Class is ", ClassHigh
   OUTPUT "Lowest mark for Class is ", ClassLow
```

> You will need to use this output from your inner loop.

> You will need to use these outputs from your middle loop.

Have a look at the pseudocode, start with the inner loop for the number of tests.

Activity 8.11

In the high-level programming language that your school has chosen to use, use the pseudocode solution to help you to write and test a short program to calculate and output largest, highest, lowest and average marks for a single subject with five tests taken by a student.

Hints:
» Look at the other statements and output needed as well as the loop.
» For testing purposes, you can reduce the number of tests to two or three.

Now look at the middle loop that surrounds the inner loop for the number of students.

Activity 8.12

When the single subject program is working, extend it to calculate and output largest, highest, lowest, and average marks for a single student with six subjects studied by a student.

Hints:
» Look at the other statements and outputs needed as well as the loop.
» For testing purposes reduce the number of subjects to two or three.

Finally look at the whole program that includes the outer loop for the whole class.

Activity 8.13

When the single student program is working, extend your program to complete the task to calculate and output the largest, highest, lowest, and average marks for the whole class of 20 students.

Hint:
» For testing purposes reduce the class size to two or three.

8.1.6 Procedures and functions

When writing an algorithm, there are often similar tasks to perform that make use of the same groups of statements. Instead of repeating these statements and writing new code every time they are required, many programming languages make use of subroutines, also known as named **procedures** or **functions**. These are defined once and can be called many times within a program.

Procedures, functions and parameters

A **procedure** is a set of programming statements grouped together under a single name that can be called to perform a task at any point in a program.

A **function** is a set of programming statements grouped together under a single name that can be called to perform a task at any point in a program. In contrast to a procedure, a function will return a value back to the main program.

Parameters are the variables that store the values of the arguments passed to a procedure or function. Some but not all procedures and functions will have parameters.

Definition and use of procedures and functions, with or without parameters

Procedures without parameters

Here is an example of a procedure without parameters in pseudocode:

```
PROCEDURE Stars
    OUTPUT"************"
ENDPROCEDURE
```

The procedure can then be called in the main part of the program as many times as is required in the following way:

```
CALL Stars
```

Instead of calling them procedures, different terminology is used by each programming language. Procedures are known as:

» void functions in Python
» subroutines in VB
» methods in Java.

▼ **Table 8.22** Procedure calls

Procedure Stars – definition	Call	Language
`def Stars():` `    print("************")`	`Stars()`	Python

`Sub Stars()`
`    Console.WriteLine("************")`
`End Sub`
	`Stars()`	Visual Basic

`static void Stars()`
`{`
`    System.out.println("************");`
`}`
	`Stars();`	Java

Activity 8.14

Write a short program in your chosen programming language to define and use a procedure to display three lines of stars.

It is often useful to pass a value to a procedure that can be used to modify the action(s) taken. For example, to decide how many stars would be output. This is done by passing an argument when the procedure is called to be used as a parameter by the procedure.

Procedures with parameters

Here is an example of how a procedure with parameters can be defined in pseudocode.

We can add parameters to a procedure:

```
PROCEDURE Stars (Number : INTEGER)
    DECLARE Counter : INTEGER
    FOR Counter ← 1 TO NUMBER
        OUTPUT "*"
    NEXT Counter
ENDPROCEDURE
```

Parameter with data type

Procedure with parameters are called like this – in this case to print seven stars:

```
CALL Stars (7)
```

Or:

```
MyNumber ← 7
CALL stars (MyNumber)
```

A procedure call must match the procedure definition. This means that when a procedure is defined with parameters, the arguments in the procedure call should match the parameters in the procedure definition. For IGCSE Computer Science the number of parameters used is limited to two.

▼ **Table 8.23** Procedures with parameters

Procedure stars with parameter – definition	Call	Language

`def Stars(Number):`
`    for counter in range (Number):`
`        print("*", end = "")`
	`Stars(7)`	Python
		
		Note: **end = ""** ensures that the stars are printed on one line without spaces between them.

`Sub Stars(Number As Integer)`
`    Dim Counter As Integer`
`    For Counter = 1 To Number`
`        Console.Write("*")`
`    Next`
`End Sub`
	`Stars(7)`	VB

`static void Stars(int Number)`
`{`
`  for (int Counter = 1; Counter <= Number; Counter ++)`
`  {`
`    System.out.print("*");`
`  }`
`}`
	`Stars(7);`	Java

Activity 8.15

Extend your short program in your chosen programming language to define and use a procedure that accepts a parameter to write a given number of lines of stars. You will find the following commands useful:

» `\n` in Python
» **Writeline** in Visual Basic
» **Println** in Java.

Functions

A function is just like a procedure except it **always** returns a value. Just like a procedure it is defined once and can be called many times within a program. Just like a procedure it can be defined with or without parameters.

Unlike procedures, function calls are not standalone and instead can be made on the right-hand side of an expression.

Instead of naming them functions, different terminology is used by some programming languages. Functions are known as:

» fruitful functions in Python
» functions in VB
» methods with returns in Java.

The keyword **RETURN** is used as one of the statements in a function to specify the value to be returned. This is usually the last statement in the function definition.

For example, here is a function written in pseudocode to convert a temperature from Fahrenheit to Celsius:

Parameter and function return both have defined data types.

```
FUNCTION Celsius (Temperature : REAL) RETURNS REAL

    RETURN (Temperature - 32) / 1.8

ENDFUNCTION
```

Because a function returns a value, it can be called by assigning the return value directly into a variable as follows:

```
MyTemp ← Celsius(MyTemp)
```

▼ **Table 8.24** Function definitions

Function temperature conversion example	Language

```def Celsius(Temperature):```
 	
    ```return (Temperature - 32) / 1.8```
	Python – data type of function does not need to be defined

```Function Celsius(ByVal Temperature As Decimal) As Decimal```
 	
    ```Return (Temperature - 32) / 1.8```
 	
```End Function```
	Visual Basic

```static double Celsius(double Temperature)```
 	
```{```
 	
  ```return (Temperature - 32) / 1.8;```
 	
```}```
	Java

Just like with a procedure, a function call must match the function definition. When a function is defined with parameters, the **arguments** in the function call should match the parameters in the procedure definition. For IGCSE Computer Science the number of parameters used is limited to two.

Activity 8.16

Write an algorithm in pseudocode as a function, with a parameter, to convert a temperature from Celsius to Fahrenheit. Test your algorithm by writing a short program in your chosen programming language to define and use this function.

When procedures and functions are defined, the first statement in the definition is a **header**, which contains:

➤ the name of the procedure or function
➤ any parameters passed to the procedure or function, and their data type
➤ the data type of the return value for a function.

Procedure calls are single standalone statements. Function calls are made as part of an expression, on the right-hand side.

Local and global variables

A **global variable** can be used by any part of a program – its **scope** covers the whole program.

A **local variable** can only be used by the part of the program it has been declared in – its **scope** is restricted to that part of the program.

For example, in this algorithm the variables **Number1**, **Number2** and **Answer** are declared both locally and globally, whereas Number3 is only declared locally.

```
DECLARE Number1, Number2, Answer : INTEGER
PROCEDURE Test
    DECLARE Number3, Answer : INTEGER
    Number1 ← 10
    Number2 ← 20
    Number3 ← 30
    Answer ← Number1 + Number2
    OUTPUT "Number1 is now ", Number1
    OUTPUT "Number2 is now ", Number2
    OUTPUT "Answer is now ", Answer
ENDPROCEDURE
Number1 ← 50
Number2 ← 100
Answer ← Number1 + Number2
OUTPUT "Number1 is ", Number1
OUTPUT "Number2 is ", Number2
OUTPUT "Answer is ", Answer
CALL Test
OUTPUT "Number1 is still ", Number1
OUTPUT "Number2 is still ", Number2
OUTPUT "Answer is still ", Answer
OUTPUT "Number3 is ", Number3
```

Global variables

Local variables

The output is

```
Number1 is 50
Number2 is 100
Answer is 150
Number1 is now 10
Number2 is now 20
Answer is now 30
Number1 is still 50
Number2 is still 100
Answer is still 150
ERROR - Number3 is undefined
```

The final line is an error because the main program has tried to access the variable **Number3**, which is local to the procedure.

Activity 8.17

Write and test a short program for the sample algorithm in your chosen programming language.

Activity 8.18

Consider your program for Activity 8.13. State the variables that should be declared and used as local variables if procedures are used for:
» The calculation of the highest, lowest, and average marks awarded for each subject
» The calculation of the highest, lowest, and average marks awarded for each student.

 Find out more

As a further challenge rewrite your program for Activity 8.13 using procedures and local and global variables.

8.1.7 Library routines

Advice

As well as library routines, typical IDEs also contain an editor, for entering code, and an interpreter and/or a compiler, to run the code.

Many programming language development systems include **library routines** that are ready to incorporate into a program. These routines are fully tested and ready for use. A programming language IDE usually includes a standard library of functions and procedures. These standard library routines perform many types of task – such as the string handling discussed in Section 8.1.4.

Each programming language has many library routines for standard tasks that are commonly required by programs. Sometimes a set of routines needs to be specifically identified in a program. For example, in Java, the statement **import java.lang.String;** is required at the start of a program to provide access to the string handling library.

You will need to use these library routines in your programs for IGCSE Computer Science:

» **MOD** – returns remainder of a division
» **DIV** – returns the quotient (i.e. the whole number part) of a division
» **ROUND** – returns a value rounded to a given number of decimal places
» **RANDOM** – returns a random number.

Here are some examples of these library routines in pseudocode:

Value1 ← **MOD(10,3)** returns the remainder of **10** divided by **3**

Value2 ← **DIV(10,3)** returns the quotient of **10** divided by **3**

Value3 ← **ROUND(6.97354, 2)** returns the value rounded to **2** decimal places

Value4 ← **RANDOM()** returns a random number between **0** and **1** inclusive

Activity 8.19

Identify the values of the variables **Value1**, **Value2** and **Value3**.

Here are the same examples, written in each programming language:

▼ **Table 8.25** MOD, DIV, ROUND and RANDOM programming examples

Programming examples for MOD, DIV, ROUND and RANDOM	Language

`Value1 = 10%3`
 	
`Value2 = 10//3`
 	
`Value = divmod(10,3)`
 	
`Value3 = round(6.97354, 2)`
 	
`from random import random`
 	
`Value4 = random()`
	Python – MOD uses the % operator and DIV the // operator
	
	The function **divmod(x,y)** provides both answers where the first answer is DIV and the second answer is MOD
	
	RANDOM needs to import the library routine **random**, and then the function: **random()** can be used afterwards

`Value1 = 10 Mod 3`
 	
`Value2 = 10 \ 3`
 	
`Value3 = Math.Round(6.97354, 2)`
 	
`Value4 = Rnd()`
	Visual Basic – DIV uses the \ operator

`import java.lang.Math;`
 	
`Value1 = 10%3;`
 	
`Value2 = 10/3;`
 	
`Value3 = Math.round(6.97354 * 100)/100.0;`
 	
`import java.util.Random;`
 	
`Random rand = new Random();`
 	
`double Value4 = rand.nextDouble();`
	Java – MOD uses the % operator
	
	DIV uses the normal division operator; if the numbers being divided are both integers then integer division is performed, as shown.
	
	Java imports the library routine **Math**
	
	Math.round only rounds to whole numbers
	
	RANDOM needs to import the library routine **Random**

Advice

A program written for a real task should be understandable to another programmer. Program code in a structured questions may not always follow these rules, to test your ability to trace the steps in a routine or correct some errors.

Activity 8.20

Write and test a short program in your chosen programming language to:
» input two integers a and b and then find **a MOD b** and **a DIV b**
» create a random integer between 100 and 300.

8.1.8 Creating a maintainable program

Once a program is written, it may need to be maintained or updated by another programmer at a later date. The programmer may have no documentation other than a copy of the source program. Even a programmer looking at their own program several years later may have forgotten exactly how all the tasks in it were completed!

A maintainable program should:

» always use meaningful identifier names for:
  – variables
  – constants
  – arrays
  – procedures
  – functions

» be divided into modules for each task using:
- procedures
- functions
» be fully commented using your programming language's commenting feature.

▼ **Table 8.26** Programming languages commenting features

Example comments	Language
`#Python uses hash to start a comment for every line`	Python
`'Visual Basic uses a single quote to start a comment for` `' every line`	Visual Basic

`// Java uses a double slash to start a single line comment`
`and`
`/* to start multiple line comments`
`and to end them`
`*/`
	Java

Activity 8.21

Check your last two programs and make sure they could be maintained by another programmer. Swap your program listing with another student and check that they can understand it.

8.2 Arrays

An **array** is a data structure containing several elements of the same data type; these elements can be accessed using the same identifier name. The position of each element in an array is identified using the array's **index**.

8.2.1 One- and Two-dimensional arrays

Arrays are used to store multiple data items in a uniformly accessible manner; all the data items use the same identifier and each data item can be accessed separately by the use of an index. In this way, lists of items can be stored, searched and put into an order. For example, a list of names can be ordered alphabetically, or a list of temperatures can be searched to find a particular value.

The first element of an array can have an index of zero or one. However, most programming languages automatically set the first index of an array to zero.

Arrays can be one-dimensional or multi-dimensional. One-dimensional and two-dimensional arrays are included the IGCSE Computer Science syllabus.

8.2.2 Declaring and populating arrays with iteration

One-dimensional arrays

A one-dimensional array can be referred to as a list. Here is an example of a list with 10 elements in it where the first element has an index of zero.

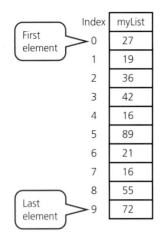

▲ **Figure 8.10** A one-dimensional array

When a one-dimensional array is declared in pseudocode:

» the name of the array
» the first index value
» the last index value
» and the data type

are included.

For example, to declare a new array called **MyList**:

```
DECLARE MyList : ARRAY[0:9] OF INTEGER
```

Each position in the array can be populated in an array by defining the value at each index position. For instance, we can add the number 27 to the fourth position in the array **MyList** as follows:

```
MyList[4] ← 27
```

To populate the entire array instead we can use a loop:

```
OUTPUT "Enter these 10 values in order 27, 19, 36, 42, 16, 89, 21, 16, 55, 72"
FOR Counter ← 0 TO 9
    OUTPUT "Enter next value "
    INPUT MyList[Counter]
NEXT Counter
```

Notice that in this code we have used the variable **Counter** as the array index.

We can display the data that lies in a particular location in an array as follows:

```
OUTPUT MyList[1]
```

This would display the value 19.

Activity 8.22

In your chosen programming language write a short program to declare and populate the array **MyList**, as shown in Figure 8.10, using a **FOR** loop.

Arrays can also be populated as they are declared.

▼ **Table 8.27** Array population

Array	Language
`myList = [27, 19, 36, 42, 16, 89, 21, 16, 55, 72]`	Python
`Dim myList = New Integer() {27, 19, 36, 42, 16, 89, 21, 16, 55, 72}`	Visual Basic
`int[] myList = {27, 19, 36, 42, 16, 89, 21, 16, 55, 72};`	Java

Two-dimensional arrays

A two-dimensional array can be referred to as a table, with rows and columns. Here is an example of a table with 10 rows and 3 columns, which contains 30 elements. The first element is located at position 0,0.

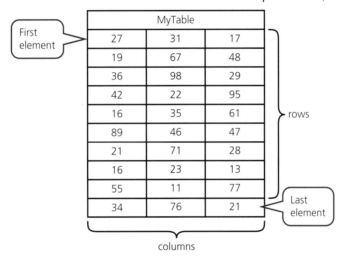

▲ **Figure 8.11** A two-dimensional array

When a two-dimensional array is declared in pseudocode:

» the first index value for rows
» the last index value for rows
» the first index value for columns
» the last index value for columns
» and the data type

are included.

For example:

```
DECLARE MyTable : ARRAY[0:9,0:2] OF INTEGER
```

The declared array can then be populated using a loop, just like for one-dimensional arrays – however this time there need to be two nested loops, one for each index:

```
OUTPUT "Enter these values in order 27, 19, 36, 42, 16, 89, 21, 16, 55, 34"
OUTPUT "Enter these values in order 31, 67, 98, 22, 35, 46, 71, 23, 11, 76"
OUTPUT "Enter these values in order 17, 48, 29, 95, 61, 47, 28, 13, 77, 21"
FOR ColumnCounter ← 0 TO 2
    FOR RowCounter ← 0 TO 9
        OUTPUT "Enter next value "
        INPUT MyTable[RowCounter, ColumnCounter]
    NEXT RowCounter
NEXT ColumnCounter
```

We can display the data that lies in a particular location in a two-dimensional array as follows:

```
OUTPUT MyList[2,1]
```

This would display the value 98.

Advice

Notes on Python and arrays

Instead of arrays, Python uses another object called a list. The differences you need to know are:
» a list can contain different data types whereas arrays must all hold the same type of data
» to achieve the same structure as a two-dimensional array, Python embeds lists within another.

Two-dimensional arrays are populated in each language as follows:

Two-dimensional arrays	Language
`MyTable = [[27, 31, 17], [19, 67, 48],[36, 98, 29],[42, 22, 95], [16, 35, 61], [89, 46, 47], [21, 71, 28], [16, 23, 13], [55, 11, 77] [34, 76, 21]]`	Python
`Dim MyTable = New Integer(8, 2) {{27, 31, 17}, {19, 67, 48}, {36, 98, 29}, {42, 22, 95}, {16, 35, 61}, {89, 46, 47}, {21, 71, 28}, {16, 23, 13}, {55, 11, 77}, (34, 76, 21)}`	Visual Basic
`int[][] MyTable = {{27, 31, 17}, {19, 67, 48}, {36, 98, 29}, {42, 22, 95}, {16, 35, 61}, {89, 46, 47}, {21, 71, 28}, {16, 23, 13}, {55, 11, 77}, {34, 76, 21}};`	Java

8.3 File handling

8.3.1 Purpose of storing data in a file

Computer programs store data that will be required again in a **file.** While any data stored in RAM will be lost when the computer is switched off, when data is saved to a file it is stored permanently. Data stored in a file can thus be accessed by the same program at a later date or accessed by another program. Data stored in a file can also be sent to be used on other computer(s). The storage of data in files is one of the most used features of programming.

8.3.2 Using files

Every file is identified by its filename. In this section, we are going to look at how to read and write a line of text or a single item of data to a file.

Here are examples of writing a line of text to a file and reading the line of text back from the file. The pseudocode algorithm has comments to explain each stage of the task.

pseudocode

```
DECLARE TextLine : STRING  // variables are declared as normal
DECLARE MyFile : STRING
MyFile ← "MyText.txt"
// writing the line of text to the file
OPEN MyFile FOR WRITE  // opens file for writing
    OUTPUT "Please enter a line of text"
    INPUT TextLine
    WRITEFILE, TextLine  // writes a line of text to the file
CLOSEFILE(MyFile)  // closes the file
// reading the line of text from the file
OUTPUT "The file contains this line of text:"
OPEN MyFile FOR READ  // opens file for reading
    READFILE, TextLine  // reads a line of text from the file
    OUTPUT TextLine
CLOSEFILE(MyFile)  // closes the file
```

Python

```python
# writing to and reading a line of text from a file
MyFile = open ("MyText.txt","w")
TextLine = input("Please enter a line of text ")
MyFile.write(TextLine)
Myfile.close()
print("The file contains this line of text")
MyFile = open ("MyText.txt","r")
TextLine = MyFile.read()
print(TextLine)
Myfile.close()
```

Visual Basic

```vb
'writing to and reading from a text file
Imports System.IO
Module Module1
    Sub Main()
        Dim textLn As String
        Dim objMyFileWrite As StreamWriter
        Dim objMyFileRead As StreamReader
        objMyFileWrite = New StreamWriter("textFile.txt")
        Console.Write("Please enter a line of text  ")
        textLn = Console.ReadLine()
        objMyFileWrite.WriteLine(textLn)
        objMyFileWrite.Close()
        Console.WriteLine("The line of text is  ")
        objMyFileRead = New StreamReader("textFile.txt")
        textLn = objMyFileRead.ReadLine
        Console.WriteLine(textLn)
        objMyFileRead.Close()
        Console.ReadLine()
    End Sub
End Module
```

Java

```
//writing to and reading from a text file, Note: the try and catch commands implement
// something called exception handling - this concept goes beyond IGCSE level
import java.util.Scanner;
import java.io.BufferedReader;
import java.io.PrintWriter;
import java.io.FileReader;
import java.io.FileWriter;
import java.io.IOException;
class TextFile {
    public static void main(String[] args) {
        Scanner myObj = new Scanner(System.in);
        String textLn;
        try {
            FileWriter myFileWriter = new FileWriter("textFile.txt", false);
            PrintWriter myPrintWriter = new PrintWriter(myFileWriter);
            System.out.println("Please enter a line of text   ");
            textLn = myObj.next();
            myPrintWriter.printf("%s" + "%n", textLn);
            myPrintWriter.close();
        } catch (IOException e) {
            e.printStackTrace();
        }
        try {
            FileReader myFileReader  = new FileReader("textFile.txt");
            BufferedReader myBufferReader  = new BufferedReader(myFileReader);
            textLn = myBufferReader.readLine();
            System.out.println(textLn);
            myFileReader.close();
        } catch (IOException e) {
            e.printStackTrace();
        }
    }
}
```

Activity 8.24

Use the program written in your chosen programming language to write a line of text to a file and read it back from the file. Use the comments in the pseudocode to help you write comments to explain how the file handling works.

Activity 8.25
Using pseudocode write an algorithm to copy a line of text from one text file to another text file.

In this chapter, you have learnt about:
✔ declare, use and identify appropriate data types for variables and constants
✔ understand and use input and outputs
✔ understand and use the programming concepts: sequence, selection, iteration, totalling, counting and string handling
✔ understand and use nested statements
✔ understand and use arithmetic, logical and Boolean operators
✔ understand and use procedures, functions and library routines
✔ write maintainable programs
✔ declare, use, identify appropriate data types for, read and write arrays with one and two dimensions
✔ store data in a file and retrieve data from a file.

Key terms used throughout this chapter

variable – a named data store that contains a value that may change during the execution of a program

constant – a named data store that contains a value that does not change during the execution of a program

declare – define the value and data type of a variable or constant

integer – a positive or negative whole number that can be used with mathematical operators

real number – a positive or negative number with a fractional part; Real numbers can be used with mathematical operators

char – a variable or constant that is a single character

string – a variable or constant that is several characters in length. Strings vary in length and may even have no characters (an empty string); the characters can be letters and/or digits and/or any other printable symbol

sequence – the order in which the steps in a program are executed

selection – allowing the selection of different paths through the steps of a program

iteration – a section of programming code that can be repeated under certain conditions

counting – keeping track of the number of times an action is performed

totalling – keeping a total that values are added to

operator – a special character or word in a programming language that identifies an action to be performed

arithmetic operator – an operator that is used to perform calculations

logical operator – an operator that is used to decide the path to take through a program if the expression formed is true or false

Boolean operator – an operator that is used with logical operators to form more complex expressions

nesting – the inclusion of one type of code construct inside another

procedure – a set of programming statements grouped together under a single name that can be called to perform a task in a program, rather than including a copy of the code every time the task is performed

function – a set of programming statements grouped together under a single name which can be called to perform a task in a program, rather than including a copy of the code every time; just like a procedure except a function will return a value back to the main program

parameters – the variables in a procedure or function declaration that store the values of the arguments passed from the main program to a procedure or function

MOD – an arithmetic operator that returns the remainder of a division; different languages use different symbols for this operation

DIV – an arithmetic operator that returns the quotient (whole number part) of a division; different languages use different symbols for this operation

ROUND – a library routine that rounds a value to a given number of decimal places

RANDOM – a library routine that generates a random number

array – a data structure containing several elements of the same data type; these elements can be accessed using the same identifier name

index – identifies the position of an element in an array

file – a collection of data stored by a computer program to be used again

Exam-style questions

1 Variables and constants are used for data storage in computer programs. Discuss the similarities and differences between these data stores. [4]

2 A programmer is writing a program that stores data about items stored in a warehouse. Suggest suitable meaningful names and data types for:
   » Item name
   » Manufacturer
   » Description
   » Number in stock
   » Reorder level
   » Whether the item is on order or not. [6]

3 Programming concepts include:
   » sequence
   » selection
   » iteration
   » totalling
   » counting.
   Describe each concept and provide an example of program code to show how it is used. [10]

4 Write a short pseudocode algorithm to input a password, check that it has exactly 8 characters in it, check that all the letters are upper case, and output the message "Password meets the rules" if both these conditions are true. [6]

5 Programs can use both local and global variables. Describe, using examples, the difference between local and global variables. [6]

6 Explain why programmers find library routines useful when writing programs. Include in your answer with **two** examples of library routines that programmers frequently use. [4]

7 A two-dimensional array stores the first name and family name of ten people.
   a Write a program in pseudocode to display the first name and family name of the ten people. [3]
   b Extend your program to sort the ten names in order of family name before displaying the names. [5]

8 A computer file, **"Message.txt"**, stores a line of text. Write an algorithm in pseudocode to display this line of text. [3]

9 **a** Describe the purpose of each statement in this algorithm.

```
FOR I ← 1 TO 300

   INPUT Name[I]

NEXT I
```
[2]

   b Identify, using pseudocode, another loop structure that the algorithm in **part a** could have used. [1]

c Write an algorithm, using pseudocode, to input a number between 0 and 100 inclusive. The algorithm should prompt for the input and output an error message if the number is outside this range. [3]

Cambridge O Level Computer Science (0478) Paper 21 Q5, June 2017

For IGCSE Computer Science, you should be able to write an understandable algorithm to solve a problem. Your algorithm should be easy to read and understand and may use any of the concepts in this chapter and Chapter 7.

Here are some further problems for you to solve:

10 The one-dimensional array `StaffName[]` contains the names of the staff in a department. Another one-dimensional array `StaffPhone[]` contains the phone numbers for the members of staff. A final one-dimensional array `StaffOffice[]` contains the office location for the members of staff. The position of each member of staff's data in the three arrays is the same, for example, the member of staff in position 5 in `StaffPhone[]` and `StaffOffice[]` is the same.
Write a program that meets the following requirements:
» uses procedures to display these lists:
 – staff phone numbers and names in alphabetic order of staff name
 – members of staff grouped by office number
» uses a procedure to display all the details for a member of staff, with the name used as a parameter
» uses a procedure to update the details for a member of staff, with the name used as a parameter.
You must use program code with local and global variables and add comments to explain how your code works. [15]

11 Use a trace table to test the program you have written in question **10**.
[*If you have used a real programming language to write your program then it is also good practice to run the program to test and help find errors.*] [5]

12 You can become a member of the town guild if you meet all the following requirements:
» aged between 18 and 65
» you have lived in the town for 20 years
 or you have lived in the town for 5 years and both your parents still live in the town
 or one parent has died and the other parent still lives in the town
 or you and a brother or a sister have lived in the town for 10 years
» you have half a million dollars in your bank account
» you have never been to prison
» at least two guild members support your application
» if five guild members support your application then you could be excused one of the above requirements, apart from age
Write a program that allows you to input answers to questions to ensure that you meet the requirements, issues a unique membership number if you do or explains all the reasons for failure if you don't meet the requirements. [15]

13 Use a trace table to test the program you have written in question 12.
[*If you have used a real programming language to write your program then it is also good practice to run the program to test and help find errors.*] [5]

9 Databases

9.1 Databases

9.1.1 Single-table databases

A **database** is a structured collection of data that allows people to extract information in a way that meets their needs. The data can include text, numbers, pictures; anything that can be stored in a computer. Relational databases will be studied at A Level but for IGCSE only single-table databases will be studied.

A **single-table database** contains only one table.

Why are databases useful?

Databases prevent problems occurring because:

» if any changes or additions are made it only has to be done once – data is consistent
» the same data is used by everyone
» data is only stored once in relational databases which means no data duplication.

What are databases used for?

To store information about people, for instance:

» patients in a hospital
» pupils at a school.

To store information about things, for instance:

» cars to be sold
» books in a library.

To store information about events, for instance:

» hotel bookings
» results of races.

 Find out more

Find five more uses for databases, and for each one decide what sort of information is being stored.

Fields and records – the building blocks for any database

Inside a database, data is stored in **tables**, which consists of many **records**. Each record consists of several **fields**. The number of records in a table will vary as new records can be added and deleted from a table as required. The number of fields in a table is fixed so each record contains the same number of fields.

An easy way to remember this is: each record is a row in the table and each field is a column in the table.

Note: while databases can contain multiple tables, all the databases considered in this chapter will contain a single table.

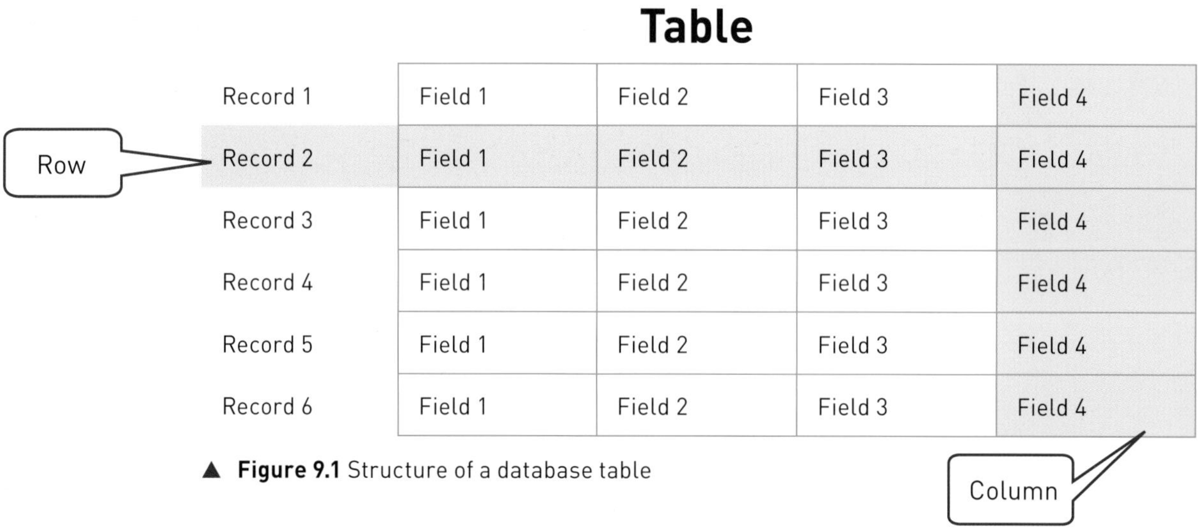

Table

▲ **Figure 9.1** Structure of a database table

A table contains data about one type of item or person or event, and will be given a meaningful name, for example:

» a table of patients called **PATIENT**
» a table of books called **BOOK**
» a table of doctor's appointments called **APPOINTMENT**.

Each record within a table contains data about a single item, person or event, for example:

» Winnie Sing (a hospital patient)
» IGCSE Computer Science (a book)
» 15:45 on January 2020 (an appointment).

As every record contains the same number of fields, each field in a record contains a specific piece of information about the single item, person or event stored in that record. Each field will have a meaningful name to identify the data stored in it, for example:

» For a hospital patient the fields could include:
   - The patient's first name field called **FirstName**
   - The patient's family name field called **FamilyName**
   - The patient's date of admission field called **DateOfAdmission**

- The name of the patient's consultant field called **Consultant**
- The patient's ward number field called **WardNumber**
- The patient's bed number field called **BedNumber**, etc.

The PATIENT table structure could look like this:

PATIENT Table

Record 1	FirstName	FamilyName	DateOfAdmission	Consultant	WardNumber	BedNumber
Record 2	FirstName	FamilyName	DateOfAdmission	Consultant	WardNumber	BedNumber
Record 3	FirstName	FamilyName	DateOfAdmission	Consultant	WardNumber	BedNumber
Record 4	FirstName	FamilyName	DateOfAdmission	Consultant	WardNumber	BedNumber
Record 5	FirstName	FamilyName	DateOfAdmission	Consultant	WardNumber	BedNumber
Record 6	FirstName	FamilyName	DateOfAdmission	Consultant	WardNumber	BedNumber

▲ **Figure 9.2** Structure of the PATIENT table

» For the table called BOOK the fields could include:
- Title of the book called **Title**
- Author of the book called **Author**
- **ISBN**, etc.

Activity 9.1

State what fields would you expect to find in each record for the doctor's appointments and give each field a suitable name.

Note: Field names should be a single word, which should not contain any spaces, for example: **BedNumber**

Validation

The role of validation was discussed in Section 7.5. It may be worth the reader revisiting this part of the book before continuing with this chapter.

Link

For more on validation see Section 7.5.

Some validation checks will be automatically provided by the database management software that is used to construct and maintain the database. Other validation checks need to be set up by the database developer during the construction of the database.

The practical use of a database management system is strongly recommended for all students. Practical examples will be used throughout this chapter. The database management software used is *Microsoft Access 365* as Microsoft Access is used by most schools with students studying IGCSE Computer Science.

For example, the **DateOfAdmission** field will automatically be checked by the software to make sure that any data input is a valid date before it can be stored in the PATIENT table.

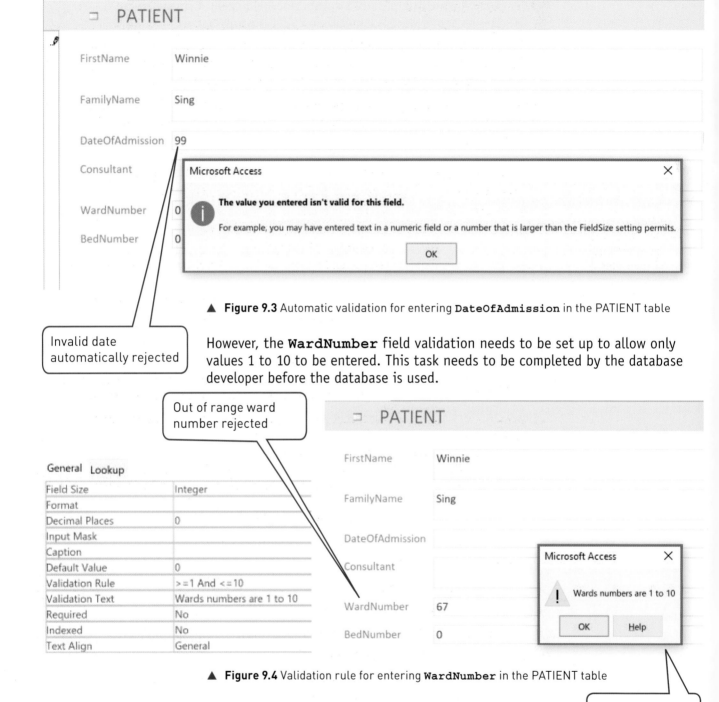

▲ **Figure 9.3** Automatic validation for entering `DateOfAdmission` in the PATIENT table

However, the `WardNumber` field validation needs to be set up to allow only values 1 to 10 to be entered. This task needs to be completed by the database developer before the database is used.

▲ **Figure 9.4** Validation rule for entering `WardNumber` in the PATIENT table

9.1.2 Basic data types
There are six basic data types that you need to be able to use in a database:

>> text/alphanumeric
>> character
>> Boolean
>> integer
>> real
>> date/time.

What is a data type?

Each field will require a **data type** to be selected. A data type classifies how the data is stored, displayed and the operations that can be performed on the stored value. For example, a field with an integer data type is stored and displayed as a whole number and the value stored can be used in calculations.

These database data types are specified in the syllabus. They are available to use as *Access* data types, but the names *Access* uses may be different from the terms in the syllabus.

Syllabus data type	Description	Access data type
text/alphanumeric	A number of characters	short text/long text
character	A single character	short text with a field size of one
Boolean	One of two values: either True or False, 1 or 0, Yes or No	Yes/No
integer	Whole number	number formatted as fixed with zero decimal places
real	A decimal number	number formatted as decimal
date/time	Date and/or time	Date/Time

Find out more

Using Access (or any other suitable database management software) find all the different date and time formats that are available to use.

Activity 9.2

Using Access (or any other suitable database management software), set up a single table database to store the PATIENT records using the fields given previously:

`FirstName, FamilyName, DateOfAdmission, Consultant, WardNumber, BedNumber.`

» Choose a suitable data type for each field.
» Include validation checks to make sure that the ward number has whole number values from 1 to 10, and that the bed number has whole number values from 1 to 8.
» Enter the following data in the PATIENT table:

Winnie Sing, 12/10/2022, Mr Smith, 6, 8

Steve Chow, 23/10/2022, Miss Abebe, 6, 3

Chin Wee, 30/10/2022, Mr Jones, 7, 1

Min Hoo, 1/11/2022, Mr Smith, 6, 1

Peter Patel, 12/11/2022, Mr Jones, 7, 8

Sue Sands, 19/11/2022, Miss Abebe, 6, 2

Farouk Khan, 22/11/2022, Mr Jones, 7, 4

Ahmad Teo 22/11/2022, Mr Jones, 7, 2

You may want to look at the instructions on how to set up the CubScout database later in this chapter if you have not set up a database before.

9.1.3 Primary keys

As each record within a table contains data about a single item, person, or event, it is important to be able to uniquely identify this item. In order to reliably identify an item from the data stored about it in a record there needs to be a field that uniquely identifies the item. This field is called the **primary key.**

A field that is a primary key must contain data values that are never repeated in the table.

The primary key can be a field that is already used, provided it is unique, for example the ISBN in the book table. The PATIENT table would need an extra field for each record as all of the existing fields could contain repeated data. To create a primary key, we could add a new field to each record, for example a unique number could be added to each patient's record. The extra field is:

» Primary key field called **HospitalNumber**

Activity 9.3

Using *Access* (or any other suitable database management software), add the **HospitalNumber** field to the single table database PATIENT.

» Choose 'text' as the data type for this field.
» Include validation checks to ensure that 8 characters must be entered starting with **HN** followed by **6 digits** for example **HN123456**.
» Choose suitable data to store in each primary key field for the 6 patients in the table.

Activity 9.4

1 Write down **four** database data types. Describe each data type and give an example of a field where it would be a suitable choice.

2 Choose suitable words/phrases from the following list to correctly complete the paragraph that follows:

Word list:	database	fields	records
	record	table	primary key
	data type	validation	text
	char	Boolean	field

You will need to use some words more than once.

A single .... contains one ....

Each .... consists of many .... Every ....

has the same number of .... Every .... is given a

.... Examples of data types are .... , ...

and .... Some .... will have .... rules.

9.1.4 SQL

Structured Query Language (SQL) is the standard query language for writing scripts to obtain useful information from a database. We will be using SQL to obtain information from single-table databases. This will provide a basic understanding of how to obtain and display only the information required from a database. SQL is pronounced as es-queue-el.

For example, somebody needing to visit a patient would only require the ward number and the bed number of that patient in order to find where they are in the hospital. Whereas a consultant could need a list of the names of all the patients that they care for.

SQL scripts

An **SQL script** is a list of SQL commands that perform a given task, often stored in a file so the script can be reused.

In order to be able to understand SQL and identify the output from an SQL script, you should have practical experience of writing SQL scripts. You can write scripts using SQL commands in *Access*. There are many other applications that also allow you to do this – *MySQL* and *SQLite* are freely available ones. When using any SQL application, it is important that you check the commands available to use as these may differ slightly from those listed in the syllabus and shown below.

You will need to be able to understand and identify the output from the following SQL statements.

SQL Query Statement	Description
SELECT	Fetches specified fields (columns) from a table; queries always begin with **SELECT**.
FROM	Identifies the table to use.
WHERE	Includes only records (rows) in a query that match a given condition.
ORDER BY	Sorts the results from a query by a given column either alphabetically or numerically.
SUM	Returns the sum of all the values in a field (column). Used with **SELECT**.
COUNT	Counts the number of records (rows) where the field (column) matches a specified condition. Used with **SELECT**.

An SQL command:

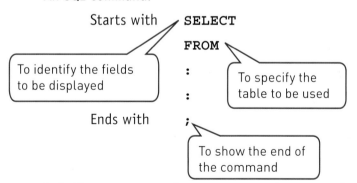

Only the **SELECT** and **FROM** commands are mandatory in an SQL script. All other commands are optional.

A **SELECT** statement takes the form:

SELECT Field1, Field2, Field3, etc. – this specifies the individual fields (columns) to be shown.

SELECT * – this specifies that **all** fields (columns) are to be shown.

A **FROM** statement takes the form:

FROM TableName – this specifies the table to use.

A **WHERE** statement takes the form:

WHERE Condition – this specifies the condition to apply.

Conditions often include values from fields, these values need to be stated in a form that matches the data type for the field.

Field type	Example value	General notes	Access notes
text	`'Mr Smith'`	Text field values should be in enclosed in single quotation marks.	Double quotation marks can also be used.
character	`'M'`	Character field values should be in enclosed in single quotation marks.	Double quotation marks can also be used.
Boolean	`TRUE`	Boolean can be **TRUE** or **FALSE**	Data type is Yes/No
integer	`12`	Integer field values should be whole numbers.	Allows integer or decimal values.
real	`12.01`	Real field values should be decimal numbers.	Allows integer or decimal values.
Date/time	`'22/11/2022'`	Date/time field values should be in enclosed in single quotation marks.	Date/time field values **must** be in enclosed in hashes (**#**).

Conditions also require operators to compare values from fields.

Operator	Description
`=`	equal to
`>`	greater than
`<`	less than
`>=`	greater than or equal to
`<=`	less than equal to
`<>`	not equal to
`BETWEEN`	between a range of two values
`LIKE`	search for a pattern
`IN`	specify multiple values
`AND`	specify multiple conditions that must all be true
`OR`	specify multiple conditions where one or more conditions must be true
`NOT`	specify a condition that must be false

An **ORDER BY** statement takes the form:

ORDER BY Field1, Field2, etc. – this specifies a sort in ascending or alphabetical order starting with the first field.

ORDER BY Field1, Field2 DESC – this specifies a sort in descending or reverse alphabetical order starting with the first field.

A **SUM** statement takes the form:

SELECT SUM (Field) – this specifies the field (column) for the calculation. The field should be integer or real.

A **COUNT** statement takes the form:

SELECT COUNT (Field) – this specifies the field (column) to count if the given criterium is met.

? Example 1: Display consultant's patients

For example, the following SQL command for the PATIENT single-table database would provide a list of all Mr Smith's patients showing the hospital number, first name and family name for each of his patients.

```
SELECT HospitalNumber, FirstName, FamilyName

FROM PATIENT

WHERE Consultant = 'Mr Smith';
```

would display:

HospitalNumber ▾	FirstName ▾	FamilyName ▾
HN123456	Winnie	Sing
HN123458	Min	Hoo

▲ **Figure 9.5** Output from the PATIENT table showing Mr Smith's patients

? Example 2: Display consultant's patients in alphabetical order

This SQL command sorts the records in alphabetical order of family name:

```
SELECT HospitalNumber, FirstName, FamilyName

FROM PATIENT

WHERE Consultant = 'Mr Smith'

ORDER BY FamilyName;
```

would display:

HospitalNumber ▾	FirstName ▾	FamilyName ▾
HN123458	Min	Hoo
HN123456	Winnie	Sing

▲ **Figure 9.6** Output from the PATIENT table showing Mr Smith's patients in alphabetical order of family name

Activity 9.5

1 Using the single table database PATIENT you have created.
   a Write an SQL query to list all Mr Jones' patients.
   b Write an SQL query to list all the patients not in ward 6.
   c Write an SQL query to list all the patients who arrived on 12/11/2022.
   d Write an SQL query to list all the patients who arrived between 12/10/2022 **AND** 30/10/2022.
2 Write down the output from this SQL query.

```
SELECT FirstName, FamilyName, BedNumber

FROM PATIENT

WHERE WardNumber = 7;
```

Activity 9.6

1 Using the single table database PATIENT you have created.
   a Write an SQL query to count the number of patients in ward 7.
   b Write an SQL query to count the number of patients not in ward 7.
2 Write down the output from this SQL query.

```
SELECT HospitalNumber, FirstName, FamilyName, Consultant

FROM PATIENT

ORDER BY Consultant, FamilyName;
```

Practical use of a database

As an IGCSE Computer Science student you need to be able to do the following:

» define a single-table database from given data storage requirements
» choose a suitable primary key for a database table
» read, complete and understand SQL scripts.

In order to do this, you will need to use a database management system. The following case study shows how to set up a database with *Microsoft Access 365* and complete the tasks described above.

Boys and girls between the ages of seven and eleven can join a cub scout group. (http://en.wikipedia.org/wiki/Cub_Scout). Each cub scout group needs to keep records about its members. Most groups will keep the following information about each cub in their group:

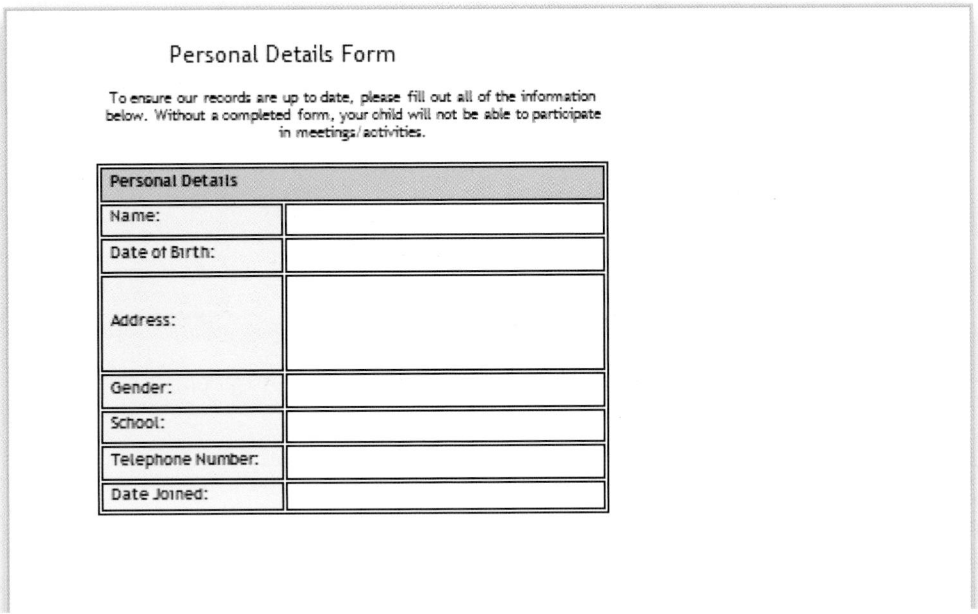

Personal Details Form

To ensure our records are up to date, please fill out all of the information below. Without a completed form, your child will not be able to participate in meetings/activities.

Personal Details	
Name:	
Date of Birth:	
Address:	
Gender:	
School:	
Telephone Number:	
Date Joined:	

▲ **Figure 9.7** Enrolment form

Define a single-table database from given data storage requirements and choose a suitable primary key

To create the cub scout database, open *Access* and select the `Blank database` template.

✓ New

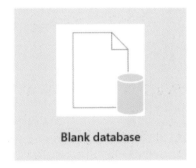

▲ **Figure 9.8** Blank database template

Then type the Filename **CubScout** and click the create button.

▲ **Figure 9.9** Creating the CubScout database

Select the table design view...   ....and name the table **CUB**.

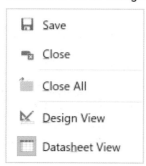

▲ **Figure 9.10** Design view   ▲ **Figure 9.11** Naming the table

Set up the fields to match the data collection form in Figure 9.7 and include an extra field for a primary key.

Each field will require a meaningful name and a suitable data type must be selected.

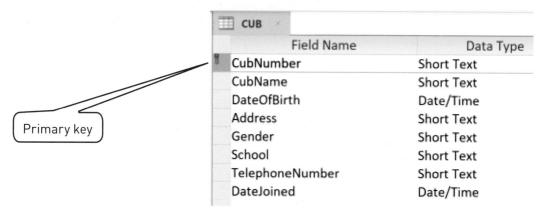

▲ **Figure 9.12** Fields for the CUB table

Validation checks need to be built in for each field, for example the **Gender** field.

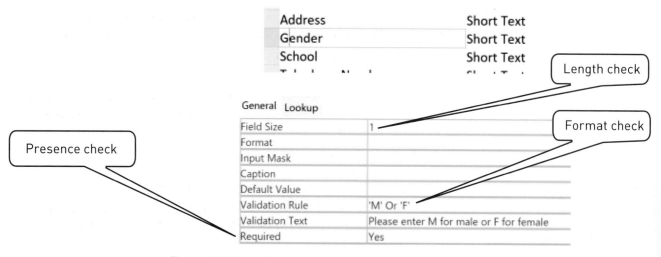

▲ **Figure 9.13** Validation rules for **Gender** field

Activity 9.7

1 a Set up a cub scout database including appropriate validation checks for each field.

  Enter data for at least 10 records.

 b The cub scout leader wants to put each cub into a group called a 'six'; each 'six' can have up to six cubs in it and is given a name for example red, yellow, blue and green.

  Add a new text field called Six, and assign each cub to either a red, blue, yellow or green six.

  i Write an SQL query to pick out any cubs in the red six.

  ii Write an SQL query to pick out any cubs in the red six or the blue six.

  iii Write an SQL query to count the number of cubs in the red six.

 c The cub scout leader wants to calculate the number of badges that all the cubs have been awarded. Add a new integer field called *Badges*, enter the number of badges awarded to each cub.

  Write an SQL query to count the number of badges awarded to the whole cub group.

Activity 9.8

1 A database of students is to be set up with the following fields:
 » Family name
 » Other names
 » Student ID
 » Date of Birth
 » Date of Entry to School
 » Current Class
 » Current school year/grade
 » Email address.

 a Select a data type for each field.

 b Which fields should be validated, and which fields should be verified?

 c Decide the validation rules for those fields which should be validated.

 d Which field would you choose for the primary key?

 e Choose a suitable format for the student ID.

 f Build a database with at least 10 records; include all your validation checks. Ensure there are at least 3 different classes and 2 different years/grades.

 g Set up and test SQL scripts to:

  i Display Other names, Family and Email address in alphabetical order of family name.

  ii Select all the students from each class in alphabetical order.

  iii Select all the students for each year/grade and print Other names, Family name and Date of Birth, grouping the students by class.

Link

For more on verification, see Chapter 7.

▶ Extension

For those students interested in studying Computer Science at A Level, this is an extension of the use of SQL to build and modify a database as well as using SQL scripts to query an existing database.

AS and A Level covers relational databases that consist of more than one table.

Industry standard methods for building and modifying a database

Database Management Systems (DBMSs) use a **Data Definition Language (DDL)** to create, modify and remove the **data structures** that form a relational database. DDL statements are written as a script that uses syntax similar to a computer program.

DBMSs also use a **Data Manipulation Language (DML)** to add, modify, delete and retrieve the **data** stored in a relational database. DML statements are written in a script that is similar to a computer program.

These languages have different functions: DDL is used for working on the relational database structure, whereas DML is used to work with the data stored in the relational database.

Most DBMSs use **Structured Query Language (SQL)** for both data definition (DDL) and data manipulation (DML). SQL was developed in the 1970s and since then it has been adopted as an industry standard.

We have already covered some SQL commands used to manipulate data. These are the SQL (DDL) commands used to set up a database.

SQL (DDL) Command	Description
`CREATE DATABASE`	Creates a database
`CREATE TABLE`	Creates a table definition
`ALTER Table`	Alters a table definition
`PRIMARY KEY`	Adds a primary key to a table

These are the data types used for attributes (fields) in SQL.

Data Types for Attributes	Description
`CHAR(n)`	Fixed length text **n** characters
`VARCHAR(n)`	Variable length text maximum **n** characters
`BOOLEAN`	True or False SQL uses the integers 1 and 0
`INTEGER`	Whole number
`REAL`	Number with decimal places
`DATE`	A date usually formatted as YYYY-MM-DD
`TIME`	A time usually formatted as HH:MM:SS

Extension Activity

Use SQL (DDL) commands to set up the PATIENT database.

This SQL script could have been used to create the Cub Scout database.

```
CREATE DATABASE CubScout
CREATE TABLE CUB(
    CubName VARCHAR(30),
    DateOfBirth DATE,
    Address VARCHAR(40),
    Gender CHAR(1),
    School VARCHAR(30),
    TelephoneNumber, CHAR(14)
    DateJoined DATE);
ALTER TABLE CUB ADD PRIMARY KEY
(CubNumber);
```

In this chapter, you have learnt about:
- ✔ define a single-table database from a given set of requirements
- ✔ suggest and use suitable data types for fields
- ✔ choose an appropriate primary key for a record
- ✔ understand SQL scripts used to query a single-table database.

Key terms used throughout this chapter

database – a persistent structured collection of data that allows people to extract information in a way that meets their needs

single-table database – a database contains only one table

table – a collection of related records in a database

record – a collection of fields that describe one item

field – a database table

data type – a classification of how data is stored and displayed, and of which operations that can be performed on the stored value

primary key – a field in a database that uniquely identifies a record

Structured Query Language (SQL) – the standard query language for writing scripts to obtain useful information from a relational database.

SQL scripts – a list of SQL commands that perform a given task, often stored in a file so the script can be reused

SELECT – an SQL command that fetches specified fields (columns) from a table

FROM – an SQL command that identifies the table to use

WHERE – an SQL command to include only those records (rows) in a query that match a given condition

ORDER BY – an SQL command that sorts the results from a query by a given column either alphabetically or numerically

SUM – an SQL command that returns the sum of all the values in a field (column); used with SELECT

COUNT – an SQL command that counts the number of records (rows) in which the field (column) matches a specified condition; used with SELECT

Exam-style questions

1 A motor car manufacturer offers various combinations of:
  » seat colours
  » seat materials
  » car paint colours.

A table, CAR, was set up as single-table database to help customers choose which seat and paint combinations were possible. (NOTE: N = no, not a possible combination, Y = yes, combination is possible)

Seat materials and colours

Pair col

Code	Cloth	Leather	Seat colour	White	Red	Black	Blue	Green	Silver	Grey
CB	Y	N	black	Y	Y	Y	Y	Y	Y	Y
LB	N	Y	black	N	Y	N	N	N	Y	Y
CC	Y	N	cream	N	Y	Y	Y	N	N	N
LC	N	Y	cream	N	Y	Y	Y	N	N	Y
CG	Y	N	grey	N	Y	Y	Y	Y	Y	N
LG	N	Y	grey	N	Y	N	Y	N	Y	Y
CR	Y	N	red	Y	N	Y	N	N	Y	Y
LR	N	Y	red	Y	N	Y	N	N	Y	Y
CB	Y	N	blue	N	N	N	Y	N	N	N
LB	N	Y	blue	N	N	Y	Y	Y	N	N

a i State the number of records shown in the table. [1]
  ii State the number of fields shown in the table. [1]
  iii State, with a reason, if any of the fields are suitable to use as primary key. [2]

b The following SQL command was used:

```
SELECT Code

FROM CAR

WHERE SeatColour = 'Red' AND ('White' OR
'silver');
```

Show what will be displayed. [2]

c A customer wanted to know all the possible combinations for a car with leather seats and either silver or grey paint colour. Complete the SQL command required.

```
SELECT *

FROM ........................................

WHERE ................ leather AND (silver ................ grey);
```
[2]

2 A company that sells bicycles keeps records of the items in stock in a table, CYCLE, using a single-table database. For each model of bicycle, the following data is kept:
  – model number, for example: BY00007
  – description of model, for example: lady's shopper
  – colour of frame, for example: gold and black

- size of wheels, for example: 700 mm
- price of model in $, for example: $309.50
- still being manufactured: Yes or No
- number in stock.

a **i** State, with a reason for your choice, the data type you would choose for each field in the table. [7]

ii Identify, with a reason for each, the validation required for each of these fields:
- model number
- price
- number in stock. [3]

iii State, with a reason, the field that would be suitable to use as primary key. [2]

b SQL commands are used to extract data from the table. Explain, using examples from your table, how each of these commands could be used:
- **SELECT**
- **FROM**
- **WHERE**
- **SUM**
- **ORDER BY** [10]

3 A database table, PERFORMANCE, is used to keep a record of the performances at a local theatre.

Show Number	Type	Title	Date	Sold Out
SN091	Comedy	An Evening at Home	01-Sep	Yes
SN102	Drama	Old Places	02-Oct	No
SN113	Jazz	Acoustic Evening	03-Nov	No
SN124	Classical	Mozart Evening	04-Dec	Yes
SN021	Classical	Bach Favourites	01-Feb	Yes
SN032	Jazz	30 Years of Jazz	02-Mar	Yes
SN043	Comedy	Street Night	03-Apr	No
SN054	Comedy	Hoot	04-May	No

a State the number of fields and records in the table.

Fields ....

Records .... [2]

b Give **two** validation checks that could be performed on the Show Number field.

Validation check 1 ....

....

Validation check 2 ....

.... [2]

Cambridge IGCSE Computer Science (0478) Paper 21 Q6 a), b), May/June 2018

10 Boolean logic

> **In this chapter, you will learn about:**
> ★ the identification, definition, symbols and functions of the standard logic gates:
> NOT, AND, OR, NAND, NOR and XOR
> ★ how to use logic gates to create logic circuits from:
>   – a given problem
>   – a logic expression
>   – a truth table
> ★ how to complete truth tables from:
>   – a given problem
>   – a logic expression
>   – a logic circuit
> ★ how to write a logic expression from:
>   – a given problem
>   – a logic circuit
>   – a truth table.

10.1 Standard logic gate symbols

Electronic circuits in computers, solid state drives and controlling devices are made up of thousands of **logic gates**. Logic gates take binary inputs and produce a binary output. Several logic gates combined together form a **logic circuit** and these circuits are designed to carry out a specific function.

The checking of the output from a logic gate or logic circuit is done using a **truth table**.

This chapter will consider the function and role of logic gates, logic circuits and truth tables. Also a number of possible applications of logic circuits will be considered. A reference to **Boolean algebra** will be made throughout the chapter; but this is really outside the scope of this text book. However, Boolean algebra will be seen on many logic gate websites and is included here for completeness, since many students may prefer this notation to logic statements.

10.1.1 Logic gate symbols

Six different logic gates will be considered in this chapter:

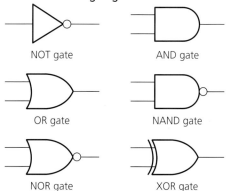

NOT gate	AND gate
OR gate	NAND gate
NOR gate	XOR gate

▲ **Figure 10.1** Logic gate symbols

Truth tables

Truth tables are used to trace the output from a logic gate or logic circuit. The NOT gate is the only logic gate with one input; the other five gates have two inputs (see Figure 10.1).

Although each logic gate can only have one or two inputs, the number of inputs to a logic circuit can be more than 2; for example, three inputs give a possible 2^3 (=8) binary combinations. And for four inputs, the number of possible binary combinations is 2^4 (=16). It is clear that the number of possible binary combinations is a multiple of the number 2 in every case. The possible inputs in a truth table can be summarised as shown in Table 10.1.

▼ **Table 10.1** All possible inputs for truth tables with two, three and four inputs

Inputs	
A	**B**
0	0
0	1
1	0
1	1

Inputs		
A	**B**	**C**
0	0	0
0	0	1
0	1	0
0	1	1
1	0	0
1	0	1
1	1	0
1	1	1

Inputs			
A	**B**	**C**	**D**
0	0	0	0
0	0	0	1
0	0	1	0
0	0	1	1
0	1	0	0
0	1	0	1
0	1	1	0
0	1	1	1
1	0	0	0
1	0	0	1
1	0	1	0
1	0	1	1
1	1	0	0
1	1	0	1
1	1	1	0
1	1	1	1

As we can see, a truth table will also list the output for every possible combination of inputs.

10.2 The function of the six logic gates

10.2.1 NOT gate

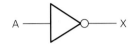

▲ **Figure 10.2**

Description:	Truth table:	How to write this:
The output, X, is 1 if: the input, A, is 0	▼ **Table 10.2** | Input	Output
---	---
A	**X**
0	1
1	0		X = NOT A (logic notation) X = $\overline{A}$ (Boolean algebra)

Note the use of Boolean algebra to represent logic gates. This is optional at IGCSE but many students may prefer to use this notation (see NOTE later).

10.2.2 AND gate

▲ **Figure 10.3**

Description:	Truth table:			How to write this:
The output, X, is 1 if: both inputs, A and B, are 1	▼ **Table 10.3**			X = A AND B (logic notation) X = A . B (Boolean algebra)

	Inputs		Outputs
	A	**B**	**X**
	0	0	0
	0	1	0
	1	0	0
	1	1	1

10.2.3 OR gate

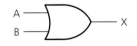

▲ **Figure 10.4**

Description:	Truth table:			How to write this:
The output, X, is 1 if: either input, A or B, or both, are 1	▼ **Table 10.4**			X = A OR B (logic notation) X = A + B (Boolean algebra)

	Inputs		Output
	A	**B**	**X**
	0	0	0
	0	1	1
	1	0	1
	1	1	1

10.2.4 NAND gate (NOT AND)

▲ **Figure 10.5**

Description:	Truth table:			How to write this:
	▼ Table 10.5			

	Inputs		Output	
	A	**B**	**X**	

Description:	A	B	X	How to write this:
The output, X, is 1 if:	0	0	1	X = A NAND B (logic notation)
input A AND	0	1	1	X = $\overline{A . B}$ (Boolean algebra)
input B are NOT both 1	1	0	1	
	1	1	0	

10.2.5 NOR gate (NOT OR)

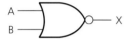

▲ **Figure 10.6**

Description:	Truth table:			How to write this:
	▼ Table 10.6			

	Inputs		Output	
	A	**B**	**X**	
The output, X, is 1 if:	0	0	1	X = A NOR B (logic notation)
neither input A nor	0	1	0	X = $\overline{A + B}$ (Boolean algebra)
input B is 1	1	0	0	
	1	1	0	

10.2.6 XOR gate

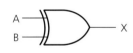

▲ **Figure 10.7**

Description:	Truth table:			How to write this:
	▼ Table 10.7			

	Inputs		Output	
	A	**B**	**X**	
The output, X, is 1 if:				X = A XOR B (logic notation)
(input A is 1 AND input B is 0)	0	0	0	X = $(A . \overline{B}) + (\overline{A} . B)$ (Boolean algebra)
or	0	1	1	
(input A is 0 AND input B is 1)	1	0	1	NOTE: this is sometimes written as: $(A + B) . (\overline{A . B})$
	1	1	0	

Activity 10.1

Show why X = (A AND NOT B) OR (NOT A AND B)
and
Y = (A OR B) AND (NOT (A AND B)) both represent the same logic gate.

You will notice in the Boolean algebra, three new symbols; these have the following meaning:

» . represents the AND operation
» + represents the OR operation
» a bar (above the letter or letters, e.g. $\bar{a}$) represents the NOT operation.

10.3 Logic circuits, logic expressions, truth tables and problem statements

When logic gates are combined together to carry out a particular function, such as controlling a robot, they form a logic circuit. The following eight examples show how to carry out the following tasks:

» Create a logic circuit from a:
  - problem statement (examples 6 and 7)
  - logic or Boolean expression (examples 3 and 8)
  - truth table (examples 4 and 5)
» Complete a truth table from a:
  - problem statement (examples 6 and 7)
  - logic or Boolean expression (examples 3 and 8)
  - logic circuit (example 1)
» Write a logic or Boolean expression from a:
  - problem statement (examples 6 and 7)
  - logic circuit (example 2)
  - truth table (examples 4 and 5).

? Example 1

Produce a truth table for the following logic circuit (note the use of black circles at the junctions between wires):

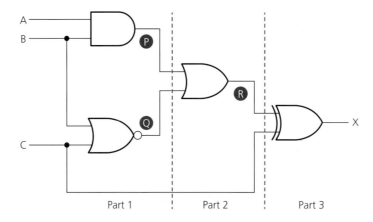

▲ Figure 10.8

There are three inputs to this logic circuit, therefore, there will be eight possible binary values that can be input.

To show stepwise how the truth table is produced, the logic circuit has been split up into three parts, as shown by the dotted lines, and intermediate values are shown as P, Q and R.

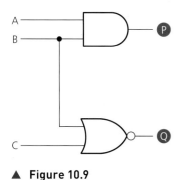

▲ Figure 10.9

Part 1

Ⓟ This is the first part of the logic circuit; the first task is to find the intermediate values P and Q.

The value of P is found from the AND gate where the inputs are A and B. The value of Q is found from the NOR gate where the inputs are B and C. An intermediate truth table is produced using the logic function descriptions in Section 10.2.

▼ **Table 10.8**

input values			Output values	
A	B	C	P	Q
0	0	0	0	1
0	0	1	0	0
0	1	0	0	0
0	1	1	0	0
1	0	0	0	1
1	0	1	0	0
1	1	0	1	0
1	1	1	1	0

Part 2

▲ Figure 10.10

The second part of the logic circuit has P and Q as inputs and the intermediate output, R:

This produces the following intermediate truth table. (Note: even though there are only two inputs to the logic gate, we have generated eight binary values in part 1 and these must all be used in this second truth table).

▼ **Table 10.9**

Inputs		Output
P	Q	R
0	1	1
0	0	0
0	0	0
0	0	0
0	1	1
0	0	0
1	0	1
1	0	1

▲ **Figure 10.11**

Part 3

The final part of the logic circuit has R and C as inputs and the final output, X:

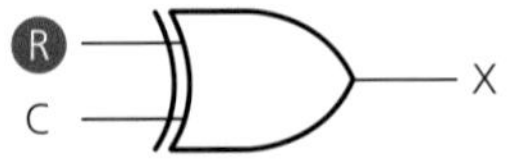

This gives the third intermediate truth table:

▼ **Table 10.10**

Inputs		Output
R	**C**	**X**
1	0	**1**
0	1	**1**
0	0	**0**
0	1	**1**
1	0	**1**
0	1	**1**
1	0	**1**
1	1	**0**

Putting all three intermediate truth tables together produces the final truth table, which represents the original logic circuit:

▼ **Table 10.11**

Input values			Intermediate values			Output
A	**B**	**C**	**P**	**Q**	**R**	**X**
0	0	0	0	1	1	1
0	0	1	0	0	0	1
0	1	0	0	0	0	0
0	1	1	0	0	0	1
1	0	0	0	1	1	1
1	0	1	0	0	0	1
1	1	0	1	0	1	1
1	1	1	1	0	1	0

The intermediate values can be left out of the final truth table, but it is good practice to leave them in until you become confident about producing the truth tables. The final truth table would then look like this:

▼ **Table 10.12**

Input values			Output
A	**B**	**C**	**X**
0	0	0	1
0	0	1	1
0	1	0	0
0	1	1	1
1	0	0	1
1	0	1	1
1	1	0	1
1	1	1	0

? Example 2

Write logic expressions from the following logic circuits:

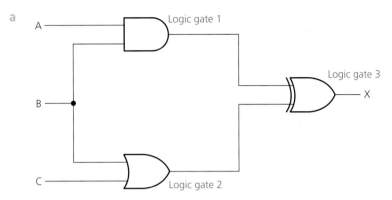

▲ **Figure 10.12**

The first action is to look at the gates connected to the inputs A, B and C:

logic gate 1:   (A AND B)

logic gate 2:   (B OR C)

We then join these together using logic gate 3:

[(A AND B)] XOR [(B OR C)] which gives us the required logic expression.

(Note: the square brackets "[ ]" in the expression are not necessary and are used here just for clarity.)

This would be written as: (A AND B) XOR (B OR C)

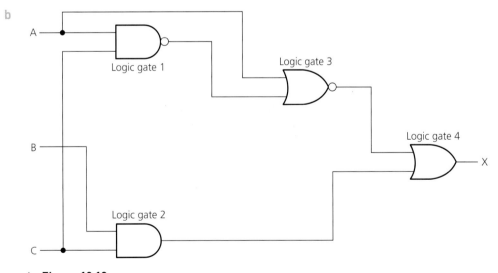

▲ **Figure 10.13**

Again, we will do this in the order of logic gates 1 and 2 first (connected to the three inputs):

logic gate 1:   (A NAND C)

logic gate 2:   (B AND C)

However, logic gate 3 is also connected to one of the inputs so that should be done next:

logic gate 3:   (logic gate 1) NOR A

If we replace (logic gate 1) by the logic expression above, we get:

$$((A\ NAND\ C)\ NOR\ A)$$

Finally, we can join all these together using:

logic gate 4:   ((A NAND C) NOR A) OR (B AND C)

Activity 10.2

1   Produce truth tables from the following logic circuits:

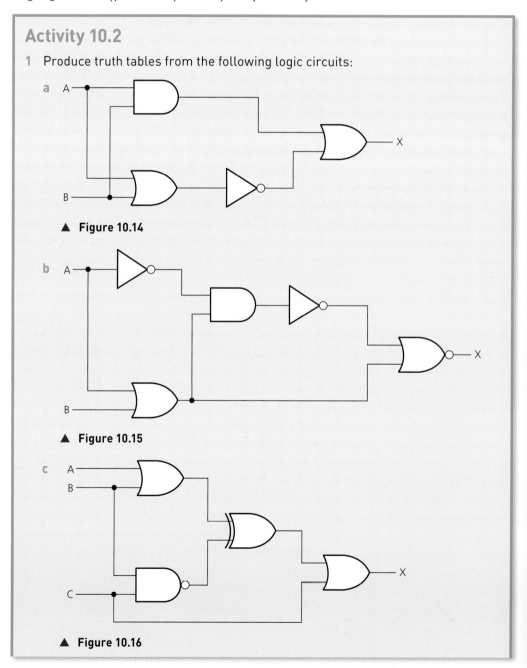

a

▲ **Figure 10.14**

b

▲ **Figure 10.15**

c

▲ **Figure 10.16**

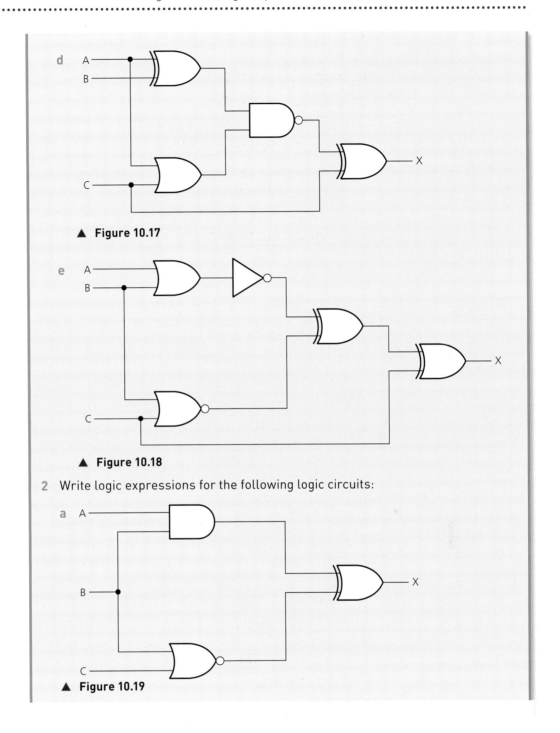

▲ **Figure 10.17**

▲ **Figure 10.18**

2   Write logic expressions for the following logic circuits:

▲ **Figure 10.19**

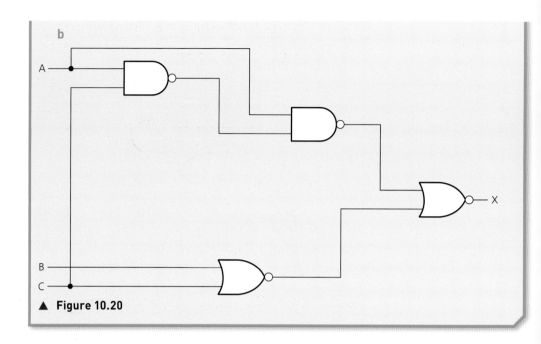

▲ **Figure 10.20**

❓ Example 3

A logic circuit can be represented by the following logic expression: (A XOR C) OR (NOT C NAND B)

Produce a logic circuit and a truth table from the above statement.

In this example we have a connecting logic gate which is OR.

So, if we produce one half of the circuit from (A XOR C) we get:

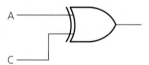

▲ **Figure 10.21**

The other half of the circuit is found from (NOT C NAND B):

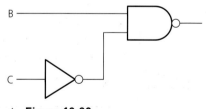

▲ **Figure 10.22**

If we now combine these together to form the final logic circuit:

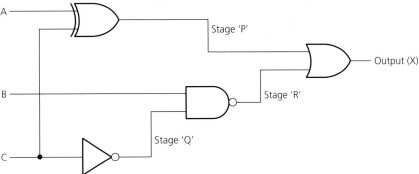

▲ Figure 10.23

The truth table is shown:

▼ Table 10.13

Input values			Values at stages:			Output
A	B	C	'P'	'Q'	'R'	X
0	0	0	0	1	1	1
0	0	1	1	0	1	1
0	1	0	0	1	0	0
0	1	1	1	0	1	1
1	0	0	1	1	1	1
1	0	1	0	0	1	1
1	1	0	1	1	0	1
1	1	1	0	0	1	1

? Example 4

Look at the two truth tables below; in each case produce a logic expression and the corresponding logic circuit:

a

▼ Table 10.14

Inputs		Output
A	B	X
0	0	0
0	1	0
1	0	1
1	1	0

> To produce the logic statement, we only concern ourselves with the truth table row where the output value is 1. In this case, A = 1 and B = 0 which gives the logical expression:
>
> A AND NOT B

So we have the logic expression: A AND NOT B

(Note that this could be written as A . $\overline{B}$ in Boolean.) It is now possible to draw the corresponding logic circuit:

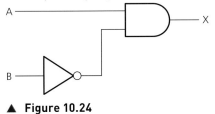

▲ Figure 10.24

b

▼ **Table 10.15**

Inputs		Output
A	**B**	**X**
0	0	0
0	1	1
1	0	0
1	1	1

> This time we have **two** rows where the output is 1; this gives the following logical expressions:
>
> (NOT A AND B)
>
> (A AND B)
>
> We now join these together using an OR gate to give:
>
> (NOT A AND B) OR (A AND B)

So we have the logic expression: (NOT A AND B) OR (A AND B)

(This could be written as: $\overline{A}.B + A.B$)

It is now possible to draw the corresponding logic circuit:

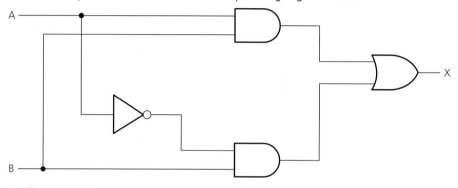

▲ **Figure 10.25**

❓ Example 5

a Which Boolean expression is represented by the following truth table?

▼ **Table 10.16**

Input values			Output
A	**B**	**C**	**X**
0	0	0	1
0	0	1	0
0	1	0	0
0	1	1	0
1	0	0	1
1	0	1	0
1	1	0	1
1	1	1	0

We only need to consider those rows where the output is a 1. This gives us the following three logic expressions:

> (NOT A AND NOT B AND NOT C)
> (A AND NOT B AND NOT C)
> (A AND B AND NOT C)

If we now join the three expressions with an OR gate, we end up with the final logic expression:

> (NOT A AND NOT B AND NOT C) OR (A AND NOT B AND NOT C) OR
> (A AND B AND NOT C)

b   i   Which logic expression is represented by the following truth table?
    ii Show that your logic expression in part i is the same as: (B AND C) OR (A AND C) OR (A AND B)

▼ **Table 10.17**

A	B	C	X
0	0	0	0
0	0	1	0
0	1	0	0
0	1	1	1
1	0	0	0
1	0	1	1
1	1	0	1
1	1	1	1

   i   We only need to consider those rows where the output is a 1. This gives us the following four Boolean expressions:

> (NOT A AND B AND C)
> (A AND NOT B AND C)
> (A AND B AND NOT C)
> (A AND B AND C)

   If we now join the four expressions with an OR gate we end up with the following logic expression:

> (NOT A AND B AND C) OR (A AND NOT B AND C) OR (A AND B AND NOT C) OR (A AND B AND C)

   ii To show that **(B AND C) OR (A AND C) OR (A AND B)** produces the same output as that shown in part i we need to produce a new truth table and show that the output is the same as the one in the given truth table:

▼ **Table 10.18**

A	B	C	B AND C	A AND C	A AND B	(B AND C) OR (A AND C) OR (A AND B)	X
0	0	0	0	0	0	0	0
0	0	1	0	0	0	0	0
0	1	0	0	0	0	0	0
0	1	1	1	0	0	1	1
1	0	0	0	0	0	0	0
1	0	1	0	1	0	1	1
1	1	0	0	0	1	1	1
1	1	1	1	1	1	1	1

As the second truth table shows, the outputs from logic expressions are both the same; thus the logic expression **(B AND C) OR (A AND C) OR (A AND B)** gives the same output as the logic expression in part i.

Activity 10.3

1 Produce:

  i   a truth table

  ii a logic circuit

  from the following logic expression:

  | (NOT A AND B) AND (NOT B OR C) |

2 Produce:

  i   a truth table

  ii a logic circuit

  from the following logic expression:

  | (A XOR B) OR ((B NOR C) AND B) |

A	B	X
0	0	1
0	1	0
1	0	0
1	1	1

3 Produce:

  i   a logic expression

  ii a logic circuit

  from the following truth table:

4 Write down a logic expression for **each** of the following truth tables:

a

A	B	C	X
0	0	0	1
0	0	1	0
0	1	0	0
0	1	1	0
1	0	0	1
1	0	1	1
1	1	0	0
1	1	1	0

b

A	B	C	X
0	0	0	0
0	0	1	1
0	1	0	1
0	1	1	0
1	0	0	1
1	0	1	1
1	1	0	0
1	1	1	0

5 a Write down a logic expression corresponding to the following truth table:

A	B	C	X
0	0	0	1
0	0	1	1
0	1	0	0
0	1	1	0
1	0	0	1
1	0	1	1
1	1	0	0
1	1	1	0

  b Show that the following logic expression produces the same output as your answer to part **a** above:

  | (NOT A AND NOT B) OR (A AND NOT B) |

? **Example 6**

A safety system uses three inputs to a logic circuit. An alarm, X, sounds if input A represents ON and input B represents OFF; or if input B represents ON and input C represents OFF.

Produce a logic circuit and truth table to show the conditions that cause the output X to be 1.

The first thing to do is to write down the logic statement representing the scenario in this example. To do this, it is necessary to recall that ON = 1 and OFF = 0 and also that 0 is usually considered to be NOT 1.

So we get the following logic expression:

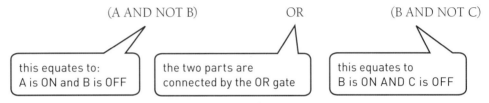

Note: this expression can also be written as follows (Boolean expression):

$$(A . \overline{B}) + (B . \overline{C})$$

The logic circuit is made up of two parts as shown in the logic expression. We will produce the logic gate for the first second part. Then join both parts together with the OR gate.

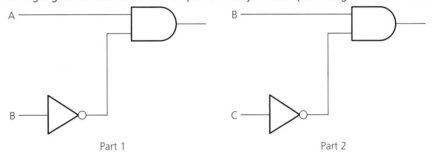

▲ **Figure 10.26**

Now combining both parts with the OR gate gives us:

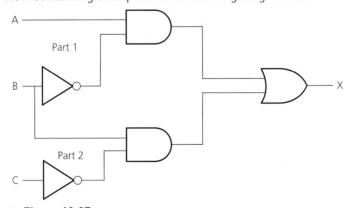

▲ **Figure 10.27**

In order to produce the truth table, there are two ways to do this:

» trace through the logic circuit using the method described in example 1 (Section 10.3)

» produce the truth table using the original logic expression; this second method has the advantage that it allows you to check that your logic circuit is correct.

We will use the second method in this example:

▼ **Table 10.19**

Inputs			Intermediate values		Output
A	**B**	**C**	**(A AND NOT B)**	**(B AND NOT C)**	**X**
0	0	0	0	0	0
0	0	1	0	0	0
0	1	0	0	1	1
0	1	1	0	0	0
1	0	0	1	0	1
1	0	1	1	0	1
1	1	0	0	1	1
1	1	1	0	0	0

(Note: it is optional whether to leave in the intermediate values or simply remove them giving a 4-column truth table with headings: A, B, C, X)

❓ Example 7

A wind turbine has a safety system which uses three inputs to a logic circuit. A certain combination of conditions results in an output, X, from the logic circuit being equal to 1. When the value of X = 1 then the wind turbine is shut down.

The following table shows which parameters are being monitored and form the three inputs to the logic circuit.

▼ **Table 10.20**

parameter description	parameter	binary value	description of condition
turbine speed	S	0	turbine speed <= 1000 rpm
		1	turbine speed > 1000 rpm
bearing temperature	T	0	bearing temperature <= 80°C
		1	bearing temperature > 80°C
wind velocity	W	0	wind velocity <= 120 kph
		1	wind velocity >120 kph

The output, X, will have a value of 1 if any of the following combination of conditions occur:

Either	turbine speed <= 1000 rpm and bearing temperature > 80°C
Or	turbine speed > 1000 rpm and wind velocity > 120 kph
Or	bearing temperature <= 80°C and wind velocity > 120 kph

Design the logic circuit and complete the truth table to produce a value of X = 1 when either of the three conditions above occur.

In this example, a real situation is given and it is necessary to convert the information into a logic expression and then produce the logic circuit and truth table. It is advisable in problems as complex as this to produce the logic circuit and truth table separately (based on the conditions given) and then check them against each other to see if there are any errors.

Stage 1

The first thing to do is to convert each of the three statements into logic expressions. Use the information given in the table and the three condition statements to find how the three parameters S, T and W are linked. We usually look for the key words AND, OR and NOT when converting actual statements into logic.

We end up with the following three logic expressions:
i turbine speed <= 1000 rpm and bearing temperature > 80°C
   logic expression: (NOT S AND T)
ii turbine speed > 1000 rpm and wind velocity > 120 kph
   logic expression: (S AND W)
iii bearing temperature <= 80°C and wind velocity > 120 kph
   logic expression: (NOT T AND W)

Stage 2

This now produces three intermediate logic circuits:

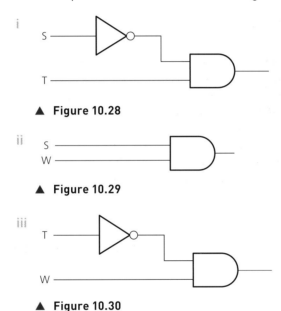

▲ **Figure 10.28**

▲ **Figure 10.29**

▲ **Figure 10.30**

Each of the three original statements were joined together by the word 'OR'. Thus, we need to join all of the three intermediate logic circuits by two OR gates to get the final logic circuit.

We will start by joining i and ii together using an OR gate:

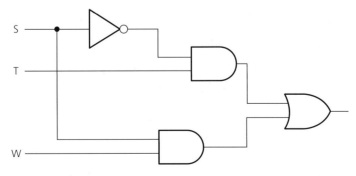

▲ **Figure 10.31**

Finally, we connect the logic circuit in Figure 10.31 to Figure 10.30 to obtain the answer:

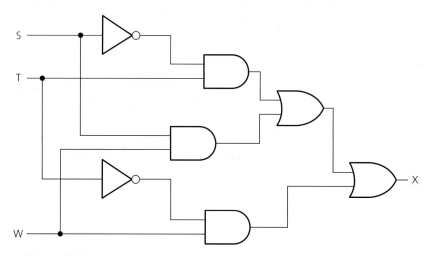

▲ **Figure 10.32**

The final part is to produce the truth table. We will do this using the original logic statement. This method has the bonus of allowing an extra check to be made on the logic circuit in Figure 10.32 to see whether or not it is correct. It is possible, however, to produce the truth table straight from the logic circuit in Figure 10.32.

There were three parts to the problem, so the truth table will first evaluate each part. Then, by applying OR gates, as shown below, the final value, X, is obtained:

i   (NOT S AND T)
ii   (S AND W)
iii (NOT T AND W)

We find the outputs from parts (i) and (ii) and then OR these two outputs together to obtain a new intermediate, which we will now label part (iv).

We then OR parts (iii) and (iv) together to get the value of X.

Inputs			Intermediate values				Output
S	**T**	**W**	**(i)** **(NOT S AND T)**	**(ii)** **(S AND W)**	**(iii)** **(NOT T AND W)**	**(iv)**	**X**
0	0	0	0	0	0	0	0
0	0	1	0	0	1	0	1
0	1	0	1	0	0	1	1
0	1	1	1	0	0	1	1
1	0	0	0	0	0	0	0
1	0	1	0	1	1	1	1
1	1	0	0	0	0	0	0
1	1	1	0	1	0	1	1

❓ Example 8

Consider the logic statement:

((A NOR B) AND C) NAND (A OR NOT B)

a   Draw a logic circuit to represent the given logic statement.
b   Complete the truth table for the given logic statement.

▼ Table 10.21

Input values			Working space	Output X
A	**B**	**C**		
0	0	0		
0	0	1		
0	1	0		
0	1	1		
1	0	0		
1	0	1		
1	1	0		
1	1	1		

First, we need to break down the logic statement. Assign:

i   P = (A NOR B)
ii   Q = (A OR NOT B)
iii R = (P AND C)

And then note that X = R NAND Q

Now draw the logic gates for statements i to iii and connect them together.

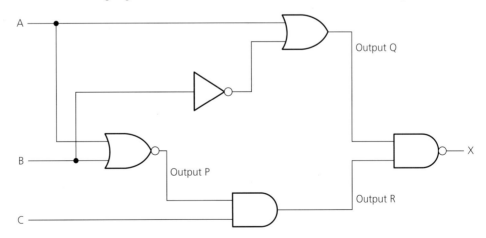

▲ Figure 10.33

We can then fill out the truth table in stages, starting with P, Q and then R, followed finally by X:

Input Values			Working Space			Output X
A	B	C	P = (A NOR B)	Q = (A OR NOT B)	R = (P AND C)	
0	0	0	1	1	0	1
0	0	1	1	1	1	0
0	1	0	0	0	0	1
0	1	1	0	0	0	1
1	0	0	0	1	0	1
1	0	1	0	1	0	1
1	1	0	0	1	0	1
1	1	1	0	1	0	1

Find out more

Boolean algebra appears throughout this chapter and is the official method for depicting logic statements. Try using truth tables to prove the following pairs of Boolean (logic) statements are the same:

i $\quad A + (A \cdot B) = A$

ii $\quad A + \bar{A} \cdot B = A + B$

iii $\quad (A + B) \cdot (A + C) = A + B \cdot C$

iv $\quad \overline{(A \cdot B)} = \bar{A} + \bar{B}$

v $\quad A + B = \bar{A} + \bar{B}$

Activity 10.4

1 Draw the logic circuits and complete the truth tables for the following logic or Boolean expressions:

a $\quad$ X = (A OR B) OR (NOT A AND B)

b $\quad$ Y = (NOT A AND NOT B) AND (NOT B OR C)

c $\quad$ T = 1 if (switch K is ON or switch L is ON) OR (switch K is ON and switch M is OFF) OR (switch M is ON)

d $\quad$ X = (A AND NOT B) OR (NOT B AND C)

e $\quad$ R = 1 if (switch A is ON and switch B is ON) AND (switch B is ON or switch C is OFF)

2 Produce the logic circuit and complete a truth table to represent the following scenario.

A chemical process is protected by a logic circuit. There are three inputs to the logic circuit representing key parameters in the chemical process. An alarm, X, will give an output value of 1 depending on certain conditions in the chemical process. The following table describes the process conditions being monitored:

Parameter description	Parameter	Binary value	Description of condition
chemical reaction rate	R	0	reaction rate < 40 mol/l/sec
		1	reaction rate >= 40 mol/l/sec
process temperature	T	0	temperature > 115°C
		1	temperature <= 115°C
concentration of chemicals	C	0	concentration <= 4 mol
		1	concentration > 4 mol

An alarm, X, will generate the value 1 if:

either $\qquad$ reaction rate < 40 mol/l/sec

or $\qquad$ concentration > 4 mol AND temperature > 115°C

or $\qquad$ reaction rate >= 40 mol/l/sec AND temperature > 115°C

3 Produce the logic circuit and complete a truth table to represent the following scenario.

A power station has a safety system controlled by a logic circuit. Three inputs to the logic circuit determine whether the output, S, is 1. When S = 1 the power station shuts down.

The following table describes the conditions being monitored.

Parameter description	Parameter	Binary value	Description of condition
gas temperature	G	0	gas temperature <= 160°C
		1	gas temperature > 160°C
reactor pressure	R	0	reactor pressure <= 10 bar
		1	reactor pressure > 10 bar
water temperature	W	0	water temperature <= 120°C
		1	water temperature > 120°C

Output, S, will generate a value of 1, if:

either   gas temperature > 160°C AND water temperature <= 120°C

or   gas temperature <= 160°C AND reactor pressure > 10 bar

or   water temperature > 120°C AND reactor pressure > 10 bar

4 A car's engine management system uses three sensors A, B and C. The data from these sensors forms the input to a logic circuit. When the output (X) from the logic circuit is 1 a signal is sent to a warning light on the dash board of the car.

The following table describes the conditions being monitored.

Parameter description	Parameter	Binary value	Description of condition
exhaust temperature	E	0	exhaust temperature > 400°C
		1	exhaust temperature <= 400°C
oil pressure	P	0	oil pressure <= 10 bar
		1	oil pressure > 10 bar
water temperature	W	0	water temperature <= 110°C
		1	water temperature > 110°C

Output, X, will generate a value of 1, if:

either   exhaust temperature > 400°C AND oil pressure > 10 bar

or   oil pressure <= 10 bar AND water temperature > 110 °C

or   oil pressure > 10 bar AND water temperature > 110 °C

Produce:

i   a truth table,

ii   a logic expression and

iii   a logic circuit

to represent the above scenario.

Also confirm that the output from your logic circuit matches the output from your truth table in part i.

5 The following truth table is for a logic gate called the *XNOR* gate.

By completing the truth table below, show that the XNOR gate can be represented by the following logic expression:

(A AND B) OR (NOT A AND NOT B)

A	B	X
0	0	1
0	1	0
1	0	0
1	1	1

A	B	(A AND B)	(NOT A AND NOT B)	(A AND B) OR (NOT A AND NOT B)
0	0			
0	1			
1	0			
1	1			

Advice

Regarding question 5, XNOR gates are not on the syllabus

▶ Extension

The following two exercises are designed to help students thinking of furthering their study in Computer Science at A Level standard. The two topics here are not on the syllabus and merely show how some of the topics in this chapter can be extended to this next level. The two topics extend uses of logic circuits in the real world and the use of full adders and half adders.

Topic 1: Logic circuits in the real world

Anybody reading this chapter with an electronics background will be aware that the design of logic circuits is considerably more complex than has been described.

This chapter has described in detail some of the fundamental theories used in logic circuit design. This will give the reader sufficient grounding to cover all existing IGCSE and O Level syllabuses. However, it is worth finally discussing some of the other aspects of logic circuit design that will interest any student considering the A Level course.

Electronics companies need to consider the cost of components, ease of fabrication and time constraints when designing and building logic circuits. We will outline two possible ways electronics companies can standardise logic circuit design:

» One method is to use 'off-the-shelf' logic units and build up the logic circuit as a number of 'building blocks'

» Another method involves simplifying the logic circuit as far as possible; this may be necessary where room is at a premium (for example, in building circuit boards for use in satellites to allow space exploration).

Using logic 'building blocks'

One very common 'building block' is the NAND gate. It is possible to build up any logic gate, and therefore any logic circuit, by simply linking together a number of NAND gates. For example, the AND, OR and NOT gates can be built from NAND gates as shown here in Figure 10.34:

The AND gate:

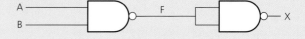

The OR gate:

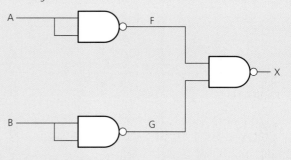

The NOT gate:

▲ **Figure 10.34**

Task 1

By drawing the truth tables, show that the three circuits in Figure 10.34 can be used to represent AND, OR and NOT gates.

Task 2

1 Show how the following logic circuit could be built using NAND gates only. Also complete truth tables for both logic circuits to show that they produce identical outputs.

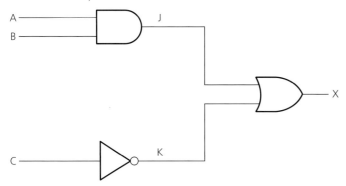

▲ **Figure 10.35**

2 Show how the XOR gate could be built from NAND gates only. Complete a truth table for your final design to show it that it produces the same output as a single XOR gate.

Task 3

By drawing a truth table, which single logic gate has the same function as the following logic circuit made up of NAND gates only?

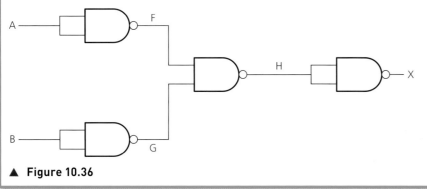

▲ **Figure 10.36**

Topic 2: Half adder and full adder circuits

In Chapter 10, the use of logic gates to create logic circuits to carry out specific tasks was discussed in much detail. Two important logic circuits used in computers are:

» the **half adder circuit**
» the **full adder circuit**.

Half adder

One of the basic operations in any computer is binary addition. The half adder circuit is the simplest circuit; this carries binary addition on 2 bits generating two outputs:

» the sum bit (S)
» the carry bit (C).

If you consider 1 + 1 this will give the result 1 0 (denary value 2). The '1' is the carry and '0' the sum. As a truth table this is:

INPUT		OUTPUT	
A	**B**	**S**	**C**
0	0	0	0
0	1	1	0
1	0	1	0
1	1	0	1

This is often shown in graphic form as:

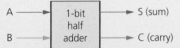

▲ Figure 10.37

Or as a logic circuit:

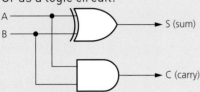

▲ Figure 10.38

Full adder

Consider the following binary sum using 5-bit numbers:

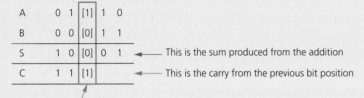

This is the sum produced from the addition

This is the carry from the previous bit position

The sum shows how we have to deal with CARRY from the previous column. There are three inputs to consider in this third column, for example, A = 1, B = 0 and C = 1 (S = 0). This is why we need to join two half adders together to form a full adder, as shown in Figure 10.40

▲ Figure 10.39

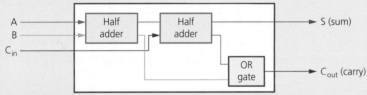

▲ Figure 10.40

As you have probably guessed already, the half adder is unable to deal with the addition of more than two bits (for example, an 8-bit byte). To enable this, we have to consider the full adder circuit.

> **Link**
> ....
> See Section 1.1 for more details of binary addition.

This has an equivalent logic circuit; there are a number of ways of doing this. For example, the following logic circuit uses OR, AND and XOR logic gates:

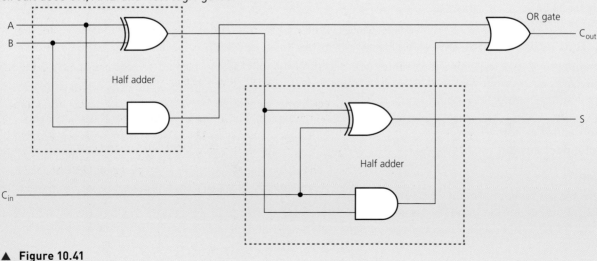

▲ Figure 10.41

Truth table for the full adder circuit:

INPUT			OUTPUT	
A	B	C_{in}	S	C_{out}
0	0	0	0	0
0	0	1	1	0
0	1	0	1	0
0	1	1	0	1
1	0	0	1	0
1	0	1	0	1
1	1	0	0	1
1	1	1	1	1

As with the half adder circuits, different logic gates can be used to produce the full adder circuit.

The full adder is the basic building block for multiple binary additions. For example, the following diagram shows how two 4-bit numbers can be summed using four full adder circuits:

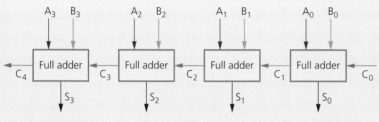

▲ **Figure 10.42**

In this chapter, you have learnt about:
- ✔ recognise the functions, symbols and truth tables for the logic gates: NOT, AND, OR, NAND, NOR and XOR
- ✔ create logic circuits from a given problem, logic expression or truth table
- ✔ complete a truth table from a given problem, logic (or Boolean) expression or logic circuit
- ✔ write a logic (or Boolean) expression from a given problem, logic circuit or truth table

> **Key terms used throughout this chapter**
>
> **logic gate** – an electronic circuit that relies on 'on/off' logic; the most common gates are NOT, AND, OR, NAND, NOR and XOR
>
> **logic circuit** – these are formed from a combination of logic gates and designed to carry out a particular task; the output from a logic circuit will be 0 or 1
>
> **truth table** – a method of checking the output from a logic circuit; a truth table lists all the possible binary input combinations and their associated outputs; the number of outputs will depend on the number of inputs; for example, two inputs have 2^2 (4) possible binary combinations, three inputs have 2^3 (8) possible binary combinations, and so on
>
> **Boolean algebra** – a form of algebra linked to logic circuits and based on TRUE or FALSE

Exam-style questions

1 a Produce:
  i a Boolean or logic expression
  ii a logic circuit
  for the truth table shown:

A	B	X
0	0	0
0	1	1
1	0	0
1	1	0

[4]

b Produce:
  i a logic expression
  ii a truth table
  for the logic circuit shown below:

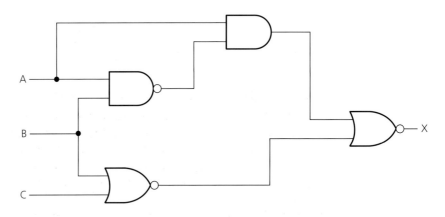

[6]

2 a Write a logic expression for the following logic circuit:

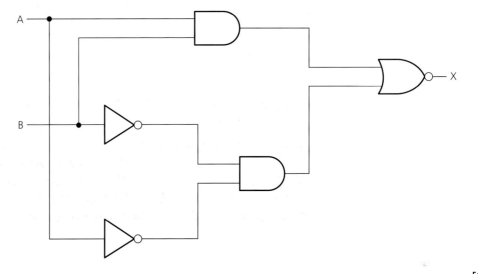

[3]

b Draw a logic circuit which represents the following Boolean expression:

X = NOT (A AND B) OR (A AND NOT B)   [3]

c Complete the truth table for the following logic circuit:

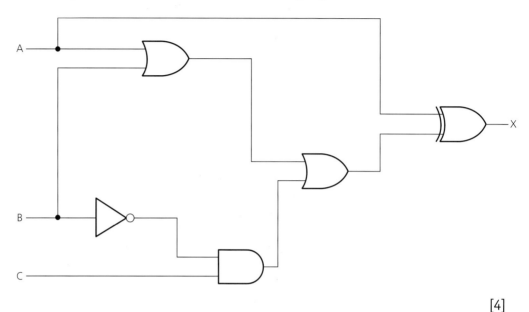

[4]

3 A motor driving a water pump has a safety system which uses three inputs to a logic circuit. A certain combination of conditions results in an output, X, from the logic circuit being equal to 1. When the value of X = 1 then the motor and pump are shut down.
The following table shows which parameters are being monitored and form the three inputs to the logic circuit.

Parameter description	Parameter	Binary value	Description of condition
motor speed	S	0	motor speed <= 2000 rpm
		1	motor speed > 2000 rpm
bearing temperature	T	0	bearing temperature <= 90°C
		1	bearing temperature > 90°C
water velocity	V	0	water velocity <= 5 m/s
		1	wind velocity > 5 m/s

The output, X, will have a value of 1 if any of the following combination of conditions occur:

» **either** motor speed > 2000 rpm and bearing temperature > 90°C
» **or** motor speed <= 2000 rpm and water velocity <= 5 m/s
» **or** bearing temperature > 90°C and water velocity <= 5 m/s
   a Design a logic circuit for the above scenario.   [7]
   b Complete a truth table for the above scenario.   [4]

4 **a** Write a logic expression for the truth table below.

X	Y	Z
0	0	1
0	1	0
1	0	1
1	1	0

b Draw a logic circuit from the above truth table. [4]

5 A factory manufactures plastic pipes. It uses logic circuits to control the manufacturing process.

a Consider the logic gate:

Complete the truth table for this logic gate.

Input A	Input B	Output
0	0	
0	1	
1	0	
1	1	

[1]

b Consider the truth table:

Input A	Input B	Output
0	0	0
0	1	1
1	0	1
1	1	0

State the **single** logic gate that produces the given output. [1]

c Plastic pipes of various sizes are manufactured by heating the plastic and using pressure. The manufacturing system uses sensors to measure the pressure (P), temperature (T) and speed (S) of production.
The inputs to the manufacturing system are:

Input	Binary value	Condition
P	1	pressure is > 5 bar
	0	pressure is <= 5 bar
T	1	temperature is > 200 degrees Celsius
	0	temperature is <= 200 degrees Celsius
S	1	speed is > 1 metre per second
	0	speed is <= 1 metre per second

The system will sound an alarm (**X**) when certain conditions are detected. The alarm will sound when:

temperature is > 200 degrees Celsius and the pressure is <= 5 bar

or

speed is > 1 metre per second and the temperature <= 200 degrees Celsius

Draw a logic circuit to represent the above alarm system.
Logic gates used must have a maximum of **two** inputs. [5]

d Give **two** benefits of using sensors to monitor the manufacture of the plastic pipes. [2]

Cambridge IGCSE Computer Science (0478) Paper 11 Q7, Oct 2019

6 A DVD recorder is protected by three sensors (S, T and P). The output from these sensors forms the inputs to a logic circuit. A certain combination of input values produces an output of 1 from the logic circuit. When this occurs a warning message is shown on the DVD display. The following table shows which parameters are being monitored and form the three inputs to the logic circuit:

Parameter description	Parameter	Binary value	Description of condition
rotation speed	S	0	rotation speed >= 1000 rpm
		1	rotation speed < 1000 rpm
tilt angle	T	0	tilt angle >= 30°
		1	tilt angle < 30°
laser power	P	0	laser power < 150 mW
		1	laser power >= 150 mW

The output X will have a value of 1 if any of the following combination of conditions occurs:

» either rotation speed >= 1000 rpm and tilt angle < 30°
» or rotation speed < 1000 rpm and laser power >= 150 mW
» or tilt angle >= 30° and laser power < 150 mW

a Write down a logic or Boolean expression for the above system. [2]

b Draw a logic circuit to monitor the above system. [6]

c   Complete the truth table for the above system:

Input values			Working space	Output X
S	T	P		
0	0	0		
0	0	1		
0	1	0		
0	1	1		
1	0	0		
1	0	1		
1	1	0		
1	1	1		

[4]

Index